SLA RESEARCH AND MATERIALS DEVELOPMENT FOR LANGUAGE LEARNING

SLA Research and Materials Development for Language Learning is the only book available to focus on the interaction between second language acquisition (SLA) theory and materials development for language learning. It consists of contributions written by experts in SLA, experts in materials development, researchers who have expertise in both fields, and introductions and conclusions by the editor. The book is organized into four major sections—position statements; materials driven by SLA theory; evaluations of materials in relation to SLA theory; and proposals for action—that offer a diverse range of perspectives while maintaining a cohesive and comprehensive overview on the subject. This book is ideal for post-graduate courses in applied linguistics and second language acquisition and for researchers interested in the relationship between SLA and materials development.

Brian Tomlinson is President of the Materials Development Association (MATSDA), a Visiting Professor at the University of Liverpool and a TESOL Professor at Anaheim University. He has over one hundred publications on materials development, language through literature, the teaching of reading, language awareness and teacher development.

SECOND LANGUAGE ACQUISITION RESEARCH SERIES

Susan M. Gass and Alison Mackey, Series Editors

Recent Monographs on Theoretical Issues:

VanPatten/Williams
Theories in Second Language Acquisition, Second Edition (2014)

Leow
Explicit Learning in the L2 Classroom (2015)

Dörnyei/Ryan
The Psychology of the Language Learner—Revisited (2015)

Recent Monographs on Research Methodology:

Larson-Hall
A Guide to Doing Statistics in Second Language Research Using SPSS and R, Second Edition (2015)

Plonsky
Advancing Quantitative Methods in Second Language Research (2015)

De Costa
Ethics in Applied Linguistics Research: Language Researcher Narratives (2015)

Mackey and Marsden
Advancing Methodology and Practice: The IRIS Repository of Instruments for Research into Second Languages (2015)

Gass/Mackey
Stimulated Recall Methodology in Applied Linguistics and L2 Research, Second Edition (2016)

Of Related Interest:

Mackey/Gass
Second Language Research: Methodology and Design, Second Edition (2015)

SLA RESEARCH AND MATERIALS DEVELOPMENT FOR LANGUAGE LEARNING

Edited by Brian Tomlinson

Routledge
Taylor & Francis Group

NEW YORK AND LONDON

First published 2016
by Routledge
711 Third Avenue, New York, NY 10017

and by Routledge
2 Park Square, Milton Park, Abingdon, Oxon, OX14 4RN

Routledge is an imprint of the Taylor & Francis Group, an informa business

Library of Congress Cataloging in Publication Data
Names: Tomlinson, Brian, 1943- editor. | University of Liverpool. | Materials Development Association (United Kingdom)
Title: SLA research and materials development for language learning / edited by Brian Tomlinson. Other titles: Second Language Association research and materials development for language learning | Research and materials development for language learning
Description: New York, NY : Routledge, [2017] | Series: Second Language Acquisition Research Series | Includes index. | "This book has developed from a joint conference between MATSDA (the Materials Development Association) and the University of Liverpool, which was held in Liverpool on June 28th-29th 2014."
Identifiers: LCCN 2015042875 (print) | LCCN 2015046203 (ebook) | ISBN 9781138811966 (hardback : alk. paper) | ISBN 9781138811973 (pbk : alk. paper) | ISBN 9781315749082 (ebk) | ISBN 9781315749082 (eBook)
Subjects: LCSH: Second language acquisition—Research—Methodology—Congresses. | Second language acquisition—Study and teaching.—Research—Congresses. | Language and languages—Study and teaching—Research—Congresses. | Teaching—Aids and devices—Research—Congresses.
Classification: LCC P118.2 .S23 2017 (print) | LCC P118.2 (ebook) | DDC 401/.93072—dc23
LC record available at http://lccn.loc.gov/2015042875

ISBN: 978-1-138-81196-6 (hbk)
ISBN: 978-1-138-81197-3 (pbk)
ISBN: 978-1-315-74908-2 (ebk)

Typeset in Bembo
by Swales & Willis Ltd, Exeter, Devon, UK

CONTENTS

PART II
Materials Driven by SLA Theory

PART III
Evaluations of Materials in Relation to SLA Theory

PART IV
Proposals for Action   **201**

ILLUSTRATIONS

FIGURES

TABLES

CONTRIBUTORS

Sasan Baleghizadeh, Shahid Beheshti University, Iran

Kathleen Bardovi-Harlig, Indiana University

Frank Boers, University of Victoria, Wellington

Lara Bryfonski, Georgetown University

Zeinab Dargahi, Shahid Beheshti University, Iran

Alper Darici, Fatih Anadolu Lisesi, Istanbul

Rod Ellis, University of Auckland and Anaheim University

Pauline Foster, St. Mary's University, Twickenham

Irma-Kaarina Ghosn, Lebanese American University, Byblos, Lebanon

Elnaz Goldouz, Shahid Beheshti University, Iran

Ann-Marie Hunter, St. Mary's University, Twickenham

Noriko Ishihara, Hosei University and Kanda University of International Studies

Alison Mackey, Georgetown University and University of Lancaster

Hitomi Masuhara, University of Liverpool

Freda Mishan, University of Limerick

Sabrina Mossman, Indiana University

Tatsuya Nakata, Kansai University, Japan

Kevin Ottley, Freelance Academic

Daniel Leigh Paller, Kinjo Gakuin University, Japan

Mark Pegrum, University of Western Australia

Hayo Reinders, Unitec Institute of Technology, New Zealand, and Anaheim University

Brian Strong, University of Victoria, Wellington

Brian Tomlinson, University of Liverpool, and Anaheim University

Stuart Webb, University of Victoria, Wellington

Handoyo Puji Widodo, University of Adelaide and Politeknik Negeri Jember, Indonesia

Mehrdad Yousefpoori-Naeim, Shahid Beheshti University, Iran

Nicole Ziegler, University of Hawai'i at Mānoa

PREFACE

Brian Tomlinson

This book has developed from a joint conference between MATSDA (the Materials Development Association) and the University of Liverpool, which was held in Liverpool on June 28th–29th, 2014. The theme of the Conference was SLA and Materials Development and many of the contributors to this book gave presentations at the Conference. What emerged from the Conference was an agreement that what Second Language Acquisition (SLA) research has revealed about what best facilitates language acquisition has been insufficiently applied to the development of language learning materials. There was considerable debate about whether or not SLA researchers have a responsibility to facilitate the application of their findings to language teaching practice and about whether or not SLA researchers have taken sufficient account of what actually does and does not facilitate language acquisition in classrooms around the world. There was, however, complete agreement that there should be more conferences and more publications which aim to bring together researchers, teachers, materials developers and publishers to share their experience and their good practice.

The book is about the interaction between Second Language Acquisition theory and materials development for language learning, and aims to contribute to the greater facilitation of language acquisition through the sharing of experience and good practice recommended above. It consists of chapters by experts in SLA, chapters by experts in materials development and chapters by researchers who have expertise in both fields. The writers put forward position statements, report on materials development projects driven by SLA theory, evaluate materials in relation to SLA theory or propose future action by SLA researchers and/or materials developers.

The book concerns itself mainly with investigating the current match between SLA theory and materials development, with considering the reasons for the reported matches and mismatches, with questioning the desirability and feasibility of achieving a match and with proposals for profitable interaction between theory and practice and practice and theory. Its objectives are to inform and stimulate students, academics and professionals in the field and ultimately to promote both more effective research and more effective practice.

There is a very large body of literature reporting SLA research and theory but very little of it concerns itself with the application of SLA findings and theory to materials development practice. There is also a recently growing literature on the principles and practice of materials development for language learning. Within this literature there are chapters and sections in books on how materials development is and is not informed by SLA theory (e.g. Harwood, 2010, 2014; McGrath, 2013; Tomlinson, 2011, 2013a, 2013b) but there is as yet no book which focuses specifically on the interaction between SLA theory and materials development for language learning. This is a serious gap in the literature and has contributed, in my view, to an impoverishment of both SLA research and materials development practice. This is a gap which I am optimistic this book will help to fill. It certainly needs filling, as the lack of such interaction has impacted negatively on SLA research in that many of its studies (though obviously not all) are laboratory experiments that could not be replicated in classroom teaching contexts which are constrained by lack of student motivation, inappropriate teacher training, pressure to cover the syllabus and the coursebook, compulsory use of inappropriate coursebooks, large numbers of students, pressure to prepare students for examinations, insufficient time, lack of exposure to English outside the classroom, etc. The gap has also impacted negatively on materials development for language learning in that many activities that are unlikely to facilitate language acquisition are still being used and others which would be more likely to facilitate language acquisition are not. It has also impacted on classroom teaching and on language testing (in which task-types typically bear little resemblance to activities which are likely to facilitate language acquisition (Tomlinson, 2005)). There is no doubt that researchers, materials developers, teachers and testers could gain from greater connections between theory and practice, between practice and theory and between each other. That is what MATSDA (www.matsda.org) and this book are dedicated to achieving.

References

Harwood, N. (Ed.) (2010). *Materials in ELT: Theory and practice.* Cambridge: Cambridge University Press.

Harwood, N. (Ed.) (2014). *English language teaching textbooks: Content, consumption, production.* Basingstoke, UK: Palgrave Macmillan.

McGrath, I. (2013). *Teaching materials and the roles of EFL/ESL teachers: Practice and theory.* London: Bloomsbury.

Tomlinson, B. (2005). Testing to learn. *ELT Journal, 59*(1), 39–46.

Tomlinson, B. (Ed.) (2011). *Materials development in language teaching* (2nd ed.). Cambridge: Cambridge University Press.

Tomlinson, B. (Ed.) (2013a). *Applied linguistics and materials development.* London: Continuum.

Tomlinson, B. (Ed.) (2013b). *Developing materials for language teaching* (2nd ed.). London: Continuum Press.

ABBREVIATIONS

CAF	Complexity, accuracy and fluency
CALL	Computer-aided language learning
CLT	Communicative language teaching
CMC	Computer-mediated communication
DAP	Developmentally appropriate practice
EAP	English for academic purposes
EFC	Error-free clauses
EFL	English as a foreign language
EGP	English for general purposes
ELF	English as a lingua franca
ELT	English language teaching
ESL	English as a second language
ESP	English for specific purposes
EVP	English for vocational purposes
FTF	Face to face
MALL	Mobile-aided language learning
PAR	Participatory action research
SCMC	Synchronous computer-mediated communication
SLA	Second language acquisition
TBLT	Task-based language teaching
TEFL	Teaching English as a foreign language
TESL	Teaching of English as a second language
TESOL	Teaching of English to speakers of other languages
TFA	Technique feature analysis
TL	Target language
VE	Vocational English

PART I
Position Statements

1

ACHIEVING A MATCH BETWEEN SLA THEORY AND MATERIALS DEVELOPMENT

Brian Tomlinson

Introduction

I am going to start my chapter by presenting an extract from the beginning of a lesson for A2/B1 learners of English. I will explain the relevance of this later.

Teacher:	Morning class.
Students:	Good morning.
Teacher:	Do you remember the sad poem I read you yesterday about the refugee mother and child? Well today I'm going to tell you a story. There won't be any comprehension questions so just relax and enjoy the story. Is there anybody here from the USA? Is there anybody from Ireland?

The story is about an American and an Irishman who were travelling by air across the Atlantic. The Irishman was tired and wanted to go to sleep. The American was wide awake and wanted to play a game.

When the Irishman refused to play, the American said, 'You'll like this game. I ask you a question and if you can't answer you give me ten dollars. Then you ask me a question and if I can't answer I give you a hundred dollars.'

'OK,' said the Irishman. 'Let's play.'

'What's the distance between the earth and the moon?' asked the American. The Irishman immediately put his hand in his pocket and gave the American ten dollars.

'My turn,' said the Irishman. 'What goes up a hill with two legs and comes down with three?'

The American couldn't answer. He thought and thought, he phoned his friends, he consulted Wikipedia. But he couldn't come up with an answer.

> The American woke up the Irishman and gave him a hundred dollars. The Irishman smiled and went back to sleep. But the American was still tormented by the question. An hour later he woke up the Irishman and said, 'OK. Tell me. What goes up a hill with two legs and comes down with three?'

> The Irishman put his hand in his pocket and gave the American ten dollars.

The teacher left the class for a couple of minutes to think about/talk about the story and then said. 'If you liked that story you can take a copy from my table at the end of the lesson. If you want to read more stories like this there's a web reference at the bottom of the story on the handout.'

What has this extract from a lesson got to do with the match between SLA and materials development? I will explain later in the chapter.

Questions

Now I would like to ask and answer some fundamental questions.

My first question is:

Are Global Coursebooks Typically Successful in Facilitating Language Acquisition?

My answer, after fifty years' experience of using global coursebooks and of observing them used in primary, secondary and tertiary classrooms around the world, is that language coursebooks are not typically very successful in facilitating language acquisition. Some teachers who use global coursebooks are successful in facilitating language acquisition but often that is because they modify and supplement their coursebooks in ways which facilitate acquisition (Tomlinson, 2015b; Tomlinson & Masuhara, forthcoming 2016). They often succeed despite, rather than because of, their coursebooks.

There is evidence that using a global coursebook can improve your ability to use the coursebook and to improve performance on tests targeted by the coursebook. For example, Hadley (2014) claims to provide empirical evidence that using a coursebook in Japan facilitated language learning because students did better on the coursebook placement test at the end of the course than they did at the beginning. I am not convinced that this proves that the coursebook facilitated language learning and I have seen no convincing evidence that a global coursebook has facilitated durable language acquisition. But to be fair, I have seen no convincing evidence that a global coursebook has ever not facilitated durable language acquisition. What I have seen though are coursebooks produced by innovative projects (Tomlinson, 1995; Bolitho, 2008) or by enlightened (and financially secure) publishers which I would consider likely to facilitate language acquisition. The two best of these in my view are *On Target* (1994), written by thirty teachers in Namibia and *Search 10* (Fenner & Nordal-Pederson, 1999), commissioned and published in Norway by an editor who had been involved in the *On Target* project. Both of these coursebooks followed the Text-Driven framework advocated in Tomlinson (2013c) and both of them were written in order to match the SLA principles I will discuss and exemplify later in this chapter.

My second question is:

Why Do Coursebooks Typically Not Facilitate Language Acquisition?

My answer is: There are many reasons but one is undoubtedly that coursebooks do not typically match what we know about what facilitates language acquisition. We know a lot about what does and does not facilitate language acquisition. We know about this from the data and theories provided by SLA research, from classroom research and from our longitudinal experience in trying to help classes of learners acquire languages. Many of us apply this knowledge and awareness to our own classroom materials but few of us have the opportunity to apply it to commercial coursebooks.

In Tomlinson (2013a), chapter after chapter provides evidence of the mismatch between published materials and what we know about languages and their acquisition. Evidence is also provided of such a mismatch in Tomlinson, Dat, Masuhara, and Rubdy (2001), Masuhara and Tomlinson (2008), Tomlinson and Masuhara (2013) and Tomlinson (2013b). This is especially true of global coursebooks. There are some notable exceptions though in local publications, e.g. *Search 10* in Norway and *On Target* in Namibia.

Dörnyei (2009, p. 268) says, 'for many, if not all, SLA researchers the ultimate goal is to develop insights and instructional strategies that will eventually improve the efficacy and efficiency of L2 learning'. Many such insights have already been developed but the problem is that most of them do not seem to have been applied.

So my next question is:

Why Do Coursebooks Not Typically Match What We Know About Language Acquisition?

My answer is: There are many understandable reasons. For example, many publications on SLA are inaccessible to teachers, writers and publishers because of their use of specialized terminology, because of their assumptions of prior knowledge and because they appear in journals not easily available to practitioners. Also there is a separation between theorists and practitioners. They each have their own conferences and publications and rarely meet to share mutually beneficial insights (with some notable exceptions such as MATSDA (www.matsda. org) conferences). In addition, the examinations that coursebooks prepare learners for do not match what we know about language acquisition because high-stakes examinations need to achieve and demonstrate their reliability by using mainly objective questions that test knowledge rather than communicative competence (Tomlinson, 2005). The ideal would be if these high-stakes examinations also focused on validity and used tasks which assessed communicative competence and therefore encouraged its development as the main objective of coursebooks. This did happen in Vanuatu in 1981 when the primary school leaving examination was changed to a communicative examination. Then teachers in a workshop wrote communication activities (which would now be called tasks) for a coursebook called *Talking to Learn* (Tomlinson, 1981), which was intended both to foster the development of communicative competence and to prepare students for their school leaving examination.

The main reasons, though, why commercial publishers do not risk producing a coursebook which matches what we know about language acquisition is that such a coursebook would not achieve face validity with administrators, teachers and parents and therefore would be unlikely to sell.

My next question is:

What Do We Know About Language Acquisition?

My answer is: There is a lot of disagreement in the SLA world but we do know there are certain prerequisites for effective and durable language acquisition. I am going to argue that a coursebook needs to achieve these prerequisites if it is going to help teachers to facilitate language acquisition regardless of the age, experience, qualifications or creativity of the teachers.

Prerequisites for Language Acquisition

I have already published criteria for facilitating language acquisition in, for example, Tomlinson (2011a, 2012, 2013b) and other criteria have been proposed by Nation (2007) and by Ellis in this volume. In this chapter I am going to focus on five criteria which I believe are prerequisites for durable and effective language acquisition and which I think should be used in both the development and the evaluation of coursebook materials. These principles are supported by second language acquisition research, by classroom research and by my experience as a teacher and teacher trainer. This is how I believe research should be applied to materials development. If principles emerging from research match with the experience of the developers then there is a responsibility to think of ways of making useful applications of these principles to practice. If principles emerging from research have no match with the experience of the developers then it would be irresponsible and possibly impractical to try to apply them. I would also argue that it could make a valuable contribution to materials development if SLA researchers investigated approaches which practitioners have found to promote language acquisition, as well as commonly used coursebook activities which practitioners suspect have little or no beneficial effect on their users' language acquisition. See Tomlinson (forthcoming 2016) for a criterion-referenced evaluation of typical coursebook activities.

I would like now to consider my five main principles and their application to materials development for language acquisition.

Principle 1: That the Learners Are Exposed to a Rich, Re-cycled, Meaningful and Comprehensible Input of Language in Use

Before I go on I would just like to refer you back to the extract from the beginning of a lesson which I presented at the beginning of this chapter. This is an example of what I call a task-free activity.

What happens is:

The teacher starts every lesson by reading a poem, telling a joke, telling a story, recounting an anecdote, reading a newspaper report, acting out a scene, giving a speech, etc. It is a task-free activity because the students do not have to do anything except listen and hopefully use visualization and their inner voice to help them enjoy what they are listening to (Tomlinson & Avila, 2007; Tomlinson, 2011b). After the teacher performance the teacher leaves a brief silence for the students to process what they have listened to (Bao, 2014), then tells the students to take a written copy of the 'text' if they want to at the end of the lesson and put it in their file. If they want to they can also follow up the suggestions for further reading or listening which are listed below the text. The idea is that the students build up a file of texts which have engaged them and they return to and experience them again throughout their course (sometimes asking the teacher about things which puzzle them). Many teachers around the world who have attended my workshops now start every lesson with a task-free activity and they have been very pleased with the impact on their students (for example, students learning German at Leeds Metropolitan University rated the teacher's reading of poems at the beginning of every lesson as the most interesting and the most useful part of their course).

Providing such a task-free activity at the beginning of every lesson is one way of offering **a rich, re-cycled, meaningful and comprehensible input of language in use** (Krashen, 1994; Nation, 2007).

> It is **rich** because of the massive accumulated amount of input over a course, because of the variety of genres which the learners can experience, and because the authenticity of the texts ensures that learners are not restricted in their access to the target language (e.g. there are four different tenses used in the Irishman and American story as well as modal verbs and infinitives, and yet the story has proved easily accessible when I have used it with A2 students).

> It is **re-cycled** because the text often contains repetitions (e.g. the questions are repeated at an interval in the Irishman and American story), because learners both listen to and read the text and, if engaged, they return to it many times.

> It is **meaningful** because the learners are encouraged to visualize and to connect the texts to their own lives.

> It is **comprehensible** because the learners can be engaged by the text without understanding everything in it, can read the text many times, can talk to each other about it and can ask their teacher about it. Of course, though, not every text will be meaningful and comprehensible to every learner.

In addition learners are more likely to notice less salient features of a text in reading than in listening and therefore a lot of extensive listening of natural language (especially of natural dialogue) can be provided if learners later read what they listened to in class (especially if the teacher performance is of transcripts of conversations, film scripts, play scripts, comic strips, graphic novels, etc).

Most importantly, task-free activities increase the learners' exposure to language in use, something which is vital for language acquisition but which for many learners is insufficient in their classroom use of the coursebook and almost non-existent outside the classroom.

Other ways of providing access to rich, re-cycled, meaningful and comprehensible input include extensive reading (Krashen, 2004), extensive listening and extensive viewing, encouraging learners to look out for English outside the classroom (Tomlinson, 2013d) and using a Text-Driven Approach to materials adaptation and development (Tomlinson, 2013c).

Principle 2: That the Learners Are Affectively Engaged

Affective engagement has also been found to be a prerequisite for language acquisition (Arnold, 1999; Pavlenko, 2005). It seems that being moved to feel amused, angry, disturbed, entertained, excited, exhilarated, empathetic, sad, sympathetic or any other emotion whilst learning or experiencing the target language is a powerful facilitator of language acquisition. On the other hand feeling nothing in response to bland, neutral texts and uninvolving activities is going to prevent acquisition for all except the exceptionally motivated learner.

Other aspects of affect include self-esteem and positive attitudes towards the learning experience, and they can be powerful determiners of acquisition too.

Principle 3: That the Learners Are Cognitively Engaged

It is important that language learners not only feel but that they think as well (Robinson, 2002; Mishan in this volume). If they are involved in challenging but achievable tasks which require high-level, critical and creative thinking, learners are much more likely move towards language acquisition than if they are mindlessly repeating meaningless drills, or completing easy exercises or reading empty texts. Problem solving, invention, persuasion and creative writing tasks are examples of activities which have the potential for the achievement of cognitive engagement.

Principle 4: That the Learners Are Sometimes Helped to Pay Attention to Form Whilst or After Focusing on Meaning

Much has been written on the need for learners to pay attention to features of the language they are exposed to and on the value of learners investigating language structures which have featured prominently in a language experience in which their main concern has been meaning rather than trying to learn a structure without having had a meaningful experience of it in use (Long, 1991; Ellis, 2002). My own preference is for a language awareness approach in which learners make discoveries for themselves about language features of texts which they have experienced (Bolitho et al., 2003; Tomlinson, 1994, 2007). My experience is that the learner investment of time and cognitive energy in solving a linguistic problem can make their discovery more salient and memorable than an explanation from a teacher or a coursebook and the resulting sense of achievement can considerably raise learner self-esteem.

Principle 5: That the Learners Are Given Plentiful Opportunities to Use the Language for Communication

Despite it being almost a mantra of the communicative approach for the last thirty-five years learner use of the target language is still not a feature of many global course-books (Tomlinson & Masuhara, 2013). Learners spend a lot of time filling in blanks, transforming sentences and participating in controlled and guided practice, but they typically do not spend much time in using the target language to achieve communicative effects. Even when they are asked to produce language without being constrained by lexical or structural prescription they are often just asked to write an essay or story, or to give a presentation or have a discussion without having addressees or purposes to relate their use of language to. As a result they do not develop the communicative competence which can only really develop from considerable experience of communication (Swain, 1995; Ortega, 2010). Ideally, much of this communication should involve contextual interaction with actual or simulated interactants and as much as possible should involve meaningful communication in the sense that it stimulates the expression of views, opinions, reactions, intentions, etc., and not just the purchase of a ticket or the specification of a time.

The vast majority of learners of an L2 are doing so in an educational institution in which the objective of achieving communicative competence is important but less so than such educational objectives as the development of high-level thinking skills (see Mishan in this volume), of problem solving skills, of open-mindedness, of social and intercultural awareness and of confidence. The development of such attributes can be facilitated at the same time as language acquisition by achieving the five criteria outlined above when using coursebook materials. They are likely to be achieved, though, by the learners doing such stereotypical exercises as filling in the blanks, matching, listen-and-repeat, dialogue recitation and answering Yes/No or True/False questions which only require word recognition. For suggestions on how to adapt such exercises so as to make them more likely to facilitate both acquisition and educational development see Tomlinson (forthcoming 2017).

My various evaluations of coursebooks have made it apparent to me that the skill least catered for is creativity – both creativity of thought and creativity of expression. In my experience in the classroom this is also the easiest skill to facilitate by making small modifications to coursebook activities and in particular by opening up such closed activities as those listed above so that there is no one correct response to them and so that justification is built into the required responses. For detailed suggestions and examples of how to do this see Tomlinson (2015a, 2015b).

Using the SLA Prerequisites as Evaluation Criteria

Evaluation of Global Coursebooks

I have already used my five prerequisites (together with other criteria investigating the match between SLA principles and materials development) to evaluate coursebooks in Masuhara, and Tomlinson, 2008; Tomlinson, 2013a; Tomlinson, Dat, Masuhara, and Rubdy, 2001; Tomlinson and Masuhara (2013). In most cases it was demonstrated that there was a very weak match between what we know facilitates language acquisition and the materials being evaluated, and that most global coursebooks were much more likely to help learners acquire knowledge of the language than an ability to use it for communication. Here is another evaluation which I have just conducted of Unit 8 in a number of Intermediate Level (i.e. B1) global coursebooks.

The books I took the units from for evaluation were taken at random from my shelf and I decided in advance to evaluate Unit 8 of each of them. The remarkable thing is how similar the three books are and how I gave very similar scores and made very similar comments about each of them.

TABLE 1.1 Evaluation of Unit 8, 'Communities' (pp. 91–102), in *Speakout* (Clare & Wilson, 2012), coursebook

Criterion	Rating	Comment
1 To what extent are the materials likely to expose the learners to a rich, re-cycled, meaningful and comprehensible input of language in use?	3/5	All the reading and listening texts are very short and are only likely to be meaningful to the well-educated, well-off and well-travelled. Many of the texts seem to have been written to exemplify structures (e.g. relative clauses in 4). However, they do seem to be comprehensible and re-cycling is achieved by using utterances from the texts in follow-up activities.
2 To what extent are the materials likely to engage the learners affectively?	2/5	There is no humour, no excitement, no controversy, nothing to stimulate affective responses. There is some localization and personalization, though.
3 To what extent are the materials likely to engage the learners cognitively?	2/5	There is nothing to stimulate learners to think, nothing to challenge learners cognitively. There are some activities inviting learners to give their views, though.

4 To what extent are the materials likely to help the learners to pay attention to form whilst or after focusing on meaning?	3/5	There are some consciousness-raising activities getting learners to work out rules for types of utterances used in the texts. The answers are predetermined.
5 To what extent are the materials likely to provide the learners with opportunities to use the language for communication?	2/5	Most of the activities involve guided practice. Some invite learners to produce a text using key phrases (e.g. a web ad with eleven key phrases provided) and one invites learners to write a web review by answering questions about the web. There is no opportunity for authentic, contextualized communication.

TABLE 1.2 Evaluation of Unit 8, 'No fear' (pp. 62–69), in *New Headway Intermediate* (4th ed.) (Soars & Soars, 2012), coursebook

Criterion	Rating	Comment
1 To what extent are the materials likely to expose the learners to a rich, re-cycled, meaningful and comprehensible input of language in use?	3/5	All the reading and listening texts are fairly short (though more extensive than in the other global coursebooks reviewed) and are only likely to be meaningful to the well-educated, well-off and well-travelled. Many of the texts seem to have been written to exemplify structures (e.g. verb patterns on pp. 62–63) but they do seem to be comprehensible and re-cycling is achieved by using utterances from the texts in follow-up activities.
2 To what extent are the materials likely to engage the learners affectively?	3/5	There is no humour, no excitement, no controversy and little to really stimulate affective responses (despite the promising title and a promising section on phobias). There is some localization and personalization, though.
3 To what extent are the materials likely to engage the learners cognitively?	2/5	There is nothing to stimulate learners to think, nothing to challenge learners cognitively. There are some activities inviting learners to give their views, though.
4 To what extent are the materials likely to help the learners to pay attention to form whilst or after focusing on meaning?	2/5	Most of the exercises and activities either test the learners' knowledge about language points, teach them about a language point or provide practice for a language point. There are no activities which ask the learners to pay attention to how language is used in authentic and meaningful texts in order to make discoveries for themselves.

(continued)

(continued)

Criterion	Rating	Comment
5 To what extent are the materials likely to provide the learners with opportunities to use the language for communication?	3/5	Most of the activities involve guided practice or controlled discussion/conversation. There is no opportunity for authentic, contextualized communication. However, there are prompted storytelling and prompted story-writing activities.

TABLE 1.3 Evaluation of Unit 8, 'Lost and found' (pp. 62–69), in *English Unlimited Intermediate* (Rea & Clementson, 2011), coursebook

Criterion	Rating	Comment
1 To what extent are the materials likely to expose the learners to a rich, re-cycled, meaningful and comprehensible input of language in use?	3/5	All the reading and listening texts are very short and are only likely to be meaningful to the well-educated, well-off and well-travelled. Many of the texts seem to have been written to exemplify structures (e.g. the causative 'have' on p. 67) but they do seem to be comprehensible and re-cycling is achieved by using utterances from the texts in follow-up activities.
2 To what extent are the materials likely to engage the learners affectively?	2/5	There is no humour, no excitement, no controversy, nothing to stimulate affective responses. There is some localization and personalization though.
3 To what extent are the materials likely to engage the learners cognitively?	2/5	There is nothing to stimulate learners to think, nothing to challenge learners cognitively. There are some activities inviting learners to give their views – but the topics hardly present a cognitive challenge (e.g. clutter, cleaning, freecycling, an interesting object).
4 To what extent are the materials likely to help the learners to pay attention to form whilst or after focusing on meaning?	2/5	Most of the exercises and activities either test the learners' knowledge about language points, teach them about a language point or provide practice for a language point. There are no activities which ask the learners to pay attention to how language is used in authentic and meaningful texts in order to make discoveries for themselves.

5 To what extent are the materials likely to provide the learners with opportunities to use the language for communication?	1/5	Most of the activities involve guided practice. There are very few production activities (a few controlled discussions, a controlled role play and the writing of a short description of something you don't need for freecycle). But there are no opportunities for authentic, contextualized communication.

I would like to make it clear that I am not attacking the units evaluated above. Each of them contains some valuable activities. What I am saying is that in my opinion all three units could have offered learners a greater contribution to their development of communicative competence if the five criteria had been given more consideration when they were being written and revised.

Evaluation of a Project Coursebook

Here is an evaluation of a national coursebook written by thirty teachers in Namibia for 16-year-old learners of English as a second or foreign language. The writers worked in groups of three and followed a principled but flexible framework in developing their units. They also made use of nationwide responses to a questionnaire asking students what topics they would like included in the coursebook.

TABLE 1.4 Evaluation of Unit 8, 'It's your choice' (pp. 153–169), in *On Target* (1994), coursebook

Criterion	Rating	Comment
1 To what extent are the materials likely to expose the learners to a rich, re-cycled, meaningful and comprehensible input of language in use?	4/5	There are many extended written and spoken texts on topics likely to be meaningful to young Namibian students. There is a rich variety of genres and text types (e.g. a poem, letters, a timetable, an application form, conversations, a legal notice, a cartoon) and the texts are authentic in the sense that they have not been written to teach language.
2 To what extent are the materials likely to engage the learners affectively?	5/5	The topics and texts are controversial (e.g. a poem about a drug dealer; a cartoon and conversation in which a teenage girl tries to persuade her friend to lie to her parents so they can go to a night club; letters about teenage pregnancy, rape and

(continued)

(continued)

Criterion	Rating	Comment
		racism) and they raise issues likely to stimulate affective responses. All the activities are of local relevance and are personalized so as to be meaningful to the students.
3 To what extent are the materials likely to engage the learners cognitively?	5/5	The texts and activities invite the students to think about issues of local and national relevance and to come up with solutions to problems.
4 To what extent are the materials likely to help the learners to pay attention to form whilst or after focusing on meaning?	4/5	There are a number of activities asking the students to make discoveries for themselves about how forms are used in meaningful texts (e.g. the use of short forms; ways of persuading).
5 To what extent are the materials likely to provide the learners with opportunities to use the language for communication?	5/5	The students are asked to participate in scenarios, simulations and role plays, to discuss issues and make plans in groups, to conduct a survey, to respond to a letter, to complete an application form and to write an informal letter. For each of these activities a context and purpose is provided and the students are not constrained by having to use key phrases provided to them.

Evaluation of Principled Units of Material

My Principled Unit of Materials

My unit follows the Text-Driven Approach (Tomlinson, 2013c) which I have mentioned above, which was used in the development of *On Target* (reviewed above), which is driven by the five principles which form the basis of the evaluation criteria used above and which is intended to provide a principled and flexible framework for materials development and adaptation. The unit is intended for young teenage learners of English as a foreign language. The approach, but obviously not the texts, can be used with any learners anywhere.

Please become young teenage learners of English at about B1 level.

1. Readiness Activity

Morning class. Let me tell you a story and a memory from my childhood.
First the story:

'Doctor, I really need your help,' I said. 'Every night for the past two weeks I've been dreaming about dogs playing football.'

'Here, take these pills tonight before you go to bed and you won't see any dogs in your sleep.'

'But can I take start taking them tomorrow?'

'Why?'

'Because tonight they're playing the Cup Final.'

Now the memory:

One of my first memories is of standing on North Station in Blackpool, where I was born. I'm with my mother and my sister and we're waiting for a train. I'm standing on the edge of the platform looking out for the train. My mother is saying, 'Come away from the edge or you'll fall in.' Suddenly a train appears pulled by a black steam locomotive. I turn to look at it and I fall onto the track below. I shout, 'Help! Help!'. My mother says, 'I told you not to stand on the edge', and does nothing to help me.

I still don't know if that actually happened or if it was a dream.

Do you remember your dreams? Try to remember one now. If you want to, tell one of your neighbours about your dream.

2. Initial Response Activity

I'm going to read you the first chapter of a novel about a teenage boy. The novel is called *May Cause Irritation* and the boy is called Norm. As you listen try to see pictures in your mind of what is happening. Don't worry, there won't be any comprehension questions afterwards.

As I read I'll sometimes pause. When I do just shout out what you think comes next.

3. Intake Response Activities

i. Chapter 2 starts: '"Norman?" said Norm's mum again. "Time to . . ."' Time to what?

ii. Think of the pictures you saw when you were listening to the story. Make use of them to draw two illustrations for the story.

iii. In groups of four choose the four pictures which you think best illustrate the story.

iv. Here's the story. Compare your pictures with the pictures in the book. Which picture do you think best represents the story?

v. Do you think dreams can be explained by what has happened in the past or do they predict what will happen in the future? Do you think Norm's dream comes from experiences and fears he has had in the past or do you think it predicts what will happen to him in the future?

vi. Read the story together and look for clues to explain Norm's dream.

4. Development Activity 1

In groups of 4 make up a circle story about a dream. Start:

In my dream I was in a dark room. When I looked out of the window I saw . . .

When you've finished tell your story to another group.

5. Development Activity 2

In chapter 3 Norm tells his family about his dream. 'I wonder what your dream means,' says Brian. 'All dreams mean something.'

Norm says, 'It means nothing.' But he begins to think it might mean something after all when he remembers that they've just moved house, that they have no money, that they're going to get a dog for his brother Brian and that Chelsea had a photo of him and his friend Mikey naked on the beach when they were babies.

And then Norm's mum says, 'if you have a dream on a Friday and tell somebody about it the next day it'll come true.' And, of course, it was Saturday.

In your group write chapter 4 as a circle story. Begin:

Norm couldn't believe it when Mikey told him that Chelsea had . . .

Complete this sentence and then pass it on.

Look at your four stories and decide which one you think is the best.

6. Input Response Activity

Go back to chapter 1 of the novel and:

i.   Decide why the author decided to use the actual words of the people in the story rather than reporting them. That is, he decided to use direct speech instead of reported speech.

ii. When else do we write the actual words that people have spoken?

iii. When do we report what was said instead of writing the actual words?

iv. Look at the words spoken by people in chapter 1. Use them to help you to write as many 'rules' as you can of direct speech. For each 'rule' provide examples from chapter 1.

v.   Share your discoveries with another group. Then make any changes you want to your 'rules' and examples.

vi. For homework find examples of direct speech and decide why the writer used direct speech and not reported speech.

vii. Put some of your new examples with your 'rules'. Add new 'rules', too, if you want to.

7. Development Activity 3

Take the group story which you chose as the best and revise it. Make sure the sentences connect with each other and that you use the rules of direct speech which you've discovered.

If you're not sure about anything ask your teacher for help.

When you've finished swap your story with another group.

8. Further Reading

i.   If you want to you can borrow the book *May Cause Irritation* from me.

ii. If you enjoy the book you can borrow other books about Norm from me.

Application of the Five Principles to My Unit

This unit is based on the Text-Driven framework which is described and exemplified in Tomlinson (2013c). The main point about this approach is that a text is chosen for its potential to engage and then the text drives the activities in the unit. Let me go back to my list of prerequisites and match them with my unit.

1. That the Learners Receive a Rich, Re-cycled, Meaningful and Comprehensible Input of Language in Use

The lengthy authentic chapter is experienced many times by the learners. They also listen to and read their own and other groups' spoken and written circle stories and they are invited to participate in extensive further reading.

2. That the Learners Are Affectively Engaged

The chapter is intended to be humorous and has been chosen because it was very popular with young teenage readers and has the potential to relate to the lives of the target learners. The unit is personalized in that the learners are invited to think about their own dreams and memories and to achieve their own visualization of the chapter. All the activities are open-ended so as to encourage personal and creative responses (Tomlinson, 2015a, 2015b).

3. That the Learners Are Cognitively Engaged

The learners are asked to think about the causes of dreams and to work out an explanation of Norm's dream.

4. That the Learners Are Sometimes Helped to Pay Attention to Form Whilst or After Focusing on Meaning

My favourite approach to help learners to do this is the discovery approach which I have used in my unit. The learners are asked to discover the reasons for using direct speech and the rules for using it from revisiting the texts and from finding examples in authentic texts outside the classroom.

It is also intended that the teacher will teach responsively in giving help on vocabulary and grammar to learners who request it during the development of their stories and it is expected that the learners will gain from meaning focused teacher recasting of form (see Tomlinson, 2007) and from meaning focused learner recasting during the development of their circle stories.

5. That the Learners Are Given Plentiful Opportunities to Use the Language for Communication

The learners are given many opportunities for open-ended discussion and they are asked to tell and to write circle stories.

Another Question

Is my unit publishable in a global coursebook? I have tried to publish such materials in global coursebooks but I have always been told that my activities are too open-ended for the teachers to use as tests, that my texts are too long and demanding and that my activities are too difficult. I have been told that what I have produced is not what teachers want.

What seems to be missing from my unit which publishers believe teachers want is:

1. Language presentation
2. Language practice
3. Language testing

As I have already claimed above, a coursebook which achieved a perfect match with SLA principles would not achieve face validity and would almost certainly not sell. What is needed is for principled activities to be the core activities but for them to be interspersed with prominently placed conventional exercises such as filling in the blanks, sentence completion, tense transformation, True/False, multiple-choice etc. (i.e. exercises which have no theoretical or research justification but which are easy to use and to mark and are expected by parents, administrators, teachers and students).

As a compromize, if I was trying to get a principled coursebook published I would re-design my unit so that it matches with what we know about language acquisition without looking radically different. I would add a summary of the conventions of direct speech in a reference box at the back of the book, I would add some recognizable practice activities (e.g. filling in the blanks, sentence completion) and I would add a ten-item multiple choice comprehension test after the intake response activities. None of these additions would be likely to facilitate language acquisition but they might get the materials published.

Your Evaluation

Here is another unit of material written to achieve the five SLA prerequisites which I have been advocating. Use the criteria in Table 1.5 below to evaluate it:

1. Readiness Activity

Think about the toys you had when you were a very young child. Try to see pictures of them.

Now picture the toys you had when you were about ten years old.

What did you want to become when you were a child?

Tell somebody about one of your toys and about what you wanted to become, about your ambition.

Anybody like to tell us about one of their toys and about their ambition?

In a small group talk about your answer to the following question:

When you were a child were you encouraged to do only things which were either typically male or typically female?

2. Initial Response Activity

Listen to me reading a song by Peggy Seeger. As you listen imagine pictures you would use in an animated version of the song.

Don't worry if there's anything you don't understand. You're not going to be tested on your comprehension and you'll get a chance to listen to the song later.

(Teacher reads aloud 'I'm Gonna Be an Engineer' by Peggy Seeger, a very emotive song about a girl who wanted to be an engineer but whose parents and then husband wanted her to do more feminine things.)

3. Intake Response Activity

In your group discuss your answers to the following:

What is your attitude towards

- the woman?
- her mother?
- her husband?
- her boss?

TABLE 1.5 Coursebook evaluation template

Criterion	Rating	Comment
1 To what extent are the materials likely to expose the learners to a rich, re-cycled, meaningful and comprehensible input of language in use?		
2 To what extent are the materials likely to engage the learners affectively?		
3 To what extent are the materials likely to engage the learners cognitively?		
4 To what extent are the materials likely to help the learners to pay attention to form whilst or after focusing on meaning?		
5 To what extent are the materials likely to provide the learners with opportunities to use the language for communication?		

4. Development Activity 1

In your group write your own song, poem or story starting:

When I was . . .

5. Input Activity 1

Read the song together and point out to each other anything you hadn't noticed about the four people when you listened to the song.

6. Input Activity 2

In your group look at all the instances of 'but' in the song. For each one decide what it means.
Now listen to Peggy Seeger singing her song in an animated version of 'I'm Gonna Be an Engineer'.
Look at other texts and find other instances of 'but'.
Use your discoveries about 'but' to write a summary of the uses of 'but'.

7. Development Activity 2

Revise your song/poem/story about 'When I was . . . ' You can make use of your discoveries about the use of 'but' and anything else from your copy of the song to help you.

8. Development Activity 3

In the UK there is a shortage of engineers. As part of your job in the marketing department of a British university you have been asked to design a poster to attract both boys and girls in secondary schools to think of doing a degree in engineering so that they can become engineers.

9. Further Reading

Do all girls want to play with dolls and tea sets? Do all boys want guns and trucks? Of course not. Then why are toymakers so aggressive in marketing these stereotypes? Kira Cochrane charts the rise of the pink–blue divide – and the fightback by angry parents.

Read 'Load of Old Pony' by Kira Cochrane from *The Guardian* newspaper (23 April 2014) and decide if you think what she says is true for your country.

10. Follow-Up Viewing

'The Lumberjack Song' by Monty Python (a song about a man who wants to become a lumberjack in the Canadian forests but also wants to dress in women's clothes).

Conclusion

To be responsible professionals and to help our students to develop the ability to communicate effectively in their L2 we need to adapt, supplement and develop materials so that they match as closely as possible what we know facilitates language acquisition. I am not proposing that all SLA findings should be applied to the development of coursebooks nor that every activity in a coursebook should be driven by SLA theory. My position is that coursebook use should be much more principled than it currently appears to be in that maximum use is made of what we know facilitates language acquisition as well as of what we know parents, administrators, teachers and students want from their coursebook.

References

Arnold, J. (Ed.) (1999). *Affect in language learning.* Cambridge: Cambridge University Press.

Bao, D. (2014). *Understanding silence and reticence: Ways of participating in second language acquisition.* London: Bloomsbury.

Bolitho, R. (2008). Materials used in central and eastern Europe and the former Soviet Union. In B. Tomlinson (Ed.), *English language learning materials: A critical review* (pp. 213–222). London: Bloomsbury.

Bolitho, R., Carter, R., Hughes, R., Ivanovic, H., Masuhara, H., & Tomlinson, B. (2003). Ten questions about language awareness. *ELT Journal 57*(2), 251–259.

Clare, A., & Wilson, J. J. (2012). *Speakout intermediate students' book.* Harlow: Pearson.

Dörnyei, Z. (2009). The psychology of instructed second language acquisition. In Z. Dörnyei, *The Psychology of instructed second language acquisition* (pp. 267–299). Oxford: Oxford University Press.

Ellis, R. (2002). Does form-focused instruction affect the acquisition of implicit knowledge? *Studies in Second Language Acquisition, 24*(2), 223–236.

Fenner, A. N., & Nordal-Pedersen, G. (1999). *Search 10.* Oslo: Gyldendal.

Hadley, G. (2014). Global coursebooks in local settings: An empirical investigation of effectiveness. In N. Harwood (Ed.), *English language teaching textbooks: Content, consumption, production* (pp. 205–240). Basingstoke, UK: Palgrave Macmillan.

Krashen, D. (1994). The input hypothesis and its rivals. In N. Ellis (Ed.), *Implicit and explicit learning of languages* (pp. 45–77). London: Academic Press.

Krashen, S. (2004). *The power of reading* (2nd ed.). Littleton: Libraries Unlimited.

Long, M. (1991). Focus on form: A design feature in language teaching methodology. In K. de Bot, R. Ginsberg, & C. Kramsch (Eds.), *Foreign language research in cross-cultural perspective.* Amsterdam: Benjamins.

Masuhara, H., & Tomlinson, B. (2008). Materials for general English. In B. Tomlinson (Ed.), *English language learning materials* (pp. 17–37). London: Continuum.

Masuhara, H., Hann, M., Yi, Y., & Tomlinson, B. (2008). Adult EFL courses. *ELT Journal, 62*(3), 294–312.

Nation, I. S. P. (2007). The four strands. *Innovation in Language Learning and Teaching, 1*(1), 2–13.

Nation, I. S. P. (2013). Materials for teaching vocabulary. In B. Tomlinson (Ed.), *Developing materials for language teaching* (2nd ed., pp. 351–364). London: Continuum.

On Target. (1994). Windhoek: Gamsberg Macmillan.

Ortega, L. (2010). *Second language acquisition: Critical concepts in linguistics.* London: Routledge.

Pavlenko, A. (2005). *Emotions and multilingualism.* Cambridge: Cambridge University Press.

Rea, D., & Clemetson, T. (2011). *English unlimited intermediate coursebook*. Cambridge: Cambridge University Press.

Robinson, P. (Ed.) (2002). *Cognition and second language instruction*. Cambridge: Cambridge University Press.

Soars, L., & Soars, J. (2012). *New headway intermediate student's book*. Oxford: Oxford University Press.

Swain, M. (1995). Three functions of output in second language learning. In G. Cook (Ed.), *Principle and practice in applied linguistics: Studies in honour of H. G. Widdowson* (pp. 125–144). Oxford: Oxford University Press.

Tomlinson, B. (1981). *Talking to learn*. Vanuatu: Ministry of Education.

Tomlinson, B. (1994). Pragmatic awareness activities. *Language Awareness, 3*(3/4), 119–129.

Tomlinson, B. (1995). Work in progress: textbook projects. *Folio, 2*(2), 26–31.

Tomlinson, B. (2005). Testing to learn. *ELT Journal, 59*(1), 39–46.

Tomlinson, B. (2007). Teachers' responses to form-focused discovery activities. In S. Fotos & H. Nassaji (Eds.), *Form focused instruction and teacher education: Studies in honour of Rod Ellis*. Oxford: Oxford University Press.

Tomlinson, B. (2011a). Introduction: Principles and procedures of materials development. In B. Tomlinson (Ed.), *Materials development in language teaching* (2nd ed., pp. 1–34). Cambridge: Cambridge University Press.

Tomlinson, B. (2011b). Seeing what they mean: Helping L2 readers to visualise. In B. Tomlinson (Ed.), *Materials development in language teaching* (2nd ed., pp. 357–378). Cambridge: Cambridge University Press.

Tomlinson, B. (2012). Materials development for language learning and teaching. *Language Teaching: Surveys and Studies, 45*(2), 1–37.

Tomlinson, B. (Ed.). (2013a). *Applied linguistics and materials development*. London: Bloomsbury.

Tomlinson, B. (2013b). Second language acquisition and materials development. In B. Tomlinson (Ed.), *Applied linguistics and materials development* (pp. 11–30). London: Bloomsbury.

Tomlinson, B. (2013c). Developing principled frameworks for materials development. In B. Tomlinson (Ed.), *Developing materials for language teaching* (2nd ed., pp. 95–118). London: Bloomsbury.

Tomlinson, B. (2013d). Looking out for English. *Studies in Self-Access Learning Journal, 4*(4), 253–261.

Tomlinson, B. (2015a) Creative use of coursebooks. In Maley, A., Creativity – for a change. In T. Pattison (Ed.), *IATEFL 2014 Harrogate conference selections* (pp. 105–109). Faversham: IATEFL.

Tomlinson, B. (2015b). Challenging teachers to use their coursebook creatively. In A. Maley & N. Peachey (Eds.), *Creativity in the language classroom* (pp. 24–28). London: British Council.

Tomlinson, B. (forthcoming 2016). Making typical coursebook activities more beneficial for the learner. In D. Bao (Ed.), *ELT material development in Asia and beyond: Directions, issues, and challenges*. Cambridge: Cambridge Scholars.

Tomlinson, B., & Avila, J. (2007). Seeing and saying for yourself: The roles of audio-visual mental aids in language learning and use. In B. Tomlinson (Ed.), *Language acquisition and development: Studies of learners of first and other languages* (pp. 61–81). London: Continuum.

Tomlinson, B., & Masuhara, H. (2013). Adult coursebooks. *ELT Journal, 67*(2), 233–249.

Tomlinson, B., & Masuhara, H. (forthcoming 2017). *The complete guide to materials development for language learning*. Hoboken, NJ: Wiley.

Tomlinson, B., Dat, B., Masuhara, H., & Rudby, R. (2001). ELT courses for adults. *ELT Journal, 55*(1), 80–101.

2

BRAIN STUDIES AND MATERIALS FOR LANGUAGE LEARNING

Hitomi Masuhara

Introduction

There seems to be marked growth in global interest and awareness of how the brain holds the key to understanding human behaviour, be it physical or mental. In this chapter, I would like to explore implications of brain studies to theories and practice in second language acquisition and materials development for language learning.

When a child alerts a mother, 'My tummy hurts', the problem is likely to lie somewhere, academically put, in the architecture and the processes that constitute the phenomena of 'digestion'. Medical advancement now enables the specialists to directly observe, analyse and measure:

- how the ingested food is processed;
- what kinds of organs or anatomical structures are involved;
- what kinds of chemicals need to be secreted.

If the mother were to seek detailed explanations, she would be able to find out about 'the digestive system and processes' from an anatomical level (e.g. stomach) and a cellular level (e.g. G-cell) to a molecular level (e.g. constitution of enzymes). Most mothers would sensibly leave such academic endeavours to specialists and request advice for appropriate solutions to their child's specific 'tummy ache' problem.

What is important, however, is that, if required, such information is abundantly available in accessible ways. It would be ludicrous for any lay people to completely disregard a basic understanding of digestive systems that are vital for sustaining our lives. Fundamental knowledge about our body and ways of maintaining health is widely made available as part of school subjects, on public health websites and in many other resources in the media.

When a second language (L2) learner alerts a teacher, 'I don't want to learn English', would a teacher be able to resort to her understanding of brain studies to support her own observation, experience and learning of second language acquisition? What is 'motivation'? Are we able to directly observe, analyse and measure 'motivation' as we can in the case of 'digestion'?

Traditionally such constructs were assumed to be not amenable to direct physical examination. 'Motivation' is a psychological/mental phenomenon that is complex, dynamic and invisible (for various definitions, see Dörnyei and Ushioda, 2011). Researchers in social, humanistic and psychological sciences refer to such unobservable and complex concepts as 'psychological/mental constructs'.

Researchers in psychology, education and applied linguistics have been studying such 'unobservable' psychological/mental constructs through systematic empirical research using indirect probes and quantitative, qualitative or mixed methods (methodological discussions are available in Cohen et al., 2011; Dörnyei and Ushioda, 2011; Mackey and Gass, 2005; Nunan and Bailey, 2009).

Though we gain a lot of insights through such empirical studies in these fields, consensus among researchers remains elusive mainly due to the fact that research requires feasible segmented focus with different methods and interpretation. Based on their survey of the studies on motivation, for example, Dörnyei and Ushioda (2011, p. 4) describe the current status by using an analogy of an 'Indian fable of the blind men encountering an elephant, each touching a different part of the animal (tusk, tail, ear, trunk, belly) and ending up with a very different mental representation of the animal'.

What is urgent is that, regardless of current situations of theories about second language acquisition, a teacher who is facing a low-motivated learner is expected to find a way somehow of helping him/her to acquire an additional language. Materials developers have been expected to provide a sound tool for teachers to conduct the task of facilitating Second Language Acquisition.

The good news is that recently there have been remarkable developments in brain studies, supported by various funds, that could change the current picture surrounding learning, teaching and materials development:

Technological Advancement in the Study of the Brain

We are seeing a concerted effort to accelerate the development and application of new technologies that will enable researchers to produce dynamic pictures of the brain that show how individual brain cells and complex neural circuits interact at the speed of thought as can be seen in the Brain Initiative (2013–2025): http://www.kavlifoundation.org/brain-initiative.

These technologies could open new doors to explore how the brain records, processes, uses, stores and retrieves vast quantities of information, and shed light on the complex links between brain function and behaviour. Psychological/mental constructs could become more observable, analysable and measurable. In other words we might be able to eventually explain what constitutes 'motivation' as we do in 'digestion'.

Collaborative and Interdisciplinary Efforts in the Investigation of Learning

Language acquisition is a complex phenomenon that requires interdisciplinary accounts. Fischer et al. (2010, p. 68) acknowledge a growing demand worldwide for interdisciplinary efforts to combine neurobiological studies with cognitive science and with social and humanistic disciplines. They describe the emergence of Educational Neuroscience as a new field in the USA that brings together biology, cognitive science, developmental science and education to investigate brain and genetic bases of learning and teaching.

Fischer et al. (2010) refer to the cases in which research and practice combine routinely in many industries and fields to create usable knowledge that has great practical value. They advocate collaboration between researchers, teachers and learners so that more useful research evidence can be fed back productively to shape schools and other learning situations.

Fischer et al. (2010) also argue for improvements in the current one-way practice in which researchers collect data in schools and make those data and the resulting research papers available to educators. Instead they recommend a two-way dialogue in which 'practitioners and researchers work together to formulate research questions and methods so that they can be connected to practice and policy' (Fischer et al., 2010, p. 68).

There must be billions of teachers globally who work with unmotivated learners and who blame themselves or their teaching context. It seems to me to make sense that such a global issue be tackled with interdisciplinary collaboration without artificial boundaries of science, occupations and specialities.

Basic Brain Knowledge for All

Neuroscience seems to be gradually becoming a part of learning in schools and in teacher development. For example, BrainFacts.org offers an authoritative source of information about the brain and nervous system for the public and educators. The organization provides Neuroscience Core Concepts for educators that are correlated to the US National Science Education Standards. The Allen Institute for Brain Science (https://www.alleninstitute.org/our-research/open-science-resources/) offers free and open resources to anyone around the world.

Obviously, we should be wary of neuro-myths that seem to be in abundance in the market. We should be realistic in our expectations of what neuroscience can tell us when there still is enormous scientific uncertainty. The scanned images or computer-simulated images may be dazzling but the research results should be presented and interpreted appropriately within the context, and findings should not be used to answer questions they were never designed to answer. Interdisciplinary studies bring in new definitions and interpretations of the same phenomenon examined in different ways.

In sum, just as dealing with 'tummy ache' should be based on the studies on 'digestion', our discussion of 'language acquisition' or 'developing materials for language learning' would benefit from consideration of the nature of the human brain and its mechanisms of language processing, learning and memory. In this sense, I agree with Jacobs and Schumann (1992) when they argue that:

> Language acquisition researchers must begin to incorporate a degree of neu-robiological reality into their perception of the language acquisition process. Research that extrapolates mental metaphors from observed behavior must be supplemented and constrained by a neutrally inspired paradigm that attempts to understand behavior based on the structure of the organ from which all behavior originates: the brain . . . A neutrally inspired perspective extends to almost all areas of inquiry into the human condition and provides a common ground for integrating various perspectives of the language acquisition process.
>
> (p. 295)

N. Ellis (2002, p. 299) notes, 'We are now at a stage at which there are important connections between SLA theory and the neuroscience of learning and memory'.

Dörnyei (2007) also emphasizes the critical importance of a shift in the SLA paradigm:

> I had to realize that applied linguists simply do not have the option of ignor-ing the new psychological approaches because the advances in these areas are leading to a fundamental restructuring of our knowledge base of lan-guage acquisition and language processing. Disregarding these developments would lead to the marginalization of the field of applied linguistics/second language research.
>
> (pp. xi–xii)

What are lacking at the moment seems to me to be projects that explore the validity and applicability of findings from brain studies in relation to language acquisition and materials development. Such investigation must have wider interdisciplinary perspectives, combining the scientific findings with what we know from our direct experience about what happens in the language learning classroom.

As part of such projects, in this chapter I'll focus on affect and mechanisms of the brain that seem to have attracted fairly wide consensus among neuroscientists and that could bring significant improvements to theories and practice of SLA and materials development.

The Construct and Role of Affect in Learning

Arnold and Brown (1999, p. 1), after evaluating various definitions, provide a broad definition of 'affect' as 'aspects of emotion, feeling, mood or attitude which condition behaviour'.

Affect is one of the teachers' major concerns around the world as they face the challenges every day of having to persuade unmotivated students to engage with second/additional or foreign language learning. They are fully aware of the vital importance of learners' motivation, emotion, moods, attitudes and aspirations. Where can a teacher find information and guidance?

Matthewson (1994) draws our attention to a stark contrast in relation to the coverage of affect between pedagogic and research publications since the 1950s. Affect-related topics maintain popularity over the years in the pedagogic publications such as *The Reading Teacher* (Dillon et al., 1992). Publication on reading research, on the other hand, included hardly anything on affect-related topics. This could be due to the behaviouristic tradition in psychology and psycholinguistics, which tended to sideline affect as an elusive and peripheral phenomenon unworthy of serious investigation. All the major models of reading in the 1970s, for example, were heavily influenced by information processing studies (e.g. artificial intelligence, connectionist studies). This meant that human emotion, interest or motivation did not feature in reading research at all. The direct consequence was teaching materials for reading that focused solely on linguistic processing without much, if any, concern for learners' interest or motivation.

Brain studies seem to provide undeniable anatomical and physiological evidence that the affect plays a vital and fundamental role in human biological and social survival (Damasio, 1994; Damasio & Carvalho, 2013; Gazzaniga et al., 2014; Immordino-Yang & Damasio, 2007; Phelps & LeDoux, 2005). With the help of the advancement of clinical and experimental studies supported by neuroimaging, neuroscientists are able to show how memory (i.e. learning) can be enhanced or diminished by affective colouring and how such structural mechanisms have developed in the evolution of the species.

Damasio and Carvalho (2013, p. 143), for example, define 'feeling' as 'mental experiences of body states'. They explain that the 'felt experience' may signify not only 'physiological need such as hunger, pain, fear, anger and well-being' but also more socially inspired reactions such as 'compassion, gratitude or love'. Ortega (2009) explains that 'Motivation is usually understood to refer to the desire to initiate L2 learning and the efforts employed to sustain it.' The dynamic, individual and complex nature of 'motivation' (Dörnyei & Ushioda, 2011) seems to fit well with a visceral biological and cognitive account based on in-built desire for better biological and social survival (Lee et al., 2009). Imagine an EFL learner who associates reading with painful translation routines. Consciously she may tell herself that she needs to learn to read fluently in L2 as her extrinsic motivation is to pass the exams in order to gain entry to an esteemed university. Right after reading she knows that she will be tested on her comprehension and on the language contained in the text. What will be her internal state and her feeling? What kinds of research data would a researcher get if this girl was a respondent in the questionnaire and interview studies on motivation in relation to classroom language learning? Would she be able to articulate why she reads in the way she does during reading lessons? The same learner, however, might read with far superior comprehension if she were to receive a love letter in English from the boy of her dreams. What would be her internal states and her feeling then? If there were unfamiliar words, would she be able to work out their meaning and moreover learn them?

Damasio and Carvalho (2013, p. 150) argue that 'Feeling paved the way for the establishment of higher levels of cognition and consciousness, culminating in the modern human mind'. In fact, the title of the article by Immordino-Yang and Damasio (2007) 'We feel therefore we learn: The relevance of affective and social neuroscience to education' sums up their view of how sentience (i.e. the ability to feel, perceive or experience subjectively in contrast to reasoning) controls learning, attention, memory, decision making and social functioning. Bolte Taylor (2009, p. 19), a neuroscientist, confirms such a claim based on her own experience of recovering from a stroke, by saying that 'Although many of us may think of ourselves as thinking creatures that feel, biologically we are feeling creatures that think'.

Implications of Placing Affect at the Heart of Research and Materials Development

What does SLA research tell teachers about affect? Has the situation changed since Matthewson (1994) reported a paucity of research on affect in reading research?

A quick survey of recent handbooks of research on Second Language Acquisition reveal that affect is not being considered as a core aspect of learning. For example, Gass and Mackey (2012) and R. Ellis (2008) do each include a chapter, respectively on 'Neurocognition of second language' and 'The neuropsychology of second language acquisition', but the main discussions seem to focus on cortical language processing, and their indexes do not include 'affect' or 'emotion'. Ortega (2009) does have chapters on 'Motivation' and 'Affect and other individual differences', but both chapters seem to be an overview of existing empirical research that considers 'motivation' as one of the variables of 'individual differences'. Task-Based Language Teaching has attracted a lot of attention from SLA researchers (e.g. Van den Branden et al., 2009). The researchers' concerns, however, seem to centre around increases in linguistic processing capacities. The indexes include 'goals' but not 'affect' or 'emotion'.

Having affect in the central position would influence how we might design research. I would like to introduce three examples below:

> Example 1: Brain studies would predict that learners' affect towards the text and towards the task should be two of the major variables for Task-Based Teaching research. How engaging the text and the task are for the learners would be seen to influence their achievement. Tomlinson (2013) argues the vital importance of engaging texts and tasks to drive materials. Research that incorporates his Text-Driven Approach has demonstrated engagement and a positive and lasting effect on language acquisition (Rico Troncoso, 2010).

> Example 2: Kuperman et al. (2014, p. 1065) maintain that emotion influences most aspects of cognition and behaviour and yet that 'emotional factors are conspicuously absent from current models of word recognition'. Their

results demonstrate a difference in word recognition rate between positive and negative words. They claim that incorporating emotional factors, especially valence, improves the performance of models of word recognition.

Example 3: Widening the context, Lee et al. (2009) attempt to offer a perspective on language acquisition based on evolutionary biology and neurobiology. Schumann (2013), for example, attempts to unify first language acquisition and second language acquisition and explore neurobiological explanations as to why a successful L1 learner may not necessarily succeed in learning an additional language.

What would be the implications of these brain studies for materials development?

Criterion-referenced surveys of global coursebooks for adult learners (e.g. Tomlinson and Masuhara, 2013) provide evidence that most coursebooks follow PPP (Presentation – Practice – Production) procedures. The problem is that PPP may be a convenient teaching procedure but it ignores what we know about when, why and how the brain learns. Listening to a presentation on an isolated and decontextualized language feature can help rational focus but is unlikely to stimulate affective engagement, especially if that feature has been selected because it comes next in the syllabus or coursebook rather than because it is conspicuously relevant to the lives, needs and wants of the learners. Likewise controlled practice of the feature without a situational purpose and guided production of the item in a prescribed and pseudo-communicative situation are unlikely to achieve the affective stimulation needed for effective and durable acquisition. Of course, if the learners have already encountered the language feature in an engaging text and/or task, have found it problematic and/or interesting and have asked the teacher for information, then the PPP procedure might have more value, providing that the presentation, practice and production relate to the text and/or task and to what the learners found problematic and/or interesting.

Based on my understanding of how affect drives learning and memory, I would strongly argue that teaching approaches should aim to ultimately provide opportunities for the self-fulfilment of learners. The brain is designed to enhance life by learning. In this sense, relevance, meaningfulness and the value of materials to the individual would play crucial roles. The activities should be engaging and contribute to well-being, so much so that the learners would want more (Fredrickson & Branigan, 2005). The bias towards reasoning skills and factual knowledge in the learning environment needs to be rebalanced with the notion of sentience (i.e., as stated above, the ability to feel, perceive, or experience subjectively in contrast to reasoning) in the mind. The implications here are that the potential for affective engagement should be the prime criterion when writing or selecting texts and tasks and that learner choice of texts and tasks should be a vital consideration when designing materials (See Masuhara, 2015 for examples). Ways of achieving this would include helping learners to select or find a text that they want to use with the tasks specified in their materials or selecting from a menu of tasks those they want to use in response to a potentially engaging text.

The opposing voices may say that 'We are language teachers. Our job is to teach the language; "self-fulfilment" and affect are beyond our duties.' Immordino-Yang and Damasio (2007, p. 9) warn that 'neither learning nor recall happen in a purely rational domain, divorced from emotion, even though some of our knowledge will eventually distil into a moderately rational, unemotional form'. They also point out that unmemorable knowledge inherently does not transfer well to the real-world situation. They say, 'As recent advances in the neurobiology of emotions reveal, in the real world, cognition functions in the service of life-regulating goals, implemented by emotional machinery' (see also Rice et al., 2007; Van Kleef et al., 2014). Do we want to ignore affect and fail in our job to teach the language? What is even worse, perhaps we may be the ones that are producing bored students with an aversion to learning, doomed to fail in society? Neurobiological insights can help us become better teachers, researchers and materials developers.

Conclusion

What I am claiming is that scientific study of the brain in action during the learning process has confirmed the significance of factors which have been drawn attention to in the literature but which are often considered as peripheral by SLA researchers. In this chapter I have focused on affect, but brain studies have also revealed the positive effect on language acquisition of such factors as macro- and multi-dimensional processing of language input, creativity, positive energy and experiential learning. In other words, brain studies have demonstrated how important it is that learners are given an engaging and holistic experience of acquiring their target language and are not just restricted to the discrete learning and practice of language items. This message needs to be passed on in accessible and persuasive ways to language teachers so that they can adapt and supplement their coursebook materials with activities which their learners really want to do and which motivate them through enjoyment, fun, laughter and achievable challenge.

References

Arnold, J., & Brown, H. D. (1999). A map of the terrain. In J. Arnold (Ed.), *Affect in language learning* (pp. 1–24). Cambridge: Cambridge University Press.

Cohen, L., Manion, L., & Morrison, K. (2011). *Research methods in education*. London: Routledge.

Damasio, A. (1994). *Descartes' error: Emotion, reason, and the human brain*. New York: Avon.

Damasio, A., & Carvalho, G. B. (2013). The nature of feelings: Evolutionary and neurobiological origins. *Nature Reviews Neuroscience, 14*(2), 143–152.

Dillon, D. R., O'Brien, D. G., Hopkins, C. J., Baumann, J. F., Humphrey, J. W., Pickle, J. M. . . . & Pauler, S. M. (1992). Article content and authorship trends in *The Reading Teacher* 1948–1991. *The Reading Teacher, 45*(5), 362–365.

Dörnyei, Z. (2007). *Research methods in applied linguistics: Quantitative, qualitative, and mixed methodologies*. Oxford: Oxford University Press.

Dörnyei, Z., & Ushioda, E. (2011). *Teaching and researching motivation* (2nd ed.). Harlow, UK: Pearson Education.

Ellis, N. (2002). Reflections on frequency effects in language processing. *Studies in Second Language Acquisition, 24*, 297–339.

Ellis, R. (2008). *The study of second language acquisition* (2nd ed.). Oxford: Oxford University Press.

Fischer, K. W., Goswami, U., Geake, J., & Task Force on the Future of Educational Neuroscience. (2010). The future of educational neuroscience. *Mind, Brain and Education, 4*(2), 68–80.

Fredrickson, B. L., & Branigan, C. (2005). Positive emotions broaden the scope of attention and thought-action repertoires. *Cognition and Emotion, 19*(3), 313–332.

Gass, S. M., & Mackey, A. (Eds.) (2012). *The Routledge handbook of second language acquisition.* Abingdon, UK: Routledge.

Gazzaniga, M. S., Ivry, R. B., & Mangun, G. R. (2014). *Cognitive neuroscience – The biology of the mind* (4th ed.). New York: W. W. Norton.

Herschensohn, J., & Young-Scholten, M. (Eds.) (2013). *The Cambridge handbook of second language acquisition.* New York: Cambridge University Press.

Immordino-Yang, M. H., & Damasio, A. (2007). We feel, therefore we learn: The relevance of affective and social neuroscience to education. *Mind, Brain, and Education, 1*(8), 3–10.

Jacobs, B., & Schumann, J. (1992). Language acquisition and the neurosciences: Towards a more integrative perspective. *Applied Linguistics, 13*(3), 282–301.

Joaquin, A. D. L., & Schumann, J. H. (2014). *Exploring the interactional instinct.* New York: Oxford University Press.

Kuperman, V., Estes, Z., Brysbaert, M., & Warriner, A. B. (2014). Emotion and language: Valence and arousal affect word recognition. *Journal of Experimental Psychology: General, 143*(3), 1065–1081.

Lee, N., Mikesell, L., Joaquin, A. D. L., Mates, A. W., & Schumann, J. H. (2009). *The interactional instinct: The evolution and acquisition of language.* Oxford: Oxford University Press.

Mackey, A., & Gass, S. M. (2009). *Second language acquisition: Methodology and design.* Mahwah, NJ: Erlbaum.

Masuhara, H. (2015). 'Anything goes' in task-based language teaching materials? – the need for principled materials evaluation, adaptation and development. *The European Journal of Applied Linguistics and TEFL, 2*, 113–127.

Matthewson, G. C. (1994). Model of attitude influence upon reading and learning to read. In R. B. Ruddel, M. R. Ruddel, & H. Singer (Eds.), *Theoretical models and processes of reading* (pp. 1131–1161). Newark, DE: International Reading Association.

Nunan, D., & Bailey, K. (2009). *Exploring second language classroom research: A comprehensive guide.* Boston: Heinle Cengage Learning.

Ortega, L. (2009). *Understanding second language acquisition.* London: Hodder Education.

Phelps, E. A., & LeDoux, J. E. (2005). Contributions of the amygdala to emotion processing: From animal model to human behaviour. *Neuron, 48*(2), 175–187.

Rice, J., Levine, L., & Pizarro, D. (2007). "Just stop thinking about it": Effects of emotional disengagement on children's memory for educational material. *Emotion, 7*(4), 812–823.

Rico Troncoso, Carlos. (2010). The effects of language materials on the development of intercultural competence. In B. Tomlinson & H. Masuhara (Eds.), *Research for materials development in language learning* (pp. 83–102). London: Continuum.

Schumann, J. H. (2013). A unified perspective of first and second language acquisition. In A. D. L. Joaquin, L. Dina, & J. H. Schumann (Eds.), *Exploring the interactional instinct* (pp. 1–15). Oxford: Oxford University Press.

Taylor, J. Bolte (2009). *My stroke of insight: A brain scientist's personal journey*. London: Hodder and Stoughton.

Tomlinson, B. (2013). Developing principled frameworks for materials development. In B. Tomlinson (Ed.), *Developing materials for language teaching* (2nd ed., pp. 95–118). London: Bloomsbury.

Tomlinson, B., & Masuhara, H. (2013). Adult coursebooks. *ELT Journal, 67*(2), 233–249.

Van den Branden, K., Bygate, M., & Norris, J. M. (Eds.) (2009). *Task-based language teaching – A reader*. Amsterdam: John Benjamins.

Van Kleef, G. A., van den Berg., H., & Heerdink, M. W. (2014). The persuasive power of emotions: Effects of emotional expressions on attitude formation and change. *Journal of Applied Psychology, 100*(4), 1124–1142.

Brain Studies Related Websites:

Allen Institute Open Resources: https://www.alleninstitute.org/our-research/open-science-resources/
The Allen Institute provides open and free resources. See also http://www.brain-map.org/ in which tutorials are provided, giving oriention videos of how their resources can be explored.

BrainFacts.org: http://www.brainfacts.org/educators/educator-resources/
An authoritative source of information about the brain and nervous system for the public.

The Brain Initiative (2013–2025): http://www.kavlifoundation.org/brain-initiative
'A broad, collaborative research initiative to advance the science and technologies needed to unlock the mysteries of the human brain. Its goal: Accelerate the development and application of new technologies that will enable researchers to produce dynamic pictures of the brain that show how individual brain cells and complex neural circuits interact at the speed of thought. These technologies will open new doors to explore how the brain records, processes, uses, stores, and retrieves vast quantities of information, and shed light on the complex links between brain function and behavior.'

The Dana Foundation: https://www.dana.org/About/
A private philanthropic organization that supports brain research through grants, publications, and educational programs. It is committed to advancing brain research and to educating the public in a responsible manner about the potential of research.

National Institute of Health http://www.nih.gov/
National Institute of Neurological Disorders and Stroke: http://www.ninds.nih.gov/education/
On this site, you'll find great educational resources related to brain health and function for parents, students, and teachers.

Society for Neuroscience: http://www.sfn.org/about/what-we-do
'The Society for Neuroscience is the world's largest organization of scientists and physicians devoted to understanding the brain and nervous system. The nonprofit organization, founded in 1969, now has nearly 40,000 members in more than 90 countries and 130 chapters worldwide.'

Brain researcher Jill Bolte Taylor studied her own stroke as it happened – and has become a powerful voice for brain recovery: http://www.ted.com/talks/jill_bolte_taylor_s_powerful_stroke_of_insight

3

APPLYING SLA PRINCIPLES TO WHOLE-CLASS ACTIVITIES

Brian Tomlinson

Introduction

Most publications on the application of second language acquisition (SLA) principles to materials development exemplify their suggestions with activities which involve group or pair work. However many teachers are in a situation in which they are not permitted by their institution to use group or pair work, or they are reluctant to do so because of problems with class management and with the monitoring of student performance in large classes, or their students express a preference for whole-class activities. In fact, in my experience, the most common reason teachers give for not being able to apply SLA principles to their classroom practice is that they are forced to teach very large classes and this causes problems of classroom management, motivation and marking. Many also say that they are required to teach these large classes using whole-class activities. What I say to teachers is that I have taught in similar situations and I have found that whole-class activities have many advantages, provided the teacher does not just stand in front of the class lecturing at them or interrogating individuals. Interestingly there seems to be a movement in many countries away from encouraging radical change in schools used to teaching large classes with whole-class activities. Instead of advocating more use of pair and group work advisors are suggesting ways in which large classes can benefit from more communicative approaches whilst retaining their traditional approach of whole-class activity. For instance, the British Council advertised on their Consultancy Opportunities website on 3 March 2015 for consultants to write teacher-training materials for teachers in Myanmar who work in institutions with a tradition of 'whole-class teaching, widespread use of chanting and rote memorisation'. The advertisement says that 'The materials should combine best practice around whole-class / direct-instruction / teacher-directed approaches and child-centred / constructivist approaches.'[1]

Here are some of the advantages I have found when doing whole-class activities instead of or in addition to pair and group activities in Japan, Oman, Singapore, Vanuatu and Zambia (often with large classes of up to ninety students). All of these advantages create conditions which are conducive to language acquisition and/or educational development.

Whole-class activities can generate more **positive energy**. After fifty years in the classroom I am convinced that positive energy is a vital prerequisite for effective learning and that an important responsibility of the teacher is the generation of positive energy. This can be achieved by initial teacher stimulus/performance followed by student response and then student interaction (see Chapter 1 in this volume) and I have found that this is much easier in a plenary session (especially with a large class) than when using pair or group work. In pairs or groups (and in small classes) a few 'unenergized' students can infect the others, whereas this is much less likely in a large whole-class activity. If positive energy is generated by the teacher's use of materials and sustained by the majority of the students then engagement, positive attitudes to the learning experience, motivation, attention, perseverance, relaxation and enjoyment can ensue and language acquisition can be facilitated. See Garmston and Wellman (2013) for a detailed and referenced rationale for the importance of generating energy in educational establishments (though ironically they advocate the use of group work to achieve this). See Doidge (2015) for scientific evidence of the importance of brain-generated energy in the learning process.

Whole-class activities also **allow students to 'hide'**. By this I mean that if they are not in the mood to 'perform' they can listen and read attentively but let others do the talking. This can relieve the pressure of monitored performance, provide valuable security and reduce the negative anxiety and stress which can be caused by the teacher insisting on everybody making a contribution in pair work, group work and small-class plenary activities. We know that there is such a thing as positive anxiety which can stimulate energy and motivation (Aida, 1994) but the anxiety caused by being pushed into language production can have a negative effect on confidence, self-esteem and motivation (e.g. Horwitz, 2000; Lyons, 2009; Ortega, 2009; Oxford, 2009, 2011). This is especially so at lower levels if students are pushed into premature language production in pair and group activities before they have achieved affective and linguistic readiness. If students are afraid of making errors they often fail to produce anything at all or say something very simple which aims at the avoidance of error rather than the communication of something significant. Bao (2013, 2014) found that this was the main reason for the perceived reticence of students in English classes in Vietnam and he designed a successful intervention which encouraged teachers not to nominate answerers to questions, to give students time to phrase answers and responses in their inner voice and to respect thoughtful silence. I have found that in whole-class activities with large classes students can 'hide' in comfort without fearing interrogation and that if the activity encourages shouting out or performing in unison (see 'Storytelling and Performance of Texts' below) the students in hiding sometimes make quiet and tentative contributions which can then be picked up and repeated by the teacher if they make a positive contribution or inconspicuously ignored if they do not. This can increase learner confidence, as can mental participation in whole-class activities which do not compel verbal participation. Of course, the teacher needs to notice those who are hiding and to check from their facial expressions, eye focus and general demeanour that they are mentally engaged. What the teacher should not do in my view is make the hiders feel guilty or push them into reluctant verbal participation. If the hiders seem motivated and engaged it makes sense to leave them alone but create opportunities in which they could come comfortably out of hiding if they wanted to. If the hiders do not seem motivated and engaged then it is even more important that the teacher leaves them alone but then thinks of ways of motivating and engaging them in that lesson or in subsequent lessons.

Confidence can also be achieved through spoken and written contributions to whole-class activities, especially if those contributions are appreciated by fellow learners and the teacher. Many of the activities I advocate below are designed to stimulate such contributions whilst still allowing for the hiding described above. The achievement of communicative confidence is undeniably beneficial in relation to language acquisition (Lyons, 2009; Ortega, 2009) and I have noted many students grow gradually more confident as a result of (and as manifested by) the increased frequency of their contributions to whole-class activities.

I have found when using whole-class activities with large classes in Japan and Oman that more **interaction in English** between students and with the teacher was stimulated than when using pair and small group activities. In the latter activities the norm was for the first language (L1) to be used (an understandable tendency in monolingual classes) and often one student would dominate, some students would make minimal contributions and feel uncomfortable about it and the conversations in English would be rehearsals of language recently 'learned' rather than communicative interactions. In whole-class activities which encouraged interruption and debate actual communicative interaction in English was quite common, especially if the activity achieved affective and cognitive engagement, and partly because I could understand neither Japanese nor Arabic. I also found that whole-class activities could promote **collaborative learning** and help to develop **team playing skills** (especially in those activities designed to stimulate individuals to contribute to a whole-class achievement such as the telling of a story, the dramatization of an event, the construction of a tableau or the painting of a mural). I found that these skills could be developed either when the whole class were working together towards the same goal or large groups were working together to achieve their own goals within the context of a whole-class activity (e.g. a competition, a quiz, a project).

Of course all the benefits claimed above (and ultimately language acquisition) can only be achieved by materials which are used in the principled ways that I have advocated in Chapter 1 of this volume so that they provide exposure to the language in use, opportunities for discovering how the language is used, opportunities to use the language for communication and, above all, affective and cognitive engagement.

Here are some examples of activity types I have used with whole classes which match with SLA principles and which have the potential to contribute positively to language acquisition and development.

The Students as an Audience

In these activities the students are all together as a class and they are all listening, viewing or reading. They might incidentally also be talking to each other but stimulating talking is not the main objective; the main objective is to provide the students with a motivated, engaging experience of the target language in use (see Principle 1 in Chapter 1 of this volume and Tomlinson (2013a) for discussions of the necessity of such exposure for the achievement of language acquisition).

1. Task-Free Activities

At the beginning of each lesson the teacher tells a joke, reads a poem, tells a story, reads an extract from the a newspaper, tells an anecdote or performs a scene from a play. The teacher leaves a few minutes silence and then starts the lesson. At the end of the lesson those students who were engaged by the teacher can take a copy of the text and put it in their loose leaf file. There are no comprehension questions and no tasks in order to ensure that students do not suffer the anxiety caused by constantly being tested on what they have listened to or read. The objective is to create a relaxed environment to enhance the likelihood of the students being engaged during their exposure to English in use.

What happens in my experience is that some students read the texts again at home and then ask questions about them in a subsequent lesson. Some also follow up the suggestions for further reading written underneath the texts and ask questions about what they have read. In my view real questions coming from engaged and curious students are much more valuable than the display questions that many teachers use in every class to interrogate their students.

I began each lesson with task-free activities when teaching recently at Sultan Qaboos University in Oman and this was very popular with the students. It was also very popular in foreign language classes at Leeds Metropolitan University (as evidenced by end-of-course questionnaires) and in the many institutions all over the world where I have recommended this approach. It is quite demanding on the teachers until they have assembled a large enough 'library' of potentially engaging texts of many different genres and text types and have developed from practice and classroom experience the confidence and competence to perform their texts effectively. It is worth it though. And, of course, you can always usefully give the students the responsibility for finding the texts by giving each group in a large class the task of finding texts for specified days.

2. Extensive Reading/Listening/Viewing

The students read potentially engaging texts, listen to potentially engaging readings or recordings or view potentially engaging films, television programmes, advertisements, etc. They do so extensively rather than intensively and ideally choose what to do and how long they do it for. The teacher reads, listens or views extensively too and makes no attempt to control, direct or question the learners. The teacher's roles are to inform the students of the value of such engaged exposure (possibly using a shared L1 for clarity), to set a good example, to establish a relaxed atmosphere and to become as inconspicuous as possible. The power of extensive reading in particular has been demonstrated in many projects (e.g. Elley et al., 1996) and it is persuasively reported in Krashen (2004). Unfortunately in order to sell their extensive readers in bulk many of the major publishers are now producing so-called 'extensive readers' which are crammed with glossaries, background information, comprehension questions, language practice exercises and other ways of interfering with the students' enjoyment of reading.

An example of good practice is the STELLAR literacy programme in Singapore (Loh & Renanyanda, 2015). It advocates the collection of a rich and varied library of potentially engaging texts (Tomlinson, 2013b) which the students in upper primary select from and read silently for ten minutes at the beginning of every lesson prior to the teacher reading aloud to them a text from a Big Book which will drive the various activities in the lesson.

My favourite example of extensive reading, though, was provided by a primary school teacher in Vanuatu who made use of a large cardboard box. She cut out a screen and painted knobs on the box under the screen. Then she rolled a large sheet of paper onto a rolling pin and inserted it into holes she had cut out of the sides of the box. On the paper was a local folk tale which she had translated into English. When her pupils (about forty of them) lined up outside her room she told them that she had got a television for them (at that time there was no television broadcasting service in Vanuatu). She let the excited students into the room and told them to sit in a semi-circle in front of the television. She then pretended to turn a knob before moving the rolling pin until the title of the story appeared on the 'screen'. She then turned the pin very slowly so that it gradually revealed the story. After a while she turned the pin more quickly so that the students would have to increase their reading speed. The students' attention was fixed on the screen and their faces revealed how much they were enjoying the story.

Another example of cardboard-box resourcefulness was that of a teacher in a Jakarta secondary school who was convinced on a teachers' course of the value of extensive reading but distressed that the school could not give her any money to buy books. She staggered into class one day with an apparently heavy box and invited her curious students to look into their new class library. They were disappointed to find the box was empty but were then persuaded by their teacher to find for homework an interesting text in English and bring it to class to put it in the box for others to read. They all did so. Some brought books, some comics, some magazines, some brochures and some just the cut-off backs of packets of foodstuffs. Each week from then on the students took a text home to read and brought it back the next week together with a new text. By the end of the term there were about four hundred texts in the box, the students had fallen in love with reading and they had experienced English outside the classroom when gathering their texts.

For more information about extensive reading see Maley (2008) and www.erfoundation.org. For ideas for extensive reading with primary school students, see Ghosn in this volume.

3. Extended Teacher/Visitor/Student Performance

In one language school where I was Director of Studies we used to put classes together in our largest room so that they could listen to their teachers having a discussion, holding a debate, reading poems, singing songs or performing extracts from plays. I have known other schools do this too and some of them have also invited native speakers (or better still non-native speakers proficient in English) to talk to the students about their jobs, their interests or an activity they are experts in. In many of the institutions where I have taught I have also invited students to give performances in English. They were asked to prepare a presentation on something they were very enthusiastic about, to rehearse their presentation and then to give a practice performance in front of a teacher. They were given support and feedback and then on performance days students gave their presentations in different rooms to audiences (made up from different classes) who had selected their presentation to listen to. I will never forget Yoshi, a Japanese student in England who hardly ever spoke in class, giving a gripping and fluent presentation on motorbikes (helped considerably by the powerful bike he brought with him into the classroom). I will also never forget groups of Japanese engineering students at Kobe University in Japan presenting mock television adverts to a class of ninety students for the weird new electric vehicles they had invented.

The whole point of performances, whether they be by teachers, visitors or students is that large classes are exposed to English in use and that, if this happens frequently with a variety of different potentially engaging topics and performers, the input this provides will be rich, re-cycled, meaningful and comprehensible (especially if students are performing to students on topics they have chosen to listen to or have given presentations on themselves). I have also found that large (or combined) classes can give such performances a sense of occasion which can focus the students' attention and enhance their engagement.

The Students as Performers

By inviting students to be performers in a large class you are increasing opportunities both for increased and motivated production of language and for increased and motivated exposure to language too. Here are some activities which have been enjoyed by students and by their teachers. In most classes when I first started doing this type of activity some students were reluctant to participate but in every country (including Colombia, Indonesia, Japan, Malaysia, Singapore and South Korea) they soon realized that their participating peers were having fun, that the teacher was not correcting anybody and that they could hide amidst the collective noise if they took part. Also so much positive energy was often generated that the spectators eventually wanted to take part. I never forced anybody to take part and never needed to. I worked on the principle that the first time I tried an activity that was novel and potentially embarrassing with a large class only half of the students would take part. The second time about two thirds would participate and the third time all the students would join in.

1. Dialogue Performance

Many textbooks still feature dialogues for students to repeat. The repetition is usually done in pairs and consists of students mouthing words without meaning because the words are decontextualized and inauthentic and/or because the situations and the characters in them have no meaning for the students (e.g. a dialogue in a London shoe shop being repeated in a village in the middle of Borneo). One way of bringing such dialogues to bizarre life is to add detail to the characterization of the interlocutors in the dialogues, as follows. For example, in the following dialogues half the class performs A together and half performs B together from a textbook script.

i. The Weekend

This dialogue is not contextualized in the coursebook. The teacher tells the students that they are recording the dialogue for the CD. The person recording A is a veteran performer in textbook dialogues and is fed up with doing it. He/she wanted to be a film star and is disappointed to end up as a textbook dialogue recorder. The person recording B is a keen newcomer and is very excited at his/her opportunity to get paid for acting.

The students are given some time to read the dialogue and then rehearse their part in it in their inner voice (Tomlinson & Avila, 2007).

A: Did you have a nice weekend?
B: Yes, it was great.
A: What did you do?
B: I went to Paris with my partner. What about you?
A: Oh, I just stayed here in London.

ii. The Shoe Shop

The textbook simply says that this dialogue takes place in a shoe shop. The teacher tells the A half of the class that they are a shoe shop salesman who has just started work in that particular shop and that they have just realized that the customer is their ex-wife who recently divorced them. The teacher tells the B half that they are the ex-wife of the salesman and they had no idea that he now worked in this shop.

As in (i) above, the students are given time for mental preparation and they are then encouraged to talk to people around them about their interpretation before the whole-class performance begins.

Salesman:	Good morning, madam.
Customer:	Good morning.
Salesman:	What can I do for you today?
Customer:	I'd like a pair of red shoes.
Salesman:	Certainly madam. What size do you take?
Customer:	Size 3.
Salesman:	What about these?
Customer:	I'd like something a bit smarter.
Salesman:	For a special occasion?
Customer:	That's right.
Salesman:	What about these?
Customer:	Yes, that's better. I'll try them on.
Salesman:	Shall I help you madam?
Customer:	No, I can manage by myself thank you.
Salesman:	How are those?
Customer:	They're fine thank you. I'll take them.
Salesman:	That'll be £180.
Customer:	That's fine. Charge them to my account.
	(The customer starts to walk out of the shop with the shoes.)
Salesman:	Wait a minute madam. What's your name?
Customer:	Mrs Thompson.
Salesman:	Thank you madam. Hope to see you again soon.

An interesting extra activity is for the students then in small groups to add the inner speech utterances in brackets to the dialogue (see Tomlinson & Avila (2007b) for the value of inner speech activities in language activities), e.g. 'Good morning, madam' ('Oh no – It's you').

Such silly collective performances as in the noisy dialogue reading above can achieve such facilitating language acquisition phenomena as bizarreness (Richman, 1994; Worthen et al., 2000), impact, memorability and affective engagement in ways in which the students just reading out the textbook dialogues could never do. Such activities can also allow the students to offer individual interpretations within the collective noise.

2. Total Physical Response (TPR) Performance

This is an approach made famous by Ascher (2009), in which the students respond physically to the teacher's spoken instructions. In the original approach the teacher gave an instruction and performed the action herself (e.g. 'Put your right hand on your head'). The students watched the teacher and then performed the action themselves when the teacher repeated the instruction. The idea was to repeat the instruction/action sequence many times and then to vary it slightly to introduce new lexical or grammatical items (e.g. 'Put your left hand on your nose. Put your right hand under your chair'). Each lesson consisted of a repetition of instructions from the previous lesson plus new instructions containing new lexical and/ or grammatical items.

When we tried this approach on the PKG Project in Indonesia (Tomlinson, 1990) we found that the students were just imitating the teacher's actions without thinking about the meaning of her instructions. We also found that they were getting rather bored with doing things which were not very significant or interesting. Most importantly we found that students were being asked to perform actions individually and were losing self-esteem if they did not succeed. So we advised the teachers to stop performing the actions themselves, to only ask the whole class or very large groups to perform actions and to try to think of sequences of actions which were meaningful and bizarre at the same time (e.g. 'Draw a car. The car is pulling a cart. On the cart there is an elephant', etc., etc.). From then on TPR activities became more meaningful and memorable and we managed to cover the six-year grammatical syllabus in the first thirty hours of a course for 12-year-old beginners (e.g. 'If I sing, give your pen to the nearest boy who is sitting to your right. If I whistle, give it to the nearest girl who is sitting to your left'). Of course the students were not yet able to produce such utterances but they were able to understand them and to achieve collective physical outcomes which gave them a sense of achievement and raised their self-esteem.

The theory behind this approach is that the students receive a massive and meaningful exposure to the target language and do not have to produce language until they are ready to do so. Allowing an input-rich silent period replicates the situation of native speakers learning their L1 and avoids the anxiety, errors and loss of self-esteem made almost inevitable by forced and premature productions. I would also argue that TPR activities promote the use of visualization and of the inner voice which Tomlinson and Avila (2007a) argue is essential for effective and durable acquisition of language and that the physical movement also helps the brain to learn from the experience (Doight, 2015). What happened on the PKG Project in Indonesia was that the students in the experimental classes (one in each secondary school) enjoyed their English lessons so much that the attendance record in these classes was much higher than in the other classes (often all forty students were present in the classroom and students from other classes were performing the actions outside by listening to the instructions through open windows). After about twenty hours of the course we found that some students were standing in front of the class giving the instructions again to their friends when the teacher had left and some were even going home to their kampungs, assembling huge crowds of young children and teaching them English through TPR. And, most importantly, in the end-of-year traditional grammar-based examinations the students in the experimental classes outperformed the students from the other classes.

3. TPR Plus Performance

One of the reasons why students on the PKG Project in Indonesia enjoyed English so much was that we developed and made use of an approach we called TPR Plus (Tomlinson, 1994). Instead of just performing a series of random actions their performance was coherent and meaningful. For example, the teacher narrated a story and as she did so the students acted out the story all together, the teacher told the students how to use the ingredients provided to cook a meal and the students cooked it, the teacher told the students what to paint on their classroom wall and the students painted it, the teacher told the students where she had hidden sweets around the school and the students went out to find them.

One of the stories the students acted out was called 'They Came From the Sea Part 1' (Tomlinson, 2001). The students were told that they were on a beach and were playing all sorts of games and enjoying themselves in ways which people typically do. The teacher narrated the story sentence by sentence in a 'dramatic voice' (e.g. 'the noise got louder and louder and louder . . . and then . . . stopped') pausing for the students to act out their representation of the sentence. The students had great fun acting out beach activities until a strange noise came from the sea and four very strange creatures appeared standing in a circle on a circular ship (played by four confident students prepared by the teacher). The story continued with the strange creatures walking into the sea towards the frightened people on the beach and eventually taking two prisoners back to their ship. What happened next was that the teacher told the story again with the whole class. She spoke the first part of each sentence and students (helped by their visualized recollections of the story) shouted out sentence completions with remarkable accuracy. They did not put their hands up or stand up but just shouted out (often two or three at a time). Initially only the confident students shouted out but after a few sentences the weaker students attempted quiet shouts and were often rewarded by having their contributions repeated by the teacher (sometimes with unobtrusive recasts (Tomlinson, 2007). The students then sat in groups in circles and numbered themselves from 1 to 4 or 5. Number 1 then repeated the first sentence of 'They Came From the Sea Part 2' provided by the teacher (e.g. 'next week the same thing happened again') and number 2 offered the next sentence and then number 3 and so on and so on round and round the circle, having been told to do so as quickly as possible and without worrying about grammatical errors. Typically the students started off repeating the same story as Part 1 but then a student in a circle would deviate and the group would go off on a tangent to create their own original story. Typically also the noise got louder and louder as the stories got sillier and sillier as the students enjoyed an experience they would never forget. Before the students had finished their story the teacher would stop the activity and invite a group she had been impressed by to tell their story to the whole class. As they narrated the story she wrote it on one side of the board verbatim. Then she congratulated the group and invited the whole class to improve the story by shouting out suggestions which the teacher made use of in writing an improved whole-class version on the other side of the board. The students then copied the improved version and individually completed it for homework. A few weeks later the teacher gave the class a written version of Part 1 with some extra details and extra lexis. The students (who were new to reading) managed to understand it by making use of visualized images from their TPR Plus performance and were then asked questions about where they thought the creatures came from and why they had visited the beach. The questions were asked in English but answered in Bahasa Indonesia. Then in groups the students made discoveries about the form and functions of the simple past and the past continuous as used in the story. Their conclusions were recorded in their English grammar loose-leaf file and revised and added to as further discoveries were made from investigations of other texts derived from TPR Plus performances. Since then I have used this and similar activities with large classes of learners of many ages and levels in many different countries and the impact has always been great.

Another example of a TPR performance activity which students of many different ages and levels have enjoyed in many different countries involves large classes acting out Roald Dahl's version of *The Three Little Pigs* (Dahl, 1984). One section of the class play the first little pig, one the second little pig, one the third little pig, one the wolf and one Little Red Riding Hood. As soon as the teacher narrator mentions a character that section of the class playing that character stand up. They then perform the actions and repeat the words narrated by the teacher. Just before the teacher gets to the end of the story she stops and tells the students to imagine the ending. Then in groups they practise miming an ending before performing their mime to another group. This group narrate the end of the story being mimed to them and then change roles and become the performing group. Each group then writes a story called 'Little Red Riding Hood in X' (i.e. the name of their town).

Sometimes after getting the students to perform a story I get them as a whole class to answer a controversial question. For example, after acting out Roald Dahl's *Snow White and the Seven Dwarfs* (Dahl, 1984) the students discuss the validity of the story's conclusion that:

> Gambling's not a sin
>
> Provided that you always win.
>
> *(p. 28)*

Another example is an activity in which, after acting out David McKee's *Not Now, Bernard*, the students as a whole class answer the question, 'Who was responsible for Bernard's death?' In the story a young boy keeps being fobbed off by his busy parents telling him, 'Not now, Bernard'. He goes into the garden and is eaten by a monster, who then goes into the house, plays with Bernard's toys and eats his dinner. When the monster is sent to bed by the mother the monster complains, only to be told by the oblivious mother, 'Not now, Bernard'. With a large class of university undergraduates in Oman a fierce debate broke out in English between the males and the females about whether it was the mother's or the father's fault until one student suggested it was the teacher's fault and another that it was society's fault for spoiling children and creating an expectation that they could always get the attention they wanted. This informal debate was conducted as a spontaneous whole-class activity with the teacher simply acting as a referee.

4. Storytelling

This activity involves the students telling stories to the whole class. It could be that:

- Each student is given five minutes a term to tell a story to the class (either a story they have found or one they have made up) and each lesson features a student story.
- The whole class and the teacher sit in a large circle. The teacher tells the beginning of a story and then the student to her left continues it. After each sentence the next student carries the story on until it goes round and round the circle. The teacher encourages students to just say what comes into their heads and to not worry about making mistakes and often the story becomes delightfully sillier and sillier and the laughter level of the class soars. Eventually the teacher stops the storytelling and gets the students to try to retell their story while she writes it verbatim on one side of the board. She then gets the class to revise the story by suggesting improvements and she writes the improved version on the other side of the board. The students copy the improved version and then complete the story individually for homework.
- The teacher leads a whole-class storytelling in English of a story which is well known in the L1 (e.g. a local folk tale or a universally known fairy tale such as 'Little Red Riding Hood'). Students just volunteer to continue the story for as long as they like with the teacher acting as a prompter (e.g. 'What happened next?'; 'What was the wolf wearing?'). After the class has finished telling the story the teacher gives out copies of the story. The students read the story and help each other with any difficulties.

5. Performance of Texts

This is similar to the other performance activities above except that the students perform extensive texts which they have already read (and sometimes discussed). For example:

- The two halves of a class alternate in reading out a text paragraph by paragraph.
- The whole class read a text with a different mood or character for each paragraph.
- The whole class work together to develop a dramatization of a poem, story or newspaper report which they have read.
- Each member of a class is prompted by the teacher to play one of a number of roles in developing a performance of a poem, story or newspaper report

which they have read (e.g. script writer, stage manager, director, costume, actors, etc.).

6. Performance of Dramas

As well as getting volunteers from large classes to actually participate in putting on a performance of a play for an audience I have involved whole classes in:

- Improvized dramas involving the whole class developing a drama spontaneously in the classroom from progressive prompts from the teacher/director.
- Classroom performances of a scene from a play in which a member of a class is given a role to play in developing a performance of a scripted play (e.g. stage manager, director, costume, actors, etc.)

In one school on the Tuesday we read and discussed a poem, story or scene from a play and on the Thursday the whole class made a video of their performance of the text. In another school we based an entire term's work on a play. We read it silently, performed it aloud from the script, interviewed characters and improvised further scenes.

The Students as Collaborators

Normally collaborative and cooperative learning is conducted in groups and, in addition to facilitating language acquisition, it can contribute to the development of both leadership and team-playing skills, as well as promoting aspects of collegiality (e.g. Imai, 2010). However I have found that the same benefits can be achieved through whole-class collaborative tasks. They can be noisy and appear chaotic and, like most potentially beneficial classroom activities, they do not always succeed. However, they can generate energy and excitement and result in the communal satisfaction which comes from collective achievement of a challenge.

1. Investigative Projects

The whole class is given an issue or problem to investigate and a period of time in which to establish the facts, come to conclusions or reach solutions. The class can be left to decide on how they will organize and carry out the investigation or an organizing committee can be appointed by the teacher and/or students for each investigation. The teacher acts as an informant and facilitator and can also be allocated a role in the investigation by the students. Examples of such investigations would be coming up with proposals for easing traffic congestion in their city, deciding on what life style to recommend to their community in order to promote healthy living, collecting and analysing the views of the local community on a proposed new building and sampling views so as to predict results in a local or general election.

2. Practical Projects

The whole class is given the task of planning and performing a task which has a practical outcome. For example, they might paint murals on the walls of the school (this happened in a school in Indonesia), organize a party and cook a meal for disadvantaged people in the community, design a new building for hypothetical construction in their area, plan the regeneration of an area or design a vehicle. The latter task I have done with students in Singapore and Indonesia. They had to first of all work out the good and the bad points of the C5, a three-wheeled, battery-powered vehicle which lost a lot of money for its inventor Clive Sinclair. They then had to design a C6 which retained the good points and overcame the bad points before creating newspaper and television advertisements for their revolutionary new vehicle. In both countries the students (inspired by my example) had great fun coming up with such silly features as an umbrella which jumped up when a sensor sensed rain and an amphibious device which was operated when the front wheel entered a deep puddle. Another challenge which created energizing fun was a project inspired by the novel *Salmon Fishing in the Yemen* (Torday, 2007), which involved working out a way of introducing salmon to the dry inlands of Oman.

The Students as Competitors

There is some controversy about the value of competition in education. Its critics argue that it fosters unwanted aggression and selfishness whilst its advocates claim that it can create energy, motivation and engagement and that, providing that students are competing in a target-language-rich environment, this can facilitate language acquisition and skills development. In Vanuatu I used competitive games with large classes of primary school students only to find that their cooperative instinct prevailed and that, for example, when the victorious player put down the winning domino the whole group celebrated their victory. However in most other parts of the world I have found that students of all ages (especially middle-aged adults) have enjoyed and gained from being competitive.

1. Competitions

In many large classes around the world I have divided the class into large groups (sometimes as many as fifteen in a group) who then compete against each other in a competition. For example, I have got large classes to act out all together a scene from a 'new' film called Mrs King Strikes Back in which an old widowed pensioner carries out a bank robbery in London (Tomlinson, 2007). The students all play Mrs King, a taxi driver, a taxi, a queue in the bank, a young hostage, a bank clerk and a policeman and have great fun acting out the teacher's narration. The students then in large groups work out and prepare a mime of what they think happens in the next scene. After the groups have performed their mimes they are told that the story of the old lady is true and that the real old lady was furious when she saw the film and realized it was about herself and largely untrue. They are given two minutes to read an authentic newspaper account of the real old lady's trial and to spot the differences between the scene from the 'film' they acted out and what happened in real life. They turn over their handouts and then there is a competition in which the groups take it in turn to report a difference. They receive two points for each reported difference unless another group challenges and corrects the reported difference.

Another very different competition involves individuals making paper aeroplanes from the teacher's oral instructions and then lining up to see whose plane will fly the furthest.

2. Games

In most countries I have found that students of all ages enjoy playing physical games and that they gain language acquisition opportunities from them if they can only win the game by understanding and producing the target language (Tomlinson & Masuhara, 2009). An example of a very popular game which involves listening to, reading and discussing complex instructions is Newspaper Hockey (Tomlinson, 2001). In this game large teams play hockey against each other with hockey sticks and balls which they have made from old newspapers following instructions given to them orally by their teacher. Each player has a number and competes with the opponent of the same number to score a goal through the opposing team's chair. The teams sit in a line facing each other until their number is shouted or in a more complex and language-richer version their team work out a mathematical problem with a single-number solution (e.g. 'The number of people in a quartet plus the number of wheels on a car divided by the number of weeks in a month'). After the winning team has scored a predetermined number of goals the teams make up and then write down the instructions for another 'newspaper' game. They are then given the written instructions for Newspaper Hockey and are told to focus on how the instructions are given (i.e. through the use of the imperative). They then revise their own instructions before getting the rest of the class to play their game.

A popular game for an elementary level large class is played on a volleyball or tennis court with a very large team on each side of the net. A version of tennis or volleyball is played in which for each point the teacher umpire changes the rules. For example the teacher might shout 'You can only use one hand', 'You must use two hands', 'You can only use your head', 'You can use your head or feet', 'You must face backwards' or 'Your team must touch the ball twice before sending it back over the net'.

3. Quizzes

In England there is a tradition of pub quizzes in which large groups listen to questions asked by the quizmaster and for each question they discuss it quietly in their group and then write down an answer. The questions are on a wide range of topics, usually including sport, music, literature, films, celebrities, geography, history, world affairs and local affairs. After the last question groups swap their answer sheets for marking, the quizmaster gives the answers and the winning group is declared. I have found this format ideal for large class competition, as it provides a rich exposure to language in use, there is frequent re-cycling through the repetition and discussion of the questions and, providing the quiz questions are locally relevant, it engages the students both affectively and cognitively.

Conclusion

If a language teacher is faced with a large class in a school culture which favours or even enforces whole-class activities there is no excuse for teacher lecturing or for occupying the class in silent individual answering of questions in the coursebook. As I hope I have demonstrated there are many types of whole-class activities which can generate positive energy, engage learners affectively and cognitively and facilitate language acquisition.

Note

1 http://www.britishcouncil.org/partner/international-development/consultancy-opportunities/current-consultancy-opportunities/material-writers-teacher-training-resources-burma

References

Aida, Y. (1994). Examination of Horwitz, Horwitz, and Cope's construct of foreign language anxiety: The case of students of Japanese. *The Modern Language Journal, 78*, 155–168.

Ascher, J. J. (2009). *Learning another language through actions* (7th ed.). Los Gatos, CA: Sky Oak Productions.

Bao, D. (2013). Voices of the reticent: Getting inside views of Vietnamese secondary students on learning. In M. Cortazzi & L. Jin (Eds.), *Researching cultures of learning: International perspectives on language learning and education* (pp. 136–154). Basingstoke, UK: Palgrave Macmillan.

Bao, D. (2014). *Understanding silence and reticence: Ways of participating in second language acquisition*. London: Bloomsbury.

Dahl, R. (1984). *Revolting rhymes*. London: Puffin.

Doidge, N. (2015). *The brain's way of healing: Stories of remarkable recoveries and discoveries*. New York: Penguin.

Elley, W., Cutting, B., Mangubai, F., & Hugo, C. (1996). Lifting literacy levels with storybooks: Evidence from the South Pacific, Singapore, Sri Lanka and South Africa. *Proceedings of the 1996 World Congress on Literacy.* http://www.literacy.org/sites/literacy.org/files/publications/elley_lit_ed_w_story_books_96.pdf/. Accessed 5 March 2015.

Garmston, R. J., & Wellman, B. M. (2013). *The adaptive school: A sourcebook for developing collaborative groups*. Lanham, MD: Rowman & Littlefield.

Horwitz, E. K. (2000). It ain't over 'til it's over: On foreign language anxiety, first language deficits and the confounding of variables. *The Modern Language Journal, 84*(2), 256–259.

Imai, Y. (2010). Emotions in SLS: New insights from collaborative learning for an EFL classroom. *The Modern Language Journal, 94*(2), 278–292.

Loh, J., & Renanyanda, W. A. (2015). Exploring adaptations of materials and methods: A case study from Singapore. *European Journal of Applied Linguistics and TEFL.* Special Issue on Materials Development.

Lyons, Z. (2009). Imagined identity and the L2 self in the French Foreign Legion. In Z. Dörnyei & E. Ushioda (Eds.), *Motivation, language identity and the L2 self* (pp. 248–273). Bristol: Multilingual Matters.

McKee, D. (1980.) *Not now, Bernard.* London: Andersen Press.

Ortega, L. (2009). *Understanding second language acquisition.* London: Hodder Education.

Oxford, R. (2009). Anxiety and the language learner: New insights. In J. Arnold (Ed.), *Affect in language learning* (pp. 58–67). Cambridge: Cambridge University Press.

Oxford, R. (2011). *Teaching and researching language learning strategies.* Abingdon, UK: Taylor & Francis.

Richman, C. L. (1994). The bizarreness effect with complex sentences: Temporal effects. *Canadian Journal of Experimental Psychology/Revue canadienne de psychologie expérimentale, 48*(3), 444–450.

Tomlinson, B. (1990). Managing change in Indonesian high schools. *ELT Journal, 44*(1), 25–37.

Tomlinson, B. (1994). Materials for TPR. *Folio, 1*(2), 8–10.

Tomlinson, B. (2001). They came from the sea and newspaper hockey. In P. Watcyn-Jones, (Ed.), *Top class activities 2.* London: Penguin.

Tomlinson, B. (2007). The value of recasts during meaning focused communication – 1. In B.Tomlinson (Ed.), *Language acquisition and development: Studies of first and other language learners* (pp.141–161). London: Continuum.

Tomlinson, B., & Avila, J. (2007a). Seeing and saying for yourself: The roles of audio-visual mental aids in language learning and use. In B.Tomlinson (Ed.), *Language acquisition and development: Studies of first and other language learners* (pp. 61–81). London: Continuum.

Tomlinson, B., & Avila, J. (2007b). Applications of the research into the roles of audio-visual mental aids for language teaching pedagogy. In B. Tomlinson (Ed.), *Language acquisition and development: Studies of first and other language learners* (pp. 82–89). London: Continuum.

Tomlinson, B., & Masuhara, H. (2009). Playing to learn: A review of physical games in second language acquisition. *Simulation & Gaming, 40,* 645–668.

Torday, P. (2007). *Salmon fishing in the Yemen.* London: Orion.

Worthen, J. B., Garcia-Revas, G., Green, C. R., & Vidos, R. A. (2000). Tests of a cognitive-resource-allocation account of the bizarreness effect. *The Journal of General Psychology, 127*(2), 117–144.

4

NO PLACE FOR COURSEBOOKS IN THE VERY YOUNG LEARNER CLASSROOM

Irma-Kaarina Ghosn

Introduction

There is an international trend to introduce English language teaching (ELT) in lower primary school and, in many cases, to make it compulsory. In some countries English is apparently introduced in pre-primary levels. For example, in many Lebanese private schools English is introduced in nursery classes to 3-year-olds. It is probably true in many other countries as well. Pearson Longman *Pocket* (for ages 3–5) is in its second edition at the time of this writing and *Little Pockets* is promoted for 2-year-olds. Although the definition of 'young learner' may refer to children anywhere from age 4 or 5 to 12, in this article 'young learner' refers to pre-school and lower primary school children between the ages of 3 and 8. The practice of teaching a foreign language to very young children is based on the notion that 'younger is better' when it comes to language learning. However, as Rixon (2013) points out, there is no research to support it. In fact, it goes against the brain-mapping studies which suggest that the optimal age for second language (L2) learning is between the ages of 6 and 15 (Thompson et al., 2000). Young children are, of course, known to acquire a new language when immersed in it within the context of interpersonal communication. However, it is quite a different matter to learn a new language within the context of the formal classroom, with exposure typically limited to a couple of hours per week, as suggested by Rixon's (2013) and Enever's (2011) studies. Another issue is the teacher qualifications. In many of the countries where English is now introduced in the lower primary school, there is a lack of teachers specially prepared to teach a foreign language to young children. This was extensively discussed in the Early Language Learning Conference which I attended at Umeå University in June 2014. Participants reported that in some cases, the classroom teacher is responsible for teaching English, while in other cases a specialist teacher travels between schools. Often teachers with secondary school language-teaching credentials end up teaching English in the primary classes. The early push for foreign language, coupled with the limited number of instructional hours and the issue of teacher qualifications, raises some concerns, particularly about instructional materials and pedagogical approaches. This paper argues against formal, coursebook-based instruction in very young learner classes and, drawing on constructivist, whole-language philosophy, proposes some practical alternatives in accordance with developmentally appropriate practice.

The Spreading Trend to Teach English to Young Children

In half of the European Union member states, foreign language instruction is now mandated at age seven (Enever, 2011), with English being by far the most popular first foreign language. A British Council survey published in 2013 (Rixon, 2013) collected data from 64 different countries representing Kachru's (1990) Outer Circle and Expanding Circle (Inner Circle referring to countries where English is the first language for a large segment of the population). In the Outer Circle countries, many of which have been colonized by Inner Circle Countries, English has a long history and plays an important role in education and commerce and often also in public administration. India, Pakistan and Zambia are three examples. In the Expanding Circle countries, English has been taught as a foreign language and has not been used in daily communication within the society. Eastern European and Nordic countries are examples. The above-cited British Council survey found that English was a compulsory part of the state-supported pre-primary curriculum in 14 countries, and that English was provided in private pre-primary education in 19 outer-circle countries (Rixon, 2013; see Table 4.1). Some European, Middle-Eastern and Latin-American countries are an exception to this trend, beginning English language instruction at the age of 8 and above.

The number and duration of weekly lessons varies across countries. Enever (2011) reports that the number of lessons in seven European countries ranged from one 35–50-minute lesson a week to two 45-minute lessons a week in year one. Rixon

TABLE 4.1 English in pre-primary education

	Outer Circle	*Expanding Circle*
Compulsory in state-supported pre-primary education	Cameroon, Hong Kong, India (Tamil Nadu), Namibia, Pakistan, Sierra Leone	Armenia, China, Jordan, Kazakhstan, North Cyprus, Qatar, Sweden, Uzbekistan
Provided in private pre-primary education	India (Goa), Zambia	Brazil, Colombia, Egypt, Greece, Indonesia, Kosovo, Lebanon, Palestine, Peru, Romania, Senegal, Serbia, South Korea, Spain, Syria, Taiwan, Turkey, United Arab Emirates, Venezuela

Adapted from Rixon (2013) and Ghosn (2013b)

TABLE 4.2 Onset of English instruction in lower primary school (state and private sector)

	Outer Circle	Expanding Circle
Age 5–6 Age 6–7	Bangladesh, Cameroon, Cyprus, India (Goa; South India; Tamil Nadu), Namibia, Sierra Leone, Zimbabwe	Georgia, Italy, Montenegro, North Cyprus, Qatar
	Hong Kong, Pakistan, Sri Lanka, Zambia	Azerbaijan, Bahrain, China, Croatia, Egypt, France, Greece, Jordan, Lebanon, Lithuania, Oman, Palestine, Poland, Portugal, Russia, Serbia, Spain, Syria, Thailand, United Arab Emirates, Uzbekistan, Zambia

Adapted from Rixon (2013) and Ghosn (2013b)

(2013) reports that in 16% of the countries she surveyed, the expected total hours of English were 30–50 a year, while another 18% targeted 50–80 annual hours (p. 29). This is not very much, considering the complexity of foreign language learning.

Young Children as Language Learners

Is Younger Better?

The British Council website learnenglishkids.britishcouncil.org (n.d.) notes that 'young learners are natural language acquirers' (¶ 1) and use the same 'innate language learning strategies' to acquire English that they use when acquiring their home language (¶ 3). This is true, but only if the learning environment is set up to allow for acquisition as opposed to instruction. The innate language acquisition strategies do not apply to formal coursebook-based instruction. In such situations, the very young learners are actually at a disadvantage, because of their rather limited knowledge about how languages work. They are not cognitively able to analyze bits and pieces of language the same way older learners can. In addition, their knowledge of the world is still limited, meaning that they may lack background knowledge of what might be presented in a coursebook. There is little research to suggest that younger is better when it comes to language learning in a formal instructional setting, which differs from the naturalistic context of L2 acquisition in early childhood.

Developmental Nature of Language Learning

Children's language learning follows a developmental sequence, irrespective of their mother tongue. Despite considerable differences in the rate of language acquisition between individual children, children's linguistic features emerge in a fairly predictable pattern. Children make predictable errors of syntax, such as over-extending a rule, in their first language, with corrective feedback rarely resulting in any change, as the following exchange between a 2½-year-old child and her grandmother illustrates:

Kiira: [Grandma], I want the other one booki [book], please.
IG: You want the <u>other</u> book? Which other book?
Kiira: Yes, I want the other one booki. That one [pointing]
[Gives Kiira the book and reads it.]
Kiira: [Grandma], I want another one booki.
IG: I'm sorry, what did you say?
Kiira: Please, read another one booki.
IG: You want me to read <u>another</u> book?
Kiira: Yes, I want you to read another one booki, please.

(Ghosn, 2013a, p. 62)

Clearly, the child is familiar with the expressions 'the other one' and 'another one' and applies them in her own way. Parents apparently know intuitively that correcting such errors is futile and, as Pinker (1994) notes, focus on the meaning instead.

Young English language learners' (ELLs') interlanguage emerges in a developmental sequence similar to that demonstrated by their native-English-speaking age peers. The productive use of language is preceded by telegraphic and formulaic phrases, and their morpheme acquisition also follows a rather predictable order, albeit different from the sequence observed with English first language (L1) speakers. Just like L1 speakers, young ELLs demonstrate creativity in their use of L2 syntax, making intralingual errors common to most young ELLs, regardless of their mother tongue (Richards, 1971). For example, just as young L1 speakers, they overextend rule application, producing sentences like *my feets hurted*. Therefore, teaching syntax to young ELLs is likely to be futile, unless the learners have reached a stage where they are ready to "assimilate the new rule into their mental grammars" (Ellis, 1994, p. 22).

The Challenge of Teaching Very Young Learners

Young learners present a unique challenge in the context of formal foreign language instruction. First, there is the language. Although by age 4 or 5 most average children have acquired considerable vocabulary in their first language and have control of the basic grammatical forms, as well as insight into pragmatics, their first language acquisition process is still far from complete. Children also differ widely in the speed at which they acquire their first language. While some learners may be at the emergent literacy stage, others might have very limited reading and writing skills, especially at the lower end of the age spectrum. Moreover, young children cannot think or reason about language in an abstract way, as adults can. They learn language through interacting with others and not by analyzing aspects of language. As Pinter (2006) insightfully points out:

A class of six-year-olds will be largely unable to reflect on how their first language works, and will show no interest or inclination to notice language forms in either their first or second language. They will pick up and learn the second or foreign language if they are having fun and if they can work out messages from meaningful contexts.

(p. 18)

Pinter further suggests that teachers monitor their young learners' use of L1 in order to gain an understanding of what realistic expectations they can place on the children in the L2 classroom.

Second, there is the development of memory and information-processing skills. The information-processing theory attempts to explain how information moves into, out of, and through sensory, short-term and long-term memories (Bee and Boyd, 2010). It is assumed by most memory research that information moves in an organized way through a process of encoding, storage and retrieval. Although researchers admit that it is difficult to measure it, most developmental psychologists agree that short-term memory capacity increases across childhood (Bee & Boyd, 2010). Dempster (1981, pp. 66–68) compared children's capacity to remember digit, letter and word spans at different ages. Children aged 4 were able, on average, to recall a span of close to four letters and three words. For children aged 5, the comparable figures were nearly four and four, and for children aged 6, four and four-and-a-half. This has implications on children's ability to remember vocabulary items, especially if they are presented out of context.

Research on memory and learning shows that meaningful information is learned faster and remembered better than less meaningful information (Anderson, 1995; Mayer, 1996), and novel, emotionally relevant, or personally significant information gets the learners' attention. It is processed to the working memory better than less meaningful information (Barkley, 1996). Procedural memory helps us remember how to do things, such as swimming or riding a bike, and Ullman's (2001) brain research shows that young children employ their procedural memory when learning grammar. In contrast, older learners use their declarative memory for grammar learning. These findings suggest that while older learners can learn grammar by explicit instruction, young children will learn grammar best by repeated exposure and practice *in context*, rather than by explicit instruction or through decontextualized drills. However, young foreign language learners typically receive language instruction only for short lesson periods, as shown above. This poses a challenge for the instructional materials and pedagogical approaches, which must provide sufficient repeated exposure to target language vocabulary and structures in a meaningful and engaging context.

It is therefore not surprising that Cameron (2001) argues that teaching young children is far from straightforward:

The teacher of young children needs to be highly skilled to reach into the children's worlds and lead them to develop their understandings towards more formal, more extensive and differently organized concepts . . . They need to understand how children make sense of the world and how they learn.

(xii)

Motivation and Materials

The third consideration involves motivation and interest. Young children are eager explorers of their environment, provided the environment offers stimulating and interesting objects, activities and events. Extensive research into the role of motivation in language learning has been carried out, but much of it has looked at older learners. Young learner motivation has been examined by Ohlstain, Shohamy, Kemp, and Chatow (1990), Mihaljevic Djigunovic (1993), and Nikolov (1999). It is undeniable that the instructional materials and lesson content play a role in young learner motivation. How much time and effort learners are willing to spend on the learning activities depends on the level of their motivation. Motivation and interest have a profound influence on academic achievement (Jalongo, 2007), and a key to intrinsic motivation is interest (Artelt, 2005). While young children in foreign language classes are unlikely to be intrinsically motivated to learn the new language, lesson content and materials can evoke situational interest, which has a strong influence on learner engagement (Jalongo, 2007). Situational interest is evoked by novelty, curiosity, and the saliency of the information. Hidi and Harckievicz (2000) cite twenty years of research on situational interest and identify certain text features related to situational interest. Texts that learners find interesting are easy to understand, present novel, surprising or unusual content, involve a high level of activity, and feature topics and characters with which learners can identify.

Developmentally Appropriate Practice (DAP)

Finally, there is the learning environment and pedagogical approach. According to the National Association for Education of Young Children (NAEYC) in the United States, the learning environment must reflect the predictable sequences of growth observed in children. Children must be exposed to experiential, interactive and appropriately challenging learning experiences, which must allow plenty of opportunities for play, especially dramatic play. In his seminal work, *Mind in Society*, Vygotsky (1978) argues that the "influence of play on a child's development is enormous" (96) and observes that "In play a child always behaves beyond his [sic] average age . . . in play it is as though he [sic] were a head taller than himself [sic]" (p. 102). The Association for Supervision and Curriculum Development (n.d.) in the United States recommends that the curriculum be organized around the developmental needs, interests and learning styles of each child, rather than around a single text, curriculum guide or time schedule. The curriculum should focus on the total child, considering cognitive, affective and psychomotor development. Each child should be actively engaged in learning through cooperative activities, projects and experiential learning.

Clearly, formal, teacher-fronted and coursebook-based instruction implied by the internationally marketed young learner materials is not aligned with the above DAP guidelines. For example, at the time of this writing many international and regional publishers offer coursebooks for kindergarten classes. One international publisher promotes a coursebook series for children between the ages of 2 and 5. Anyone familiar with 2- and 3-year-old children can see the difficulty (if not absurdity) in having them sit down with a coursebook.

Constructivist Pedagogy

In contrast, a constructivist, whole-language-based approach is more in line with DAP. Popular in the 1980s in American first language reading classes, whole language (Goodman, 1989, 1992; Edelsky, Altwerger & Flores, 1991) was introduced into North American ESL classrooms by Freeman and Freeman (1992) and Carrasquillo and Hedley (1993). Although much misunderstood, the whole-language approach is based on theories about how humans learn ideas and concepts, and on a constructivist view of learning. It is also aligned with Vygotsky's (1978) sociocultural theory of learning, the basic premise being that humans develop concepts through their intellectual interactions with and upon their world (Weaver et al., 1996). In other words, learning and learners are not passive recipients of input, but active participants in the construction of their knowledge and understanding.

First language research clearly indicates that children acquire language by interacting with others, both adults and peers, and by using language within the context of meaningful interactions—not by doing pencil-and-paper tasks or by drill exercises. Both Vygotsky (1978) and Halliday (1975) have stressed the importance of social interaction in language development. Children learn about language, both oral and written, when they are presented with natural—'whole'—language rather than the simplified chunks of language typical in lower primary school language teaching coursebooks. In fact, Cameron (2001) points out that if children are only taught simple, basic language, that is all they learn.

In a constructivist whole-language classroom, students engage in authentic activities rather than decontextualized drills, and vocabulary and skills are acquired within the context of these activities. Although there are many misconceptions about the whole language approach (Freeman & Freeman, 1992), it is grounded in research and is embraced by the California Association for Bilingual Education and the National Council of Teachers of English, as well as many ESL teachers in North America. However, it has failed so far to find its way to English as a foreign language (EFL) coursebooks, possibly because it is believed by some experts to be a fad, but also because it is quite challenging to develop EFL materials aligned with the whole language philosophy. Yet a whole-language approach is ideal, particularly in young learner classes, because it promotes *acquisition* of language, as opposed to instructed learning of language, and because it is aligned with theories of learning (Ghosn, 2014).

Practical Examples for Motivating and Engaging in Lessons

The suggestions below are adapted from my presentation at the TESOL Arabia Conference in Dubai, UAE, in 2014.

Mother Goose Rhymes (also known as Nursery Rhymes)

Children naturally enjoy rhymes, which makes nursery rhymes a natural medium in young learner classes. Nursery rhymes are usually short and present humorous or familiar situations. A wide variety of rhyming texts are available in English, from counting rhymes to finger-play verses, riddles and cumulative tales. Some nursery rhymes are an ideal medium for teaching English to children between the ages of 3 and 6 and can easily be adapted to meaningful, enjoyable and motivating lessons. The rhythm of the rhymes will develop young learners' understanding of intonation, and the repetition of the rhymes will reinforce vocabulary and structures in an enjoyable context, thus helping children remember them.

Although some may object to 'messing with *Mother Goose*' and adapting the original texts, it is quite justified when working with young language learners. One excellent example that can help meet a variety of objectives with minor adaptations is the familiar "Baa-Baa Black Sheep."

"Baa-Baa Black Sheep" is a good rhyme for beginners, because it can be used to introduce colors, numbers and pronouns, among other possibilities. The time required will depend on the number of objectives selected. The rhyme provides a natural context to learn numbers from one to three, or more, since any number of bags of wool are possible. The rhyme can also be used to teach colors: Black, white, red, brown, and any other color of choice (imaginary sheep colors are fine). The structures *for me/ you/ him/ her* can be introduced naturally in context. The rhyme can be adapted slightly to read:

> Baa-baa black (white/ red/ blue . . .) sheep, do you have some wool?
> Yes, I do. Yes I do (one/ two/ three/ four/ five) bag(s) full.
> One for me and one for you.
> Two for me and one for you.
> One for you and three for her, etc.

The teacher will need a basket of yarn balls in the target colors, sturdy paper bags (up to the highest target number) that can hold three or four yarn balls each, a cardboard shape of a sheep in the target color/s, construction paper and poster paints or markers.

The teacher chants the question addressing the cardboard sheep. The teacher then hides behind the 'sheep' and replies with the sheep's voice. This is repeated a few times and children are encouraged to join in. Black, white and red (or any other colors) are taught using the cardboard 'sheep'. Children play a game to practice vocabulary with the sheep and colored yarn. Bags are labeled, and a basket of yarn balls is placed in front of the bags. Children stand in line, and, as the teacher calls out colors, they take turns to pick the right colored yarn and put it in the correct bag. Children can also be divided into teams, if they enjoy competition. However, frequent competitive activities may frustrate or discourage less proficient children and should be used with caution.

Children are given paints in the target colors and sheep shapes cut from A4-size sturdy paper or cardstock. Children paint their sheep using the color of their own choice. Teacher circulates among the children, talking about colors. Teacher then gathers children into a group and encourages them to talk about the colors of the sheep, modeling first: *I have a white sheep* (showing a white sheep). *What color sheep do you have? What about Maria's sheep? Is her sheep black or red* (showing the two colors). And so on.

Children dramatize the rhyme wearing simple character cards. Two holes are punched in the sheep figures and a loop of yarn is attached, long enough to slip around a child's neck. Children wear their sheep card, and the teacher chants the rhyme again, this time addressing questions to children's sheep: *Red sheep, red sheep,* etc. Children can take turns to ask the teacher's sheep the question, as she holds the different colored sheep in turn in front of her. Children can then take turns asking each others' sheep the question, and the sheep respond. The colored yarn balls are used as appropriate.

Once children are familiar with the colors, the above activities can be repeated, but by adding numbers. Teacher models by stamping feet or clapping hands at the numbers while chanting the rhyme and encouraging children to respond by a number of their choice. Then the yarn ball activity described above can be repeated, but with numbers this time. As teacher calls out colors, children take the correct number of yarn balls from the basket and give the teacher some and keep some for themselves. (Teacher models first.) When children are familiar with the target colors and numbers, the lines *for me, for you* can be addressed. The rhyme can be adapted to other concepts, with activities adjusted accordingly:

> Moo-moo red cow, do you have some milk?
> Yes I do. Yes I do. (Yes, I have). One/ two/ three pail(s)/ bucket(s) full.

or

> Cluck-cluck brown hen, do you have some eggs?
> Yes, I do. Yes I do. One/ two/ three basket(s) full.

or

> Bzz-bzz busy bee, do you have some honey?
> Yes, I do. Yes I do. One/ two/ three pot(s) full.

It is not necessary to have all the words rhyme. Some Mother Goose rhymes are ready to use in their original form. "Little Miss Muffet," "Hickory, Dickory,

Dock" and "Twinkle, Twinkle, Little Star" do not require any adaptations. From longer rhymes, such as "Little Bo-Peep," one may select only the first verse. In rhymes with children's names, one can repeat the rhyme and substitute names of children in the class. For example, when doing "Jack Be Nimble," one can replace Jack with names of children, who take turns jumping over the candlestick. In "Lazy Mary," the teacher could also use children's names and perhaps change 'lazy' to 'sleepy'. A good source of activity ideas for nursery rhymes is *Let Loose on Mother Goose* (Graham, 1982). If you are interested in the history of Mother Goose rhymes, visit www.rhymes.org.uk/. Accessed January 15, 2015.

Songs and Chants

Songs and chants are perfect for young learner language classes, because they are enjoyable and usually involve physical movement. The following are some of the best-known examples that have rich possibilities in the language classroom, especially for Total Physical Response (TPR) activities. (All the tunes can be found on Youtube.) "Head and Shoulders, Knees and Toes" is ideal for teaching essential body-part vocabulary. "Do the Hokey Pokey" introduces *left/ right* and *in/ out*, as well as *around*. Other useful chants are "Teddy Bear, Teddy Bear, Turn Around," "If You're Happy and You Know It," "Twinkle, Twinkle Little Star" and "Intsy, Wintsy Spider." "This is the Way I Wash My Face" is one of those songs that can be adapted to introduce many other ideas. For example, in a course for 6-year-old beginners it goes like this:

> This is the way we come to school,
> Come to school, come to school.
> This is the way we come to school, walking
> In the morning.
> This is the way we go to class,
> Go to class, go to class.
> This is the way we go to class,
> Marching one by one.
> This is the way we sit in class,
> Sit in class, sit in class.
> This is the way we sit in class,
> So nicely and quietly.
>
> *(Ghosn, 2011, pp. 24–25)*

Picture Books and Big Books

Children are naturally drawn to stories, making well-illustrated picture books an excellent language-teaching medium in young learner classes. A wide selection is available on the market, and used copies can be purchased on the Internet literally for pennies. Good examples are Eric Carle's fabulous *The Very Hungry Caterpillar*,

Pat Hutchins' highly amusing *Rosie's Walk*, and Margaret Wise Brown's *Goodnight Moon*, all perfect for teaching the very young learner.

Many picture books that are popular with teachers are also produced as big easel books, measuring 50 × 35 cm with 2 cm-high letters. This format is ideal in the young learner class, because the illustrations are easy to see for all the children. The frequent pairing of oral language with print will gradually develop children's sight vocabulary even when literacy is not yet the goal. Old favorites, such as *The Little Red Hen*, *The Gingerbread Man*, and *The Enormous Turnip* have entertained generations of children and can be enlarged into Big Books. Books with rich, rhyming and/or repetitive language are ideal for L2 teaching and learning. Illustrations make the language salient, which enhances learning. Classic folktales can also be adapted to different cultural context, by simply adapting characters' names, clothing or setting to make the content relevant to young learners. There are a number of different ways teachers can approach the story, depending on the level and needs of their students, and their own preferred teaching approach. While many teachers prefer to pre-teach vocabulary, it is not the only available approach. As a matter of fact, allowing the language to emerge from the story can be much more enjoyable for children, as they try to construct the meaning from the language contextualized by the illustrations. For example, pre-teaching the word 'butterfly' before exposing children to Carle's *The Very Hungry Caterpillar* would completely spoil the surprise ending. It would also deny children the pleasure of making predictions and confirming them.

Shared Reading

One approach that I have found to work very well in a very young learner classroom is the dialogic, shared reading approach originally developed by Don Holdaway (1979) in New Zealand. The shared reading experience is as close to the bedtime story as one can get in a classroom setting. The story is enlarged into a big book (or separate pages). The book is placed on an easel, and children gather around the teacher, who reads the story to the class with appropriate expression and intonation. In other words, the teacher models how a competent reader reads (Mueller & Wegner, 1989). Shared reading differs from read-aloud in that children *see* the text. As the teacher reads, she uses a pointer to point to the words, stopping also to point to the illustrations and asking questions such as "See the plums here?" and confirm, "The hungry caterpillar is eating the plums." This should not be done so frequently that it interrupts the flow of the story. It is important to keep in mind that when children are very intensely engaged with a story, too many questions can frustrate them.

With the second reading, the teacher can also ask children to come and point to the illustrations: "Who can show me where the caterpillar is?" "Where are the strawberries?" It is important that children are allowed to use their mother tongue when commenting on or discussing the story. First, this will enable even the very beginners to remain motivated and make meaningful contributions to the discussion.

Second, it will maintain the flow of discourse and will give the teacher important information about the level of children's comprehension. Most importantly, it provides ample opportunities for the negotiated interactions essential in language learning. However, whenever students use their L1, or use incorrect English, the teacher should validate their contribution and recast it into English. For example if an Arabic-speaking student says "My grandfather *he has* a *hemār* [donkey]," the teacher can validate the contribution, provide the needed word, and extend the exchange: "Oh, your grandfather *has a donkey!* Does the donkey help your grandfather on his farm?"

With beginning language learners, the teacher goes over the story again and asks questions at different levels of language acquisition: "Is this the dog?" "Is this the dog or the cat?" "Who is this?" "Is the donkey helping the Little Hen?" The story is then read again.

Follow-Up Work

Key vocabulary can be practiced after the initial exposure to the story by using toys, other objects, or picture cards. The pictures can be pasted on large index cards and the relevant vocabulary word printed on the card. If children can already recognize letters and their sounds, a picture can be pasted on one card and the corresponding word on another for children to play a matching game or *Go fish* card game. Low intermediate learners, who already have some English communication ability, can be engaged in brief discussion about their experiences with the story concepts or plot.

The story can be revisited many times to practice target vocabulary and structures. For a retelling activity, the pages are copied and pasted on cardboard. Lamination ensures that pages can be used multiple times. Teacher places the cards on the table or the floor and rereads the story. Children take turns to come and select the correct illustration and place it on the chalkboard tray (or use masking tape to stick them on the board or the wall). Children can also be invited to retell the story, step by step, as teacher takes down their dictation on flipchart paper or the board. When language errors or L1 are included in children's utterances, the teacher validates the contribution and recasts it into correct English as they write it down. Whenever there is a disagreement or something is forgotten, children can revisit the story to check the facts/vocabulary.

A sequencing activity can be adapted to different levels of literacy instruction. The teacher gives children picture cards (one per child) and invites them to arrange themselves in the correct order (facing the class) from left to right as she reads the story. The class will then read the story together. The enlarged easel version of the story can be used for word study. Target words are covered with small 'Post-it'® notes. The teacher reads the story and stops at a covered word. Children try to think what the word might be. Gradually, teacher uncovers the word, letter by letter until children guess it correctly. Children use a non-permanent marker to circle or underline target words. Note: Young children may not have a clear concept of a 'word' or a 'sentence.' This activity will tell the teacher where the students are in this regard. Children can take turns to circle or underline given sounds; capital letters; punctuation marks; past tense verbs; phrases; sentences, etc.

When children have acquired beginning literacy, they can be given picture cards with words or simple phrases (one word/ phrase per child) and invited to arrange themselves in the correct order (facing the class) from left to right to make a word or a phrase. The class will read the word together. Split sentences printed on strips of cardboard can be used with slightly more advanced learners, with beginning capital letters/ ending punctuation/ quotation marks as clues.

Children can use the original story as a base to write their own story by changing some of the elements. Teacher first discusses possibilities with children. For example, in *The Little Hen Gets Help* (Ghosn, 2009), the little hen finds some kernels of corn, gets help from other animals at the farm, and at the end bakes corn bread. Corn can be changed to some other grain, or even a vegetable. Wheat can be baked into bread while carrots could be made into carrot cake, lettuce into a salad, and so on. In the story, a dog barks, a pig grunts and a goat bleats their answers to the hen's question. Children can change the animals in the story and pick out their sounds from the animal-sound chart provided by Derek Abbott in his *Animal Noise* webpage.[1] Children will print their story on heavy-duty white paper, illustrate the pages and make a cover page for the story. Pages are stapled or stitched into a book children can take home. Needless to say, children can use either the original story or their own copies for the sequence of events and spelling of the words.

Games

The following games are appropriate for language practice regardless of the lesson content. The approaches are 'generic' and adaptable to many different age and proficiency levels. Some of the examples given will not apply to the beginning learner, while other examples are not appropriate for more advanced learners. Teachers can adapt the activities to suit their particular teaching situation and learning objectives.

Memory

In this old, popular game, the first person says the first line; e.g. *I went to the store and bought [names an item]/ I went on a trip to [names a place]*; the second person says the same thing and adds another item, and so on. Students need to be very alert in order to remember all items. The one who forgets is out. This is both vocabulary practice and memory sharpening. This game can be modified in many ways; for example, all items must begin with a given letter, be of a certain category, etc.

Telephone

This is another popular game. The first person whispers a word or a sentence to a second person; the second person whispers it to a third, and so on. The last person says aloud the word or sentence s/he heard. It is always amusing and surprising to see how much the message can change in the process, especially in a large L2 class.

Students vs. Teacher

The teacher draws two columns on the board, labeling one as 'Teacher' (or the name) and the other 'Students.' As the teacher shows the class a vocabulary card, a phonics card or a picture, students take turns calling out the word or the sound. The teacher should call on students systematically up and down the rows of students rather than relying on volunteers. If the student answers correctly, a point is recorded on the 'Student' column, if not, the 'Teacher' column gets the point. Students love to win this game against their teacher (Ghosn, 2011).

Team Race

Desk rows form teams and children stand next to their desks. The teacher shows picture cards, word cards or phonics cards, one at a time, and children in the front of the row race to the board to write the answer. Alternatively, a set of cards are posted on the board and the teacher names the object or makes a statement about one of the cards. Children race to the board to point out the correct cards. The child who is first to answer correctly goes to the back of his/her team's line. The winning line is the one where the child who started at the beginning of the line is back at his/her place. Alternatively, instead of racing to the board, students can answer from their seat in the same way (Ghosn, 2011).

Bingo

Bingo is a popular board game that can be applied with learners of different ages. Multiple Bingo boards can be made of rhyme, song and story pictures, pasted on cardboard and laminated. Depending on the objectives, one can use only pictures, a combination of pictures and words, or only words. Children need small coins, buttons, paperclips or small squares of paper to cover the pictures/words the teacher calls out. Alternatively, washable markers can be used with laminated boards.

Conclusion

The activities described above are aligned with the whole language approach as it can be realized in the young language learner classroom. As the practice of teaching English to young learners spreads to ever-younger age groups, careful attention must be paid to instructional materials and pedagogical approaches employed. When a coursebook is required in order to ensure a relatively uniform exposure and achievement of learning outcomes for a large student population in the beginning stages of language learning, the syllabus can be built around the above-described approaches as starting points. For example, classic folk tales can be adapted to the local cultural context and developed into Big Easel Books with large print. Collections of songs, chants and rhymes can be adapted to a variety of purposes and into Big Books. The Big Book stories and songs can then be replicated in the coursebook. The initial instruction is carried out using the Big Books. The coursebook replication of the big book texts provides children with practice and enables them to demonstrate their learning to their families.

It is important to ensure children's motivation and their opportunities for success while preventing frustration and any sense of failure. There should be no pressure on children, and literacy-related activities, while providing the teacher with valuable information, should not be part of any formal assessment. (Regrettably, in some contexts, children as young as 4 and 5 are subjected to having their language output marked and graded.) David Elkind (1988) gives us a reminder about the false concept of young children's competence in *Miseducation: Preschoolers at Risk*:

> Young children learn in a different manner from that of older children and adults, yet we can teach them many things if we adapt our materials and mode of instruction to their level of ability. But we miseducate young children when we assume that their learning abilities are comparable to those of older children and that they can be taught with materials and with the same instructional procedures appropriate to school-age children.
>
> *(p. 59)*

Note

1 http://www.eleceng.adelaide.edu.au/personal/dabbott/animal.html/. Accessed January 15, 2015.

References

Anderson, J. R. (1995). *Learning and memory: An integrated approach*. New York: Wiley.

Artelt, C. (2005). Cross-cultural approaches to measuring motivation. *Educational Assessment*, *10*(3), 231–255.

Association for Supervision and Curriculum Development (n.d.). *The whole child initiative*. www.ascd.org/programs/whole-child.aspx/. Retrieved January 12, 2015.

Barkley, R. A. (1996). Critical issues in research on attention. In G. R. Lyon & N. Krasnegor (Eds.), *Attention, memory and executive function*. Baltimore, MD: Brookes Publishing.

Beed, H., & Boyd, D. (2010). *The developing child* (12th ed.). Boston, MA: Allyn & Bacon.

The British Council. (n.d.). *How young children learn English as another language*. www.learnenglishkids.britishcouncil.org/. Retrieved January 10, 2015.

Cameron, L. (2001). *Teaching language to young learners*. Cambridge: Cambridge University Press.

Carrasquillo, A., & Hedley, C. (1993). *Whole language and the bilingual learner*. Norwood, NJ: Ablex.

Dempster, F. (1981). Memory span: Sources of individual and developmental differences. *Psychological Bulletin*, *89*(1), 63–100.

Edelsky, C., Altwerger, B., & Flores, B. (1991). *Whole language: What's the difference?* Portsmouth, NH: Heinemann.

Elkind, D. (1988). *Miseducation: Preschoolers at risk*. New York: Alfred A. Knopf.

Ellis, N. (1994). *Implicit and explicit learning of language*. London: Academic Press.

Enever, J. (2011). *ELLiE. Early language learning in Europe*. London: The British Council.

Freeman, Y., & Freeman, D. (1992). *Whole language for second language learners*. Portsmouth, NH: Heinemann.

Ghosn, I.-K. (2009). *The Little Hen Gets Help*. http://www.youtube.com/watch?v= RPWH 71tUJaE/. Retrieved January 15, 2015.

Ghosn, I.-K. (2011). *Enjoy English! Grade 1*. Beirut: UNRWA Education Program.

Ghosn, I.-K. (2013a). Language learning for young learners. In B. Tomlinson (Ed.), *Applied linguistics and materials development* (pp. 61–74). London: Bloomsbury.

Ghosn, I.-K. (2013b). *Storybridge to second language literacy: The theory, research and practice of teaching English with children's literature*. Charlotte, NC: Information Age.

Ghosn, I.-K. (2014). Teaching the very young learners: An alternative to kindergarten textbooks. Dubai, UAE: TESOL Arabia.

Goodman, K. S. (1989). Whole language research: Foundations and development. *The Elementary School Journal, 90*, 208–221.

Goodman, K. S. (1992). I didn't found whole language. *The Reading Teacher, 46*, 188–199.

Graham, T. (1982). *Let loose on Mother Goose*. Nashville, TN: Incentive.

Halliday, M. (1975). *Learning how to mean: Explorations in the functions of language*. London: Edward Arnold.

Hidi, S., & Harackiewicz, J. (2000). Motivating the academically unmotivated: A critical issue for the 21st century. *Review of Educational Research, 70(2)*, 151–180.

Holdaway, D. (1979). *The foundations of literacy*. Auckland, New Zealand: Ashton Scholastic.

Jalongo, M. (2007). Beyond benchmarks and scores: Reasserting the role of motivation and interest in children's academic achievement. An ACEI Position Paper. *Childhood Education*, International Focus Issue, 395–407.

Kachru, B. (1990). *The alchemy of English: The spread, functions, and models of non-native Englishes*. Chicago: University of Illinois Press.

Mayer, R. E. (1996). Learning strategies for making sense of our expository text: The SOI model for guiding three cognitive processes in knowledge construction. *Educational Psychology Review, 8*, 357–371.

Mihaljevic Djigunovic, J. (1993). Investigation of attitudes and motivation on early foreign language learning. In M. Vilke & I. Vrhova (Eds.), *Children and foreign languages* (pp. 45–71). Zagreb: Faculty of Philosophy, University of Zagreb.

Mueller, H., & Wegner, A. (1989). Big books: Literacy and young children. In *The shared reading experience* (pp. 10–16). Glenview, IL: Scott, Foresman.

National Association for Education of Young Children (2009). *Developmentally appropriate practice in early childhood programs serving children from birth through age 8*. http://www.naeyc.org/dap/. Retrieved January 20, 2015.

Nikolov, M. (1999). Why do you like English? Because the teacher is short. A study of Hungarian children's foreign language learning motivation. *Language Teaching Research, 3(1)*, 33–56.

Ohlstain, E., Shohamy, E., Kemp, J., & Chatow, R. (1990). Factors predicting success in EFL among culturally different learners. *Language Learning, 40*, 23–44.

Pinker, S. (1994). *The language instinct*. New York: HarperCollins.

Pinter, A. (2006). *Teaching young language learners*. Oxford: Oxford University Press.

Richards, J. (1971). Error analysis and second language strategies. *Language Sciences, 17*, 12–22.

Rixon, S. (2013). *British Council survey of policy and practice in primary English language teaching worldwide*. London: The British Council.

Thompson, P., Giedd, J. N., Woods, R. P., MacDonald, D., Evans, A., & Toga, A. W. (2000). Growth patterns in the developing human brain detected using continuum-mechanical tensor mapping. *Nature, 404,* 190–193. Also retrieved from: http://www.nature.com/nature/journal/v404/n6774/full/404190a0.html

Ullman, M. (2001). The neurocognitive perspectives on language: The declarative/ procedural model. *Nature Reviews Neuroscience, 2,* 717–726.

Vygotsky, L. (1978). *Mind in society.* London: Harvard University Press.

Weaver, C., Gillmesiter-Krause, L., & Vento-Zogby, G. (1996). *Creating support for effective literacy education.* Portsmouth, NH: Heinemann.

COMMENTS ON PART I

Brian Tomlinson

The position papers in this section express a variety of differing views about the interface between second language acquisition research and materials for language learning. In my chapters, I express the opinion that there is currently little match between SLA research findings and the content and pedagogy of materials for language learning. I argue that materials developers and the teachers using their materials should try to ensure that the learners' experience of the materials replicates as nearly as possible the conditions found by SLA research to facilitate language acquisition and the development of communication skills. I admit that this is not easy because there is still much controversy about what all the optimum conditions actually are. I stress however that there *is* common agreement about what the basic prerequisites are for language acquisition and development, and suggest that materials developers and teachers should try to ensure that learners are given access to these prerequisites, providing that they accord with their own experience of what promotes acquisition and development. Hitomi Masuhara takes a similar position but stresses the importance of incorporating findings from neurolinguistic research into SLA theory and then applying them to the development and use of language learning materials. Irma Ghosn also advocates the application of theory to practice, and in particular the application of what we know about how very young learners develop and how they are most likely to succeed in acquiring a second language.

What all the authors in this section seem to agree on is that most commercially available language learning materials (especially coursebooks) do language learners a disservice by not taking sufficient account of what we know about language acquisition, regardless of whether this awareness comes from academic research, from classroom research, from teacher enquiry or from teacher intuition. This echoes the discontent voiced by teachers of English at conferences and workshops around the world. Recently I have heard teachers complaining about the failure of the materials they use to relate to, to engage or even to interest their learners in China, Indonesia, Malaysia, Portugal, Turkey and Vietnam. They blame the institutional obsession with testing for the predominance of activities in course-books which can be used as tests and/or for examination preparation but which seem to contribute very little to the language acquisition and skills development of the students using them. They also blame their ministries of education and/or their institutions for providing such unsuitable materials, and they try their best to make these materials more relevant, engaging and interesting, so that at least some of their learners will gain the motivation they need to inspire them to look for English outside the classroom.

PART II

Materials Driven by SLA Theory

5

A CASE STUDY OF PRINCIPLED MATERIALS IN ACTION

Alper Darici and Brian Tomlinson

Background to the Case Study

In the last few years we have worked together at the Fatih Koleji middle schools and high schools in Istanbul,[1] to engage their students affectively and cognitively more than their coursebooks typically do. We have tried to do this through using a text-driven framework with a focus on providing rich exposure to English in use plus opportunities to respond in open-ended and personal ways (Tomlinson, 2013a). Brian has visited the schools where Alper is responsible for the teaching of English, and has seen how bored and reticent the students can be when their teacher just uses a global coursebook. He has also observed Alper's classes and seen the effects on the students of him using a text-driven approach. To paraphrase a well-known work of art, the room is alive with the sound of English. This is true, too, of some of the other classrooms in which teachers influenced by Alper's example and Brian's workshops have been engaging their previously reticent students through materials using a text-driven approach.

Alper aims to conduct PhD research with Hitomi Masuhara (a co-presenter of workshops with Brian at the Fatih schools) at the University of Liverpool in order to evaluate the effectiveness of the text-driven materials he is developing and using. In this chapter, though, we are just reporting on the perceived effect of one unit of text-driven materials developed for one lesson at a Fatih school in Istanbul.

Procedures for the Development of the Unit of Materials

What we did was as follows:

Specification of Learning Principles to Inform the Development of the Unit

We consulted the literature on principled materials development (e.g. Harwood, 2010, 2014; McGrath, 2014; Tomlinson, 2008, 2010, 2011, 2012, 2013b). We also reflected on our previous experience of materials development and on the principles that we have used in materials development workshops for teachers at Fatih schools and then we specified the following principles which we would use to inform the development of the unit:

Gen Course Design

We can facilitate second language (L2) acquisition through the unit of materials by:

1. providing a rich exposure to language in use;
2. providing texts and tasks likely to stimulate affective engagement;
3. providing texts and tasks likely to stimulate cognitive engagement;
4. providing meaningful and spaced recycling;
5. attempting to stimulate a willing investment of time and energy (i.e. motivation);
6. helping the students to pay attention to form after meaning focused activities;
7. providing opportunities to use English for communication;
8. attempting to stimulate student/text interaction, student/student inter-action and student/teacher interaction.

We decided on these principles because we both agree that they establish pre-requisites for fostering eventually effective and durable language acquisition and because we have found that English language teaching (ELT) global coursebooks are rarely informed by these principles (Tomlinson et al., 2001; Masuhara et al., 2008; Tomlinson & Masuhara, 2013; Tomlinson, 2013b).

Specification of a Principled Framework to Drive the Materials

We decided to make use of a text-driven framework because materials driven by such a framework had been observed by Brian to appear to engage students on textbook projects in China, Ethiopia, Namibia and Norway and by Alper to engage previously unmotivated and reticent students in classes in Fatih schools in Istanbul. The following is the principled framework which we used for developing the unit of materials:

LP

1. A **readiness activity** to activate the students' minds in relation to the theme/ topic/location of the text. Such activities could include student visualization of relevant situations in their lives and/or students talking to themselves or to other students about such situations.
2. An **initial response activity** to influence the way the students encounter the text and, where appropriate, to assist them to experience it multidimensionally in the mind rather than study it (e.g. creating a visual image of a place, event or character as they read; interpreting the behaviour of characters in the text; evaluating ideas discussed in the text; comparing an event in the text to one in their own lives).
3. An **intake response activity** helping the students to deepen and articulate their personal response to their experience of the text.

4.   A **development activity** stimulating the students to develop texts of their own in response to the core text.
5.   An **input response activity** helping the students to make discoveries about language use by focusing on a linguistic, discourse or pragmatic feature of the core text.
6.   A **development activity** involving the students in making use of their discoveries in 5 to improve the text they produced in 4.

See Tomlinson (2013c) for a detailed description and theoretical justification of this framework, and see Al-Busaidi and Tindle (2013), Gottheim (2013), McCullagh (2013) and Rico Troncoso (2013), for reports of the effects of using text-driven approaches to develop materials in Oman, Brazil, the UK and Colombia respectively.

Specification of Important Features of the Unit of Materials

Based on our experience, on our beliefs and on what we consider to be typically missing from global coursebooks, we specified the following important features of the unit of materials:

1. The Text(s) Will Be Authentic in the Sense of Not Having Been Developed to Teach Language but Having Been Written (or Spoken) to Entertain, Instruct, Stimulate, Persuade, Make Arrangements, etc.

We wanted to make sure that the students were exposed to English being used for communication rather than English being contrived to illustrate features of the language (see Mishan, 2005; Gilmore, 2007).

2. The Texts and Tasks Will Be Connected to the Lives of Teenage Students in Istanbul

The texts and tasks did not have to be about the lives of teenage students in Istanbul, but we wanted them to suggest connections so as to increase the likelihood of engagement.

3. The Texts and Tasks Will Have the Potential to Get Teenage Students in Istanbul to Think and to Feel Whilst Experiencing Them (Tomlinson, 2013a)

We were convinced that achieving affective and cognitive engagement was vital both because we really believed in the value of such engagement in promoting acquisition and because it seemed to rarely be achieved when global coursebooks were used in Fatih schools.

4. The Texts and Tasks Will Pose an Achievable Challenge to All the Students in the Class

We both believed that most global coursebooks underestimate students and that the students often get bored and demotivated because the activities they are asked to do are both mindless and too easy. We believe in pushing the students to make use of their English so as to eventually manage to understand and appreciate a text and/or to accomplish a task.

5. The Tasks Will Be Coherent in the Sense That Each One Follows On From the Preceding Task and Prepares the Students for the Next One

Too many global coursebooks consist of units which are crammed with activities that have no useful connection with each other and whose completion has no value in relation to subsequent activities (Tomlinson et al., 2001; Masuhara et al., 2008; Tomlinson & Masuhara, 2013).

6. The Materials Will Provide Opportunities for Revisiting the Text(s) and Reusing Language Related to Them

It is generally agreed by SLA researchers that recycling of language both receptively and productively is vital for language acquisition and that it is most valuable if the encounters are varied, spaced and over a lengthy period of time (see, for example, Nation and Webb, 2011) rather than crammed into a short period of time (as, for example, with drills).

7. The Materials Will Provide Options for Learners to Choose From

Each learner in a class is different, because each learner is at a different level, is motivated to a different degree, has different preferred learning styles, has different needs and wants, has different interests, etc., etc. So it is logical that at some point in a lesson the learner is given choices of content, route, objectives and activity.

8. The Materials Will Stimulate Out-of-Class Activities Which Provide Further Opportunities to Experience English in Use

No school can provide enough time and experience for learners to rely on what they do in the classroom to acquire communicative competence. They need to look for English outside the classroom too and to supplement their experiences in class with, for example, extensive reading, listening and viewing, with interactions with speakers of English and with experience of English being used for communication (Lamb, 2009; Tomlinson, 2014).

The Development of the Unit of Materials

The Profile of the Class

High school students in Turkey seem to be very similar to each other according to observations made by Alper when he did research for his MA dissertation in Turkish high schools in 2009. The learners in Fatih usually fit this typical foreign-language learner profile in Turkey.

Learners who want to go on to high school in Fatih are exposed to instructional English for 5–8 years in primary education. Most of them have the same kind of restricted learning experience, with the exception of those few fortunate students whose innovative teachers intuitively adapt the coursebook materials they are obliged to use. Most learners can be said to be habitual users of global coursebooks, usually resulting in inefficiency of productive skills and a feeling of failure in learning a foreign language.

From a pedagogical point of view, the feeling of failure can cause the loss of hope, the lack of excitement and the weariness that seem to be main obstacles to the progress of the students. The students are mostly analytic (or trained to be so) and they are score-addicted. Even though not all of them are fully successful, they like maths and science as these subjects do not require speaking and writing. As long as they do pen-and-paper studies in a mechanical routinized style, are not pushed into creative thinking and do not have to risk making big mistakes in front of their classmates, they usually feel comfortable. As a result of this habit, they hardly ever intend to respond to questions in a full or extended form. They never fancy writing more than a paragraph in writing studies. They mainly try to make their writing as simple and direct as possible just to complete the task in a very short time. Also, since the main goal is to get high enough scores to pass the class, they rarely take unnecessary risks in producing language to complete communicative tasks which have the potential of promoting L2 acquisition. When students rarely take the risk of getting involved in communicative tasks, they only occasionally become aware of their real performance and capabilities. This usually results in a failure to notice the gap between their performance and proficient performance, and this lack of awareness means they rarely achieve comprehensible output. As the students never urge themselves to be productive, they fail to achieve the multidimensional representation and use of inner speech which can help to facilitate language acquisition (Tomlinson & Avila, 2007). Multidimensional representation and inner speech involve imagination and creativity and making connections with their own lives. They are rarely aimed at by global coursebooks and rarely achieved in Turkish high schools.

Overall, as learners are almost exclusively exposed to deductive language learning which involves frequent use of such conventional practice exercises as True/False, matching words to sentences or pictures, filling in blanks, completing sentences, role play and working in pairs to compare ideas, it is not very surprising that they develop the feeling of failure, loss of hope, lack of excitement and weariness after many years of English.

The class for which Alper developed a unit of materials was a first-year high school class (known as 9th grade in Turkey). There were 44 14-year-old boys who had graduated from various private secondary schools in Istanbul and who had had a successful education in all subjects except English. Even though they all came within the top 10,000 students in the high school examination taken by 1,200,000 students, they were still at an A2 level after 5–8 years of learning English at school.

The Writing of the Unit

Teachers and global coursebook writers are not fully aware of the current interests of learners and their potential effect on the motivation of learners. When books focus on global topics and issues they may not easily appeal to learners with different cultural and social backgrounds, interests and styles in different parts of the world. When teachers use these books without any reference to local issues the learners are unlikely to be motivated.

To be able to create necessary learning energy teachers should first do small-scale classroom research in their schools to identify what kind of topics and texts their learners are interested in.

Before Alper designed this unit of material, he applied a small survey, which provided a general profile of his learners and gave him clues about their interests and learning styles. He realized that they enjoy listening or reading stories which are gripping, full of surprise, even involving a little violence, murder and crime and that they want to be engaged affectively and cognitively. There is strong evidence found in the research on affective engagement for second language acquisition (SLA) that learners who are stimulated to laugh, smile, feel joy, feel excited and feel empathetic are much more likely to acquire communicative competence than learners who are restricted to bland, safe, neutral materials which do not stimulate any emotional response (Tomlinson, 2013b). Positive emotions seem most likely to stimulate deep processing (Craik & Lockhart, 1972) and therefore to facilitate language acquisition. However, negative emotions such as anger, disagreement and sorrow are much more facilitative than no emotional responses at all (Tomlinson, 2013b).

Before developing his unit Alper started looking for an authentic text which was not specifically written to teach English and which is potentially engaging, in order to drive personal response tasks, thinking tasks, visual imaging tasks, inner speech tasks and creative writing tasks. In addition he aimed to find material which would stimulate genuine interaction and which would require extensive reading and writing for a purpose. Alper also aimed to match the material with the linguistic needs of his learners so he decided to use the first two chapters of the book, *The Street Lawyer* by John Grisham (2007). He utilized a lengthier extract of the story in the actual unit of materials used with the class.

The Use of the Unit in the Classroom

Alper tried to design his material and lesson plan in accordance with procedures agreed with Brian, which were:

- A readiness activity
- An initial response activity
- An intake response activity
- A development activity
- An input response activity
- A development activity.

We both believe that a good opening, which makes students think, feel and connect with their world, is always the key point of a successful lesson. So Alper used a cartoon which he thought had the potential to stimulate the students from the beginning of the lesson. As we never expect learners to come to classroom ready for English, this bit of the lesson is useful for smooth transition from Turkish to English. Moreover it is an opening gate to exchange ideas with other mates in the classroom.

One possible way of increasing motivation in the classroom is to create a positive atmosphere in which no idea is ever fully right or wrong. As long as the learners try to communicate in English in the classroom we should encourage them. For this

FIGURE 5.1 Life without feeling empathy (from CartoonStock.com)

FIGURE 5.2 'Ostracized lawyer': Example of student drawing for task 2 of the unit

FIGURE 5.3 'Astonishing meeting': Example of student drawing for task 2 of the unit

to happen we need to give them open questions and tasks rather than the closed exercises typical of many global coursebooks used in Turkey.

The subsequent three tasks (see 2. 3. and 4. in the Unit of Materials below) are the most powerful part of the lesson, since they pursue the energy of a good beginning. While Alper was reading the story, learners tried to make their own pictures in their mind and afterwards drew them in their notebook. The images that they visualized were another tool to build a meaningful interaction between the learners and the materials. This part of the lesson can be said to be the most enjoyable, because although most of the learners were quite weak in drawing and used stick man figures, the happiness and the joy of the learners

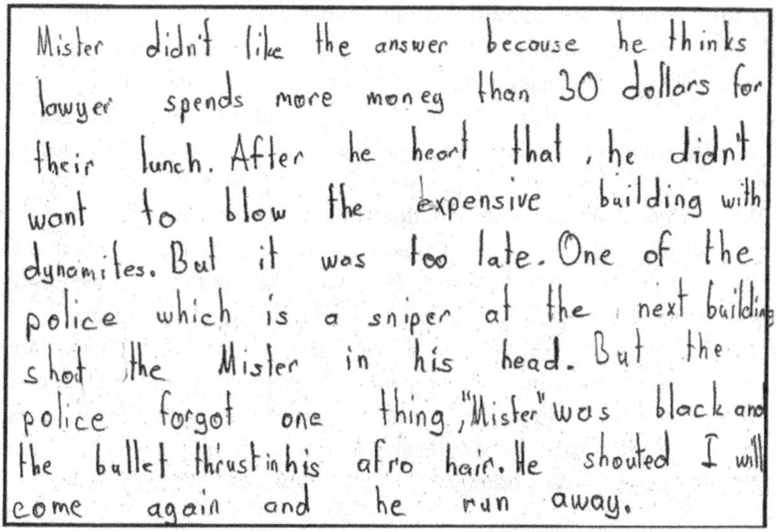

> Mister didn't like the answer because he thinks lawyer spends more money than 30 dollars for their lunch. After he heard that, he didn't want to blow the expensive building with dynamites. But it was too late. One of the police which is a sniper at the next building shot the Mister in his head. But the police forgot one thing, "Mister" was black and the bullet thrust in his afro hair. He shouted I will come again and he run away.

FIGURE 5.4 Student's manuscript

created a positive, relaxed atmosphere. One possible reason for the happiness and joy was that they did not do typical classroom activities which require low-level thinking skills, such as filling gaps, choosing the right word or choosing true/false, etc.

After the stage in which learners tried to guess what might happen, there was no need for further points to encourage them to read the rest of the story. They wanted to see if they were right with their predictions. The challenge created the energy to carry out the next tasks, which required them to think, analyse and speak. Provided that learners are productive in the tasks, they are likely to enjoy doing them. There is no risk of losing concentration and enthusiasm. This encouraged them to write their own ending and read the rest of the story to make another comparison.

The first nine tasks were mainly based on the affective and cognitive involvement of the learners. Learners were active and more productive than ever, compared to their previous learning experience. Learners were given the chance to be critical and to think about possible solutions in task nine. They also attempted to personalize their learning. In addition, they had to take risks, an important feature of the interlanguage development of learners.

The third part of the lesson plan mainly targeted the improvement of the linguistic competence of the learners. They had to make a personal investment and explore the text to discover 'new' features of language items which they might have had some familiarity with before. To make the discoveries they had to revisit the text and therefore gain re-cycled exposure. We may claim that as long as they discover on their own they are unlikely to forget what they gain. In this part of the lesson, Alper needed to assist them more than elsewhere, as the experience was unfamiliar and demanding.

Personally we think that giving people alternatives can reduce their anxiety, and this was why Alper let them choose their homework from a list of options, each catering for a different intelligence or learning style (e.g. finding music and photos to match the text; creating a cartoon story for a newspaper).

With the help of this material, Alper tried to reduce the gap between what theorists claim and what language policy makers and some materials developers do. In theory we all accept the idea of language variation, the basic need for creating opportunities which facilitate SLA and the diversity of language and cultures worldwide, but in practice, when defining policies or developing language materials, there is often an attempt to homogenize and standardize the way we teach our learners. In fact, if we can be a little more empathetic and think how we ourselves would like to learn, then we will be able to find or develop the best materials to apply in the language classroom.

The Unit of Materials

Here is the unit of materials which was used with the class.

Level: Low-Intermediate

Class Profile: High school students. Most of them are analytic learners. They like neither reading long texts nor writing them. They rarely participate in a lesson verbally unless they find it stimulating to talk on.

1. **Look at Figure 5.1. Think about the message then share it with your class.**
2. **Your teacher will read you the first part of the story. Close your eyes then try to see pictures in your mind. Draw a picture of the story.**
3. **Show your picture to your seatmate. Tell him about your picture.**
4. **Guess why people were looking at him so strangely.**
5. **Read the rest of the story.**

The old black man got into the elevator behind me. . . . His beard and hair were half-gray and very dirty. He was wearing sunglasses, and a long dirty coat hung down to his knees. . . .

The elevator stopped at six. . . . When I stepped out and turned right, he followed me. There were eight lawyers at the table inside and they all looked surprised. They were looking behind me, so I turned. My friend from the elevator was standing there. He was pointing a gun at me.

"Put that gun down," said one of the lawyers at the table. . . .

Suddenly, a shot hit the ceiling.

"Lock the door," the man said to me. I locked the door of the meeting room. . . .

He had five or six red sticks around his waist, tied there with string. . . .

"Please be quiet," said the man, calmly. Then he took a long yellow rope and a knife from the pocket of his pants. "You," he said to me. "Tie them up."

Rafter stepped forward. "Listen, friend," he said, "what do you want?"

The second shot went into the wall, behind Rafter's ear.

"Do not call me 'friend,'" said the man.

"What would you like us to call you?"

"Call me 'Mister.'" . . .

We could hear police cars outside and noises as the police entered the building. . . .

"I pull this," he said, "and we die." . . .

I thought of all those terrible shootings you read about in the newspapers. A crazy worker returns to work after lunch with a gun and kills everybody in his office. . . .

"What did you eat for lunch today?" Mister asked me, breaking a long silence, dynamite. . . .

"I had chicken and salad," I said, surprised.

"How much did it cost, for both of you?"

"Thirty dollars."

Mister didn't like that. "Thirty dollars," he repeated. "For two people."

6. **Discuss with your partner:**

   a. What do you think Mister's problem was?
   b. What would be the first thing to pop up in your mind if you were one of the hostages?
   c. What would you do if you were the lawyer who tied his friends?
   d. Why do you think Mister did not like the answer, 'Thirty dollars'?

7. **Imagine that this is the first chapter of a book. Complete the first chapter with your own words.**

8. **Read the rest of the first chapter then compare it with your ending.**
   In the rest of the story Mister asked questions about their level of income and indicated that they were all unaware of what poor people ate and how they struggled with life. To give all the lawyers experience of this, he wanted them to get soup and bread from the shelter at L Street and 17th. Half an hour later after ordering the food there was a knock at the door. Mister threatened to kill the lawyers if he saw a policeman. When Mister opened the door a policeman shot him in the head.

9. **Answer the following questions.**

   a. Are there a lot of homeless people in your city? Do you think we are sufficiently aware of homeless people?
   b. If you were the chairman of an NGO (Non-Governmental Organization) how would you deal with the problem 'homelessness'?

10. **Revisit the story. Underline the questions.**
11. **Read 'learn this' box below.**
12. **Choose 8 questions from the text then put the questions into reported form.**

Ex: 'What do you want? ━━━▶ He asked me what I wanted.

Q: _____

R: _____

13. **Choose one of the homework tasks below.**

    a. Imagine that that you were one of the hostages. Draw a cartoon story for a newspaper.
    b. Think about a news headline for this event. Write a short story of the event for a cover page.
    c. Find some photos and a music. Make a video clip to attract public attention to problems of homelessness.
    d. Go to the dailymail web site and watch the video. Tell about it to the class. http://www.dailymail.co.uk/news/article-2408786/Homeless-man-Billy-Ray-Harris-returned-4k-diamond-engagement-ring-woman-moves-new-house.html

The Evaluation of the Unit

This was a small-scale research study so we did a simple humanistic evaluation. As soon as Alper had completed his lesson he delivered a questionnaire, to learn what the students thought about the text and tasks and whether they found the lesson interesting and useful. We also wanted to find out about the parts they liked most and least. The questions and answers were in English, part of writing for a real purpose, which was also our message to our learners.

Although learners stated that they were very happy about the choice of text and tasks and they found the lesson interesting, Alper was more interested in the negative feedback, as this revealed the parts he needed to revise. He tried to improve the weakest points indicated by the feedback and applied the new lesson plan with another class. As a result the second lesson was more successful than expected.

L2 learners, like first language (L1) learners, need to be given the advantage of exposure, motivation, opportunities for use and availability of feedback on the effectiveness of their outcomes. When teachers aim to make changes with their materials and lesson plans in relation to the real learning needs of L2 learners they will help to make them real acquirers, developing much greater lexical, grammatical and pragmatic competence. Moreover, all L2 learners may acquire English effortlessly and effectively if they have both sufficient exposure to the language and opportunities to use it in and outside the classroom. If acquisition is natural and inevitable given the appropriate conditions but development requires

WORD ORDER

Normal word order is used in reported questions, that is, the subject comes before the verb, and it is not necessary to use 'do' or 'did':

EXAMPLES

Direct speech	Indirect speech
"Where does Peter live?"	She asked him where Peter lived.
"Where are you going?"	She asked where I was going.
"Why is she crying?"	He asked why she was crying.

YES / NO QUESTIONS

This type of question is reported by using 'ask' + 'if / whether' + clause:

EXAMPLES

Direct speech	Indirect speech
"Do you speak English?"	He asked me if I spoke English.
"Are you British or American?"	He asked me whether I was British or American.
"Is it raining?"	She asked if it was raining.
"Have you got a computer?"	He wanted to know whether I had a computer.
"Can you type?"	She asked if I could type.
"Did you come by train?"	He enquired whether I had come by train.
"Have you been to Bristol before?"	She asked if I had been to Bristol before.

QUESTION WORDS

This type of question is reported by using 'ask' (or another verb like 'ask') + question word + clause. The clause contains the question, in normal word order and with the necessary tense change.

EXAMPLES

Direct speech	Indirect speech
"What is your name?" he asked me.	He asked me what my name was.
"How old is your mother?", he asked.	He asked how old her mother was.
The policeman said to the boy, "Where do you live?"	The policeman asked the boy where he lived.
"What time does the train arrive?" she asked.	She asked what time the train arrived.
"When can we have dinner?" she asked.	She asked when they could have dinner.
Peter said to John, "Why are you so late?"	Peter asked the John why he was so late.

FIGURE 5.5   Question forms and reported speech (from Edufind.com)

tuition (Tomlinson, 2007), teachers need to design better materials and develop their lesson plans in relation to such basic proven principles of SLA as we agreed on before developing the materials.

Language development is the deliberate optimizing of communication skills already gained. It builds on from acquisition and requires conscious attention, frequent demanding use, self-reflection and informed feedback in order to construct large syntactical, lexical and strategic repertoires from which to select for potential effect (Tomlinson, 2007). Materials therefore need to cater both for acquisition and development, as Alper aimed to do when developing his materials.

Implications of the Case Study

This is a case study of the development, use and evaluation of one unit of materials and therefore no strong claims can be made as to its effectiveness. However we would like to suggest that observation of the materials in use, and post-use evaluation of the materials indicate the possibility that:

1. teenage Turkish students are likely to be affectively engaged by rich texts which are exciting and/or disturbing;
2. teenage Turkish students are likely to be cognitively engaged by texts and activities which stimulate them to think;
3. teenage Turkish students are likely to respond to open-ended activities by expressing their attitudes, views and thoughts in the target language and thus gaining opportunities to develop their ability to communicate effectively;
4. teenage Turkish students are likely to enjoy responding personally to engaging texts and are likely to be motivated to learn English by doing so.

TABLE 5.1 Learner questionnaire and results

Questions	Proportion of Students responding favourably
1. Did you enjoy the text? Enjoyable / exciting / easy to read / interesting / stimulating / gripping / realistic text	28/28
2. Did you enjoy the tasks? Not as enjoyable as the text / enough to enjoy / nice to produce/ producing subjective ideas / had great fun / not much	22/28
3. Did you find the lesson interesting?	25/28
4. Did you find the lesson useful?	For various reasons, 1 student out of 28 reported negative feedback
5. What did you like most about the lesson? The story / length of the story / exchanging ideas in pairs / drawing / story completion / makes me think / the way teachers ran the lesson	
6. Was there anything you did not like about the lesson? Some questions were absurd / don't like writing too much / the end of the story	

If 1–4 above are true for these students then they are likely to be creative in their response to, and their use of, English. If this happens for these students then the likelihood of them achieving effective L2 acquisition will be increased. If this is true for this class of students then there is a possibility that it might be true for other similar classes of students in Turkey and maybe elsewhere too.

Obviously this is a one-off case study and needs to be replicated many times with different texts and activities, with different students and with different teachers before any strong conclusions can be reached. This we intend to do, and Alper will be continuing the research longitudinally as the basis of his PhD.

Tentative Conclusion

We believe (and hope to be able to demonstrate) that using a text-driven approach can increase students' chances of achieving engagement, motivation, linguistic awareness, self-confidence and therefore acquisition.

Note

1 Fatih schools are run by a charitable Islamic foundation, which has schools all over the world.

References

Al-Busaidi, S., & Tindle, K. (2010). Evaluating the effect of in-house materials on language learning. In B. Tomlinson & H. Masuhara (Eds.), *Research for materials development in language learning* (pp. 137–149). London: Continuum.

Craik, F. I. M., & Lockhart, R. S. (1972). Levels of processing: A framework for memory research. *Journal of Verbal Learning, 11*, 671–684.

Gilmore, A. (2007). Authentic materials and authenticity in foreign language learning. *Language Teaching, 40*, 97–118.

Gottheim, L. (2010). Composing textbooks as a non-expert. In B. Tomlinson & H. Masuhara (Eds.), *Research for materials development in language learning* (pp. 224–236). London: Continuum.

Grisham, J. (2007). *The Street lawyer* (pp. 1–2). Penguin Active Reading Series. Harlow, Essex: Pearson Education Ltd.

Harwood, N. (Ed.) (2010). *English language teaching materials: Theory and practice.* Cambridge: Cambridge University Press.

Harwood, N. (Ed.) (2014). *English language teaching textbooks: Content, consumption, production.* Basingstoke, UK: Palgrave Macmillan.

Lamb, M. (2009). Situating the L2 self: Two Indonesian school learners of English. In Z. Dörnyei and E. Ushioda (Eds.), *Motivation, language identity and the L2 self* (pp. 229–47). Bristol: Multilingual Matters.

Masuhara, H., Haan, M., Yi, Y., & Tomlinson, B. (2008). Adult EFL courses. *ELT Journal, 62*(3), 294–312.

McCullagh, M. (2010). An initial evaluation of a set of published materials for medical English. In B. Tomlinson & H. Masuhara (Eds.), *Research for materials development in language learning* (pp. 381–393). London: Continuum.

McGrath, I. (2014). *Teaching materials and the roles of EFL/ESL teachers.* London: Bloomsbury.

Mishan, F. (2005). *Designing authenticity into language learning materials.* Bristol: Intellect.

Nation, I. S. P., & Webb, S. (2011). *Researching and analysing vocabulary.* Boston, MA: Heinle Cengage Learning.

Question forms and reported speech at: http://www.edufind.com/english-grammar/question-forms-and-reported-speech/. Accessed 7 May 2013.

Rico Troncoso, C. (2010). The effects of language materials on the development of intercultural competence. In B. Tomlinson & H. Masuhara (Eds.), *Research for materials development in language learning* (pp. 83–102). London: Continuum.

Tomlinson, B. (2007). Introduction: Some similarities and differences between L1 and L2 acquisition and development. In B. Tomlinson (Ed.), *Language acquisition and development: Studies of learners of first and other languages* (pp. 1–12). London: Continuum.

Tomlinson, B. (2008). Language acquisition and language learning materials. In B. Tomlinson (Ed.), *English language learning materials: A critical review* (pp. 3–14). London: Continuum.

Tomlinson, B. (2010). Principles of effective materials development. In N. Harwood (Ed.), *English language teaching materials: Theory and practice* (pp. 81–108). Cambridge: Cambridge University Press.

Tomlinson, B. (2011). Introduction: Principles and procedures of materials development. In B. Tomlinson (Ed.), *Materials development in language teaching* (2nd ed., pp. 1–34). Cambridge: Cambridge University Press.

Tomlinson, B. (2012). Materials development. *Language Teaching, 45*(2), 1–37.

Tomlinson, B. (2013a). Developing principled frameworks for materials development. In B. Tomlinson (Ed.), *Developing materials for language teaching* (2nd ed., pp. 95–118). London: Bloomsbury.

Tomlinson, B. (2013b). Second language acquisition and materials development. In B. Tomlinson (Ed.), *Applied linguistics and materials development* (pp. 11–30). London: Bloomsbury.

Tomlinson, B. (2014). Looking out for English. *Folio, 16*(1), 5–8.

Tomlinson, B., Dat, B., Masuhara, H., & Rubdy, R. (2001). EFL courses for adults. *ELT Journal, 55*(1), 80–101.

Tomlinson, B., & Avila, J. (2007). Seeing and saying for yourself: The roles of audio-visual mental aids in language learning and use. In B. Tomlinson (Ed.), *Language acquisition and development: Studies of learners of first and other languages* (pp. 61–81). London: Continuum.

Tomlinson, B., & Masuhara, H. (2013). Review of adult ELT textbooks. *ELT Journal, 67*(2), 233–249.

6

RESEARCH-INFORMED MATERIALS FOR TEACHING PRAGMATICS

THE CASE OF AGREEMENT AND DISAGREEMENT IN ENGLISH

Noriko Ishihara and Daniel Leigh Paller

From the perspective of researchers in second language acquisition (SLA), many of the commercially available materials may be less than desirable, as they do not necessarily reflect principles of SLA nor adequately capitalize on research-based information (Tomlinson, 2013). In fact, commercially available English language teaching (ELT) materials have been severely criticized by researchers of pragmatics for their lack of authenticity or the stiltedness of the language presented as a model for learners, as well as for the scarcity of activities designed to facilitate the analysis of contextualized language use by learners (Vellenga, 2004). Nevertheless, teaching materials are a major part of language teaching and learning, and, in many places around the world, the textbook gives the course its "face," dictating the curriculum. At one extreme, teachers might use the textbook as their students' only source of language input. In other cases, teachers use the information in the textbook as a starting point for their lessons and supplement it with more creative communicative activities. In either case, with some notable exceptions, commercially produced textbooks offer students few opportunities to develop their pragmatic competence, their ability to exercise appropriate use and interpretation of the language in a given sociocultural context.

The purpose of this chapter is not to reiterate this argument but to direct the attention of practitioners, materials developers, and SLA researchers to a few currently published materials that have been developed in better alignment with current SLA theories and research-based information in the realm of pragmatics. By highlighting such materials, we intend to underscore the value of pedagogically oriented publications in SLA that can serve as a promising bridge between theory, research, and practice. Simultaneously, we will critically examine ways in which these materials may be enhanced even more to support language learning in interactive contexts.

In this chapter, we will first review available research on textbooks with particular attention paid to the perspective of pragmatics. We will then focus on the discourse of oppositional talk and summarize the structure of disagreement. These reviews will be followed by a discussion about the match and mismatch between currently available language teaching materials and authentic language use. Finally, suggestions will be offered with regard to the evaluation and selection of materials designed for teaching pragmatics.

Current Research Evaluating English Language Teaching (ELT) Textbooks

A mismatch between authentic and textbook language is often reported in textbook evaluation research. One current representative work in textbook evaluation is Tomlinson (2013), in which six commercial textbooks are analyzed in relation to SLA theory. Tomlinson noted their shortcomings, including the similar approach of the textbooks' units and their activity types, a limited amount of language being re-cycled, activities focused more on practice than on use, and limited opportunities for creative and critical thinking. Other studies have also found a mismatch, including, for example, an overuse of grammar and written skills in Colombian English as a foreign language (EFL) textbooks (Gómez-Rodriguez, 2010), limited free writing and an emphasis on translation in Japanese writing textbooks (Kobayakawa, 2011), a lack of communicative activities in Japanese oral communication textbooks (Ogura, 2008), and an incongruence between government guidelines and textbook activities in Japanese senior high school EFL textbooks (Glasgow & Paller, 2014a).

Pragmatic Language Use in ELT Textbooks

Similarly, in investigations of textbooks aiming to foster pragmatic competence (Bjørge, 2012; Cohen & Ishihara, 2013; Diepenbroek & Derwing, 2013; Glasgow & Paller, 2014b; Petraki & Bayes, 2013; Vellenga, 2004; Williams, 1988) mismatches can also be found. It can, therefore, be argued that more research-informed pragmatic material is needed in addition to what is currently available, since pragmatic failure could have greater repercussions than grammar-based mistakes (Crandall & Basturkmen, 2004). While grammar mistakes can be dismissed as innocent language problems, pragmatic-based miscommunication can readily be characterized as a sign of rudeness or flawed personality. Fortunately, pragmatic competence is known to be amenable to instruction (Jeon & Kaya, 2006; Kasper & Rose, 2002), and textbook materials could play a crucial supporting role in facilitating the development of learners' pragmatic competence.

One study analyzed five government-approved high school oral communication textbooks in Japan (McGroarty & Taguchi, 2005), particularly for task communicativeness, range of situations, and range of functions. The study found that in all five textbooks the tasks contained mostly mechanical practice in which students filled in blanks, in addition to limited opportunities for ongoing communication. In all five textbooks, the tasks were highly structured and showed little variation in activity types, as well as not being cognitively demanding. Moreover, the textbooks incorporated a sparse amount of pragmatic information. Many of the pragmatic functions were practiced through straightforward fill-in-the-blank activities without allowing students to express themselves creatively. Furthermore, the limited number of situations for language use in the textbooks makes it difficult for learners to communicate outside of the classroom in different social situations.

A more recent study examined three Vietnamese high school textbooks and their accompanying workbooks for the inclusion of 27 speech acts (Nguyen, 2011). The textbooks were analyzed in terms of the extent of speech act instruction in the materials, how the speech acts were presented, and the pragmatic information included. Nguyen found that there was a decrease in the number of speech acts treated in the textbooks throughout the series as the proficiency level became more advanced. However, some speech acts were found across all grades, including "giving opinions," "agreeing," and "disagreeing," thus allowing for more consistent practice. However, the overall distribution of the speech acts showed that they were randomly placed across grades. Like McGroarty and Taguchi (2005), Nguyen found that the textbooks did not contain sufficient pragmatic information to enhance the learners' pragmatic competence, and stressed the need to provide such support.

On the other hand, a study recently conducted in Canada showed mixed results. In a survey of pragmatics-based and oral fluency activities in 48 textbooks, Diepenbroek and Derwing (2013) found a great variety in their treatment of pragmatic language use. Some textbook series include frequent speech acts and conversation strategies, even though they lack a clear justification for their selection. They noted the *Touchstone* series (McCarthy, McCarten, & Sandiford, 2005, 2006) as a commendable exception that shows both frequency and prioritization of expressions based on their corpus data. Nevertheless, the authors pointed out that in many of the textbooks, pragmatic activities are often decontextualized and do not provide instruction as to which expressions are appropriate for use in a given context or for whom, when, and why certain expressions should be selected over others.

Focusing on particular aspects of pragmatic language use, another recent study investigated five ESL textbooks used in Australia with regard to the inclusion of the speech act of request, specifically oral requests (Petraki & Bayes, 2013). The authors analyzed five textbooks in terms of the extent to which the textbooks raised cross-cultural awareness of requests, exposed learners to various request forms, analyzed factors that affect the degree of politeness, emphasized preferred and dispreferred responses, and presented multi-turn requests (Petraki & Bayes, 2013, p. 504). Petraki and Bayes found that none of the five textbooks contained activities designed to raise students' cross-cultural awareness. Additionally, the analysis showed that the textbooks contained an insufficient range of requests that would vary in their level of directness. Therefore, the five textbooks in question did not provide students with ample pragmatic information or activities for practice.

In a 2012 study, Nguyen and Ishitobi compared authentic fast-food ordering transactions with EFL textbook dialogues on that subject. Table 6.1 shows a natural fast-food ordering sequence as analyzed by the authors.

They found that the textbook dialogues and the natural conversations were not in alignment with one another, with a substantial difference noted in the sequencing of the transaction and in the manner of completing an action or interaction. For example, the textbook transactions were only partially complete in that one or more of the sequences (i.e., opening or closing) were not present. Additional findings included a lack of confirmation from the worker or customer in the textbooks, incongruence in the sequences of utterances, and inappropriate timing of expressions. For example, in one textbook dialogue, the worker says "Enjoy your meal," before the customer receives it (p. 177). Thus, the textbook dialogues could be misleading for teachers who are less familiar with authentic routines at fast-food restaurants. This could also be troublesome for learners when they are put in the actual situation. Nguyen and Ishitobi concluded that authentic materials should be incorporated into textbooks, in order for students to learn natural sequences of actions and experience a variety of language choices for authentic situations.

Thus far, we have reviewed textbook evaluation research centered on pragmatics in general. In the following section, we will focus on agreement and disagreement in particular, as this is the focal point of this chapter.

TABLE 6.1 Fast-food ordering sequence

OPENING

(a) worker greets customer – customer responds

FOOD ORDERING

(b) customer makes request – worker gives acknowledgment
(c) worker offers choices – customer responds / makes requests – worker confirms (steps b–c may be repeated)
(d) worker asks if order is complete – customer confirms / makes new requests – worker acknowledges
(e) worker states order summary – customer acknowledges / reminds worker – worker acknowledges
(f) worker offers choices of food – customer responds / makes request – worker gives acknowledgment

PAYMENT

(g) worker requests payment – customer gives payment – worker acknowledges amount

CLOSING

(h) worker thanks customer – customer thanks worker
(i) customer leaves counter and waits for food in another area of restaurant

Adapted from Nguyen and Ishitobi (2012, p. 157)

Current Research on Disagreement

In this section, we examine the case of disagreement, an important and frequently occurring pragmatic function, and investigate how closely (or scarcely) research is reflected in current language teaching materials.

Expressing opinion is a function used prevalently in language textbooks, with learners being asked to exchange their views in interaction or build arguments academically in writing. Compared to frequently researched speech acts such as requests, apologies, and compliments, the language of disagreement has rarely been studied in cross-cultural and acquisitional pragmatics, at least until recently (Bardovi-Harlig & Salsbury, 2004; Maíz-Arévalo, 2014). However, with increasing attention being paid to this speech act, there has lately been a considerable body of research on this topic (Maíz-Arévalo, 2014). We would be remiss if this collective knowledge were to be neglected instead of being applied to the everyday practice of language teaching and learning. In fact, while second language (L2) learners have been found to largely avoid disagreement, when they did disagree, they often underused the language of mitigation and indirectness (Bardovi-Harlig & Salsbury, 2004; Beebe & Takahashi, 1989; Salsbury & Bardovi-Harlig, 2001). Moreover, as a lack of mitigation could potentially lead to misunderstanding or communication breakdown in high-stakes contexts, it warrants effective pragmatic instruction on how to express disagreement.

While agreement with others' views is a *preferred* linguistic action and is typically accompanied by an immediate response that embodies alignment and serves to maximize its effect, disagreement is typically viewed as *dispreferred*. For example, hesitation or a pause causes a delay, causing speakers to distance themselves from the preceding utterance (Pomerantz, 1984; Schegloff, 2007). Such a delaying device can, therefore, signal an upcoming dispreferred action, such as a disagreement or refusal, psychologically prepare the hearer for the imminent face threat, and minimize the potential offense.

For instance, a response to *Let's go for a beer* may be immediate acceptance, such as *Sure, why not?* without a delay (a *preferred* response). Agreement components alone can occupy an entire turn, and this serves to emphasize the agreement. In contrast, a hedged response, such as *Well, you know,* as well as an initial pause can alert the interactant to the fact that a rejection of the invitation is imminent, or at least suggest a lack of enthusiasm. Thus, a dispreferred turn tends to be structurally more complex and elaborate so as to downplay the intensity of the disagreement. As shown below, a variety of mitigation devices preface a disagreement and serve to soften the impact of the disagreement, thus helping to maintain the interactant's face (Bjørge, 2012; Brown & Levinson, 1987; Holtgraves, 1997; Johnson, 2006; Locher, 2004; Maíz-Arévalo, 2014; Pomerantz, 1984; Schnurr & Chan, 2011):

- delay through:
  - A pause or silence (e.g., A: *God, isn't it dreary.* B: [pause] *It's warm though.* [adapted from Pomerantz, 1984, p. 70]);
  - Hedging (e.g., *um, uh, er*);
  - Discourse marker (e.g., *well, but, and, or*);

- understaters and downtoners (e.g., maybe, perhaps, just, possibly, seem, a little, kind of, sort of);
- modal verbs (e.g., I **may have to** admit, it **could** be that . . ., there **might** be some . . .);
- partial or conditional agreement often followed by but (e.g., Yeah but . . ., I would agree except that . . . [Holtgraves, 1997, p. 230]);
- an initial expression of appreciation (e.g., Thanks for that, nice try) or apology or regret (e.g., I'm sorry, I'm afraid) often followed by but;
- an explanation, justification, or elaboration serving as added support (e.g., I don't er I don't agree at all with this **because furniture is the kind of product that people are not used to buy** [sic] **without seeing it and touching it** [Bjørge, 2012, p. 420]);
- indirect (off-record) disagreement:

  o joking (e.g., Sure, if you enjoy crowds and street gangs [Malamed, 2010, p. 204]);
  o metaphors, irony, and rhetorical questions (e.g., What can I say? [Brown & Levinson, 1987, p. 223]);
  o laughter;
  o gaze avoidance and posture (Fujimoto, 2012; Houck & Fujii, 2013).

Bjørge (2012) provides a particularly revealing example of the textbook treatment of disagreement. In this study, Bjørge compared the utterances of speakers of English as a lingua franca (ELF) in a simulated negotiation setting with that of disagreement structures in 13 business ELT textbooks. She found that 80% of the ELF utterances used for disagreement consisted of *no* or *but*, thus revealing limited correspondence between ELF usage and the textbook items. Nevertheless, Bjørge points out that these speakers recognized the disagreement act as being face-threatening and therefore used mitigation strategies, which were also predominantly employed in the textbooks, albeit in an implicit manner (e.g., using partial agreement followed by *but* and modal verbs).

While mitigation is required or even expected in many interactional situations in which the interactants' face is to be protected and maintained, on certain specific occasions in English, disagreements can serve as a preferred rather than dispreferred response (Dippold, 2011; Fujimoto, 2012; Kotthoff, 1993; Pomerantz, 1984; Schegloff, 2007). For instance, disagreements may be expected or even welcomed in academic discussions and debates as providing critical insights that could further the discussion or analysis. In such a case, unmitigated disagreements without any delays can also be contextually appropriate (e.g., *No that's not possible, no we can't* [Bjørge, 2012, p. 422]).

In a study of language use in authentic business contexts (Williams, 1988), speakers familiar with each other were occasionally found to be quite blunt and neither excessively polite nor explicit. The speakers sometimes said *no, no, it's* . . . or simply, *but* . . . without prefacing their disagreement through partial or tentative agreement, as in *yes, but* . . . Likewise, members of an international consulting corporation in

Hong Kong sometimes disagreed quite explicitly in English, using little mitigation with each other or even the CEO, actively co-constructing their expert identities and dynamically negotiating co-leadership (Schnurr & Chan, 2011). However, it is important to note that such preferences for direct language use may not apply to more formal occasions involving higher-stakes confrontations.

In addition, a lack of mitigation in a series of direct disagreements may be characteristic of a conversation between intimates such as family members. In a study investigating a naturally occurring interaction between a mother and her teenage daughter (DelPrete & Box, 2014), both interactants spoke in a sharp tone of voice for several turns, leading to upgraded personal criticism and unresolved conflict. It may be that the daughter's resistance along with a lack of mitigation in her speech is linked to her identity construction (DelPrete & Box, 2014). Her direct opposition can thus be viewed as a face-*enhancing* act on her part rather than as a face-*threatening* one for her mother. Direct conflict and disharmony may be part of everyday interactions between parents and their teenage children, and as a result of their intimate relationship, minor cases of dissonance may be expected and can even be regarded as a positive sign of an open, uninhibited, and trusting relationship.

Furthermore, some occasions may call for intensified or upgraded disagreement. For instance, in response to self-deprecation (e.g., *I'm so dumb!*), an immediate and strong rejection (e.g., *No, absolutely not*) would be interpreted as an affable preferred response. Similarly, aggravated disagreement can be expressed through upgraders or intensifiers (e.g., *absolutely, not at all, really, so, such, quite*) without delay or mitigating devices (Kotthoff, 1993; Pomerantz, 1984; Schegloff, 2007).

Mismatches Between Research and ELT Materials

As stated earlier, despite the sheer volume of commercially available textbooks, their instructional content does not necessarily align with the actual language use of pragmatically competent speakers of English, who could serve as models for language learners. The language of disagreement is no exception (Bjørge, 2012; Maíz-Arévalo, 2014; Williams, 1988). In the study of language use in authentic business contexts (Williams, 1988), native English-speaking business associates taking part in informal meetings were found to carefully build up their main points through elaboration rather than expressing their views in isolation, as was often done in the ELT textbooks investigated in this study. In addition, Williams pointed out that there was rarely a need to be overly explicit about one's stance in such authentic contexts as speakers often implicitly expressed agreement using nods or utterances such as *mmm*. In fact, expressions such as *in my opinion*, a typical expression taught in ELT textbooks as a way of presenting either agreement or disagreement, was often used to express disagreement. This may particularly be the case when the stress falls on the possessive (*in **my** opinion*), which could carry the potentially face-threatening implication of "I know what **your** opinion is, but **mine** is . . . " (Williams, 1988, p. 52, author's emphasis).

Similarly, ELT textbooks sometimes fail to represent a range of mitigation devices, or they present a list of expressions of agreement and disagreement without introducing the contexts in which they are used. In a popular series of ELT textbooks focusing on discussion skills, a few examples of short reactions to the issue under discussion are introduced and accompanied by a list of useful expressions, so that learners can exchange their views and reactions using these expressions. Although the selection of expressions varies according to proficiency levels and units, one unit from an intermediate level textbook presents, "I agree most/completely agree/sort of agree/kind of agree/strongly disagree/don't agree at all with Luis/Ken/Susan" (Day, Shaules, & Yamanaka, 2009b, p. 19). Another unit at beginning level from the same series asks learners to select a response that corresponds to their own view from a list: "I think so; I'm not sure; and No way!" (Day, Shaules, & Yamanaka, 2009a, p. 16).

Several issues are compounded in such textbook representations. Neither of the units described above provides instruction regarding the contexts in which the expressions are to be used. In addition, in the former example, upgraders of agreement and disagreement are introduced all together, disregarding the notions of preference and dispreference. While upgrading agreement (*I agree most with . . . [sic]*, *I completely agree with . . .*) is likely to be interpreted as a face-enhancing strategy, intensified disagreement (*I strongly disagree with . . . ; I don't agree at all with . . .*) can potentially be highly face-threatening. Yet, no delays or other forms of mitigation are introduced along with these expressions. In the case of the beginning level textbook, no mitigations are included in *I agree/disagree with . . .*, and *I'm not sure* is introduced simply as a neutral expression to be used when the speaker has no opinion, rather than as a mitigated expression of disagreement. Furthermore, while these upgraded disagreements may be more suitable for discussing third-party opinions provided by the textbook, learners can be misled into believing that the same expressions are equally appropriate for more personal interactions in which disagreement may be addressed directly. However, similar potentially problematic representations of disagreement are not unique to this series but are commonly shared with other commercially available materials (e.g., Dummett, Hughes, & Stephenson, 2015; Johannsen, & Chase, 2015; Paul, 2003; Richards & Bohlke, 2012; Stempleski, 2014).

Matches Between Research and ELT Materials

This section will discuss some of the materials that have been designed specifically for pragmatic development based on SLA principles. On a positive note, even though most commercial ELT textbooks do not reflect research-based information on how we actually disagree, there is a growing number of informed, more research-based materials proposed and written primarily by those inclined to the learning of pragmatics and discourse.

One example of a pragmatically focused language textbook is *Workplace Talk in Action* (Riddiford & Newton, 2010). The conversations in this textbook derive from a corpus of 1,500 natural conversations collected in 20 workplaces in New Zealand. Among seven units organized by pragmatics principles (e.g., small talk, requesting, refusing, making suggestions), Unit Five discusses disagreements in the workplace and is divided into five sections: (A) observation of workplace interaction; (B) analysis of additional workplace conversations; (C) analysis of workplace e-mails; (D) categorization of useful phrases for agreeing and disagreeing; and (E) practice using these phrases. In each unit, one of the sample conversations is accompanied by an audio file made available online.

In Part A, learners consider workplace interaction. They are first asked to look at a situation and analyze the context based on the two speakers in terms of status difference, level of familiarity, and level of difficulty in communicating the disagreement (p. 69). This awareness-raising task reflects a current approach to the teaching of pragmatics drawing on the Noticing Hypothesis (Schmidt, 1993, 2001). The next task is a role-play, which allows the learners to speak at length and encourages creative use of the language. After performing the role-play, the learners write down their exchanges and compare and contrast these to the dialogue in the textbook. The language used in the dialogue is drawn from actual workplace exchanges in Riddiford and Newton's much larger business English corpus. Specifically, the learners are asked to look for the following:

- phrases they use to agree and acknowledge each others' comments, and the frequency of such phrases;
- how the disagreement was phrased;
- words or phrases used to soften the blow of the disagreement;
- use of humor;
- extent to which the two speakers are trying to be cooperative.

Adapted from Riddiford and Newton, 2010, p. 69

Once again, learners are provided with an awareness-building task centering on linguistic structures, discourse, and sociocultural norms. The next task emphasizes how the speakers take turns, with a specific focus on how they interrupt, agree, and disagree. The final task is a comparison of the communicative styles of the learners' cultures, creating yet another opportunity for noticing and understanding.

In Part B, the learners are provided with three additional conversations including disagreements, and asked to analyze the conversation using the same categories as in Part A: the speakers' status, level of familiarity, difficulty in communicating the disagreement. In Part C, the learners investigate written disagreements, especially in e-mails. First, the learners must identify the phrases expressing disagreement in three examples of e-mails. Following this, they are asked to write two e-mails based on the situations provided and actually use the language for simulated communication.

In Part D, the learners are provided with useful phrases for agreeing and disagreeing, as well as with a sample conversation for them to add some of these phrases for practice. Finally, Part E offers some of the phrases for use in interactional practice. Using the five role-play scenarios of disagreements provided at the end of the book, the teacher could encourage students to use these phrases in interactive communication.

Overall, the approach taken in *Workplace Talk in Action* makes it a prime example of research-informed materials for pragmatic development. These exercises would effectively trigger learners' noticing of the language of disagreements and enhance their sociocultural awareness of the context in which these forms are used. Regarding the production of pragmatic language use, the textbook often provides practice in which learners use spoken and written disagreement in simulated settings. Still, one may wonder about the extent to which learners are given opportunities to produce language in authentic interactive contexts, especially in speaking. Even though five role-play scenarios are offered for each unit in this textbook, it appears to include little guidance about when or how they are used and what feedback is to be provided to learners. However, as this textbook is focusing on workplace English in the L2 context, learners may have authentic opportunities to use newly learned language outside of the classroom and may successfully put their pragmatic awareness to use, if skillful teachers are to provide guidance for successful application.

Another notable textbook is the *Touchstone* series (McCarthy, McCarten, & Sandiford, 2005/2014). As mentioned earlier, this series features corpus-informed language. In addition to the corpus-based selection of vocabulary, the textbooks incorporate instruction on pragmatic functions and discourse features, labeled "conversation strategies," in each unit. For example, the beginning level textbook starts with a unit in which more or less formal everyday expressions (e.g., *yes, yeah; thank you; thanks; hello, hi; I'm fine, OK, pretty good, good*) are provided side by side and accompanied by a statistical note informing the learners that "*yeah* is ten times more common than *yes*" (McCarthy et al., 2005/2014, Student's Book 1, p. 9) along with a graph visually showing these frequencies. Other conversation strategies instructed in this series include:

- use *I mean* to repeat your ideas or to say more (Level One);
- respond with *right* or *I know* to agree or show you are listening (Level One);
- take time to think using *uh, um, well, let's see*, or *let me think* (Level One);
- say *no* in a friendly way (Level Two);
- use *just* to soften things you say (Level Two);
- agree to something with *all right* and *OK* (Level Two);
- use expressions such as *exactly, definitely*, or *absolutely* to agree with people's opinions (Level Three);
- soften comments with expressions such as *I think, probably, kind of*, or *in a way* (Level Three);
- give different opinions using expressions such as *on the other hand . . .* or *I know what you mean, but . . .* (Level Three);
- use *of course* when giving information that is not surprising, and/or to show understanding and agreement (Level Four);
- use *that's a good point* to show someone has a valid argument (Level Four);
- use *just* to make your meaning stronger or softer (Level Four).

In two of the units in the Level Three textbook, expressions such as *really, sure, exactly, definitely,* and *absolutely* are taught in the context of agreement. In contrast, dispreferred responses are largely mitigated, as in the following excerpt.

EXCERPT 1, DISPREFERRED RESPONSES

Greg: We play [games online] together all the time. They're kind of like friends.

Hugo: I don't know. You don't even know their real names. You know?

Greg: That's true. It's still fun, though. We're like a team. You know what I mean?

Hugo: Maybe. On the other hand, they're not *real* friends.

Adapted from McCarthy et al. (2005/2014, Student's Book 3, p. 90)

In this unit, a few other mitigation strategies (e.g., *Yeah. I know what you mean, but . . . , I'm not so sure*) are also modeled and practiced, albeit not extensively. Although the quality of input in this textbook is desirable, whether learners can acquire socially preferred use of disagreement through the limited amount of exposure and practice is an empirical question. It seems that it is left up to each classroom teacher to decide what interactive output practice to provide, when, and to what extent, in order to support learners' pragmatic development.

Another potentially successful textbook is *Conversation Strategies* (Kehe & Kehe, 2011). This textbook contains various activities designed to enhance learners' spoken communicative ability. One unit focuses on "Expressing Opinions." This unit is divided into an introductory part and then a four-step task sequence. In the introductory section, learners are provided with statements of opinion, agreements,

---

EXCERPT 2, EXPRESSING OPINIONS

Fill in the blanks with the following words or phrases in **bold type**

Perhaps	True	afraid I disagree	my opinion

1. A: In _____, camping is more fun than swimming.
2. B: I'm _____. I think camping is dangerous.
3. A: _____, but if you're careful, you'll have no problems.
4. B: That's _____.

Adapted from Kehe and Kehe (2011, p. 79)

and disagreements and are asked to fill in blanks with the appropriate expression (see Excerpt 2).

As this practice is a controlled fill-in-the-blank exercise, the correct answers can be worked out from the grammatical clues in the dialogue. To supplement this exercise with relevant input, a typical conversation containing opinions and reasons for disagreement is also provided. The second half of the unit consists of a series of pair-work tasks. In the first step, one student fills in a blank with a statement of opinion, to which then the other student responds by agreeing or disagreeing (see Excerpt 3), with the roles reversed in the following step.

EXCERPT 3, EXPRESSING AGREEMENT, DISAGREEMENT, AND THE REASONS

Student A	Student B	
	Agree	*Disagree*
1. I feel _____ is the best city in the world. 2. In my opinion, _____ is the best season. 3. Don't you think girls are harder workers than boys?	1. I agree. 2. That's true. 3. That's a good point.	1. I'm afraid I disagree. 2. I'm not sure I agree. 3. Perhaps, but . . .

Adapted from Kehe and Kehe (2011, pp. 81–82)

In Step Three, the students write down their own opinions and then share them with a new partner in Step Four. Additionally, students are to either agree and state their reasons or disagree and give their rationale.

Although Excerpts Two and Three were not designed as pragmatics-focused and offer little support for learners or teachers, this textbook has the potential to create opportunities for pragmatic development, provided that the teacher offers meta-pragmatic information regarding when certain expressions are appropriate and why. That is, the teacher could explain, for example, in what situations the particular mitigations are expected or preferred given the relationship between the speakers and the stakes involved in the disagreement. As it is, learners are provided with different statements of opinion, agreements, and disagreements and then practice them in relatively controlled activities. Thus, the controlled nature of the exercises may not engage learners affectively and cognitively. In later activities, as the learners continue to recycle language in increasingly authentic discussion settings, the tasks are likely to become more meaningful and engaging. Although this is not an explicit part of the textbook, pragmatic noticing could be promoted if students are encouraged to analyze the form–context mapping and invited to use the target expressions especially in an interactive environment relevant to their lives.

In addition to the textbooks introduced above, Bouton, Curry, and Bouton (2010) and Malamed (2010) provide research-informed samples of instructional materials and lesson plans on agreeing and disagreeing as well as expressing opinions. In addition to Bouton et al. (2010) and Malamed (2010), notable others on additional aspects of pragmatics are included in practically oriented publications (e.g., Bardovi-Harlig & Mahan-Taylor, 2003; Houck & Tatsuki, 2011; Ishihara & Cohen, 2010; Martínez-Flor & Usó-Juan, 2010; Ronald, Rinnert, Fordyce, & Knight, 2012; Tatsuki & Houck, 2010), which can serve as resources for research-based instruction in pragmatics.

Conclusion

While many of the currently available materials may not be pragmatically authentic, we have demonstrated some promising signs in this chapter by introducing praiseworthy instructional materials designed by language educators researching pragmatics. Given the increasingly higher profile of pedagogical materials in this area, we would like to highlight the value of pedagogically-oriented publications in applied linguistics that afford informed practitioners opportunities to participate in collective knowledge construction in SLA. Pedagogical sections in journals are also an invaluable vehicle for the dissemination of field-tested, research-based pedagogy.

Moreover, rather than simply lamenting the paucity of pragmatically focused materials, teachers are invited to seek research-informed materials intended to connect theory, research, and practice extensively. However, as we have seen above, even research-informed materials appear to require teachers to be critical consumers who would use their discretion to supplement materials in order to secure authentic opportunities for exposure and use, as well as for pragmatic noticing and understanding. Once practitioners become critical appraisers of such materials, they may begin to define themselves as potential participants in this professional practice, thus contributing to and co-constructing knowledge in the field. Through reflective and exploratory practice (Allwright, 2005; Allwright & Hanks, 2009) based on the use of such research-informed materials, the instruction can be further refined to reflect the real-world issues teachers and learners encounter in authentic everyday classrooms, which in turn could contribute to the development of research in instructed SLA.

References

Allwright, D. (2005). Developing principles for practitioner research: The case of exploratory practice. *The Modern Language Journal, 89*(3), 353–366.

Allwright, D., & Hanks, J. (2009). *The developing language learner: An introduction to exploratory practice*. London: Palgrave Macmillan.

Bardovi-Harlig, K., & Mahan-Taylor, R. (Eds.). (2003). *Teaching pragmatics*. Washington, DC: Office of English Programs, US Department of State.

Bardovi-Harlig, K., & Salsbury, T. (2004). The organization of turns in the disagreements of L2 learners: A longitudinal perspective. In D. Boxer & A. D. Cohen (Eds.), *Studying speaking to inform second language learning* (pp. 199–227). Clevedon, UK: Multilingual Matters.

Beebe, L., & Takahashi, T. (1989). Do you have a bag? Social status and patterned variation in second language acquisition. In S. Gass, C. Madden, D. Preston, & L. Selinker (Eds.), *Variation in second language acquisition: Discourse, pragmatics, and communication* (pp. 103–125). Clevedon, UK: Multilingual Matters.

Bjørge, A. K. (2012). Expressing disagreement in ELF business negotiations: Theory and practice. *Applied Linguistics 33*(4), 406–427.

Bouton, K., Curry, K., & Bouton, L. (2010). Moving beyond "in my opinion": Teaching the complexities of expressing opinion. In D. Tatsuki & N. Houck (Eds.), *Pragmatics: Teaching speech acts* (pp. 105–123). Alexandria, VA: TESOL.

Brown, P., & Levinson, S. (1987). *Politeness: Some universals in language use*. Cambridge: Cambridge University Press.

Cohen, A., & Ishihara, N. (2013). Pragmatics. In B. Tomlinson (Ed.), *Applied linguistics and materials development* (pp. 113–126). London: Bloomsbury.

Crandall, E., & Basturkmen, H. (2004). Evaluating pragmatics-focused materials. *ELT Journal, 58*(1), 38–49.

Day, R. R., Shaules, J., & Yamanaka, J. (2009a). *Impact issues 1: 20 key issues to help you express yourself in English*. Hong Kong: Pearson Education Asia.

Day, R. R., Shaules, J., & Yamanaka, J. (2009b). *Impact issues 3: 20 stimulating issues for discussion and debate in English*. Hong Kong: Pearson Education Asia.

DelPrete, D. L., & Box, C. (2014, March). *"What are you doing?": Exploring mother–adolescent daughter (dis)harmonious discourse*. Paper presented at the annual conference of the American Association for Applied Linguistics, Portland, OR.

Diepenbroek, L., & Derwing, T. (2013). To what extent do popular ESL textbooks incorporate oral fluency and pragmatic development? *TESL Canada Journal, 30*(7), 1–20.

Dippold, D. (2011). Argumentative discourse in L2 German: A sociocognitive perspective on the development of facework strategies. *The Modern Language Journal, 95*(2), 171–187.

Dummett, P., Hughes, J., & Stephenson, H. (2015). *Life: Student book 2*. Boston, MA: Cengage Learning.

Fujimoto, D. (2012). *Agreements and disagreements: Novice language learners in small group discussion*. Unpublished doctoral dissertation. Temple University, Japan.

Glasgow, G. P., & Paller, D. L. (2014a). MEXT-approved EFL textbooks and the new Course of Study for Foreign Languages. In N. Sonda & A. Krause (Eds.), *JALT2013 conference proceedings* (pp. 113–122). Tokyo: JALT.

Glasgow, G. P., & Paller, D. L. (2014b). *Pragmatic information and MEXT-approved textbooks*. Poster presented at the JALT2014 International Conference, Tsukuba, Ibaraki, Japan.

Gómez-Rodríguez, L. F. (2010). English textbooks for teaching and learning English as a foreign language: Do they really help to develop communicative competence? *Educación y Educadores, 13*(3), 327–346.

Holtgraves, T. (1997). Yes, but . . . : Positive politeness in conversation arguments. *Journal of Language and Social Psychology, 16*(2), 222–239.

Houck, N., & Fujii, S. (2013). Working through disagreement in English academic discussions between L1 speakers of Japanese and L1 speakers of English. In T. Greer, D. Tatsuki, & C. Rover (Eds.), *Pragmatics & language learning, vol. 13* (pp. 103–132). Honolulu, HI: University of Hawai'i, National Foreign Language Resource Center.

Houck, N., & Tatsuki, D. (Eds.) (2011). *Pragmatics: Teaching natural conversation*. Alexandria, VA: TESOL.

Ishihara, N., & Cohen, A. D. (2010). *Teaching and learning pragmatics: Where language and culture meet*. Harlow, UK: Pearson Education.

Jeon, E. H., & Kaya, T. (2006). Effects of L2 instruction on interlanguage pragmatic development: A meta-analysis. In J. M. Norris & L. Ortega (Eds.), *Synthesizing research on language learning and teaching* (pp. 165–211). Amsterdam: John Benjamins.

Johannsen, K. L., & Chase, R. T. (2015). *World English level 2* (2nd ed.). Boston, MA: Cengage Learning.

Johnson, F. (2006). Agreement and disagreement: A cross-cultural comparison. *BISAL, 1*, 41–67.

Kasper, G., & Rose, K. (2002). *Pragmatic development in a second language*. Malden, MA: Blackwell.

Kehe, D., & Kehe, P. D. (2011). *Conversation strategies*. Brattlebaro, VT: Pro Lingua Associates.

Kobayakawa, M. (2011). Analyzing writing tasks in Japanese high school English textbooks: English I, II, and Writing. *JALT Journal, 33*(1), 27–48.

Kotthoff, H. (1993). Disagreement and concession in disputes: On the context sensitivity of preference structures. *Language in Society, 22*(2), 193–216.

Locher, M. A. (2004). *Power and politeness in action: Disagreements in oral communication*. Berlin: Mouton de Gruyter.

Maíz-Arévalo, C. (2014). Expressing disagreement in English as a lingua franca: Whose pragmatic rules? *Intercultural Pragmatics, 11*(2), 199–224.

Malamed, L. H. (2010). Disagreement: How to disagree agreeably. In A. Martínez-Flor & E. Usó-Juan (Eds.), *Speech act performance: Theoretical, empirical and methodological issues* (pp. 199–215). Amsterdam: John Benjamins.

Martínez-Flor, A., & Usó-Juan, E. (Eds.), *Speech act performance: Theoretical, empirical and methodological issues* (pp. 179–198). Amsterdam: John Benjamins.

McCarthy, M., McCarten, J., & Sandiford, H. (2005/2014). *Touchstone: Student book 1, 2, 3, & 4*. New York: Cambridge University Press.

McGroarty, M., & Taguchi, N. (2005). Evaluating communicativeness of EFL textbooks for Japanese secondary schools. In J. Froedson & C. Holten (Eds.), *The power of context in language teaching and learning* (pp. 211–224). Boston, MA: Thomson Heinle.

Nguyen, H. T., & Ishitobi, N. (2012). Ordering fast food: Service encounters in real-life interaction and in textbook dialogs. *JALT Journal, 34*(2), 151–186.

Nguyen, M. T. T. (2011). Learning to communicate in a globalized world: To what extent do school textbooks facilitate the development of intercultural pragmatic competence? *RELC Journal, 42*(1), 17–30.

Ogura, F. (2008). Communicative competence and senior high school oral communication textbooks in Japan. *The Language Teacher, 32*(12), 3–8.

Paul, D. (2003). *Communication strategies*. Singapore: Thomson Learning.

Petraki, E., & Bayes, S. (2013). Teaching oral requests: An evaluation of five English as a second language coursebooks. *Pragmatics, 23*(3), 499–517.

Pomerantz, A. (1984). Agreeing and disagreeing with assessments: Some features of preferred/dispreferred turn shapes. In M. Atkinson & J. Heritage (Eds.), *Structures of social action: Studies in conversation analysis* (pp. 57–101). Cambridge: Cambridge University Press.

Richards, J. C., & Bohlke, D. (2012). *Speak now: Student book 2*. New York: Oxford University Press.

Riddiford, N., & Newton, J. (2010). *Workplace talk in action: An ESOL resource*. Wellington: School of Linguistics and Applied Language Studies, Victoria University of Wellington.

Ronald, J., Rinnert, C., Fordyce, K., & Knight, T. (2012). *Pragtivities: Bringing pragmatics to second language classrooms*. Tokyo: JALT Pragmatics SIG.

Salsbury, T., & Bardovi-Harlig, K. (2001). "I know what you mean, but I don't think so": Disagreements in L2 English. In *Pragmatics and Language Learning, vol. 10* (pp. 131–151). Urbana-Champaign, IL: University of Illinois, Division of English as an International Language.

Schegloff, E. A. (2007). The organization of preference/dispreference. In E. A. Schegloff (Ed.), *Sequence organization in interaction: A primer in conversation analysis* (pp. 58–96). Cambridge: Cambridge University Press.

Schmidt, R. W. (1993). Consciousness, learning, and interlanguage pragmatics. In G. Kasper & S. Blum-Kulka (Eds.), *Interlanguage pragmatics* (pp. 21–42). Oxford: Oxford University Press.

Schmidt, R. W. (2001). Attention. In P. Robinson (Ed.), *Cognition and second language instruction* (pp. 3–32). Cambridge: Cambridge University Press.

Schnurr, S., & Chan, A. (2011). Exploring another side of co-leadership: Negotiating professional identities through face-work in disagreements. *Language in Society, 40*(2), 187–209.

Stempleski, S. (2014). *Stretch: Student book 2*. New York: Oxford University Press.

Tatsuki, D., & Houck, N. (Eds.) (2010). *Pragmatics: Teaching speech acts*. Alexandria, VA: TESOL.

Tomlinson, B. (2013). Second language acquisition and materials development. In B. Tomlinson (Ed.), *Applied linguistics and materials development* (pp. 11–29). London: Bloomsbury.

Vellenga, H. (2004). Learning pragmatics from ESL and EFL Textbooks: How likely? *TESL-EJ, 8*(2). Retrieved November 30, 2014 from http://www.tesl-ej.org/wordpress/issues/volume8/ej30/ej30a3/.

Williams, M. (1988). Language taught for meetings and language used in meetings: Is there anything in common? *Applied Linguistics, 9*(1), 45–58.

7

FROM SLA RESEARCH ON INTERACTION TO TBLT MATERIALS

Alison Mackey, Nicole Ziegler and Lara Bryfonski

Following the appearance of more than seventy empirical studies of task-based interaction and second language (L2) learning outcomes in laboratory and classroom settings over the past quarter century, several research syntheses and meta-analyses have emerged (including Keck et al., 2006 and Mackey & Goo, 2007). This body of work collectively provides empirical support for claims about the efficacy of task-based interaction in promoting L2 learning. Cognitively oriented research into task-based interaction has investigated relationships amongst working memory, cognitive creativity, noticing and attention, aptitude, and interaction-driven language learning. Socially oriented research has examined factors such as the roles of learners' conversational partners, their peers, and conversational contexts in task-based interaction-driven learning. Findings of these studies can explain how and why task-based interaction can work to positively impact learning and why it sometimes doesn't. This chapter will first outline the background and then move on to discuss the relationships amongst L2 interaction research and authentic learning contexts to illustrate some of the research-based principles behind current claims about task-based language teaching and learning, and discuss how these can be translated into specific guidelines to inform task-based materials design. The main focus will be the strong connections between the Interaction Hypothesis and task-based language teaching (TBLT), specifically, how work on interactional feedback underpins the design of a number of different types of task, as well as considerations of task implementation.

Task-Based Language Teaching: An Introduction

Task-based language teaching utilizes task, as opposed to language, as the unit of instruction in language classrooms. It has garnered much attention in the past several decades due to its grounding in second language acquisition (SLA) theory and its empirical success (Long, 2015). TBLT emphasizes authentic, communication-driven tasks that simultaneously promote language acquisition and prepare students to use their linguistic skills in meaningful interactions outside the classroom (Bygate, Norris, & Van den Branden, 2014). In contrast to other models of language teaching, task-based teaching emphasizes the fact that language is used to "get things done in the real world" with authentic tasks playing the important role of "keeping things real" (Van den Branden, Bygate, & Norris, 2009, p.16). That being said, TBLT is not simply meaning-based language teaching. There are properties in a task that will predispose, and sometimes induce, learners to engage in certain types of language use and mental processing that are known to be beneficial to acquisition (Ellis, 2000). During task-based language learning, students interact and negotiate for meaning, while carefully designed tasks elicit perception and production of the linguistic forms learners need to notice, use and learn.

Traditional synthetic syllabuses present language in discrete grammatical units, assuming learners will be able to synthesize forms to create meaning when called upon to do so (Long & Norris, 2000). This type of syllabus utilizes a "focus-on-forms" approach as the basis of instruction. This has been the dominant approach to language teaching for the past 60 years (Long, 2015). At the other end of the spectrum, analytic teaching methods rely purely on a "focus of meaning" eliminating any grammatical analysis (Van den Branden et al., 2009). Communicative language teaching and other immersion methods utilize meaning-driven methodologies as a route to language acquisition, and are often touted as the "natural approach" (Krashen & Terrell, 1983) or the kind of implicit learning employed in first language (L1) acquisition. However, an exclusive focus on meaning has proven to be deficient in delivering advanced L2 competencies and leads to inefficient treatments of learner errors, particularly those made by adult learners (Long, 2015). Established research in the field of SLA proposes that language is actually acquired according to a learner internal syllabus, with each individual learner passing through common stages of acquisition (Pienemann & Johnston, 1986; Long & Norris, 2000; Robinson, 2001). As a result of this research, TBLT emerged from communicative language teaching with the aim to "focus on form" (not forms) by entailing "attention to formal elements of a language, whereas focus on forms is *limited* to such a focus, and focus on meaning *excludes* it" (Long & Norris, 2000, p. 598). For the learner, a task provides a narrative with a clear time sequence from beginning to middle to end, easing the language processing burden and enabling greater attention to accuracy and fluency in performance (Foster & Skehan, 2009). In addition, tasks might provide learners with opportunities to discover grammatical features or rules through task completion. In other words, learners may actively direct their attention during a task to discovering how or why certain features might be used in a story or conversation, thereby supplying opportunities for learners to develop their knowledge of the target language gradually and through self-discovery (Tomlinson, 2012). TBLT therefore avoids many of the pitfalls in existing language teaching approaches, providing a testable model of language education that is consistent with SLA research findings and is grounded in philosophies of education (Long, 2015).

Research on tasks has identified benefits for a range of features, based on planned manipulations of learning. By examining task features like the goal(s) of communication, the amount and type of information presented, as well as task conditions such as planning time, and a host of additional features, task designers are able to elicit specific grammatical forms and influence different aspects of language learning, as noted, in the early days of task research, by Pica, Kanagy, and Falodun (1993). In order to carry out or complete a task, the learners must typically clarify when they are misunderstood and ask for help when they are confused. As part of task-based instruction, teachers have the opportunity to implement a variety of interactional feedback techniques. These processes allow learners to notice the gaps between their current state of linguistic knowledge and the target language (Schmidt, 1990).

Over the years, language-teaching methodologies have alternated between synthetic and analytic approaches without providing consistent, generalizable results. TBLT's blend of analytic and focus-on-form teaching is empirically researched with evidence of its effects on potential and actual language learning (Van den Branden et al., 2009). It has been applied in many countries around the world, for example in Belgium, for Dutch as an L2 classrooms, and it has been shown to be associated with success in children through adults (van Avermaet & Gysen, 2009). A host of research programs, targeted at tasks and task design, aim to continue to improve and expand on this exciting approach to language teaching.

Theoretical Underpinnings of TBLT: The Interaction Approach

Grounded in the notion that communication is the driving force behind language learning, with research of the past few decades investigating the relationship between communication, learning, and mediating factors, such as noticing, attention, and the role of affective and cognitive engagement on learners' processing, the interaction approach, which posits that exposure to linguistic information (as input), opportunities for language production (as output), and positive and negative feedback on learners' production (through interaction) are constructs critical to understanding L2 learning processes (Mackey & Gass, 2006; Gass & Mackey, 2007; Mackey, Abbuhl, & Gass, 2012), provides a firm theoretical foundation for TBLT.

Within the interaction approach, input, which can be defined as the language that a learner is exposed to through various mediums, can be modified to accommodate the needs of language learners. For instance, learners experiencing communication breakdowns can seek additional input from their interlocutors through negotiation, such as confirmation checks (expressions that clarify whether an utterance has been correctly heard or understood) and clarification requests (remarks aimed at developing a better understanding of a previous utterance), thereby encouraging speakers to modify incomprehensible utterances using lexical substitutions or different grammatical structures, or by providing repetitions. In addition, negotiation may prime learners to be more attentive to future input, raising their awareness of specific features of the target language and providing them with multiple opportunities to confirm or disconfirm hypotheses they have formed regarding the L2. Although input is a key component of L2 acquisition, the interaction approach suggests that it is the ways in which learners interact with input and their interlocutors through negotiating for meaning, as in the descriptions of various interactional features above, that are most likely to support L2 development (Mackey, 2012; Mackey et al., 2012).

Another key component of the interaction approach is output. Research has demonstrated that in addition to exposure to the target language, learners need opportunities to produce language. For instance, Swain's (1985, 1995) investigations of children in a French immersion program revealed that learners' productive skills were deficient when compared to native French-speaking children of the same age, a result attributed to a lack of opportunities to produce output. Modified output, or learners' reformulations of previous utterances in response to feedback or self-monitoring (Mackey, 2012), is believed to facilitate L2 development by providing learners with opportunities to develop fluency and automaticity, test hypotheses about the L2, and receive corrective feedback, thereby drawing their attention to mismatches between their production and the target language (TL) and facilitating noticing (Izumi et al., 1999), a process demonstrated to be supportive of L2 learning. In addition, production, particularly instances where learners are 'pushed' to produce output, is posited to aid learners in moving from semantic top-down processing to syntactic bottom-up processing (Swain, 1995). In order to produce language, learners must attend in some manner to the linguistic form they are attempting to utter to maximize their comprehensibility, thereby experiencing syntactic processing on some level. Other researchers have also argued that production requires deeper levels of processing than comprehension (Izumi, 2002), and that without affective and cognitive engagement there is minimal chance of deep, syntactic processing (Tomlinson, 2008, 2012). Furthermore, as Mackey (2012) points out, the process of modifying output can be as important to language development as the actual modification, with learners still benefiting whether they produce correct target forms or not. This important finding highlights the potential benefits learners might receive from interaction, even with minimal pre-teaching on the part of the instructor. For example, instructors may hesitate to use tasks in the classroom without first pre-teaching vocabulary or certain grammatical structures, due to concerns that learners may not be able to successfully complete the task goals. Although they might make more errors or fail to produce target-like utterances without pre-teaching exercises, they are still likely to benefit from the processes of negotiation and output modification sparked by these potential linguistic issues.

In addition to providing learners with opportunities to practice the L2, output also offers learners the chance to receive negative evidence in the form of feedback from their instructor or other learners (Leeman, 2003, 2007). In other words, negative evidence provides learners with information regarding their use of ungrammatical forms, indicating that there was an issue with their language production.

Ideally, this helps to draw learners' attention to potential differences between their L2 utterances and the TL, thereby creating an environment supportive of learning.

Negative evidence can take a variety of forms, with scholars proposing various ways of classifying different types. For example, Ranta and Lyster (2007) suggest that types of feedback can be categorized as either reformulations or prompts. Both categories consist of implicit and explicit types of corrective feedback designed to draw learners' attention to an incorrect utterance, and vary instead in the extent to which they provide learners with reformulations of their erroneous utterances or whether learners are instead prompted to initiate self-repair without a model of the target-like language (Lyster, Saito, & Sato, 2013). In other words, teachers' use of negative evidence may or may not include the provision of positive evidence, defined as the modeling of target-like language, in conjunction with the negative evidence. For example, recasts and explicit correction, considered reformulations in this taxonomy, provide learners with more target-like versions of their non-target-like production (positive evidence), while prompts, such as elicitation, metalinguistic clues, clarification requests, and repetition, encourage learners to discover their own errors and produce modified output. However, as other scholars have pointed out, although positive evidence may be helpful to a learner, it is limited in its efficacy as it only demonstrates correct forms and/or use (Long, 2015). That is, negative evidence shows a learner the correct form as well as indicating that their production is incorrect, helping learners to focus their attention on differences between their production and target-like forms. In addition, learners interacting with other learners might not feel that they have the metalinguistic knowledge to provide positive evidence when giving corrective feedback, potentially limiting learners' exposure to interactions with instructors or learners with higher proficiency levels. As also discussed below, research examining the effects of various types of corrective feedback has suggested that the potential benefits may vary according to context, target feature, or whether learners are interacting with their instructor or other learners, with scholars calling for further research into the variable effectiveness of corrective feedback in the L2 classroom (Lyster, 2013; Lyster et al., 2013).

Research has also indicated that negative evidence can be classified according to explicitness, with types of feedback including implicit and explicit forms, such as recasts and metalinguistic feedback. Recasts, defined as the reformulation of all or part of a learner's immediately preceding utterance in which one or more non-target like item(s) are replaced by the corresponding target form, and where the focus is on meaning rather than form or object (Long, 2007), have been shown to be facilitative of L2 development as they enhance the salience of the target feature and help learners to contrast their incorrect utterance with the reformulation (e.g. Doughty & Varela, 1998; Long, 2007; Goo & Mackey, 2013), thereby focusing learners' attentional resources on the target form. However, research has also demonstrated that the impact of recasts on learning may be affected by a variety of factors, such as target feature (Egi, 2007), learners' proficiency and developmental readiness (Mackey & Philp, 1998), setting (Oliver, 2000), task characteristics (Révész, Sachs, & Mackey, 2011), and learners' individual differences (Mackey,

2012). Although some researchers have argued that other kinds of feedback may be more beneficial than recasts (e.g. Lyster & Ranta, 1997; Lyster, 2004) research has empirically demonstrated the effectiveness of recasts on learners' L2 development (see Mackey & Goo, 2007 for a review). In general, as explained below, recasts are one tool in a teacher's toolbox, and though they may lead to development in one way, and other kinds of feedback may lead to development in other ways, direct comparisons of feedback types may not be helpful for authentic teaching scenarios.

Overall, research indicates that a range of interactional processes, such as receiving feedback and participating in negotiation, are beneficial to learners' L2 development, with a large body of empirical research and meta-analyses supporting the use of interaction-based tasks and activities (see Keck et al., 2006; Mackey & Goo, 2007; Ziegler, 2015 for reviews). As a research-based pedagogical approach (Long, 2015), TBLT is firmly situated in the theoretical foundations of the interaction approach, providing educators with a framework focused on meaning and communication that provides a site for the ideal type of interactive learning processes known to facilitate acquisition.

External and Social Factors: The Role of Context and Setting in Task-Based Interaction

The role learners' individual cognitive differences play in mediating the impact of interactional feedback in task-based learning is an interesting one, but sadly beyond the scope and word limit for the current chapter. However the role of instructional contexts and settings is important and directly relevant for materials design. For example, the growing body of research examining task-based computer-mediated communication (CMC) and interaction suggests positive benefits within technology-supported environments (e.g. Smith, 2004, 2005; Lai & Li, 2011; Sauro, 2011,) with tasks commonly found in face-to-face (FTF) interaction research, such as decision-making and information-gap tasks, demonstrated to be successful in eliciting learner interaction and negotiation in a CMC environment (Pellettieri, 1999; Blake, 2000). In addition, some studies indicate advantages within computer-mediated contexts over FTF contexts. For instance, research has demonstrated that text-based synchronous computer mediated communication (SCMC), a context considered most similar to face-to-face interaction because learners communicate and engage in tasks in real time, such as might occur in a live text or video chat, may result in increased and more equitable learner participation (e.g. Beauvois, 1992; Kelm, 1992; Warschauer, 1996), as well as greater quality of language production (e.g. Chun, 1994; Kern, 1995), than in FTF interaction. In addition, SCMC may also provide learners with a less stressful environment than FTF interaction (Chun, 1998), potentially leading to reduced anxiety and improved willingness to communicate. Text chat environments may also help learners with lower WM to compensate by providing a visual, written representation of input and output (Payne & Whitney, 2002), thereby directing learners to attend more closely to the form and content of the input, while still maintaining the real-time feel of conversation (Pellettieri, 2000; Smith, 2003). This increased processing time may provide learners with additional opportunities to receive modified input, and produce modified output and corrective feedback, increasing their potential for L2 development. Overall, research findings suggest that task-based SCMC interaction leads to learning outcomes similar to those found in FTF modes (see Ziegler, 2015 for a review), providing instructors with encouraging evidence that computer-mediated tasks can be successfully used independently or as a supplement within the traditional classroom.

Previous meta-analyses have also demonstrated that foreign language (FL) and L2 settings act as influencing factors on the efficacy of interaction, with research in FL producing larger effect sizes for interaction than research in L2 settings (Mackey & Goo, 2007). Sheen (2004) examined the relationship between corrective feedback and learner uptake in FL and L2 communicative classrooms, with results indicating that the amount of corrective feedback, as well as uptake and instances of repair, varied significantly across contexts. Research has also demonstrated that the effectiveness of different types of corrective feedback (Lyster & Mori, 2006), as well as teachers' provision of and learners' response to corrective feedback (Llinares & Lyster, 2014), is dependent on the communicative orientation of the classroom.

Some researchers have also argued that interaction may not be as effective in classroom contexts as in laboratory settings (Foster, 1998). However, other researchers have shown that task type affects the amount of negotiation more than the educational setting (Gass, Mackey, & Ross-Feldman, 2005). Nicholas, Lightbown, and Spada (2001) have also suggested that the benefits attributed to interaction in lab settings could be caused more by the intense, focused, and consistent application of the treatment rather than the treatment itself, especially as the classroom environment is unpredictable due to factors often beyond researchers' control, such as the effects of peer relationships or disruptive students. However, despite the possible advantages that lab-based environments may offer due to their controlled and calculated nature, research has indicated that interaction and corrective feedback are facilitative of L2 development in classroom environments (Gass et al., 2005; Russell & Spada, 2006; Mackey & Goo, 2007; Lyster & Saito, 2010).

Overall, these findings suggest that the relationship between the individual learner, the setting, and overall learning outcomes is complex. Researchers, educators, and curriculum developers are best advised to inform their practice by understanding that considering all of these cognitive and affective underpinnings of TBLT, as well as external factors such as task design, task sequencing and implementation, including time pressure and modality, and complexity can influence the outcomes of task-based language teaching.

Task Variables Impacting Learning and Performance

There are a multitude of task factors that influence the relationships between interaction and learning within a task-based environment. These factors must be taken into account when designing tasks. For example, individual differences such as motivation or aptitude act to influence perceived task difficulty. How complex a task is can be affected by conditions that can increase or decrease the cognitive demands placed on the learner. According to Robinson (2001), teacher decisions about sequencing tasks in a syllabus or curriculum should be based on the relative complexity of the tasks. In his framework, a gradual increase of the cognitive demands of the task brings learners closer to the authentic version they would have to perform in the real world. The more cognitively demanding the task, the more attention learners pay to input and output, the more input is incorporated into the learners' language, and the more learners modify their own output. Task complexity can be manipulated in a variety of ways, for instance by either directing resources (increasing/decreasing the elements in a task, changing the task from present to past tense, or increasing/decreasing reasoning demands), or depleting resources (providing/not providing planning time, increasing/decreasing the number of tasks, or increasing/decreasing the amount of required background knowledge or task familiarity) among other possibilities (Robinson, 2001).

Take, for example, a typical map task where learners have to give their partner directions using a map. If the tasks are sequenced starting with the least complex task, the learner will receive a small map of an area they are familiar with, with a clear route marked, and time to plan how they will explain the route to their partner (Robinson, 2001; Long, 2015). Learners begin with a limited number of task elements (small map), they have the required background knowledge (a familiar map), the reasoning demands are low (the route is pre-marked), and they have time to decide what to say (planning time). To increase the complexity of the task, any of these factors can be manipulated, for example, eliminating planning time. To make the task even more complex, the learners could use a map of an unfamiliar area or create their own route, and so on. In this way, tasks can be sequenced according to their approximation of real world tasks (Robinson, 2001). This could also be accomplished in a two-way interaction with a spot-the-difference task. In this type of task, learner pairs have pictures that are different in predetermined ways (see Iwashita, 2003) and are asked to find the differences without looking at their partner's picture. A low-complexity version might involve a picture of a familiar scene, such as a classroom, including familiar vocabulary, and a small number of differences. Complexity increases as more differences are added, if the scene and vocabulary are unfamiliar, or if learners do not know how many differences to look for.

The effect of changing task complexity on learners' processing has been explored in a variety of different empirical studies. One way of manipulating task complexity is to offer, or take away, supports such as graphic organizers or visuals, with research demonstrating a clear relationship between task complexity, uptake, and interactional feedback (Révész, Sachs, & Mackey, 2011), suggesting that providing or withholding visual support from learners impacts their task performance. The effects of task complexity have also been investigated with children as well as adults. For example, Mackey, Kanganas, and Oliver (2007) investigated the issue of task familiarity in a study with 40 English as a second language (ESL) learners. The children, in pairs, carried out tasks that had either familiar or unfamiliar procedures and content. Children working on tasks with unfamiliar procedures and content (more complex tasks) produced more clarification requests and confirmation checks, and provided more corrective feedback to each other. However, the children working on tasks that had familiar procedures had more opportunities to use the feedback provided, and the learners working on tasks that had familiar procedures and content actually used the feedback the most, suggesting that thoughtful manipulation of task design can elicit a range of learning outcomes.

Repeating a task is another way of manipulating the variable of familiarity or background knowledge, whether it is a direct repetition or a repetition of the same type of task. Practicing a task gives learners meaningful experience with language production and allows them to identify gaps in their knowledge base (Bygate, 2001). In a study by Gass et al. (1999), the effect of task repetition was explored with L2 Spanish learners learning the Spanish verb forms *ser* and *estar*. Three groups of learners were presented with Mr. Bean videos and instructed to simultaneously record their own online rendition in Spanish of the episode. One group watched the same video three times over the course of several weeks, while the other group watched three different Mr Bean videos. After analyzing the development of overall proficiency, morphosyntax, and lexical sophistication of the student-produced renditions, the repetition group demonstrated higher performance than the other groups, although these effects did not transfer to new contexts.

The sequencing of tasks according to increasing complexity has become a cornerstone of TBLT curricula (Norris, 2009). When designing tasks, instructors can take advantage of the complexities tasks can offer learners by carefully planning sequences to maximize the interactive and learning potential of the tasks. As learners progress through stages of increasingly complex tasks, they become gradually more prepared to perform the task in a real world setting; this is the ultimate goal of language acquisition and underscores why TBLT has met such empirical success, as has been demonstrated empirically by a number of scholars in diverse contexts, such as in Thailand (McDonough & Chaikitmongkol, 2007) and Belgium (Van den Branden, 2006).

Pedagogical Implications

Interactional approaches and TBLT are only useful if they can be successfully applied to real-world classrooms. The transformation of TBLT research into practical language education has been a top priority for both teachers and researchers (Norris, 2009). Designing materials, sequencing tasks, and understanding the chosen tasks' effects on the complexity, accuracy, and fluency of learners' production are all essential elements for creating an effective language classroom.

In order to sequence and effectively execute tasks in the classroom, instructors designing tasks would benefit from asking: What are my sequencing criteria? How complex will the task be? What conditions will be present? These questions can be decided and planned for ahead of time. Instructors can also examine the methodological criteria for task design such as: What individual learner differences might mediate task difficulty? What are the abilities of my students? How will I group them? These decisions may affect how the task plays out in real time and can be made online in the classroom (Robinson, 2001).

The complexity, accuracy, and fluency of a learner's output during a task are also helpful variables to keep in mind when designing a task. Robinson (2001) predicts that increasing the complexity of the task along one or more of the dimensions described above will push learners to improve the accuracy and complexity of their output, at the expense of fluency. The more authentic the task, the more complex the language produced. Empirically testing this hypothesis has been the subject of many TBLT studies (Foster & Skehan, 1996; Bygate, 2001; Ortega, 2005). For instance, Foster and Skehan (1996) explored the relationship between unplanned, short planning, and detailed planning on learners' production during a task. They found that the opportunity to plan improved the learners' fluency; however, the most accurate productions were provided by the less detailed planners, suggesting a trade-off effect between complexity and accuracy. Other studies have suggested that a number of factors influence whether or not pre-task planning leads to increased accuracy (Skehan & Foster, 1996, 1997; Mehnert, 1998; Ortega, 2005). Yuan and Ellis (2003) examined the effects of planning time on fluency, complexity and accuracy during L2 monologic oral production. Their study compared pre-task planning (time to plan out what to say before the task) with online planning (formulation and monitoring of speech plans). The results demonstrated that pre-task planning positively influenced grammatical complexity and encouraged more fluent and lexically varied language, while on-line planning positively influenced accuracy and grammatical complexity. The studies described above underscore how the specific type of task chosen, along with designated task conditions, will mediate complexity, accuracy, and fluency and must be carefully considered when choosing a task and designing materials.

Many different task types and features have been examined for their contribution to acquisition processes such as feedback, interlanguage modification, and comprehension. According to Long (2015), the most important feature of any task is its relevance to students' communicative needs. Long also argues that the best task materials are those that are locally produced, as the program designers and teachers know their students and students' needs the best. Available resources, whether human, financial, or technological, all need to be taken into account when designing materials. That being said, the type of task utilized can greatly affect the interaction that is produced. Types of tasks are usually grouped by the relationship between the interactors, the requirements for communicating information, the goals of the task, and the possible task outcomes (Pica et al., 1993). For example, in a jigsaw task, there is a two-way information gap. In other words, each learner in a group begins with information that other group members do not have and cannot see. In this task type, all learners have to interact to complete the task and there is one solution as the task goal. According to Long (2015), this type of task elicits implicit and explicit negative feedback among learners as they work together to sustain conversation and complete the task. The spot-the-difference task described above is an example of a jigsaw task that would lead to the type of interaction known to be facilitative of L2 development.

Other types of tasks manipulate the interactive factors described above into a variety of permutations. In an information-gap task, such as a picture-drawing task, one student holds all the information and must describe the scene to the other student. Since interaction is not necessarily required, a teacher would expect to see less feedback and modified output in this task type. Therefore, it is important for task designers to keep interaction requirements and relationships in mind when designing tasks for specific purposes. A decision-making task, on the other hand, would require learners to converge on a single outcome for the task, thereby increasing the likelihood that interaction and modification of output would occur. An example of this, for students in a program for business English learning, is to involve them in negotiating the details of a contract, perhaps role playing with specific outcomes required, or converging to decide on a new company policy and how to implement it.

Above all, TBLT materials need to be relevant so that they can motivate learners to accomplish tasks they know they will need to succeed in real-world language interactions. Through careful observation of the effects of task type on interaction and linguistic complexity, accuracy and fluency of student production, instructors are the best-suited designers of task materials for their learners. Many materials need to be developed and altered in real time based on the specific needs of the given learners. TBLT is therefore not a one-size-fits all approach. The individual differences and authentic linguistic needs of the students are the essential components for effective TBLT execution.

Conclusion

Overall, we have argued that there are a number of theoretically grounded principles for instructors and curriculum developers to keep in mind when designing and using interactional tasks in the classroom. For example, based on the large body of empirical evidence, it is clear that learners need rich and authentic input and meaningful interactional feedback as well as opportunities to produce and modify output. By providing learners with numerous communicative activities that vary in their cognitive and social demands, teachers will be creating an environment that encourages learners to practice and test their hypotheses about the TL, as well as giving them opportunities to notice differences between their production and more target-like utterances, thereby supporting L2 development.

In addition, the interaction approach underpinning TBLT highlights the importance of feedback and negotiation for L2 learning. A large body of empirical research has demonstrated the facilitative effects of feedback on L2 development, providing encouraging evidence for the use of feedback in task-based instruction. However, although the efficacy of feedback has been demonstrated (see Li, 2010; Mackey & Goo, 2007 for reviews), instructors must nonetheless make daily decisions regarding how many and which errors they address, as it will not always be appropriate to provide feedback on every error. Rather, instructors might consider learners' proficiency and expectations when deciding whether, and how, to implement feedback in the classroom. For example, for some forms, lower-level learners might benefit more from judiciously provided metalinguistic explanations that directly identify and correct an error while more proficient learners might feel recasts, which maintain a focus on meaning, to be more useful. For instructors interested in integrating technology into the classroom, the developmental benefits of interaction might even be enhanced with the use of certain technologies. For instance, SCMC text chat activities might aid learners' noticing of feedback due to the purely textual nature of the task, helping to draw learners' focus to the feedback or target features, possibly providing more opportunities to focus on form and meaning in the absence of other forms of input.

Educators and program designers interested in TBLT have numerous options regarding the development and implementation of task-based pedagogy. In order to best meet the needs of their individual classrooms, instructors should consider the influence of learners' cognitive and affective differences, as well as the potentially influencing role of setting or modality, on the quality and quantity of language that learners might produce during task-based interactions.

References

Beauvois, M. H. (1992). Computer-assisted classroom discussion in the foreign language classroom: Conversation in slow motion. *Foreign Language Annals, 25*, 455–464.

Blake, R. (2000). Computer mediated communication: A window on L2 Spanish interlanguage. *Language Learning & Technology, 4*, 120–136.

Bygate, M. (2001). Effects of task repetition on the structure and control of oral language. In K. Van den Branden, M. Bygate, & J. Norris (Eds.), *Task-based language teaching: A reader* (pp. 249–274). Philadelphia/Amsterdam: John Benjamins.

Bygate, M., Norris, J. M., & Van den Branden, K. (2014). Task-based language teaching. In C. Chapelle (Ed.), *The Blackwell encyclopedia of applied linguistics*. Malden, MA: Wiley-Blackwell.

Chun, D. M. (1994). Using computer networking to facilitate the acquisition of interactive competence. *System, 22*, 17–31.

Chun, D. M. (1998). Using computer-assisted class discussion to facilitate the acquisition of interactive competence. In J. Swaffar, S. Romano, P. Markley, & K. Arens (Eds.), *Language learning online: Theory and practice in the ESL and L2 computer classroom* (pp. 57–80). Austin, TX: Labyrinth Publications.

Doughty, C., & Varela, E. (1998). Communicative focus on form. *Focus on Form in Classroom Second Language Acquisition, 1*, 114–138.

Egi, T. (2007). Recasts, learners' interpretations, and L2 development. In A. Mackey (Ed.), *Conversational interaction in second language acquisition: A collection of empirical studies* (pp. 249–67). Oxford: Oxford University Press.

Ellis, R. (2000). Task-based research and language pedagogy. In K. Van den Branden, M. Bygate, & J. Norris (Eds.), *Task-based language teaching: A reader* (pp. 109–129). Amsterdam: John Benjamins.

Foster, P. (1998). A classroom perspective on the negotiation of meaning. *Applied Linguistics*, *19*, 1–23.

Foster, P., & Skehan, P. (2009). The influence of planning and task type on second language performance. In K. Van den Branden, M. Bygate, & J. Norris (Eds.), *Task-based language teaching: A reader* (pp. 275–300). Amsterdam: John Benjamins.

Gass, S., & Mackey, A. (2007). *Data elicitation for second and foreign language research*. New York: Routledge.

Gass, S., Mackey, A., & Ross-Feldman, L. (2005). Task-based interactions in classroom and laboratory settings. *Language Learning*, *55*, 575–611.

Gass, S., Mackey, A., Álvarez-Torres, M., & Fernández-Garcia, M. (1999). The effects of task repetition on linguistic output. *Language Learning*, *49*, 549–580.

Goo, J., & Mackey, A. (2013). The case against the case against recasts. *Studies in Second Language Acquisition*, *35*(1), 127–165.

Iwashita, N. (2003). Negative feedback and positive evidence in task-based interaction. *Studies in Second Language Acquisition*, *25*, 1–36.

Izumi, S. (2002). Output, input enhancement, and the noticing hypothesis: An experimental study of ESL relativization. *Studies in Second Language Acquisition*, *24*, 541–577.

Izumi, S., Bigelow, M., Fujiwara, M., & Fearnow, S. (1999). Testing the output hypothesis. *Studies in Second Language Acquisition*, *21*, 421–452.

Keck, C., Iberri-Shea, G., Tracy-Ventura, N., & Wa-Mbaleka, S. (2006). Investigating the empirical link between task-based interaction and acquisition. In J. M. Norris & L. Ortega (Eds.), *Synthesizing research on language learning and teaching* (pp. 91–131). Philadelphia: John Benjamins.

Kelm, O. R. (1992). The use of synchronous computer networks in second language instruction: A preliminary report. *Foreign Language Annals*, *25*, 441–454.

Kern, R. G. (1995). Restructuring classroom interaction with networked computers: Effects on quantity and characteristics of language production. *The Modern Language Journal*, *79*, 457–476.

Krashen, S., & Terrell, T. (1983). *The natural approach: Language acquisition in the classroom*. Hayward, CA: Alemany Press.

Lai, C., & Li, G. (2011). Technology and task-based language teaching: A critical review. *CALICO Journal*, *28*, 1–24.

Leeman, J. (2003). Recasts and second language development. *Studies in Second Language Acquisition*, *25*, 37–63.

Leeman, J. (2007). Feedback in L2 learning: Responding to errors during practice. In R. DeKeyser (Ed.), *Practice in a second language: Perspectives from linguistics and psychology* (pp. 111–37). Cambridge: Cambridge University Press.

Li, S. (2010). The effectiveness of corrective feedback in SLA: A meta-analysis. *Language Learning*, *60*, 309–365.

Llinares, A., & Lyster, R. (2014). The influence of context on patterns of corrective feedback and learner uptake: A comparison of CLIL and immersion classrooms. *The Language Learning Journal*, *42*, 181–194.

Long, M. H. (2007). *Problems in SLA*. Mahwah, NJ: Erlbaum.

Long, M. H. (2015). *Second language acquisition and task-based language teaching*. Malden, MA: Wiley-Blackwell.

Long, M. H., & Norris, J. (2000). Task-based language teaching and assessment. In M. Byram (Ed.), *Encyclopedia of language teaching* (pp. 597–603). London: Routledge.

Lyster, R. (2004). Differential effects of prompts and recasts in form-focused instruction. *Studies in Second Language Acquisition*, *26*, 399–432.

Lyster, R. (2013). Roles for corrective feedback in second language instruction. In C. Chapelle (Ed.), *The Blackwell encyclopedia of applied linguistics*. Malden, MA: Wiley Blackwell.

Lyster, R., & Mori, H. (2006). Interactional feedback and instructional counterbalance. *Studies in Second Language Acquisition, 28*, 269–300.

Lyster, R., & Ranta, L. (1997). Corrective feedback and learner uptake: Negotiation of form in communicative classrooms. *Studies in Second Language Acquisition, 19*, 37–67.

Lyster, R., & Saito, K. (2010). Oral feedback in classroom SLA: A meta-analysis. *Studies in Second Language Acquisition, 32*, 265–302.

Lyster, R., Saito, K., & Sato, M. (2013). Oral corrective feedback in second language classrooms. *Language Teaching, 46*, 1–40.

Mackey, A. (2012). *Input, interaction and corrective feedback in L2 classrooms*. Oxford: Oxford University Press.

Mackey, A., & Gass, S. M. (2006). Pushing the methodological boundaries in interaction research: An introduction to the special issue. *Studies in Second Language Acquisition, 28*, 169–178.

Mackey, A., & Goo, J. (2007). Interaction research in SLA: A meta-analysis and research synthesis. In A. Mackey (Ed.), *Conversational interaction in SLA: A collection of empirical studies* (pp. 408–452). Oxford: Oxford University Press.

Mackey, A., & Philp, J. (1998). Conversational interaction and second language development: Recasts, responses, and red herrings? *Modern Language Journal, 82*, 338–356.

Mackey, A., Abbuhl, R., & Gass, S. (2012). Interactionist approach. In S. Gass & A. Mackey (Eds.), *The Routledge handbook of second language acquisition* (pp. 7–24). New York: Routledge.

Mackey, A., Kanganas, A., & Oliver, R. (2007). Task familiarity and interactional feedback in child ESL classrooms. *TESOL Quarterly, 41*, 285–312.

McDonough, K., & Chaikitmongkol, W. (2007). Teachers' and learners' reactions to a task-based EFL course in Thailand. *TESOL Quarterly, 41*, 107–132.

Mehnert, U. (1998). The effects of different lengths of time for planning on second language performance. *Studies in Second Language Acquisition, 20*, 83–108.

Nicholas, H., Lightbown, P.M., & Spada, N. (2001). Recasts as feedback to language learners. *Language Learning, 51*, 719–758.

Norris, J. M. (2009). Task-based teaching and testing. In M. Long and C. Doughty (Eds.), *Handbook of language teaching* (pp. 578–594). Malden, MA: Blackwell.

Oliver, R. (2000). Age differences in negotiation and feedback in classroom and pairwork. *Language Learning, 50*, 119–151.

Ortega, L. (2005). What do learners plan? Learner-driven attention to form during pre-task planning. In R. Ellis (Ed.), *Planning and task performance in a second language* (pp. 77–109). Amsterdam: John Benjamins.

Payne, J. S., & Whitney, P. J. (2002). Developing L2 oral proficiency through synchronous CMC: Output, working memory, and interlanguage development. *CALICO Journal, 20*(1), 7–32.

Pellettieri, J. (1999). *Why-Talk?: Investigating the role of task-based interaction through synchronous network-based communication among classroom learners of Spanish*. Unpublished doctoral dissertation. University of California at Davis.

Pellettieri, J. (2000). Negotiation in cyberspace: The role of chatting in the development of grammatical competence. In M. Warschauer & R. Kern (Eds.), *Network-based language teaching: Concepts and practice* (pp. 59–86). Cambridge: Cambridge University Press.

Pica, T., Kanagy, R., & Falodun, J. (1993). Choosing and using communication tasks for second language instruction. In G. Crookes and S. Gass (Eds.), *Tasks and language learning: Integrating theory & practice*. Clevedon, UK: Multilingual Matters.

Pienemann, M., & Johnston, M. (1986). An acquisition based procedure for second language assessment (ESL). *Australian Review of Applied Linguistics, 9*, 92–122.

Ranta, L., & Lyster, R. (2007). A cognitive approach to improving immersion students' oral language abilities: The Awareness-Practice-Feedback sequence. In R. DeKeyser (Ed.), *Practice in a second language: Perspectives from applied linguistics and cognitive psychology* (pp. 141–160). Cambridge: Cambridge University Press.

Révész, A., Sachs, R., & Mackey, A. (2011). Task complexity, uptake of recasts, and second language development. In P. Robinson (Ed.), *Second language task complexity: Researching the cognition hypothesis of language learning and performance* (pp. 203–238). Amsterdam: John Benjamins.

Robinson, P. (2001). Task complexity, cognitive resources, and syllabus design: A triadic framework for examining task influences on SLA. In K. Van den Branden, M. Bygate, & J. Norris (Eds.), *Task-based language teaching: A reader* (pp. 193–226). Amsterdam: John Benjamins.

Russell, J., & Spada, N. (2006). The effectiveness of corrective feedback for the acquisition of L2 grammar: A meta-analysis of the research. In J. M. Norris & L. Ortega (Eds.), *Synthesizing research on language learning and teaching* (pp. 133–164). Amsterdam: John Benjamins.

Sauro, S. (2011). SCMC for SLA: A research synthesis. *CALICO Journal, 28*, 1–23.

Schmidt, R. W. (1990). The role of consciousness in second language learning. *Applied Linguistics, 11*, 129–158.

Sheen, Y. (2004). Corrective feedback and learner uptake in communicative classrooms across instructional settings. *Language Teaching Research, 8*, 263–300.

Skehan, P., & Foster, P. (1996). *The influence of post-task activities and planning on task-based performance* (Working Papers in English Language Teaching, No. 3). London: Thames Valley University.

Skehan, P., & Foster, P. (1997). Task type and task processing conditions as influence on foreign language performance. *Language Teaching Research, 1*, 185–211.

Smith, B. (2003). Computer-mediated negotiated interaction: An expanded model. *The Modern Language Journal, 87*, 38–57.

Smith, B. (2004). Computer-mediated negotiated interaction and lexical acquisition. *Studies in Second Language Acquisition, 26*, 365–98.

Smith, B. (2005). The relationship between negotiated interaction, learner uptake, and lexical acquisition in task-based computer-mediated communication. *TESOL Quarterly, 39*, 33–58.

Swain, M. (1985). Communicative competence: Some roles of comprehensible input and comprehensible output in its development. In S. Gass & C. Madden (Eds.), *Input in second language acquisition* (pp. 235–253). Rowley, MA: Newbury House.

Swain, M. (1995). Three functions of output in second language learning. In G. Cook & B. Seidlhofer (Eds.), *Principle and practice in applied linguistics: Studies in honour of H. G. Widdowson* (pp.125–144). Oxford: Oxford University Press.

Tomlinson, B. (2008) Language acquisition and language learning materials. In B. Tomlinson (Ed.), *English language teaching materials* (pp. 3–14). London: Continuum.

Tomlinson, B. (2012) Materials development. In C. A. Chapelle (Ed.), *The encyclopedia of applied linguistics*. Malden, MA: Wiley-Blackwell.

Warschauer, M. (1996). Comparing face-to-face and electronic communication in the second language classroom. *CALICO Journal, 13*, 7–25.

van Avermaet, P., & Gysen, S. (2009). From needs to tasks: Language learning needs in a task-based approach. In K. Van den Branden, M. Bygate, & J. Norris (Eds.), *Task-based language teaching: A reader* (pp. 143–170). Philadelphia/Amsterdam: John Benjamins.

Van den Branden, K. (2006). *Task-based language education: From theory to practice*. Cambridge: Cambridge University Press.

Van den Branden K., Bygate, M., & Norris, J. (2009). *Task-based language teaching: A reader*. Philadelphia/Amsterdam: John Benjamins.

Yuan, F., & Ellis, R. (2003). The effects of pre-task planning and on-line planning on fluency, complexity and accuracy in L2 monologic oral production. *Applied Linguistics, 24*, 1–27.

Ziegler, N. (2015). Synchronous computer-mediated communication and interaction: A meta-analysis. *Studies in Second Language Acquisition*.

COMMENTS ON PART II

Brian Tomlinson

It is reassuring that some practitioners and researchers are working towards the development of more research-informed learning materials. In the three chapters in this section practitioners and researchers seem to be working together towards this goal. This, to me, is the hope for the future in that a connection of practical and theoretical expertise, whether combined in a differentiated team or interacting in the work of an individual, is more likely to lead to effective learning materials than the isolated efforts of practice-focused or theory-focused writers. Resource rooms throughout the world are littered with textbooks developed by writers with a lot of experience of what typically happens in the classrooms they have experienced but without an awareness of what research has found to actually facilitate language acquisition and development in classrooms throughout the world. Some of these resource rooms also contain a few unused textbooks written by theorists without experience or awareness of what actually happens in language learning classrooms.

Chapter 5 illustrates one potentially productive model. I started out as a classroom teacher, became a teacher trainer, became a curriculum developer and am now a university academic. Alper Darici is an experienced teacher and Head of Department who has become increasingly interested in and aware of the potential value of applying relevant SLA research findings to improving the effectiveness of the materials used in the classrooms he is responsible for in Istanbul. Together we pooled our expertise and experience to develop a flexible framework for materials development and then to use it to produce, evaluate and revise materials for specific classroom situations. This is a model I would like to see made much more use of by commercial publishers. It is a model I have made productive use of on textbook projects in China, Ethiopia, Namibia and Singapore, but one which is rarely used to develop global coursebooks.

Chapters 6 and 7 illustrate a slightly different model, in that they team together researchers with experience and expertise in both classroom teaching and academic research, who approach the task of developing materials after a specification of what can be learned from research and then applied to materials being developed for particular pedagogic approaches; for example, pragmatic awareness or task-based learning. This is also a potentially productive model in that it could also lead to more principled and effective materials.

Each of the three chapters focuses on a different pedagogical approach, Chapter 5 on a text-driven approach, Chapter 6 on a pragmatic awareness approach and Chapter 7 on a task-based approach. Interestingly, though, all three chapters recommend the application of similar SLA research-based principles. The importance of a rich and re-cycled input, of plentiful opportunities for communicative output, of learner noticing, of learner discovering, of on-task learner and teacher feedback, of relevance to the learner and of affective and cognitive engagement are stressed by all three chapters, suggesting that there is more agreement about what can facilitate language acquisition than is commonly acknowledged. Unfortunately these are facilitators of language acquisition which rarely feature in global coursebooks. Fortunately it is not difficult to develop textbooks which do apply these principles, as has been demonstrated by many local textbook projects, for example *On Target* (1995) in Namibia and *Search 10* (Fenner & Nordal-Pedersen, 1999) in Norway. All it needs is for research to demonstrate to commercial publishers of textbooks that it is possible to apply these principles in such a way as to preserve the face validity of their textbooks, to improve the effectiveness of their textbooks and to increase the profits generated by their textbooks.

References

Fenner, A. N., & Nordal-Pedersen, G. (1999). *Search 10*. Oslo: Gyldendal.
On Target. (1995). Windhoek: Gamsberg Macmillan.

PART III

Evaluations of Materials in Relation to SLA Theory

8

VOCABULARY LEARNING EXERCISES

EVALUATING A SELECTION OF EXERCISES COMMONLY FEATURED IN LANGUAGE LEARNING MATERIALS

Tatsuya Nakata and Stuart Webb

Introduction

This chapter examines common second language (L2) vocabulary learning activities using a framework proposed by Nation (2013a). In particular, Nation's first guideline, which focuses on efficacy, will be examined in detail. Nation and Webb's (2011) Technique Feature Analysis (TFA) will be used to determine which components of the activities contribute to learning. The chapter aims to gauge the relative efficacy of three vocabulary learning activities: Learning from flashcards, cloze exercises, and crossword puzzles; shed some light on their strengths and weaknesses; and show how they might be modified to be made more effective.[1]

Nation (2013a) argues that vocabulary teaching activities need to meet five guidelines. The first guideline states that activities need to facilitate vocabulary learning (see below for the discussion on how the effectiveness of vocabulary teaching activities is measured). Second, according to Nation, activities should not require a lot of work on the part of teachers. In other words, if there are two activities that are equally effective, and Activity A requires less work from teachers than Activity B, the former is more desirable in terms of practicality. Nation's third guideline states that activities should provide a balance of the four strands of meaning-focused input, meaning-focused output, language-focused learning, and fluency development. Meaning-focused input refers to activities where the focus is on understanding a message, such as extensive reading or listening. In meaning-focused output, there is a focus on conveying a message such as giving a speech or writing a story. Language-focused learning involves intentional learning of an aspect of language such as explicit grammar instruction, or memorization of vocabulary. Fluency development refers to activities such as improving the rate of word recognition, reading, or speaking, where the focus is on increasing the speed at which learners use L2 knowledge (e.g., Nation, 2013b). Because having a balance of the four strands is effective for L2 learning, good vocabulary learning activities should also provide a balance of the four strands. Nation's (2013a) fourth guideline states that activities should be efficient. In other words, if there are two activities that are equally effective, and Activity A requires less time than Activity B, the former is more efficient and thus more desirable. Last, Nation (2013a) also argues that activities need to be able to be used many times.

Flashcards

Now let us examine common L2 vocabulary learning activities using Nation's (2013a) framework. The first activity to be analyzed is learning from flashcards in the productive direction. Flashcards (also known as word cards) are a set of cards where the L2 word is written on one side and its meaning, usually a first language (L1) translation, is written on the other. Learning flashcards in the productive direction involves viewing the meaning of a target item and then trying to recall its L2 form. Nation's first guideline is concerned with effectiveness. Although it is not very easy to determine which activities are effective for vocabulary development, the present study will analyze the potential effectiveness of activities using the TFA framework (Nation & Webb, 2011).

TFA consists of 18 criteria that have been found to facilitate L2 vocabulary learning based on previous empirical research. If a vocabulary learning activity meets a certain criterion, 1 point is given for that criterion. The more points an activity receives out of a total score of 18, the more effective it is considered to be for vocabulary learning. Table 8.1 shows the results of our analysis of flashcard learning based on TFA.

Let us now consider how many criteria shown in Table 8.1 flashcard learning satisfies. The first three criteria in TFA are concerned with motivation. Criterion 1 asks whether there is a clear vocabulary learning goal in the activity. Because learners use flashcards for the purpose of learning vocabulary, the flashcard activity meets this criterion. The second criterion asks whether the activity is motivating for learners. There may exist conflicting views regarding this criterion. On one hand, some learners tend to perceive rote learning, including flashcard learning, as boring (e.g., Krashen, 1989). On the other hand, some researchers point out that flashcard learning may be motivating because it may give learners a sense of accomplishment (e.g., Mondria & Mondria-de Vries, 1994; Nation & Webb, 2011). The use of computer-based flashcards (e.g., Nakata, 2011, 2013a) may be particularly motivating. Here, following Nation and Webb's analysis, 1 point is given for this criterion. The third criterion asks whether learners select the words to be studied. This criterion is based on the assumption that studying L2 words selected by learners may be more motivating than studying L2 words selected by others such as teachers or materials developers. Unless ready-made flashcards are used, learners study L2 words selected by themselves. Hence, 1 point is also given for this criterion. In the case of computer-based flashcards, a wide selection of ready-made flashcards are available. Nakata (2011) argues that electronic ready-made flashcards are useful because they may allow learners to study many lexical items without the time-consuming task of flashcard creation. Whether the use of computer-based ready-made flashcards has a negative effect on learners' motivation is an empirical question that needs to be investigated.

TABLE 8.1 Analysis of flashcard learning using Technique Feature Analysis

	Criteria	Explanation	Flashcard
	Motivation		
1	Vocabulary learning goal	Does the activity have a clear vocabulary learning goal?	1
2	Motivate learning	Is the activity motivating for learners?	1
3	Words selected by learners	Do learners select the target words to be studied?	1
	Noticing		
4	Attention on target words	Does the activity encourage the learners to pay attention to the target words?	1
5	Awareness of new vocabulary learning	Does the activity make learners notice new features of target words?	1
6	Negotiation	Does the activity provide opportunities for negotiation?	0
	Retrieval		
7	Retrieval	Does the activity provide opportunities for retrieval?	1
8	Productive retrieval	Does the activity involve productive retrieval?	1
9	Recall	Does the activity involve recall?	1
10	Multiple retrievals	Does the activity involve multiple retrieval opportunities for each target word?	1
11	Spacing between retrievals	Does the activity introduce spacing between retrieval opportunities?	1
	Generation		
12	Generation	Does the activity promote generation?	0
13	Productive generation	Does the activity involve productive generation?	0
14	High degree of generation	Does the activity involve a high degree of generation?	0
	Retention		
15	Successful form–meaning linking	Does the activity provide opportunities for successful linking of form and meaning?	1
16	Instantiation	Does the activity promote instantiation?	0
17	Imaging	Does the activity promote imaging?	0
18	Avoidance of interference	Does the activity avoid interference between words?	1
	Total score		12

Adapted from Nation and Webb (2011, p. 7)

Criteria 4–6 in TFA are concerned with noticing. Criterion 4 asks whether the activity focuses learners' attention on the target words. When learning from flashcards, learners deliberately attempt to learn target words, which involves noticing. Hence, 1 point is given for this criterion. The next criterion is concerned with whether the activity makes learners notice some features of L2 words that need to be learned. Because flashcard learning typically involves learning (at least partially) unfamiliar L2 word forms and their meanings, flashcard learning also meets this criterion. Criterion 6 is concerned with negotiation. Because flashcard learning is usually done individually, this criterion is not met.

The next five criteria are concerned with retrieval. Retrieval refers to the act of accessing previously learned information about L2 words from memory. Retrieval can be categorized into two types: Productive and receptive. The former involves retrieving L2 word forms, whereas the latter involves retrieving the meanings of L2 words. Criterion 7 asks whether the activity involves retrieval. This criterion is based on research showing that retrieval enhances the retention of L2 vocabulary (e.g., Folse, 2006; Barcroft, 2007; Karpicke & Roediger, 2008). Because learning flashcards in the productive direction involves productive retrieval, it satisfies this criterion. Retrieval is also a common feature among existing computer-based flashcards (Nakata, 2011).

The next criterion is concerned with the direction of retrieval (i.e., receptive or productive). Research suggests that if only one direction has to be chosen, productive retrieval may be more desirable than receptive retrieval. This is because productive retrieval results in adequate gains in receptive knowledge as well as large gains in productive knowledge, whereas receptive retrieval results in large gains in receptive knowledge but only small gains in productive knowledge (e.g., Mondria & Wiersma, 2004; Steinel, Hulstijn, & Steinel, 2007; Webb, 2009). Because productive retrieval may be more desirable than receptive retrieval, Criterion 8 gives a point for productive retrieval. In Nation and Webb's (2011) analysis, no point is given to flashcard learning regarding this criterion because they limit their analysis to receptive flashcard learning. However, as Nation and Webb acknowledge, flashcards can be used to practice productive retrieval if learners look at the meanings and attempt to retrieve L2 words. Furthermore, most computer-based flashcards support not only receptive but also productive retrieval (Nakata, 2011). One point, therefore, is given for Criterion 8 in our analysis.

The next criterion is concerned with the recall / recognition distinction. Recall requires learners to produce L2 word forms or their meanings, whereas recognition asks learners to choose L2 word forms or their meanings from a number of options as in a multiple-choice question. Memory research shows that recall may enhance the retention of L1 vocabulary, reading materials, and lecture materials more than recognition (e.g., Carpenter & DeLosh, 2006; Butler & Roediger, 2007; Kang, McDermott, & Roediger, 2007). As a result, TFA considers recall to be a positive feature. Because learning from paper-based flashcards usually involves recall, flashcard learning meets this criterion. In the case of computer-based flashcards, recognition formats are also common (Nakata, 2011). It should be noted, however, that although recall is often considered to be more effective than recognition, L2 vocabulary research has found little or no difference between the effects of recall and recognition (Van Bussel, 1994; Nakata, 2013b). The use of recognition formats among computer-based flashcards, therefore, may not necessarily be a negative feature.

Criterion 10 in TFA asks whether the activity involves multiple retrievals of each target word. By going through a stack of flashcards multiple times, learners can practice repeated retrieval. As a result, flashcard learning satisfies this criterion. This criterion is based on the assumption that vocabulary learning increases as a function of retrieval frequency. Yet empirical studies have produced mixed results regarding this assumption. Non-L2 vocabulary research has shown that although multiple retrievals may facilitate short-term memory, they may not necessarily enhance long-term retention (Rohrer, Taylor, Pashler, Wixted, & Cepeda, 2005). L2 vocabulary research, however, demonstrated the advantage of multiple retrievals 4 weeks after the treatment on productive and receptive recall posttests (Nakata, 2013b). It may be reasonable, therefore, to assume that for L2 vocabulary learning, the benefits of multiple retrievals may persist at least four weeks after learning.

Criterion 11 asks whether there is any spacing between retrievals. This is based on the spacing effect. According to the spacing effect, spaced learning, which introduces spacing between retrievals of a certain item, yields superior retention to massed learning, which does not involve any spacing (e.g., Karpicke & Bauernschmidt, 2011; Nakata, in press). Spacing is found to have a very large effect on learning. Nakata (in press), for instance, found that spaced learning was more than twice as effective as massed learning on a posttest conducted one week after the treatment. Flashcards allow learners to introduce spacing between retrievals unless learners practice the same word repeatedly without any interval. Hence, flashcard learning also satisfies Criterion 11.

Given that introducing spacing increases learning, one might ask how we should space retrieval opportunities in order to maximize learning. Previous research shows that larger spacing generally leads to better long-term retention than shorter spacing (e.g., Pashler, Zarow, & Triplett, 2003; Pyc & Rawson, 2007; Karpicke & Bauernschmidt, 2011; Nakata, 2013b). In other words, studying a set of L2 words every month leads to better long-term retention than studying them every week. This is a phenomenon known as the lag effect. The lag effect suggests that not only the presence or absence of spacing but also the amount of spacing may affect vocabulary learning.

Some researchers argue that gradually increasing spacing between retrievals (e.g., one month, two months, three months) may maximize L2 vocabulary learning (e.g., Ellis, 1995; Schmitt, 2000; Hulstijn, 2001). This type of spacing is known as expanding spacing. In contrast, a schedule where spacing between retrievals of a given item is held constant (e.g., two months, two months, two months) is referred to as equal spacing. Although expanding spacing is often regarded as the most effective type of spacing schedule, L2 vocabulary studies comparing equal and expanding spacing have produced inconsistent results. Three studies failed to find any advantage of expanding over equal spacing in their posttest scores (Pyc & Rawson, 2007; Karpicke & Bauernschmidt, 2011; Kang, Lindsey, Mozer, & Pashler, in press). Nakata (in press) showed statistically significant, yet only limited, advantage of expanding over equal spacing. Overall, research suggests that the amount of spacing may have a larger effect on learning than the type of spacing (i.e., expanding or equal; Karpicke & Bauernschmidt, 2011). Because flashcards offer flexibility in the order of items, they may allow learners to manipulate the amount and type of spacing relatively easily, which is another potentially positive feature of flashcard learning. Computer-based flashcards are also useful because they can be programmed to keep a record of a learner's performance and ensure that L2 words are practiced at regular intervals (e.g., Nakata, 2008, 2011).

The next three criteria in TFA are concerned with generation (also referred to as *generative* or *creative use*), where learners meet or use familiar words in novel contexts (e.g., Joe, 1998). In flashcard learning, L2 words are always met in the same context, unless learners make multiple cards for one word, each of which illustrates its different usages. As a result, flashcard learning meets none of Criteria 12–14. Although computer-based flashcards could be programmed to promote generation, it is not a common feature among existing vocabulary learning programs (Nakata, 2011).

The last four criteria in TFA are concerned with factors affecting retention. Criterion 15 asks whether learners have a chance to be exposed to correct L2 word forms and their meanings. In flashcard learning, learners can verify the correct response by looking at the other side of cards. Flashcard learning, therefore, meets this criterion. Looking at the correct response after retrieval can be considered as a form of feedback. Non-L2 vocabulary research has shown that receiving feedback after a delay (delayed feedback) may increase retention more than receiving feedback immediately after retrieval (immediate feedback), a phenomenon known as the delay retention effect (e.g., Kulik & Kulik, 1988; Butler, Karpicke, & Roediger, 2007; Metcalfe, Kornell, & Finn, 2009). Nakata (2015), however, failed to observe this effect, suggesting that feedback timing may have little effect on L2 vocabulary acquisition in flashcard learning conditions.

Criteria 16 and 17 in TFA ask whether the activity involves instantiation and imaging, respectively. In instantiation, target words are used in a meaningful, visual situation. When the meanings of target words are illustrated visually, the activity involves imaging. Although flashcards can include example sentences or pictures, they usually do not promote instantiation or imaging. As a result, flashcard learning meets neither Criterion 16 nor 17. Due to their multimedia capabilities, computer-based flashcards may have some potential to facilitate instantiation and imaging (Nakata, 2011).

The last criterion in TFA asks whether the activity is designed to avoid interference. Studies have shown that learning semantically related words such as synonyms or antonyms together has a negative effect on L2 vocabulary learning because it tends to cause interference between words (for a review, see Nation, 2000). Unless learners study semantically related words together, interference can be avoided using flashcards. Flashcard learning, therefore, sometimes meets this criterion. However, it should be noted that some vocabulary learning computer programs offer sets of ready-made flashcards that are semantically related (e.g., words related to food, animals, or colors). Because some learners, teachers, and materials developers tend to believe that semantically related words should be studied together (Folse, 2004), it may be useful to raise awareness that interference inhibits L2 vocabulary learning.

Let us now look at the other four guidelines proposed by Nation (2013a). Flashcard learning typically does not require a large amount of work from teachers because flashcards are usually prepared by students. Various kinds of readymade flashcards, both paper- and computer-based, are also available. Regarding the four strands, flashcard learning is typically used for language-focused learning and does not provide opportunities for meaning-focused input, meaning-focused output, or fluency development. It may be useful, therefore, for teachers and curriculum developers to ensure that L2 words studied using flashcards are also met in the other three strands. Flashcard learning satisfies Nation's guideline of efficiency because a large number of words can be learned using flashcards in a short amount of time (e.g., Fitzpatrick, Al-Qarni, & Meara, 2008; Nation, 2013b). The activity also meets Nation's fifth guideline because it can be used many times. If the same words are practiced more than once, it may be desirable to practice receptive retrieval first and then productive retrieval (e.g., Nation, 2013b).

Cloze Exercises

The next activity to be analyzed is the cloze exercise, where learners are asked to complete sentences by filling in blanks. Cloze exercises can be done in two ways: In one, students have to fill in blanks from memory (recall), in the other, students fill in blanks based on a list of possible choices (recognition). In our example, we are using the former format. An example is given in Figure 8.1.

In the example shown in Figure 8.1, L1 (Japanese) translations of the missing words are also given (セメント, 費用, and 市場) in order to prevent learners from supplying words that are acceptable in the sentence but are different from target words that we want them to practice. For instance, some learners may produce *shop* instead of the target word *market* for the third question. It may also be useful to provide the first letter (e.g., m_____) and/or the number of letters in the word (e.g., six letters) instead of L1 translations. Now let us consider the effectiveness of this activity. Table 8.2 (middle) indicates the efficacy of cloze exercises using TFA.

Table 8.2 shows that cloze exercises have a TFA score of 9 out of 18. This is the second highest among 12 exercises analyzed by Nation and Webb (2011), suggesting that cloze exercises are a relatively effective vocabulary learning technique. At the same time, Table 8.2 also shows that the activity could be improved, especially in the retrieval and

---

1. This building is made of (   ). セメント
2. The (   ) of living is expensive in big cities. 費用
3. I buy my vegetables at the (   ) every week on Sunday morning. 市場

FIGURE 8.1 Example of a cloze exercise adapted from Webb (2012)

Note: The correct answer is *cement* for 1, *cost* for 2, and *market* for 3. Adapted from Webb (2012, p. 130).

TABLE 8.2 Analysis of cloze exercises and crossword puzzles using Technique Feature
Analysis

		Cloze exercises		Crossword puzzles	
	Criteria	Score	Comment	Score	Comment
	Motivation				
1	Vocabulary learning goal	1		1	
2	Motivate learning	1	Yes, because it is challenging.	1	Yes, because some learners find puzzles interesting.
3	Words selected by learners	0	No, but it could involve self-selected words (see text).	0	
	Noticing				
4	Attention on target words	1		1	
5	Awareness of new vocabulary learning	1		1	
6	Negotiation	0		0	No, but it could involve negotiation (see text).
	Retrieval				
7	Retrieval	1	Yes, because learners have to retrieve L2 word forms.	1	Yes, because learners have to retrieve L2 word forms.
8	Productive retrieval	1	Yes, because learners have to retrieve L2 word forms.	1	Yes, because learners have to retrieve L2 word forms.
9	Recall	1	Yes, because learners have to recall L2 word forms.	1	Yes, because learners have to recall L2 word forms.
10	Multiple retrievals	0	No, but it could involve multiple retrievals (see text).	0	No, but it could involve multiple retrievals (see text).
11	Spacing between retrievals	0	No, but it could involve spacing (see text).	0	No, but it could involve spacing (see text).
	Generation				
12	Generation	1	Yes, because learners meet L2 words in novel contexts.	0	No, but it could involve generation (see text).
13	Productive generation	0	No, because learners meet, not use, L2 words in novel contexts.	0	
14	High degree of generation	0		0	

Retention

15	Successful form–meaning linking	0	No, but successful form–meaning linking could be ensured (see text).	0	No, but successful form–meaning linking could be ensured (see text).
16	Instantiation	0		0	
17	Imaging	0		0	
18	Avoidance of interference	1	Yes, unless semantically related words are practiced together.	0	No, because semantically related words (names of vegetable) are practiced together in our example. But it could be improved (see text).
	Total score	9		7	

Adapted from Nation and Webb (2011, pp. 318–319)

retention categories. One way to modify the activity would be to give multiple questions for a given target word (Folse, 2006). For instance, the target word *cement* could be practiced in three cloze questions such as those in Figure 8.2.

Because the activity shown in Figure 8.2 involves three retrievals of the target word *cement*, it now meets Criterion 10 (multiple retrievals). When giving multiple sentences for a given target word, it is useful to ensure that sentences for a given target word are separated by those for other words. For instance, in the example below, *cement* is practiced in Questions 1, 3, and 5, not in 1, 2, and 3. By doing so, the activity now introduces spacing between retrievals and satisfies Criterion 11. Note that the sentences are designed to promote generation. In Question 1, *cement* is a noun and used in its most frequent, basic meaning. In Question 3, the word is used as a verb and takes a concrete noun (*path*) as the object. In Question 5, the word is used as a verb, takes an abstract noun (*friendship*) as the object, and is used figuratively. Although these features may be useful, they do not contribute

---

1. This building is made of (   ). セメント
2. The (   ) of living is expensive in big cities. 費用
3. We (   ) the path. 舗装した
4. I buy my vegetables at the (   ) every week on Sunday morning. 市場
5. We (   ) our friendship with a drink. 強固にした
6. . . .

FIGURE 8.2 Example of cloze questions activity with target word 'cement' adapted from Nation (2013) and Webb (2012)

Note: The correct answer is *cement* for 1, *cost* for 2, *cemented* for 3 and 5, and *market* for 4. セメント is the Japanese translation for the noun *cement*. 舗装した is the Japanese translation for the past tense of the verb *cement* when used literally. 強固にした is the Japanese translation for the past tense of the verb *cement* when used figuratively.

to the TFA score because the activity is already given a point for generation (Criterion 12).

Another way to increase the learning potential of cloze exercises would be to give correct answers. By doing so, we can ensure that learners have opportunities to make the correct form-meaning connection, and the activity will receive a point for Criterion 15 (successful form-meaning linking). If cloze exercises are given in a computer program, feedback can be provided relatively easily (for an example, see http://www.lextutor.ca/conc/multi/).

Motivational aspects of cloze exercises could be improved by allowing learners to practice self-selected target words. Multi-Concordance (http://www.lextutor.ca/conc/multi/) created by Tom Cobb enables learners to do this. If learners type L2 words, the software automatically generates cloze exercises for each word based on sentences extracted from a corpus. Figure 8.3 shows an example of cloze exercises created by the software for the word *cement*.

If all of the above changes are made, the activity will receive a total TFA score of 13, which is higher than any other activity analyzed by previous research so far (Nation & Webb, 2011; Webb, 2012).

Let us now look at the other four guidelines proposed by Nation (2013a). Cloze exercises require a reasonable amount of work from teachers because the exercises need to be created. It is true that software such as Multi-Concordance allows teachers to create cloze exercises automatically. However, exercises generated by software may need to be edited by teachers because they might contain a large number of low-frequency words and may not necessarily be suitable for learners. Regarding the four strands, cloze exercises are mainly concerned with

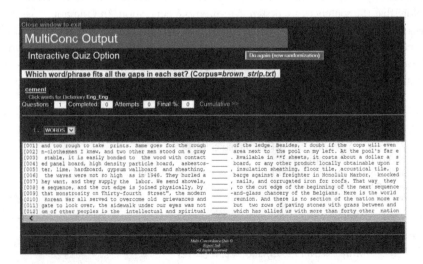

FIGURE 8.3 Example of cloze exercises based on Brown Corpus created by Tom Cobb's Multi-Concordance (http://www.lextutor.ca/conc/multi/)

language-focused learning and do not provide opportunities for the other three strands. Cloze exercises satisfy Nation's guideline of efficiency because the task can be completed relatively quickly. At the same time, because the task requires more time than learning from flashcards, it may be less efficient than flashcard learning. The activity also meets Nation's fifth guideline because it can be used many times. However, when the same target words are practiced in cloze exercises, it may be desirable not to use the same contexts repeatedly because it may not be very motivating.

Crossword Puzzles

The next activity to be analyzed is the crossword puzzle, where learners produce L2 words based on the meaning given. An example is given in Figure 8.4.

First, we will consider the effectiveness of this activity. Table 8.2 (right-hand pair of columns) indicates the efficacy of crossword puzzles using TFA. Table 8.2 shows that crossword puzzles have a TFA score of 7 out of 18 and may be less effective than flashcards (12) or cloze (9). Note that the activity receives no point for the generation and retention categories. Let us see how this activity could be improved to increase the learning potential. First, by having students solve crosswords in a pair or group instead of individually, the activity may involve negotiation of word meanings and satisfy Criterion 6 of TFA.

Another way to modify the activity would be not to practice semantically related words (e.g., names of vegetable) together. For instance, instead of *carrot*, *tomato*, and *cucumber*, target words such as *carrot*, *cost*, and *market* could be practiced. This would avoid interference, and the activity would receive one point for Criterion 18 (interference). It may also be useful to give multiple questions

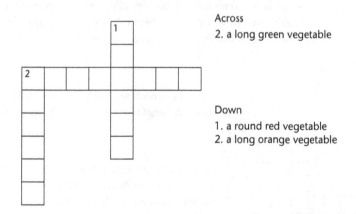

Across
2. a long green vegetable

Down
1. a round red vegetable
2. a long orange vegetable

FIGURE 8.4 Example of a crossword puzzle. The correct answer is *cucumber* for 2 Across and *tomato* and *carrot* for 1 and 2 Down, respectively. Adapted from Webb (2012, p. 129)

for a given target word. By doing so, the activity would meet Criteria 10 (multiple retrievals) and 11 (spacing). Another way to increase the learning potential of crosswords would be to give correct answers. This will ensure that learners have opportunities to make the correct form–meaning connection, and the activity will receive a point for Criterion 15 (successful form–meaning linking). Last, in addition to the meanings of target words, cloze sentences can also be provided, which may help promote generation. The modified activity might look like Figure 8.5.

Note that the target word *cost* is practiced twice in this activity (2 Across and 2 Down), thus involving repeated retrievals (Criterion 10) and spacing (Criterion 11). Also, while *cost* is used as a verb in 2 Across, it is used as a noun in 2 Down. This facilitates generation (Criterion 12). Using inflected forms (e.g., *costing, carrots,* and *markets* instead of *cost, carrot,* and *market*) as answers may also help promote generation. If all of the above changes are made, the activity will receive a total TFA score of 13, the same score as the revised cloze exercises.

One potential problem with crossword puzzles, though, is that learners may be able to solve some questions without carefully considering the clues. For instance, suppose that learners solved 2 Across (*cost*) and 3 Across (*carrot*) before 2 Down in the example below. By solving these questions first, learners may be able to infer that the correct answer for 2 Down is a four-letter word that starts with *c* and ends with *t*. As a result, learners may be able to come up with the correct answer for 2 Down (*cost*) without carefully examining the definition or cloze sentence. This is not very effective because it may deprive learners of opportunities to strengthen form–meaning connection or study how L2 words are used in context.

Let us now look at the other four guidelines proposed by Nation (2013a). Because creating crossword puzzles may require a substantial amount of work from teachers, the activity does not meet Nation's (2013a) second guideline. However, a website such as *Puzzlemaker* (http://puzzlemaker.discoveryeducation. com/CrissCrossSetupForm.asp) can help teachers to create crossword puzzles in a relatively short time. Regarding the four strands, crossword puzzles are mainly

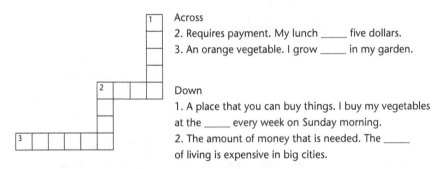

Across
2. Requires payment. My lunch _____ five dollars.
3. An orange vegetable. I grow _____ in my garden.

Down
1. A place that you can buy things. I buy my vegetables at the _____ every week on Sunday morning.
2. The amount of money that is needed. The _____ of living is expensive in big cities.

FIGURE 8.5 Example of a crossword puzzle. The correct answer is *cost* for 2 Across and 2 Down, *carrot* for 3 Across, and *market* for 1 Down. Adapted from Webb (2012, p. 130)

concerned with language-focused learning and do not provide opportunities for the other three strands. Crossword puzzles may be less efficient than flashcard learning and cloze exercises because they take more time. The activity meets Nation's fifth guideline because it can be used many times.

Discussion

In this chapter we looked at the relative efficacy of three common vocabulary learning activities using guidelines proposed by Nation (2013a). The analysis found that Nation's guidelines may be useful for highlighting possible strengths and weaknesses of vocabulary learning activities. For instance, the analysis revealed that although flashcard learning may be very effective in terms of retrieval, its ability to promote generation may be limited. In contrast, although crossword puzzles may be motivating, they may not be very effective in terms of generation and retention, at least unless some modifications are made. Flashcard learning may have additional value because it requires less work from teachers and time on task compared with cloze exercises and crossword puzzles. Examining activities using these guidelines may be useful because it may allow teachers and materials developers to determine which activities might be used based on learning goals or learners' needs. Teachers and materials developers could also combine different activities so that they can complement each others' weaknesses. For instance, by practicing same words in flashcards first and then revised cloze exercises, learners may be able to benefit from the positive effects of both retrieval and generation. The chapter also showed how TFA may be used to evaluate and indicate where modification of vocabulary learning activities may be useful to increase learning potential. For example, by making modifications to cloze exercises and crossword puzzles, both activities might be made to be more effective by including generation and retrieval within the activity.

Present and previous analyses using TFA (Nation & Webb, 2011; Webb, 2012) also reveal that few vocabulary learning activities involve instantiation or imaging. For instance, none of the activities analyzed in the present and previous analyses promotes instantiation. Similarly, only one activity (keyword technique; Nation & Webb, 2011) analyzed so far facilitates imaging. This suggests that it may be useful for teachers and materials developers to consider instantiation and imaging when designing vocabulary learning activities. Including an instantiation or imaging component within an activity may be particularly useful for developers of computer-assisted language learning (CALL) materials, where instantiation and imaging can be promoted relatively easily because of multimedia capabilities (WUFUN provides one example of how this might be done; Ma & Kelly, 2006).

As this chapter has shown, Nation's (2013a) framework may be very useful for evaluating and indicating where modification is necessary within vocabulary learning activities. Further analysis of more activities using this framework would be useful. Teachers and materials developers may then be able to use this information to improve the efficacy of vocabulary learning programs.

Note

1 It should be noted that most activities can be done in several different ways. We have selected commonly used formats for these three activities. However, it would be fair to argue that we are analyzing a particular way of using each of the three activities, and other manifestations of the activities may have slightly different strengths and weaknesses.

References

Barcroft, J. (2007). Effects of opportunities for word retrieval during second language vocabulary learning. *Language Learning*, *57*, 35–56. doi:10.1111/j.1467-9922.2007.00398.x

Butler, A. C., & Roediger, H. L. (2007). Testing improves long-term retention in a simulated classroom setting. *European Journal of Cognitive Psychology*, *19*, 514–527. doi:10.1080/09541440701326097

Butler, A. C., Karpicke, J. D., & Roediger, H. L. (2007). The effect of type and timing of feedback on learning from multiple-choice tests. *Journal of Experimental Psychology: Applied*, *13*, 273–281. doi:10.1037/1076-898X.13.4.273

Carpenter, S. K., & DeLosh, E. L. (2006). Impoverished cue support enhances subsequent retention: Support for the elaborative retrieval explanation of the testing effect. *Memory and Cognition*, *34*, 268–276. doi:10.3758/BF03193405

Cobb. T. (n.d.) Corpus concordance English [Computer software] at: http://www.lextutor.ca/conc/eng/. Accessed August 29, 2014.

Ellis, N. C. (1995). The psychology of foreign language vocabulary acquisition: Implications for CALL. *Computer Assisted Language Learning*, *8*, 103–128. doi:10.1080/0958822940080202

Fitzpatrick, T., Al-Qarni, I., & Meara, P. (2008). Intensive vocabulary learning: A case study. *Language Learning Journal*, *36*, 239–248. doi:10.1080/09571730802390759

Folse, K. S. (2004). *Vocabulary myths: Applying second language research to classroom teaching.* Ann Arbor, MI: University of Michigan Press.

Folse, K. S. (2006). The effect of type of written exercise on L2 vocabulary retention. *TESOL Quarterly*, *40*, 273–293. doi:10.2307/40264523

Hulstijn, J. H. (2001). Intentional and incidental second language vocabulary learning: A reappraisal of elaboration, rehearsal, and automaticity. In P. Robinson (Ed.), *Cognition and second language instruction* (pp. 258–286). Cambridge: Cambridge University Press.

Joe, A. (1998). What effects do text-based tasks promoting generation have on incidental vocabulary acquisition? *Applied Linguistics*, *19*, 357–377. doi:10.1093/applin/19.3.357

Kang, S. H. K., McDermott, K. B., & Roediger, H. L. (2007). Test format and corrective feedback modify the effect of testing on long-term retention. *European Journal of Cognitive Psychology*, *19*, 528–558. doi:10.1080/09541440601056620

Kang, S. H. K., Lindsey, R. V., Mozer, M. C., & Pashler, H. (in press). Retrieval practice over the long term: Should spacing be expanding or equal-interval? *Psychonomic Bulletin & Review*. doi:10.3758/s13423-014-0636-z

Karpicke, J. D., & Bauernschmidt, A. (2011). Spaced retrieval: Absolute spacing enhances learning regardless of relative spacing. *Journal of Experimental Psychology: Learning, Memory, and Cognition*, *37*, 1250–1257. doi:10.1037/a0023436

Karpicke, J. D., & Roediger, H. L. (2008). The critical importance of retrieval for learning. *Science*, *319*, 966–968. doi:10.1126/science.1152408

Krashen, S. (1989). We acquire vocabulary and spelling by reading: Additional evidence for the Input Hypothesis. *The Modern Language Journal*, *73*, 440–464. doi:10.1111/j.1540-4781.1989.tb05325.x

Kulik, J. A., & Kulik, C.-L. C. (1988). Timing of feedback and verbal learning. *Review of Educational Research, 58*, 79–97. doi:10.3102/00346543058001079

Ma, Q., & Kelly, P. (2006). Computer assisted vocabulary learning: Design and evaluation. *Computer Assisted Language Learning, 19*, 15–45. doi:10.1080/09588220600803998

Metcalfe, J., Kornell, N., & Finn, B. (2009). Delayed versus immediate feedback in children's and adults' vocabulary learning. *Memory & Cognition, 37*, 1077–1087. doi:10.3758/MC.37. 8.1077

Mondria, J.-A., & Mondria-de Vries, S. (1994). Efficiently memorizing words with the help of word cards and "hand computer": Theory and applications. *System, 22*, 47–57. doi:10.1016/0346-251X(94)90039-6

Mondria, J.-A., & Wiersma, B. (2004). Receptive, productive and receptive + productive L2 vocabulary learning: What difference does it make? In B. Laufer (Ed.), *Vocabulary in a second language: Selection, acquisition, and testing* (pp. 79–100). Amsterdam: John Benjamins.

Nakata, T. (2008). English vocabulary learning with word lists, word cards and computers: Implications from cognitive psychology research for optimal spaced learning. *ReCALL, 20*, 3–20. doi:10.1017/S0958344008000219

Nakata, T. (2011). Computer-assisted second language vocabulary learning in a paired-associate paradigm: A critical investigation of flashcard software. *Computer Assisted Language Learning, 24*, 17–38. doi:10.1080/09588221.2010.520675

Nakata, T. (2013a). Web-based lexical resources. In C. Chapelle (Ed.), *The encyclopedia of applied linguistics* (pp. 6166–6177). Oxford: Wiley-Blackwell.

Nakata, T. (2013b). *Optimising second language vocabulary learning from flashcards*. Unpublished doctoral dissertation. Victoria University of Wellington, New Zealand.

Nakata, T. (2015). Effects of feedback timing on second language vocabulary learning: Does delaying feedback increase learning? *Language Teaching Research, 19*, 416–434. doi:10.1177/1362168814541721

Nakata, T. (in press). Effects of expanding and equal spacing on second language vocabulary learning: Does gradually increasing spacing increase vocabulary learning? *Studies in Second Language Acquisition.* doi:10.1017/S0272263114000825

Nation, I. S. P. (2000). Learning vocabulary in lexical sets: Dangers and guidelines. *TESOL Journal, 9*, 6–10.

Nation, I. S. P. (2013a). What are the ten most effective vocabulary activities? Paper presented at the JALT College and University Educators' Special Interest Group Event, Sapporo, Japan.

Nation, I. S. P. (2013b). *Learning vocabulary in another language* (2nd ed.). Cambridge: Cambridge University Press.

Nation, I. S. P., & Webb, S. A. (2011). *Researching and analyzing vocabulary*. Boston, MA: Cengage Learning.

Pashler, H., Zarow, G., & Triplett, B. (2003). Is temporal spacing of tests helpful even when it inflates error rates? *Journal of Experimental Psychology: Learning, Memory, and Cognition, 29*, 1051–1057. doi:10.1037/0278-7393.29.6.1051

Pyc, M. A., & Rawson, K. A. (2007). Examining the efficiency of schedules of distributed retrieval practice. *Memory & Cognition, 35*, 1917–1927. doi:10.3758/BF03192925

Rohrer, D., Taylor, K. M., Pashler, H., Wixted, J. T., & Cepeda, N. J. (2005). The effect of overlearning on long-term retention. *Applied Cognitive Psychology, 19*, 361–374. doi:10.1002/acp.1083

Schmitt, N. (2000). *Vocabulary in language teaching*. Cambridge: Cambridge University Press.

Steinel, M. P., Hulstijn, J. H., & Steinel, W. (2007). Second language idiom learning in a paired-associate paradigm: Effects of direction of learning, direction of testing, idiom imageability, and idiom transparency. *Studies in Second Language Acquisition, 29*, 449–484. doi:10.1017/S0272263107070271

Van Bussel, F. J. J. (1994). Design rules for computer-aided learning of vocabulary items in a second language. *Computers in Human Behavior, 10*, 63–76. doi:10.1016/0747-5632(94)90029-9

Webb, S. A. (2009). The effects of pre-learning vocabulary on reading comprehension and writing. *Canadian Modern Language Review, 65*, 441–470. doi:10.1353/cml.0.0046

Webb, S. A. (2012). Learning vocabulary in activities. In H. P. Widodo & A. Cirocki (Eds.), *Innovation and creativity in ELT methodology* (pp. 121–133). New York, NY: Nova.

9

AN EVALUATION OF TEXTBOOK EXERCISES ON COLLOCATIONS

Frank Boers and Brian Strong

Introduction

The past two decades have seen a proliferation of publications about lexical phrases such as idioms (e.g., *pull strings; sit on the fence; below the belt*) and collocations (e.g., *make an effort; pretty girl; wide awake*). This recent proliferation has been particularly noticeable regarding the latter type of lexical phrase – collocations, i.e., combinations of words whose co-occurrence is so common that substituting one of the words by a near-synonym sounds wrong (e.g., *?do an effort*) or at least odd (e.g., *?a pretty man*).

The growing interest in the phraseological dimension of language has undoubtedly been stimulated by advances in two research disciplines. One is the discipline of corpus linguistics, which has revealed that lexical phrases abound in natural discourse (e.g., Sinclair, 1991). The other is psycholinguistics, where knowledge of formulaic expressions has been shown to be vital for fluent language processing (e.g., Wray, 2002). Given the importance of multi-word lexis in language and language processing, it stands to reason that second language (L2) or foreign language (FL) learners can benefit considerably from developing a sizeable repertoire of lexical phrases. Indeed, several studies have shown that a growing command of phraseology is part and parcel of becoming proficient in an L2 or FL (e.g., Boers, Eyckmans, Kappel, Stengers, & Demecheleer, 2006) and that knowledge of lexical phrases benefits both receptive and productive fluency (e.g., Ellis, Simpson-Vlach, & Maynard, 2008; Wood, 2010). It also helps learners to produce 'idiomatic' language instead of un-native-like word strings such as *?say a joke* and *?with other words.*

Unfortunately, a growing body of evidence also suggests that, in the absence of massive amounts of exposure to the target language, learners tend to be slow at acquiring its phraseological dimension and consequently produce discourse that is lacking in idiomaticity (e.g., Prodromou, 2007; Forsberg, 2010; Li & Schmitt, 2010). This justifies the pleas by several pedagogy-minded applied linguists for interventions that raise learners' awareness of the importance of multiword lexis (e.g., Nattinger & DeCarrico, 1992; Lewis, 1993; Boers & Lindstromberg, 2009) as an encouragement for them to start paying closer attention to formulaic word strings in the samples of target language they are exposed to.

Because it is often doubtful whether learners will accurately identify formulaic word strings unaided (Eyckmans, Boers, & Stengers, 2007), designers of pedagogic materials may choose to direct learners' attention to high-utility expressions by manipulating the texts they work with. Expressions can be made more salient by 'flooding' a text with instances (Webb, Newton, & Chang, 2013), by typographically enhancing (e.g., underlining) expressions (Peters, 2012), by adding clarifying glosses to expressions whose meaning is not transparent (Peters, 2009), or by means of a combination of such techniques (Jones & Haywood, 2004).

Research on the extent to which these interventions foster durable retention of lexical phrases has yielded rather mixed results, however, with attested learning gains sometimes leaving much to be desired (see Boers & Lindstromberg, 2012, for a review of quasi-experimental studies on ways of helping learners to master formulaic word strings). This is not entirely surprising. While attention is known to be a vital first step on the way to retention (Schmidt, 2001), additional cognitive operations on the part of the learner are often required for new lexical items (and language forms more generally) to stick in long-term memory. The nature of those cognitive operations influences not only the chances that information is retained at all (hence the importance of cognitive engagement or 'depth of processing', e.g., Craik & Tulving, 1975) but also the nature of the resulting knowledge representation and thus the purposes (e.g., receptive or productive tasks) that this knowledge will serve best (hence the importance of aligning learning methods and learning goals and of ensuring 'transfer-appropriate processing', e.g., Morris, Bransford, & Franks, 1977).

Given the observation that more seems to be needed to satisfactorily accelerate learners' acquisition of lexical phrases, it would appear a welcome trend for contemporary English as a foreign language (EFL) textbooks to include a focus on collocations – usually called 'phrases' in textbooks – that goes beyond efforts to make these more salient in input texts. For example, many contemporary textbooks contain worksheets with exercises on selected expressions where learners are asked to perform operations such as completing partially given expressions in gapped sentences, matching words from jumbled lists so as to establish accurate word partnerships, and various other exercise formats that all require the learner to distinguish between correct and incorrect word combinations (see, e.g., Lewis, 1997, pp. 89–106, and Lewis, 2000, pp. 88–116, for ample examples). It is assumed that doing such exercises will lead learners to make a mental note of which associations are correct and thus to be retained in memory, and which associations are wrong and thus to be dismissed and forgotten. It is textbook exercises founded on that assumption which the present chapter examines the merits of.

It is important to clarify that the focus of this chapter is on 'exercises', which we – following Lewis, (2000) – distinguish from 'activities'. The latter are of a more interactive nature and/or engage learners with longer stretches of discourse than the decontextualized sentences that are typical of exercise worksheets. Due to constraints of space, this chapter is confined to 'exercises'. A wide range of ideas for 'activities' with a focus on lexical phrases can be found, for example, in the aforementioned books by Lewis (1997; 2000) as well as in Lindstromberg & Boers (2008a) and Davis & Kryszewska (2012). While it is likely that the activities proposed in these publications are more engaging and plausibly bring about greater learning gains than the exercise formats we scrutinize in this chapter, it is worth noting that most of them are still awaiting empirical validation as well.

Horses for Courses

Exercises on lexical phrases can be distinguished by the purpose they intend to serve. One strand (including completion exercises) is intended to help learners *produce* well-formed expressions; others (including exercises where learners are asked to match phrases with their meanings) are intended to help learners *comprehend* expressions whose meaning is not straightforwardly transparent. Up to a point, the distinction that is sometimes made between idioms and collocations is helpful in this regard. Idioms are expressions such as *through thick and thin* and *spill the beans*, whose meaning is virtually impossible to infer by adding up the meanings of the constituent words. Collocations, by comparison, are deemed transparent in meaning because their overall meaning supposedly follows from adding up the meanings of the constituent words. If you understand *perform* and *a play*, then *perform a play* should pose no comprehension problems. The picture is blurred, however, by the fact that many expressions which seem straightforwardly transparent to a native speaker may yet be quite puzzling to a learner because constituent words are often not used in their primary sense. Unlike *performing a play*, *performing surgery* is not usually done for public entertainment. Unlike *paying a bill*, *paying one's last respects* (at a funeral) does not usually involve a financial transaction, and, unlike *running a marathon*, *running a business* does not often require fast bipedal motion. The primary meaning of *break* may suggest something negative (as in *breaking a glass* and *breaking a leg*), but *breaking the silence* is not necessarily a bad thing to do. As a consequence, expressions that linguists and native-speaker teachers might categorize as collocations rather than idioms because they seem transparent at first glance may yet be confusing for learners who rely too much on primary word meanings for interpretation. Research has indeed demonstrated that native-speaker teachers (and possibly also materials writers) find it hard to put themselves in the shoes of L2 learners when it comes to gauging the transparency of idioms and collocations (Boers & Webb, 2015). In this chapter, we will be looking exclusively at exercises intended to foster productive knowledge (e.g., knowledge that it is *make*, not *do*, which goes with *an effort*) and ask how well they serve that specific purpose. Whether the meaning of the phrases targeted in these exercises is always well understood by the textbook user is a question we will not further address here, but it would seem from the preceding discussion that it cannot be taken for granted.

Neither will we be able in this chapter to address the question of whether the phrases selected for targeting in textbook exercises are always ones that merit prioritization for serving learners' needs (Gouverneur, 2008; Martinez, 2013; Tsai, 2015). It is safe to say that the materials writer's decision to give explicit attention to a given collocation should be informed by at least the following considerations: (a) the usefulness of the expression and (b) the likelihood of the expression posing difficulty for the given learner. A good proxy for the relative usefulness of an expression is its frequency of use in contemporary discourse, and this can be gauged by consulting a relevant corpus. Corpus information also helps to gauge the degree of fixedness of expressions or the strength of word partnerships. When substitutions are possible (e.g., one can *do research* or *conduct research* or *carry out research*), there may be a smaller risk of 'erring' than in the case of very exclusive partnerships (e.g., *commit suicide*; *have a nightmare*) – all else being equal. To estimate the strength of a word partnership a corpus-based mutual information (MI) measure can be helpful. This measure represents the extent to which two words seek each others' company in discourse to the exclusion of others (e.g., Hunston, 2002). The higher the MI score, the stronger the collocation is. Word substitutions that cause deviations from the above-chance co-occurrences (e.g., *highly religious* instead of *deeply religious*) will tend to stand out as 'non-idiomatic'.

Estimating the likelihood that a given expression will pose a problem for a learner is probably a more intricate question. It is well documented that differences in the lexical makeup of near-equivalent expressions in the mother tongue (L1) and the target language (L2) are a major source of production errors (Nesselhauf, 2005; Yamashita & Jiang, 2010). For example, L1 interference may lead a Dutch learner of English to say *a big woman* to refer to *a tall woman*, a French learner of English to say she 'made a nightmare' and a Spanish learner who wishes to order *sparkling water* to ask for 'water with gas'. The problem for textbook writers – especially those whose books are marketed globally – in trying to anticipate what expressions merit attention on this ground is that cases of incongruence are bound to vary from one learner's L1 to another's.

Win Some, Lose Some

While a fair amount of research on the design and validation of exercises on figurative expressions (figurative idioms and phrasal verbs) is already available (see, e.g., Boers, 2013, for a review), little research-informed advice is as yet available for the design of textbook exercises on collocations. In what follows we review the few available studies from which we can begin to distil such advice.

The point of departure of this section is a study by Boers, Demecheleer, Coxhead and Webb (2014), who investigated the effectiveness of textbook exercises on verb–noun collocations (e.g., *make a suggestion*; *take a photo*; *pay attention*; *do someone a favor*, and *tell lies*). Exercises on verb–noun collocations were chosen as the object of that study because L2 verb–noun collocations have been shown to be a particularly problematic area for learners (Laufer & Waldman, 2011; Peters, 2016). It is typically the verb in such collocations that is prone to being substituted (e.g., ?*make a nightmare* instead of *have a nightmare*). It is not surprising that exposure alone is insufficient to prompt learners to adjust their choice of verb. Many of the verbs that figure in verb-noun collocations (e.g., *make*, *have*, and *do*) are high-frequency forms and are thus likely to be familiar to learners. Familiar words are known not to attract much attention, and thus their collocational behavior is likely to go unnoticed as well. Besides, these verbs lack semantic distinctiveness (they are 'de-lexicalized'), while it is the noun (e.g., *mistake*, *dream*, and *effort*) that carries most communicative value, and will therefore attract most attention as part of the interpretation process. Infelicitous collocations are not very likely to trigger feedback from an interlocutor during natural interaction either. For example, saying *I've done a terrible mistake* (instead of *I've made a terrible mistake*) will not cause misunderstanding and is thus unlikely to prompt a request for clarification – a request which could raise the learner's awareness of the unconventionality of the wording he or she used. Furthermore, substitutions of certain high-frequency verbs can go unnoticed in real-time speech because of phonological similarities (e.g., *make* and *take*). Given these many obstacles to incidental acquisition of verb–noun collocations, exercises that require learners to contemplate the choice of verb in those expressions would seem well justified. The question we ask here is whether the design and implementation of such exercises are optimally effective.

The majority of the exercises on verb–noun collocations in textbooks require learners to reunite broken-up phrases. In essence, these are matching exercises, where sets of verbs and noun phrases are given and the learner is asked to decide which goes with which to form the correct partnership. In the simplest format the task is to connect verbs (e.g., *pay*; *meet*; *make*; *have*; *do*) listed together on one side of a worksheet to their jumbled noun-partners listed on the opposite side (e.g., *a dream*; *a deadline*; *a contribution*; *homework*; *attention*). In a more contextualized variant, part of the collocation (usually the noun phrase) is incorporated in a sentence (e.g., *My husband just pretends to _____ attention when I talk to him*), and the learner is asked to choose, from a number of options, the word that fits the blank.

In a series of four trials with different cohorts of English as a second language (ESL) students (totaling 135 participants), Boers et al. (2014) tested the effectiveness of several variants of exercises that require learners to reassemble broken-up verb–noun collocations. Target collocations were selected from McCarthy and O'Dell's (2005) book for independent study of English collocations. The students' knowledge of these collocations was first gauged in a pre-test, which consisted of gapped sentences where the verb (e.g., *make*) was missing before a given noun phrase (e.g., *a suggestion*). As part of their coursework in class, the students were later given exercises on the same verb–noun collocations, and these exercises mimicked the formats commonly found in textbooks (e.g., matching verbs and nouns to form word partnerships). After finishing each exercise, the students were given corrective feedback. A post-test, which was identical to the pre-test, was administered two to three weeks later.

In all four trials, the comparisons of pre-test and post-test performance revealed only marginal learning gains. Overall post-test scores were typically only between 5% and 10% better than the pre-test scores. The pre-test to post-test comparison also revealed that the exercises created confusion in the students' minds about collocations which they had actually shown correct intuitions about in the pre-test. It was not uncommon for verbs that were correct in the pre-test to be substituted in the post-test by another verb that corresponded to one of the verbs in the set of options from which the students had been asked to choose in the exercise. For example, students would correctly supply the verb *take* to precede *an approach* in the pre-test, be asked to choose between *give, make,* and *take* for this item in the exercise, and in the post-test wrongly produce *give* to fill the blank before *an approach*.

It therefore looks as though exercises which invite students to contemplate different options for reassembling broken-up collocations carry the risk of engendering undesirable memory traces. These exercises in effect invite learners to consider the plausibility of verb–noun associations which they are subsequently expected to discard from memory (or to retain in memory with the label 'wrong' attached to them). The above findings suggest that this approach is not particularly helpful. Moreover, some of the wrong associations which the learner is invited to contemplate in an exercise and which may consequently linger in memory may be ones which this learner might never have considered had it not been for the exercise in the first place.

These observations also cast doubt on the effectiveness of certain exercise formats which were not included in the article by Boers et al. (2014), such as 'find the odd one out', where learners are asked to identify from a set of noun phrases (e.g., *a promise, a sacrifice, an accident,* and *a discovery*) the one which does *not* collocate with a given verb (e.g., *make*), and 'find the mistake' (in, e.g., *If you're not careful you're going to make an accident*). These exercises may perhaps serve the purpose of remedial teaching, in the case that the error tackled in the exercise item is actually manifested in the given learner's discourse. If, however, such exercises are used in the spirit of 'prevention is better than cure', then the aforementioned research findings certainly caution about the risk of negative side-effects when learners are asked to devote time and attention to infelicitous verb–noun combinations.

As already mentioned, an important part of the challenge for learners to discriminate between right and wrong verb–noun combinations and then retain only the right ones lies in the fact that many constituent words (in particular the verbs) are easily confusable because they lack semantic distinctiveness (e.g., *do* and *make*) or belong to the same semantic set (e.g., *say, speak, talk* and *tell*). A substantial body of research on the learning of single words has shown that studying sets of new words that are semantically related is harder than studying sets of semantically distinct words (e.g., Finkbeiner & Nicol, 2003; Erten & Tekin, 2008; Ishii, 2015). This finding can be extended to the learning of collocations as well. In an experiment concerning adjective–noun collocations, for example, Webb and Kagimoto (2011) found that studying collocations in sets that contain semantically similar words (e.g., *narrow* in *narrow escape* and *slim* in *slim chance*) is especially hard for learners, probably due to the effort that is required to block erroneous cross-associations of the synonymous words. The risk of such cross-item interference can be reduced by allowing time for an item to get entrenched in memory before a new, potentially interfering, item is introduced. By contrast, exercises which target multiple new collocations in one go are likely to increase the risk of interference, especially if they are made up of constituents that are not semantically distinct.

One must be hopeful, of course, that any confusion resulting from exercises such as the ones evaluated here will over time be cleared up for the learners as they encounter the targeted collocations again. However, textbooks do not tend to create many opportunities for re-engaging with the collocations that were 'covered' in exercises. We analyzed a corpus of 40 recent editions of EFL textbooks for their treatment of lexical phrases (including collocations, idioms and phrasal verbs) and found that only 23% of a total of 750 exercises include items which were already dealt with in a preceding activity in the textbook. And yet, the benefits of retrieval practice, i.e., recalling previously encountered or studied material, are well documented in memory research (Roediger & Karpicke, 2006; Karpicke & Roediger, 2008). Apparently, this line of memory research has not yet influenced L2 materials development for collocation learning much. This seems particularly odd in light of the contribution that phrasal competence (including collocation knowledge) is believed to make to fluency (e.g., Wood, 2010), as L2 users learn to accelerate their retrieval of phrases from memory as prefabricated chunks. It is hard to see how encounters with collocations in a one-off exercise could achieve this.

Don't Hazard a Guess

The study by Boers et al. (2014), which we gave a synopsis of above, also found that, when learners made a wrong choice in the exercise, this almost doubled the likelihood of them making a mistake also in the post-test, and this on items where their pre-test response had actually been correct. Together with the overall marginal learning gains, this suggests that the corrective feedback which the students received after the exercises was not very effective in having them 'learn from their mistakes'. This supports arguments in favor of learning practice in which the rate of error is deliberately kept minimal, an approach which is in keeping with a strand of memory research that has found errorless learning to be superior to learning through trial-and-error (Baddeley & Wilson, 1994). Recent work on deliberate word learning also suggests that practice which minimizes the risk of error is more efficient than practice which relies on the benefits of error correction (Warmington & Hitch, 2014).

One obvious way in which the risk of errors can be reduced in exercises on collocations is to ensure the learner has access to model input that they can mine for the correct answers. In that regard, the bleak picture presented in the study by Boers et al. (2014) could be objected to because no model input was given to the participants for them to consult as they did the exercises. On the other hand, our analysis of textbooks found this to be the way exercises on lexical phrases are commonly implemented: 54% of the exercises make no reference to any preceding input material, often leaving learners to blind guessing unless they already know the target items.

Is it then more judicious to avoid error-prone guessing and instead present learners first with exemplars of the target expressions before these are tackled in an exercise? In an effort to answer this question, Boers, Deconinck, and Stengers (2015) compared two implementations of the common exercise format where students are asked to supply the missing verbs of phrases in gapped sentences. In one implementation (the 'error-prone' procedure), the learners first tried to fill in the blanks and they were subsequently given the answer key to check their responses, and to cross out wrong responses and write down the correct response on their worksheets instead. In the other implementation (the 'error-free' procedure), the exercises were accompanied by a handout with two exemplars of each of the target expressions, which the learners were urged to read before filling the blanks on their worksheet. The latter approach resembles that taken in the books for independent study by McCarthy and O'Dell (2005; 2008), where exercises printed on the right-hand page are accompanied on the left-hand page by explanations and examples which the learner can consult while doing the exercises. The participants in Boers et al.'s (2015) experiment were 19 high-intermediate students of English. They were given four exercises each targeting a different set of 14 verb–noun collocations, spread over four lessons. They took a pre-test two weeks prior to doing the first exercise and a post-test two weeks after completing the fourth exercise. Like the exercises, the tests consisted of gapped sentences with the verb of the verb-noun collocations missing.

The pre-test to post-test comparison showed a mean gain of 20.5% for the students who did the exercises first and then received corrective feedback, compared to a mean gain of 36% for the students who were given exemplars and thus avoided writing down wrong responses in the exercises. This overall outcome needs to be qualified, however, because it matters whether a student supplies the correct response in an error-prone exercise on collocations. The students in the 'error-prone' condition occasionally supplied correct responses in the exercises on items where they had failed in the pre-test, and these correct exercise responses were particularly well remembered in the post-test: 73%. However, when these students made a wrong choice in the exercise, the corrective feedback appeared largely ineffective, because only 16.5% of incorrect exercise responses were followed by correct responses in the post-test. It thus looks as though positive feedback (i.e., confirmation of the correct answer) fostered retention of the correct form, while negative feedback (i.e., correction of the wrong answer) usually failed to entrench the correct form in memory. All this suggests that implementing collocation exercises in a way that generates errors and relies on the power of corrective feedback may not be an optimal use of learners' time.

Apart from the scenario where students in the error-prone condition sup-plied correct exercise responses, the exemplar-based procedure for completing the exercises appeared more conducive to learning. That having been said, the mean pre-test to post-test gain (i.e., 36%) indicates that this exemplar-based procedure does not work wonders either. This is not entirely surprising, for at least two rea-sons. One is the learning burden. Roughly half of the collocations in each of the 14-item exercises were not yet familiar to the learners and this may have left too many novel items to be retained in memory. The extent to which it is possible for textbook authors to estimate users' prior knowledge of lexical phrases targeted in a given exercise in order to strike an appropriate balance is an underexplored area of investigation. In any case, what needs to be conceded here is that the sets of exercises comprised more items than is typical of textbooks, where, accord-ing to our corpus analysis, it is uncommon for more than ten phrases to be tar-geted in one exercise. The second explanation for the less-than-dramatic learning gain observed in the exemplar-modelled, error-free exercise procedure lies in the non-challenging nature of the exercise. Research suggests that direct copying (i.e., with the to-be-copied material available in your field of vision) is too shallow an operation to leave strong memory traces (Kang, 2010; Stengers, Deconinck, Boers, & Eyckmans, 2016). It is thus quite plausible that the exemplar-based procedure required too little 'engagement' (Schmitt, 2008) on the part of the students. This may well be the challenge for designing exercises on collocations that 'work' – minimizing the risk of error and yet ensuring sufficient engagement. We explore some possibilities in the next section.

A Balancing Act

Apart from the provision of exemplars to steer students clear of errors in colloca-tion exercises, several other options spring to mind, possibly ones that present a slightly greater challenge to the learner but that still prevent the formation of erroneous word associations. One option is to give learners a more active role by asking them to look for the required information themselves, for example by referring them to collocation dictionaries (Komuro, 2009) or online corpus-based resources (Chen, 2011; Gao, 2011). In a similar vein, students may first be asked to explore the contextualized use of collocations in an actual text before target-ing these collocations in an exercise. The exercise can then serve the purpose of retrieval practice and consolidate knowledge rather than confront learners with lacunae and deficiencies in their resources. Encountering the phrases in discourse first may also provide better opportunities for learners to appreciate the semantics and pragmatic functions of the expressions.

A second option for reducing the risk of error is to design exercises where learners are given a set of *intact* collocations (e.g., *draw conclusions*) to choose from to complete gapped sentences (e.g., *Let's not _____ yet before we've heard all the facts*). In the majority of textbook exercises on lexical phrases intended to foster 'productive' knowledge, the collocations are broken up and learners are asked to reassemble them or to supply the missing pieces. The potential advantage of presenting intact collocations instead for students to work with in an exercise is that the constituents of the collocations are less likely to get substituted (e.g., a student who is presented with the intact phrase *make a mess* and is asked to look for a gapped sentence where this phrase belongs is not very likely to write down *?do a mess* instead). A disadvantage may be that the learner's attention is not necessarily directed to the precise lexical makeup of the collocation. Recall that in many collocations one of the constituents is a stronger cue for meaning than the other. For example, the word *truth* is probably sufficient as a cue for a learner to match the collocation *tell the truth* with the gapped sentence *They're going to find out sooner or later, so why not _____ now?* As a result, the learner may not pay much attention to the choice of verb and still produce, e.g., *?say the truth* on a later occasion, despite having supplied the correct response in the exercise. Part of the study by Boers et al. (2014), which we reviewed above, actually included an evaluation of this exercise format where learners are asked to match intact collocations with gapped sentences. Although the results were rather mixed, at least there were fewer signs of confusion ensuing from doing the exercises (i.e., correct pre-test responses stayed correct in the post-test).

An adaptation of gap-fill exercises, the effectiveness of which has not yet been put to the test, (as far as we know) is to give hints in the exercise items so as to reduce the risk of error and yet preserve a minimal degree of engagement on the part of the learners. A straightforward means is to provide the onset of missing words (e.g., *She's too shy to m_____ any contributions to discussions in the classroom*). Using parts of the target words as cues in gap-fill exercises is a technique that could possibly also serve to increase the salience of particular sound patterns that have the potential to make phrases memorable. A sound pattern that has been found to be particularly conspicuous in English phraseology (and in the phraseology of other Germanic languages) is alliteration (i.e., the inter-word repetition of word-initial phonemes in phrases such as *a slippery slope, time will tell, make a mess, cause a commotion, face the facts, cut corners,* and *life-long learning*). According to counts in the *Macmillan English Dictionary for Advanced Learners* (Rundell, 2007), alliteration is manifested in over 12% of English multi-word expressions overall (Boers & Lindstromberg, 2009, pp. 114–115). Counts in dictionaries devoted specifically to lexical phrases, such as *Collins Cobuild Dictionary of Idioms* (Sinclair, 2002), reveal that 17% of English idioms alliterate (e.g., *through thick and thin, beat about the bush, on the back burner, from pillar to post*). Some segments of the English phrasal repertoire show an even greater abundance of alliterative phrases. For example, over a third of binomial phrases (e.g., *black and blue, dim and distant, part and parcel*) and standardized similes (e.g., *good as gold; hot as hell; dead as a dodo*) alliterate. Pointing out the presence of alliteration in lexical phrases such as compounds (e.g., *health hazard* and *credit crunch*) and collocations (e.g., *private property* and *to wage war*) has been shown to help language learners remember these expressions relatively well (Boers, Lindstromberg, & Eyckmans, 2014a; Lindstromberg & Boers, 2008b). It should not be difficult to signal (e.g., by means of typographic enhancement) the presence of alliteration in collocations that are targeted in the kinds of exercises that we have taken a critical look at in this chapter, and thus to unlock the mnemonic potential that such a sound pattern holds. Rhyme (e.g., *take a break* and *brain drain*) and near-rhyme (e.g., *small talk* and *high time*) could be exploited in the same way to make the lexical phrases that manifest these patterns more memorable (Boers, Lindstromberg, & Eyckmans, 2014b; Lindstromberg & Boers, 2008c). The latter sound patterns may be particularly exploitable in the case of languages where these patterns are comparatively prevalent. This is likely to hold for languages with word-final stress (e.g., French), for instance.

Conclusions and Perspectives

Overall, our evaluation of textbook exercises on collocations suggests that there is little ground for pinning one's hopes on their power as instruments for learning *new* collocations. We have seen that, unless the collocations are already known by the learner, the task of deciding which words form partnerships – while potentially serving a useful awareness-raising purpose – often fails to establish the desired partnerships in the learner's mental lexicon. Exercise formats and their implementation that entail a high risk of the learner making mistakes while doing the exercise appear particularly prone to unwanted side-effects.

If it is nevertheless deemed worth including such exercises in a textbook, they would seem better suited as instruments to *consolidate* knowledge of collocations which the learner has already engaged with before. That having been said, it remains a possibility, of course, that future research will indicate that the exercise formats that we have examined in this chapter might not be optimal instruments even for that purpose. Decontextualized, discrete-point exercises – while providing the possibility of reviewing a relatively large number of lexical units in a short time – may never be a substitute for more genuine communicative practice, where learners incorporate (and evaluate the appropriateness of) learned phrases in their own discourse to express their own messages. An empirical evaluation of the effectiveness of such more genuine communicative activities should be high on the applied linguists' to-do list.

References

Baddeley A., & Wilson B.A. (1994). When implicit learning fails: Amnesia and the problem of error elimination. *Neuropsychologia, 32*, 53–68.

Boers, F. (2013). Cognitive linguistic approaches to second language vocabulary: Assessment and integration. *Language Teaching: Surveys and Studies, 46*, 208–224.

Boers, F., & Lindstromberg, S. (2009). *Optimizing a lexical approach to instructed second language acquisition*. Basingstoke, UK: Palgrave Macmillan.

Boers, F. & Lindstromberg, S. (2012). Experimental and intervention studies on formulaic sequences in a second language. *Annual Review of Applied Linguistics, 32*, 83–110.

Boers, F., & Webb, S. (2015). Gauging the semantic transparency of idioms: Do natives and learners see eye to eye? In R. Heredia & A. Cieslicka (Eds.), *Bilingual figurative language processing* (pp. 368–392). Cambridge: Cambridge University Press.

Boers, F., Deconinck, J., & Stengers, H. (2015). Error-prone and error-free exercises on verb–noun collocations. Paper presented at *EuroSLA 25*, Aix-en-Provence, 26–29 August, 2015.

Boers, F., Lindstromberg, S., & Eyckmans, J. (2014a). Is alliteration mnemonic without awareness-raising? *Language Awareness, 23*, 291–303.

Boers, F., Lindstromberg, S., & Eyckmans, J. (2014b). When does assonance make L2 lexical phrases memorable? *The European Journal of Applied Linguistics and TEFL, 3*, 93–107.

Boers, F., Demecheleer, M., Coxhead, A., & Webb, S. (2014). Gauging the effects of exercises on verb–noun collocations. *Language Teaching Research, 18*, 54–74.

Boers, F., Eyckmans, J., Kappel, J., Stengers, H., & Demecheleer, H. (2006). Formulaic sequences and perceived oral proficiency: Putting a lexical approach to the test. *Language Teaching Research, 10*, 245–261.

Chen, H. (2011). Developing and evaluating a web-based collocation retrieval tool for EFL students and teachers. *Computer Assisted Language Learning, 24*, 59–76.

Craik, F. I. M., & Tulving, E. (1975). Depth of processing and the retention of words in episodic memory. *Journal of Experimental Psychology: General, 104*, 268–294.

Davis, P., & Kryszewska, H. (2012). *The company words keep: Lexical chunks in language teaching*. Peaslake, UK: Delta Publishing.

Ellis, N.C., Simpson-Vlach, R., & Maynard, C. (2008). Formulaic language in native and second language speakers: Psycholinguistics, corpus linguistics, and TESOL. *TESOL Quarterly, 42*, 375–396.

Erten, İ.H., & Tekin, M. (2008). Effects on vocabulary acquisition of presenting new words in semantic sets versus semantically unrelated sets. *System, 36*, 407–22.

Eyckmans, J., Boers, F., & Stengers, H. (2007). Identifying chunks: Who can see the wood for the trees? *Language Forum, 33*, 85–100.

Finkbeiner, M., & Nicol, J. (2003). Semantic category effects in second language word learning. *Applied Psycholinguistics, 24*, 369–383.

Forsberg, F. (2010). Using conventional sequences in L2 French. *IRAL, 48*, 25–51.

Gao, Z. M. (2011). Exploring the effects and use of a Chinese-English parallel concordancer. *Computer Assisted Language Learning, 24*, 255–275.

Gouverneur, C. (2008). The phraseological patterns of high-frequency verbs in advanced English for general purposes: A corpus-driven approach to EFL textbook analysis. In F. Meunier & S. Granger (Eds.), *Phraseology in foreign language learning and teaching* (pp. 223–246). Amsterdam: John Benjamins.

Hunston, S. (2002). *Corpora in applied linguistics*. Cambridge: Cambridge University Press.

Isshi, T. (2015). Semantic connection or visual connection: Investigating the true source of confusion. *Language Teaching Research, 19*, 712–722.

Kang, S. H. K. (2010). Enhancing visuospatial learning: The benefit of retrieval practice. *Memory & Cognition, 38*, 1009–1017.

Karpicke, J. D., & Roediger, H. L., III (2008). The critical importance of retrieval for learning. *Science, 319*, 966–968.

Jones, M., & Haywood, S. (2004). Facilitating the acquisition of formulaic sequences: An exploratory study. In N. Schmitt (Ed.), *Formulaic sequences* (pp. 269–300). Amsterdam: John Benjamins.

Komuro, Y. (2009). Japanese learners' collocation dictionary retrieval performance. In A. Barfield & H. Gyllstad (Eds.), *Researching collocations in another language: Multiple perspectives* (pp. 86–98). Basingstoke, UK: Palgrave Macmillan.

Laufer, B., & Waldman, T. (2011). Verb–noun collocations in second language writing: A corpus analysis of learners' English. *Language Learning, 61*, 647–672.

Lewis, M. (1993). *The lexical approach*. Hove, UK: Language Teaching Publications.

Lewis, M. (1997). *Implementing the lexical approach*. Hove, UK: Language Teaching Publications.

Lewis, M. (Ed.) (2000). *Teaching collocation*. Hove, UK: Language Teaching Publications.

Li, J., & Schmitt, N. (2010). The development of collocation use in academic texts by advanced L2 learners: A multiple case study approach. In D. Wood (Ed.), *Perspectives on formulaic language: Acquisition and communication* (pp. 22–46). New York, NY: Continuum.

Lindstromberg, S., & Boers, F. (2008a). *Teaching chunks of language*. Rum, Austria: Helbling Languages.

Lindstromberg, S., & Boers, F. (2008b). The mnemonic effect of noticing alliteration in lexical chunks. *Applied Linguistics, 29*, 200–222.

Lindstromberg, S., & Boers, F. (2008c). Phonemic repetition and the learning of lexical chunks: The mnemonic power of assonance. *System, 36*, 423–436.

Martinez, R. (2013). A framework for the inclusion of multi-word expressions in ELT. *ELT Journal, 67*, 184–198.

McCarthy, M., & O'Dell, F. (2005). *English collocations in use: Intermediate*. Cambridge: Cambridge University Press.

McCarthy, M., & O'Dell, F. (2008). *English collocations in use: Advanced*. Cambridge: Cambridge University Press.

Morris, C. D., Bransford, J. D., & Franks, J. J. (1977). Levels of processing versus transfer appropriate processing. *Journal of Verbal Learning and Verbal Behavior, 16*, 519–533.

Nesselhauf, N. (2005). *Collocations in a learner corpus*. Amsterdam: John Benjamins.

Nattinger, J. R. & DeCarrico, J. S. (1992). *Lexical phrases and language teaching*. Oxford: Oxford University Press.

Peters, E. (2009). Learning collocations through attention-drawing techniques: A qualitative and quantitative analysis. In A. Barfield & H. Gyllstad (Eds.), *Researching collocations in another language: Multiple perspectives* (pp. 194–207). Basingstoke, UK: Palgrave Macmillan.

Peters, E. (2012). Learning German formulaic sequences: The effect of two attention-drawing techniques. *Language Learning Journal, 40*, 65–79.

Peters, E. (2016). The learning burden of collocations: The role of interlexical and intralexical factors. *Language Teaching Research, 20*, 113–138.

Prodromou, L. (2007). A sort of puzzle for English as a lingua franca. In B. Tomlinson (Ed.), *Language acquisition and development: Studies of learners of first and other languages* (pp. 225–246). London: Continuum.

Roediger, H. L. III, & Karpicke, J. D. (2006). The power of testing memory: Basic research and implications for educational practice. *Perspectives on Psychological Science, 1*, 181–210.

Rundell, M. (Ed.) (2007). *Macmillan English dictionary for advanced learners*, (2nd ed.). Oxford: Macmillan.

Schmidt, R. W. (2001). Attention. In P. Robinson (Ed.), *Cognition and second language instruction* (pp. 3–32). Cambridge: Cambridge University Press.

Schmitt, N. (2008). Instructed second language vocabulary learning. *Language Teaching Research, 12*, 329–363.

Sinclair, J. (1991). *Corpus, concordance, collocation*. Oxford: Oxford University Press.

Sinclair, J. (Ed.) (2002). *Collins Cobuild dictionary of idioms* (2nd ed.). Glasgow: Harper Collins.

Stengers, H., Deconinck, J., Boers, F., & Eyckmans, J. (2016). Does copying idioms promote their recall? *Computer Assisted Language Learning, 29*, 289–301.

Tsai, K-J. (2015). Profiling the collocation use in ELT textbooks and learner writing. *Language Teaching Research, 19*, 723–740.

Warmington, M., & Hitch, G. J. (2014). Enhancing the learning of new words using an errorless learning procedure: Evidence from typical adults. *Memory, 22*, 582–594.

Webb, S., & Kagimoto, E. (2011). Learning collocations: Do the number of collocates, position of the node word, and synonymy affect learning? *Applied Linguistics, 32,* 259–276.

Webb, S., J., Newton, A., & Chang, C.-S. (2013). Incidental learning of collocation. *Language Learning, 63,* 91–120.

Wood, D. (2010). *Formulaic language and second language speech fluency: Background, evidence and classroom applications.* New York: Continuum.

Wray, A. (2002). *Formulaic language and the lexicon.* Cambridge: Cambridge University Press.

Yamashita, J., & Jiang, N. (2010). L1 influence on the acquisition of L2 collocations: Japanese ESL users and EFL learners acquiring English collocations. *TESOL Quarterly, 44,* 647–668.

10

WHAT GRAMMAR ACTIVITIES DO ELT WORKBOOKS FOCUS ON?

Sasan Baleghizadeh, Elnaz Goldouz and Mehrdad Yousefpoori-Naeim

Introduction

Teaching and learning grammar have always been one of the commonest issues to focus on among English language teaching (ELT) researchers and professionals. The question of whether grammar should be taught has been a controversial debate among many researchers, and there have been many arguments for and against grammar teaching. Some applied linguists, including Krashen (1981), believe that language should be acquired through natural exposure and that there is no need to teach grammar explicitly because it only contributes to the growth of declarative knowledge rather than the procedural ability to use the target forms. Similar arguments were made regarding Universal Grammar (UG), which focused on the fact that if UG is available to second language (L2) learners, then there is no need for formal instruction, and like first language (L1) learners, they can learn grammatical forms through receiving input (Cook, 1991; Schwartz, 1993). As Krashen (1981) and Corder (1967) asserted, learners can follow their own built-in syllabus in order to acquire target forms as long as they receive comprehensible input. In addition, according to Richards (2002), with the advent of the communicative approach, focusing on grammatical activities such as drills and mechanical practice diminished and was supplanted by fluency-centered activities that highlight the need for negotiation of meaning and information sharing in the classroom. Thus, the students' needs for grammar are determined by their performance on fluency-based activities rather than a grammatical syllabus. As Truscott (1996, 1998) suggests, satisfactory results from form-focused instruction are obtained from tests that examine explicit metalinguistic knowledge, while learners are not able to use those structures in spontaneous communication. However, over the last few decades, the status of grammar has undergone a major change, and there is a great body of research on form-focused instruction which indicates that incorporating formal instruction into language learning needs to be emphasized (Bygate, Skehan, & Swain, 2001;

Bialystok, 1990, 1994; DeKeyser, 1998). Nassaji and Fotos (2011), for example, have asserted that the role of teaching grammar is essential to language pedagogy and Schmidt (2001) has argued that formal and conscious attention to form is a necessary condition in language learning. He strongly believes that:

> The concept of attention is necessary in order to understand virtually every aspect of second language acquisition (SLA), including the development of interlanguages (ILs) over time, variation within IL at particular points in time, the development of L2 fluency, the role of individual differences such as motivation, aptitude and learning strategies in L2 learning, and the ways interaction, negotiation for meaning, and all forms of instruction contribute to language learning.
>
> *(p. 3)*

Despite the enormous amount of support for formal instruction, traditional approaches to grammar teaching are in opposition to the trend of current research on explicit instruction, which incorporates an element of communication as well. As Ellis, Basturkmen, and Loewen (2002) pointed out:

> While there is substantial evidence that focus-on-forms instruction results in learning as measured by discrete-point language tests (e.g., the grammar test in the TOEFL), there is much less evidence to show that it leads to the kind of learning that enables learners to perform the targeted form in free oral production (e.g., in a communicative task).
>
> *(p. 421)*

The History of the Development of Grammar Materials

Historically, grammar instruction was limited to focusing on language forms and structures with little need to focus on meaningful communication. Many grammar-based methods focus on this view of grammar instruction. According to Nassaji and Fotos (2011), various methods that emerged after the Grammar Translation and the Audio-Lingual Methods, despite some differences regarding their syllabuses, were all grammar-based: Oral Method, Situational Method, Reading Method, Total Physical Response, and Silent Way.

The traditional methods of grammar teaching had nothing to do with the communicative needs of learners. As Pennington (2002) noted, "they are therefore entirely inappropriate to the practical communicative needs of today's language students" (p. 77). Nevertheless, with the advent of Communicative Language Teaching (CLT), there was a shift away from a pure focus on forms, and instead the need to focus on meaning and language use in context was realized. However, in contrast to the traditional approaches that gave rise to purely grammatical forms, the earlier approaches to CLT were totally communicative without focusing on linguistic forms. According to Nassaji and Fotos (2011), the main defect of this approach during the 1970s and 1980s was that the learners were not able to make accurate output despite many years of studying. However, the current view of the communicative approach is that there is a need also to focus on linguistic features, as emphasized in L2 task-based teaching. A new approach called "focus on form" (Long, 1991) lays emphasis on drawing learners' attention to form during the context of communicative interactions. Therefore, both purely communicative and traditional grammar-based approaches to teaching that had their own shortcomings have resulted in a well-balanced focus-on-form approach.

These different approaches to grammar instruction have led many materials writers to adopt different points of view, and according to the level of the learners and the context, put a higher or lower emphasis on grammatical rules, on communication, or on a parallel focus on form. Therefore, the argument is over the need to focus on grammatical activities in a specific context and the balance between fluency and accuracy. Focus-on-form instruction as featured in task-based approaches (e.g., Long & Robinson, 1998), differs from grammar-based approaches in that learners develop linguistic forms in the context of meaningful communication, though according to Skehan (1996), there is a distinction between the strong and the weak versions of the task-based instruction:

> A strong form sees tasks as the basic unit of teaching and drives the acquisition process. A weak form sees tasks as a vital part of language instruction but is embedded in a more complex pedagogical context. Tasks are necessary, but may be preceded by focused instruction, and after use, may be followed by focused instruction that is contingent on task performance.
>
> *(p. 39)*

In other words, it is the weak version of the tasks that highlights the need to focus on specific target structures.

Grammar and Textbooks

Effective grammar materials need to possess many features. As noted earlier, based on the current approaches to grammar, there is a strong need to prioritize various dimensions of teaching grammar. However, despite the paucity of models and specific frameworks for developing grammar materials, there is a popular framework by Larsen-Freeman (2001), which focuses on three interrelated aspects of grammar, namely form, meaning and use, which could serve as a useful model for many materials writers to adopt and follow. This framework along with its three interrelated dimensions, suggests that in addition to the form of a target grammatical structure, other dimensions such as meaning (semantics) and use (pragmatics) should receive equal attention.

As for the analysis of textbooks in terms of teaching grammar, the study by Nitta and Gardner (2005) elaborates on the distinction between practice and consciousness-raising (CR) activities in nine ELT coursebooks. According to their findings, each book was essentially based on a presentation-practice approach to grammar teaching, both inductive and deductive approaches were seen in the presentation stages followed by practicing tasks, and there was little evidence of focused communication tasks. There have been many objections to this focus on grammar practice. Ellis (1993), for example, advocates replacing practice with CR tasks and Ellis and Gaies (1998) emphasize the need to include discovery-type tasks in order to raise learners' consciousness about grammar. Likewise Baleghizadeh (2012b) puts a great emphasis on CR activities and argues that if grammar is a must in English classes, there should be a considerable role for CR activities. As he puts it, "CR activities are valuable for language learning in that they encourage learners to discover grammatical rules for themselves, with the teacher as a source of support rather than as the sole source of knowledge" (p.115).

A Framework for Analyzing the Grammatical Components of Textbooks

In this study, the framework proposed by Baleghizadeh (2012a) was adopted to focus on grammatical activities in all levels of three series of ELT workbooks. The aim of the study was to discover which dimension of grammar received more attention in grammatical activities and which dimension needs to receive higher or equal importance compared to the other dimensions in ELT workbooks. Figure 10.1, which shows two dimensions of fluency–accuracy and reproductive–creative activities, appears in the form of a grid.

This grid is based on the difference between fluency and accuracy and another dimension that distinguishes reproductive from creative activities (Nunan, 1999).

The difference between fluency and accuracy is an important issue in language performance. The distinction between fluency (speaking at a normal speed with very

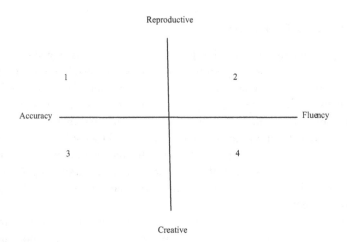

FIGURE 10.1 Framework for developing grammar materials (Baleghizadeh, 2012a, p. 63)

little hesitation, repetition, or self correction) and accuracy (speaking without making obvious grammatical mistakes) as well as deciding which one should be prioritized has always been a controversial issue among language teaching researchers. In addition to the distinction between fluency and accuracy, grammatical activities need to be analyzed in terms of being creative or reproductive. Nunan (1999) analyzed the 3P instructional cycle and suggested that although such tasks are necessary for learners to employ phonological elements and syntactic patterns, there should be opportunities for learners to use language creatively. He defines creativity as "the opportunity to recombine familiar language elements in new and unfamiliar ways" (p. 241).

The proposed framework appears in four cells and offers a model that represents accuracy-centered and fluency-centered reproductive activities in the first and second cells. The third and fourth cells deal with accuracy-centered and fluency-centered creative activities. A brief description of the four cells follows.

Accuracy-Centered Reproductive Activities

Most grammar activities in coursebooks belong to this cell. According to many scholars (e.g., Ellis, 2009; Ur, 2012), these activities are out-of-context grammar practice in the sense that they do not foster the development of any real-life communication by the learners. In addition, they are totally prescribed grammatical structures transmitted from teachers to learners. Examples of these types of activities according to Ur (2012) are discrete-point mechanical gap-fill, multiple choice, sentence completion, and matching tasks. The following activity is an example of a discrete item gap-fill by Ur (2012).

1. A car is .... than a bicycle. (fast)

2. Chinese is .... than English. (difficult)

3. A lion is .... than a dog. (big)

Fluency-Centered Reproductive Activities

This type of activity differs from the previous cell in that it has an element of fluency rather than accuracy. However, the activities are similar in the sense that they are reproductive and involve learners in manipulating a set of specific structures. According to Ellis (2009), they are focused tasks that provide learners with the opportunity to speak in the classroom, using a specific structure. A sample activity belonging to this cell could be:

Discuss what you would do in the following situations:

1. What would you do if you were kidnapped?

2. What would you do if you were a millionaire?

3. What would you do if you were handicapped?

Accuracy-Centered Creative Activities

According to Baleghizadeh (2012a), this cell requires learners to produce accurate sentences through creative activities. Typical activities of this category are grammaticization tasks and grammar dictations.

In the following grammaticization activity, learners are provided with some stories and are required to write headlines so as not to lose the sense of the stories:

> Now, write headlines for these stories. How short can you make them, without losing the sense of the story?
>
> 1.   The government has announced plans to cut spending on the military.
>
> 2.   The captain of a tanker involved in an oil spill off the French coast has been found guilty of negligence.
>
> (From Uncovering Grammar [Thornbury, 2001])

Another type of accuracy-centered creative activity is grammar dictation or dictogloss. Wajnryb (1990) defines dictogloss as follows:

> Dictogloss is a task-based procedure designed to help language-learning students towards a better understanding of how grammar works on a text basis. It is designed to expose where their language-learner shortcomings (and needs) are, so that teaching can be directed more precisely towards these areas.
>
> (p.6)

As Baleghizadeh (2012a) argues, dictogloss is a constructive activity in which learners are asked to produce an accurate version of a text by reconstructing it as it is read to them. The nature of this activity differs from reconstructive activities in which learners need to manipulate a set of grammatical sentences. In this type of accuracy- centered creative activity, they need to create their own sentences, and according to Nunan (1999), to produce language in a new and unfamiliar way.

Fluency-Centered Creative Activities

As mentioned earlier, this type of activity includes focused tasks in which learners are required to produce language while using a specific structure. On the one hand, these activities differ from cell 2 in that they are creative, and as Baleghizadeh (2012a) mentions, they do not explicitly require learners to use a specific grammatical structure, but the learners themselves need to recognize which linguistic feature to use. On the other hand, they are fluency-centered, as they encourage learners to use language communicatively.

The following activity requires learners to use the comparative structure and clauses of reason:

Look at the list below. Work with a partner and decide which ones are the five most exciting sports. Be ready to explain why.

Swimming   Soccer   Tennis

Basketball   Wrestling   Volleyball

Fencing   Hockey   Diving

(From Baleghizadeh, 2012a, p.64)

Methodology

The Workbooks

Three series of general English workbooks ranging from beginner to advanced levels were used in this study and were analyzed based on the framework proposed

TABLE 10.1 The first series used in the study (*Interchange* workbooks)

Title	Authors	Publisher	Year	Level
Interchange Intro (3rd ed.)	Jack C. Richards	Cambridge University Press	2005	Beginner
Interchange 1 (3rd ed.)	Jack C. Richards, J. Hull, and S. Proctor	Cambridge University Press	2005	Elementary
Interchange 2 (3rd ed.)	Jack C. Richards, J. Hull, and S. Proctor	Cambridge University Press	2005	Intermediate
Interchange 3 (3rd ed.)	Jack C. Richards	Cambridge University Press	2005	Upper-intermediate
Passages 1 and 2	Jack C. Richards and Chuck Sandy	Cambridge University Press	2008	Advanced

TABLE 10.2 The second series used in the study (*Top-Notch* workbooks)

Title	Author	Publisher	Year	Level
Top-Notch Fundamentals A and B	Joan Saslow and Allen Ascher	Longman	2013	Fundamentals
Top-Notch: 1A and B	Joan Saslow and Allen Ascher	Longman	2013	Elementary
Top-Notch: 2A and B	Joan Saslow and Allen Ascher	Longman	2013	Pre-intermediate
Top-Notch: 3A and B	Joan Saslow and Allen Ascher	Longman	2013	Upper-intermediate
Top-Notch Summit A and B	Joan Saslow and Allen Ascher	Longman	2013	Advanced

TABLE 10.3 The third series used in the study (*Headway* workbooks)

Title	Author	Publisher	Year	Level
Headway	John and Liz Soars	Oxford University Press	1991	Elementary
Headway	John and Liz Soars	Oxford University Press	1991	Pre-Intermediate
Headway	John and Liz Soars	Oxford University Press	1991	Intermediate
Headway	John and Liz Soars	Oxford University Press	1991	Upper-Intermediate
Headway	John and Liz Soars	Oxford University Press	1991	Advanced

by Baleghizadeh (2012a). The rationale behind adopting these books was the popularity of the books at their own time and their well-known authors. In Table 10.1, the list of the selected workbooks is provided.

Procedure

All the grammatical activities in all the units of the workbooks were examined. The review part of each unit was ignored. This process led to the coverage and analysis of almost all grammar modules of the workbooks. An additional grammar booster part, which appeared in one of the series, was also examined. The proportion of different grammatical activities was different in each series. A grammatical activity was taken to mean anything that the learners were required to do in order to produce a set of accurate sentences, either creatively or reproductively. An attempt was made to focus on different activities labeled as grammatical activities that prioritized one of the four cells of accuracy-centered reproductive, fluency-centered reproductive, accuracy-centered creative, and fluency-centered creative. However, it should be noted that some activities were not classified under a grammar heading and were distributed in other parts; those sections were also considered as grammar activities. Not surprisingly, there were no activities that focused on more than one dimension. In other words, there could not simultaneously be an activity that was based on two dimensions of "out of context" and "meaningful communication," other than those that focused on more than one dimension in specific questions that are clear for learners; these infrequent types of activities were considered as two-dimensional. Therefore, each dimension received its own attention in specific activities. In some workbooks, one special grammar activity includes two modules, each of which concerns two different dimensions; therefore, they were counted separately. At times, it was difficult for the researchers to reach a compromise over various activities. In analyzing the workbooks, a deliberate attempt was made to strive for consistency all over different grammatical activities.

Results and Discussion

As Table 10.4 shows, the number of activities found in each workbook series focusing on different dimensions along with their percentages was calculated. Based on the results, the number of grammatical activities in the *Headway* series is the highest,

TABLE 10.4 Number and frequency of grammatical activities in each workbook series

			Workbook series			Total
			Headway	Interchange	Top-Notch	
Activity	Cell 1	Frequency	423	343	417	1183
Types for		Percentage	84.3%	64.4%	72.0%	73.3%
each cell						
	Cell 2	Frequency	71	160	152	383
		Percentage	14.1%	30.0%	26.3%	23.7%
	Cell 3	Frequency	0	1	1	2
		Percentage	0%	0.2%	0.2%	0.1%
	Cell 4	Frequency	8	29	9	46
		Percentage	1.6%	5.4%	1.6%	2.9%
Total		Frequency	502	533	579	1614
		Percentage	100.0%	100.0%	100.0%	100.0%

compared to the other two series. With regard to the activities belonging to cell 1, this dimension receives the most attention in all of the series, compared to the other three, with cell 3 receiving the least attention in *Headway* of all the workbooks analyzed. When it comes to cell 1, the number of activities belonging to this dimension (accuracy-centered reproductive activities) in the *Headway* series exceeded the number of this kind of activity in the other two series. Fluency-centered reproductive activities received a considerable amount of attention in the *Interchange* series. With regard to the activities in cell 3 (accuracy-centered creative activities), there was no significant difference among the workbooks: In both *Top-Notch* and *Interchange* series, only one activity belonged to this cell and no grammatical activities were counted for the *Headway* series. Cell 2 received considerable attention in the *Interchange* series, and cell 4 also got the highest attention in this series, compared to the other two. The calculated chi-square was significant $X^2(6) = 63.7$, $p = .001$; therefore, the three surveyed workbook series were found to be different from one another. Figure 10.2 indicates the number of different activities of each dimension in the form of a bar chart.

Cells 1 and 2 (accuracy-centered and fluency-centered reproductive activities) were the most prominent cells found in the workbooks; however, looking across the different levels of workbooks revealed that there was a trend for more accuracy-centered activities than fluency-centered ones at the beginning levels of the workbooks. Therefore, it is obvious that materials writers believe that as students start learning English, it is sufficient to have them focus on accuracy-centered reproductive activities. As they progress though, more fluency-centered activities need to be introduced to get them more familiar with structures in a meaningful context. This view is obviously against the current approach towards teaching grammar, which puts higher emphasis on the communicative needs of the learners from the beginning. As Pennington (2002) rightly asserted, traditional grammars would only highlight structures of the language they are going to describe; "they

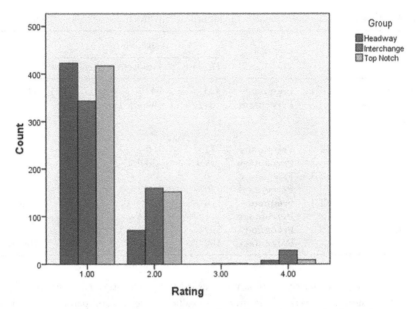

FIGURE 10.2 Bar chart representing the number of activities in each dimension

are therefore entirely inappropriate to the practical communicative needs of today's language students" (p. 77). This point of view is also in contrast to what Ellis (2009) believes regarding the predominance of developing implicit knowledge while not neglecting explicit knowledge; as he believes, irrespective of different positions on how implicit knowledge develops, "there is consensus that learners need the opportunity to participate in communicative activities to develop implicit knowledge. Thus, communicative tasks need to play a central role in instruction directed at implicit knowledge" (p. 214). However, as the results indicated, not only have fluency-centered activities in cells 2 and 4 been neglected but it was also observed that the number of accuracy-centered reproductive activities in non-communicative contexts was far greater than the fluency-centered ones.

With regard to cells 3 and 4, the results suggest that materials writers do not seem to provide learners with creative activities, whether fluency- or accuracy-centered. Although it is entirely beneficial for learners to recognize which grammatical structure to use in different contexts, in the three series of workbooks, except for a negligible number of activities in the *Interchange* series, there existed no activities belonging to this dimension, and for most of the activities analyzed, due to the particular structure for specific units or lessons, it was totally clear for learners which structure to use. For cell 3, accuracy-centered creative activities received almost no attention in any series. As mentioned earlier, the neglect of creativity in these three series is also subject to criticism; as in one of the successful language learning principles set forth by Ellis (2009), it is important to focus on free as well as controlled production. For the effectiveness of instruction, Norris and Ortega (2000) identified four types of measurement, one of which focuses on free constructed response (e.g., a communicative task). As they believe, this kind of measurement has the greatest effect in that it corresponds to the kind of language use that learners encounter outside the classroom, and these can be best elicited by means of tasks. However, the researchers in this study could not find many activities belonging to cell 4 throughout the three series. Therefore, we believe that more activities of the creative type would be necessary for learners in order to produce language successfully without being told which structure to use in advance.

In the case of accuracy-centered creative activities, only 1% of the activities of the three series focused on this cell. In the *Headway* series, none of the activities belonged to this dimension, and in the other two series, only one activity in each series could be considered as accuracy-centered creative. According to the bar chart, with regard to the within-group comparisons, when it comes to the *Headway* series, one can easily find that it is cell 1 (accuracy-centered reproductive activities) that receives considerable attention, compared to the other three dimensions. After that, cells 2, 4, and 3 received attention in diminishing order. The *Interchange* and *Top-Notch* series also followed the same pattern regarding the number of the activities in each cell. Regarding the between-group comparisons, cell 1 received the highest attention in *Headway*, less in *Top-Notch* and *Interchange*, respectively. Cell 2 gained a considerable amount of attention in *Interchange*, less in *Top-Notch* and least in *Headway*. For cell 3, in the *Top-Notch* and *Interchange* series, few activities were spotted; no activities were found in the *Headway* series for this cell. Finally, only the *Interchange* series paid some attention to cell 4 activities, compared to the other two series, which ignored activities of this cell. As previously highlighted, for many logical and widely accepted reasons, fluency-centered activities in a meaningful context need to receive a significant amount of attention; learners need to focus on grammatical features in meaningful contexts. According to Richards (2002), when learners are provided with communicative tasks, they are involved in the process of negotiation of meaning and they employ different strategies, such as "comprehension checks, confirmation checks, and clarification requests. These strategies lead to a gradual modification of learners' language output, which over time takes on more and more target-like features" (p. 37). Despite all the aforementioned evidence and reasoning regarding the importance of activities of this type, the results indicated that workbooks have a totally different perspective on the type of grammar activities they provide for learners. The researchers found no significant difference between the recently published series and the older ones – namely the new series of *Top-Notch* and the older version of *Headway* – in terms of focusing on accuracy–centered reproductive activities out of context.

Conclusion

This study surveyed three general English workbooks series with regard to different types of grammatical activities they give attention to. It was found that the workbooks mostly focus on accuracy-centered reproductive activities, then on fluency-centered reproductive activities, and finally on fluency-centered and accuracy-centered creative activities. This finding certainly has implications for materials writers and teachers, in that it broadens their views for laying more emphasis on fluency-centered and creative activities. By doing so, learners, especially those who learn English in EFL settings, would benefit from specific structures in meaningful contexts and also get the opportunity to gain a more comprehensive knowledge of grammatical structures. Moreover, if they are provided with creative activities, it would be a favorable opportunity for them to recognize the specific structure among the grammatical features they have previously been exposed to. In other words, they will not be limited to activities belonging to specific lessons and structures.

The obvious limitation of the present study is the limited sample size involved, particularly considering the four cells of grammatical structures at all different levels of the three workbook series. Future research is needed to focus on more series to better explore the proportion of different activities belonging to various cells. More importantly, this study focused on analyzing activities in global popular workbooks. Based on the framework used in this study, future research may compare grammatical activities in different students' books to see to what extent grammatical activities in students' books take advantage of different dimensions introduced in this study. Local workbooks and students' books could also be analyzed to find out whether, in EFL settings, there is any opportunity for learners to focus more on fluency-centered and creative activities.

References

Baleghizadeh, S. (2012a). A grammar grid. *Modern English Teacher, 21*(1), 62–65.

Baleghizadeh, S. (2012b). Grammatical syllabus and EFL textbooks: The need for consciousness-raising activities. *Per Linguam, 28*(1), 110–116.

Bialystok, E. (1990). The competence of processing: Classifying theories of second language acquisition. *TESOL Quarterly, 24*, 635–648.

Bialystok, E. (1994). Representation and ways of knowing: Three issues in second language acquisition. In N. Ellis (Ed.), *Explicit and implicit learning of languages* (pp. 549–569). London: Academic Press.

Bygate, M., Skehan, P., & Swain, M. (Eds.) (2001). *Researching pedagogic tasks: Second language learning, teaching and testing.* New York: Longman.

Cook, V. (1991). *Second language learning and language teaching.* London: Edward Arnold.

Corder, S. P. (1967). The significance of learners' errors. *International Review of Applied Linguistics, 5*, 161–169.

DeKeyser, R. (1998). Beyond focus on form: Cognitive perspectives on learning and practicing second language grammar. In C. Doughty & J. Williams (Eds.), *Focus on form in classroom second language acquisition* (pp. 42–63). New York: Cambridge University Press.

Ellis, R. (1993). Talking shop: Second language acquisition research: How does it help teachers? An interview with Rod Ellis. *ELT Journal, 47*(1), 3–11.

Ellis, R., & Gaies, S. (1998). *Impact grammar.* Hong Kong: Longman Addison Wesley.

Ellis, R. (2009). Task-based language teaching: Sorting out the misunderstandings. *International Journal of Applied Linguistics, 19*, 221–246.

Ellis, R., Basturkmen, H., & Loewen, S. (2002). Doing focus-on-form. *System, 30*, 419–432.

Krashen, S. (1981). *Second language acquisition and second language learning*. Oxford: Pergamon.

Larsen-Freeman, D. (2001). Teaching grammar. In M. Celce-Murcia (Ed.), *Teaching English as a second or foreign language* (3rd ed., pp. 251–266). Boston, MA: Heinle.

Long, M. (1991). Focus on form: A design feature in language teaching methodology. In K. DeBot, R. Ginsberge, & C. Kramsch (Eds.), *Foreign Language research in cross-cultural perspective* (pp.39–52). Amsterdam: John Benjamins.

Long, M. H., & Robinson, P. (1998). Focus on form: Theory, research, process. In C. Doughty & J. Williams (Eds.), *Focus on form in classroom SLA* (pp. 15–41). New York: Cambridge University Press.

Nassaji, H., & Fotos, S. (2011). *Teaching grammar in second language classrooms: Integrating form-focused instruction in communicative context*. New York: Routledge.

Nitta, R., & Gardner, S. (2005). Consciousness-raising and practice in ELT coursebooks. *ELT Journal, 59*(1), 3–13.

Norris, J. M., & Ortega, L. (2000). Effectiveness of L2 instruction: A research synthesis and quantitative meta-analysis. *Language Learning, 50*, 417–528.

Nunan, D. (1999). *Second language teaching and learning*. Boston, MA: Heinle & Heinle.

Pennington, M.C. (2002). Grammar and communication: New directions in theory and practice. In E. Hinkel & S. Fotos (Eds.), *New perspectives on grammar teaching in second language classrooms* (pp.77–98). Mahwah, NJ: Erlbaum.

Richards, J.C. (2002). Accuracy and fluency revisited. In E. Hinkel & S. Fotos (Eds.), *New perspectives on grammar teaching in second language classrooms* (pp. 35–50). Mahwah, NJ: Erlbaum.

Schmidt, R. W. (2001). Attention. In P. Robinson (Ed.), *Cognition and second language instruction* (pp. 3–32). Cambridge: Cambridge University Press.

Schwartz, B. (1993). On explicit and negative data effecting and affecting competence and linguistic behavior. *Studies in Second Language Acquisition, 15*, 147–163.

Skehan, P. (1996). A framework for the implementation of task-based instruction. *Applied Linguistics, 17*, 38–62.

Thornbury, S. (2001).*Uncovering grammar*. Oxford: Macmillan.

Truscott, J. (1996). The case against grammar correction in L2 writing classes. *Language Learning, 46*, 327–369.

Truscott, J. (1998). Noticing in second language acquisition: A critical review. *Second Language Research, 14*, 103–135.

Ur, P. (2012). Grammar teaching: Theory, practice and English teacher education. In J. Huttner, B. Mehlmauer-Larcher, S. Reichl, & B. Schiftner (Eds.), *Theory and practice in EFL teacher education: Bridging the gap* (pp. 83–100). Bristol: Multilingual Matters.

Wajnryb, R. (1990). *Grammar dictation*. Oxford: Oxford University Press.

11

COMPREHENSIBILITY AND COGNITIVE CHALLENGE IN LANGUAGE LEARNING MATERIALS

Freda Mishan

Introduction

Nowhere do second language acquisition (SLA) research and language learning materials design intersect more clearly than on the issue of 'comprehensibility'. The idea of providing input that is notionally 'comprehensible' (as conceived by Krashen, 1982, 1985) seems to have a common-sense appeal to teachers and materials writers. One of the aims of this chapter is to critically examine the notion to see how well it has stood the test of time, particularly in light of radically altered access to and relationship with language data in the digital age.

The chapter will examine the correlation between comprehensibility, comprehension and language acquisition, with reference to research by Gilmore (2007), Oh (2001) and others. We pursue the concept of 'comprehension' for the second part of the chapter, examining it in the context of Bloom's taxonomy of the cognitive domain (originally Bloom, 1956, revised version by Anderson & Krathwohl, 2001). Bloom's taxonomy represents comprehension (understanding) as not particularly cognitively demanding; it figures on the second lowest rung of the six-level classification. The work of Bloom and his successors has had tremendous influence in the sphere of education in general in drawing attention to the importance of promoting higher-order thinking to achieve effective learning. Yet this has never appeared to extend in any systematic way to language learning or language learning materials development, despite the recognized link between cognitive challenge and memory (e.g. Craik, 2002) which has implications for SLA, as I illustrate below. In this chapter, I therefore consider the influence of these two core concepts, the first from SLA, comprehensibility, and the second from education, Bloom's taxonomy of the cognitive domain, on the design of language learning materials. I argue for the importance of providing learners with the sort of cognitive stimulation and challenge that respects their intellects, and I propose a materials design 'checklist' based on Bloom's taxonomy which does this.

Comprehensibility

Krashen's original statement of (the second part of) the Input Hypothesis as 'we acquire by understanding language that contains structure a bit beyond our current level of competence ($i + 1$)' (Krashen, 1982, p.21), is probably one of the best-known SLA theories in language teaching. And thereby hangs the problem. This was a theory of SLA that was effectively 'transplanted' as a pedagogical concept (an error which Ellis warns us of; 'doubts exist as to whether the findings of SLA are sufficiently robust to warrant applications to language pedagogy' (Ellis, 2010, p. 34)). It was, arguably, misapplied or misinterpreted (over simplified) to equate 'comprehensibility' with linguistic 'simplification', exercising a disproportionate influence on pedagogy in the sense that 'comprehensibility' often appears to be the overriding criterion for selection and design of materials. In one study, Clavel-Arriotia and Fuster-Márquez (2014) calculated that around 90% of the authentic texts in a cross-section of six recent coursebooks at C1 and B2 level had been adapted/simplified to fit the level (and coursebook layout requirements). Bell and Gower, in their record of designing a so-called 'global' coursebook, note the difficulty of finding texts 'of the right length and level of comprehensibility' (2011, p.148). From the teacher's perspective, suiting coursebook to level is also a major consideration, ranking second of the 11 criteria for coursebook selection discussed in McGrath (2013, p.118). Preoccupation with this criterion can, furthermore, be at the expense of other essential criteria for SLA such as the one we examine later on, cognitive challenge, or affective factors, e.g. relevance, interest, appeal (which Krashen also recognized, conceptualizing an 'affective filter', e.g. 1982, for acquisition). Freeman's (2014) analysis of coursebook question types, for example, revealed affective response to be solicited mainly via the 'superficial' (2014, p.93) personal response-type question.

Alongside this, there are a number of other, even more serious reservations (à propos of the Comprehensibility Hypothesis), which we will discuss in turn. Most critically with regard to language teaching materials, we need to examine the correlation between *comprehension* and *acquisition*. Refining our terms somewhat may be helpful here, distinguishing 'comprehended' input (specifically, that which the learner has understood) from 'comprehensible' input (controlled by the input provider; Gass, 1988). If it is indeed the case that 'comprehended' input can become 'intake', i.e. the filtered input that is potentially available for acquisition, as posited within input/interaction models of SLA (see, for example, Gass, 1997), then we need to look at the ways in which input is rendered 'comprehensible'. If this is via 'modification' (simplification) as Krashen originally suggests (1982), we still need to examine (a) whether simplification (even) aids comprehension at all and (b) the quality of the input we are supplying. The final step in this critical analysis of the ramifications of the input hypothesis is its application to 21st-century digitally-adept language learners with their superior skills for dealing with non-comprehension, which we will look at further on.

We will look first at the identification of *comprehension* with *acquisition,* the perceived underlying 'fatal flaw' in the application of the comprehensible Input

Hypothesis to pedagogy. It has not gone unnoticed that much research in the area of what might loosely be called 'comprehensibility studies' seems to 'assume a causal link between comprehension and language acquisition' (Gilmore, 2007, p.110). Yet, 'the processes of comprehension and acquisition are not the same' as Sharwood Smith stresses, (1986; cited in Ellis, 2008, p. 251). Learners might understand input using primarily 'top-down processes' – utilizing contextual information and their own background knowledge – paying little attention to linguistic form, and quite possibly acquiring nothing new (Ellis, 2008, p. 251). Ellis synthesizes some of the early research thus: 'The research evidence relating to the relationship between comprehension and acquisition is quite mixed. Much of the early research was correlational in nature and therefore cannot be said to demonstrate that comprehensible input *causes* acquisition' (italics in the original) (Ellis, 2008, pp. 248–9). Furthermore, summarizing Larsen-Freeman's 1983 research, Ellis adds; 'some L2 learning may take place without comprehensible input [such as information relating to the phonology of the L2] and, more importantly, comprehending input may not result in acquisition' (Ellis, 2008, p. 249). This is particularly interesting in light of today's learners' extensive exposure to input in the digital media; see also below. If comprehensibility does not necessarily make for acquisition, then the practice of aspiring to it as a core parameter for materials design surely needs to be questioned. In other words, there seems to be 'a tension between the requirements of input for comprehension on the one hand, and acquisition on the other' (Oh, 2001, p. 71). Particularly because one way in which materials writers tend to render material 'comprehensible', is, of course, to 'simplify' it, and simplified input may not necessarily (a) be more comprehensible (b) offer the best 'quality' input or (c) facilitate intake. In order to investigate this empirically with respect to language learning materials, the modifications in a typical sample of coursebook material based on an authentic text are analysed and matched to research evidence on the ways in which learning materials are traditionally 'simplified'. This allows us the examine questions (a) to (c), stated above.

The text below appears in *New English File Upper Intermediate* (Oxenden & Latham-Koenig, 2008, p.47). It was adapted from an article in *The Guardian* newspaper (2006): http://www.theguardian.com/world/2006/sep/02/japan.just inmccurry (accessed May 16, 2014):

Japan's children play safe

When Ryosuke and Taemi Suzuki take their 18-month-old daughter to Fantasy Kids Resort in Japan they are guaranteed total peace of mind. Fantasy Resort is one of several playgrounds in Japan that provides for the growing number of parents who constantly worry about possible dangers threatening their children such as disease and accidents.

First-time visitors to the playground must provide proof of identification before they enter, and shoes must be removed at the door because they carry germs. Even the wheels of baby-buggies are sprayed with an antibacterial solution.

Inside, children are watched over by about 20 staff dressed in bright yellow overalls and more than a dozen security cameras are mounted on the ceiling. Although pets are banned from the playground, its large sandpit contains sterilised sand which is cleaned daily to remove any potentially harmful objects. Most of the bigger toys are inflatable to reduce the risk of injury. This is to protect the resort as much as the children, because parents of a child injured while at nursery might easily sue the school.

"We've been here before and we'll definitely come again," says Mr Suzuki, "This place has everything under one roof, but most importantly, it puts absolute priority on safety."

Mr and Mrs Suzuki are not alone in wanting to remove just about every element of risk from their children's lives. According to a recent government survey . . .

New English File Upper Intermediate *(Oxenden &*
Latham-Koenig, 2008, p. 47)

The original article (excluding headlines) runs to 771 words. The abridged version for the coursebook is less than a third of that, consisting of just 231 words. This sort of 'cropping' is pervasive in the adaptation of authentic texts for coursebooks, being the process used in 96.6% (58 of 60) of those analysed (in B1/C2-level coursebooks) in a study by Clavel-Arriotia and Fuster-Márquez (2014). While the rationale for cropping is understandably to fit the parameters of the traditional coursebook text (as well as being dictated by publishers' space restrictions), this cannot but impact on the cohesion and coherence of the discourse. In our sample, the conjunction introducing this paragraph in the coursebook text:

Although pets are banned from the playground, its large sandpit contains sterilised sand which is cleaned daily to remove any potentially harmful objects.

Is not linked to any previous clause or idea, because the following paragraph which occurs earlier in the original article, has been cut out:

The playground is a world away from ordinary playgrounds, with their concrete surfaces, rusty swings and sandpits that often conceal unwelcome deposits by dogs.

This has long been an issue in the research; the editing out of cohesive devices to simplify syntax and shorten sentences has been shown to actually make comprehension *more* difficult (Blau, 1982) by removing the semantic connections between ideas. The 'atypical' 'short, choppy' sentences resulting from simplification can actually complexify the syntax and impede comprehension (Crossley, Louwerse, McCarthy, & McNamara, 2007, p. 27) as well as constituting unnatural models; see below.

This dovetails with research that has looked at the sorts of changes that *do* seem to facilitate comprehension, and these are the sorts of elaborative changes that are second nature to experienced teachers (in their classroom discourse at least), such as increased redundancy (via repetition and paraphrase); using canonical word order (*The film was brilliant* as opposed to *It was brilliant, the film was*) and increased intra-/ intersentential markers (*because, therefore*, etc.). The transfer of such strategies to written texts has had startling results:

> The provision of elaborative information in written input enhances the read-ing comprehension of even low-proficiency learners while exposing them to native-like features that are usually absent in simplified input. Although elab-oration often produces texts that are longer and linguistically more complex than the simplified versions, elaborative amplification of pivotal terms and concepts can compensate for the greater linguistic complexity and length. Elaborative modification, by multiplying opportunities for dealing with text information through redundancy and clearly signaled thematic structure, seems to improve the comprehensibility of written input.
>
> *(Oh, 2001, pp. 90–91)*

Oh concludes by dismissing simplification as a comprehension technique: 'Elaboration retains more native-like qualities than[,] and is at least equally [as] successful as—if not more successful than—simplification in improving comprehension' (Oh, 2001, p. 69).

Moving on from the syntactic modifications, in our sample text, there are lexi-cal and content adjustments, as comparison of these extracts from the original and adapted versions illustrate:

> The growing number of parents who constantly fret about the threats posed to their tiny offspring by disease, accidents and other people.
>
> *(original)*

> The growing number of parents who constantly worry about possible dan-gers threatening their children such as disease and accidents.
>
> *(coursebook version)*

The lexical changes ('worry' substituting 'fret', 'children' for 'tiny offspring', 'danger' instead of 'threat') using more commonly used vocabulary are typical of course-book strategies; Clavel-Arriotia and Fuster-Márquez (2014) found that nearly 93% of the B2/C1 level coursebook texts they analysed had undergone some 'linguistic substitution'. Lexical simplification possibly aids speedy comprehension at the level of our sample text (B2), but on the other hand arguably impoverishes the input and its potential for enriching the learners' vocabulary; acquisition is only possible, as Gor and Long emphasize, with 'meaningful exposure [. . .] to *unknown* forms' (2009, p. 447). The value of materials as viable target-language (TL) models can be diminished –'stilted, fragmented, unnatural and psychologically inappropriate' (Gor & Long 2009, p. 447) – with sentences that are 'atypical' and 'choppy' (see also above) (Crossley et al., 2007, p. 27).

Semantic (content) changes, finally, as in the above extracts, the outright removal of 'other people' as potential threats to children, are often effective censorship: What Wajnryb (1996) noted as the 'parental guidance' (PG) rating of coursebook material, and eschew opportunities for deploying the sort of higher-order thinking skills (evaluation, morality and so on) that we discuss later on.

We conclude this section with Gor and Long lamenting that despite the counter evidence, 'commercially published teaching materials continue the practice of linguistic simplification as the primary modification strategy' (Gor & Long, 2009 p. 446). Oh's clarion-call to the profession could be no clearer: 'EFL reading material developers as well as English teachers need to re-evaluate the widely held assumption that linguistic simplification is the only viable way of modifying target language written input' (Oh, 2001, p. 91).

Bearing in mind this sort of evidence that 'simplifying' input does not necessarily enhance comprehension nor provide value input, returning to the third question ((c) above), as to whether this sort of modified input is conducive to intake, we find the evidence from empirical research far from convincing. Leow's research (1993, 1997) showed that the use of simplified texts, while more comprehensible, did not result in greater levels of intake. He hypothesized that, with our relative lack of knowledge of the internal processes that determine the conversion of input to intake, our manipulation of input was basically 'haphazard', and 'inadequate to address what facilitates learners' intake' (Leow, 1993, p. 342). This brings us full circle, sundering the implicit link between simplification and acquisition: '[Other] experimental studies have failed to find that simplified input aids acquisition' (Ellis, 2008 p. 250) – making references to this research by Leow (1993, 1997).

i+∞. . .?

'Learners can work by themselves on unmodified input – such as that found in TV programmes – and so gain input that helps them learn.' Interestingly, this research conclusion comes from two decades ago (Ellis, 2008, p. 249, discussing Larsen-Freeman's 1983 research) but is all the more true today. This generation of learners' disposition to technology, a sort of evolving 'hardwiring' for technology, as mooted by Prensky, for example (2009) (even among populations previously unfamiliar with it: See the experience recounted of the One Laptop per Child (OLPC) project in Ethiopia (Stokes, 2012)) should open us to the idea that the upcoming generation of learners is more experimental, more adventurous and less phased by non-comprehension. These abilities will surely become more widespread in tandem with predicted worldwide technological spread and normalization in the next decades (see, for example, Prensky, 2011). A 2011 Organization for Economic Cooperation and Development (OECD) report, which assessed 470,000 15-year-old students in 19 countries internationally, revealed the level of technological integration. On average, 94% of students had a computer at home and an average of 89% had Internet access, with high levels of students reporting they browsed the Internet for fun, chatted online, played games, and so on (OECD, 2011). 'A population of learners, especially young people', as Maggi, Cherubin and Garcia Pascual assess it, 'fully engaged in a multi-media world' (2014, p. 199). Given that skills are transferable, and that life skills can and should be transferred to language learning (and vice versa), the language teaching/materials preoccupation with 'comprehensibility' can be seen as over-cautious; arguably a concept that is 'overrated and outdated' (Mishan & Timmis 2015, p. 21). Might it be time, therefore, to consider revisiting Krashen's 'i+1' as i+2, i+3, i+∞ . . .?

Cognitive Challenge

The final nail in the coffin (so to speak) of 'comprehensibility', is that comprehension – understanding – is a low-ranking cognitive skill (above only 'remembering') in Bloom's well-known taxonomy of the cognitive domain (originally 1956; revised 2001 version reproduced in Figure 11.1 for convenience); this throws into question its predominance in the language teaching context.

Bloom's taxonomy ranks thinking skills from simple to complex in a cumulative hierarchy, each simpler category a prerequisite for the next one; so 'remembering' is conceived as a prerequisite for 'understanding' and so on. However, these are,

cite?,

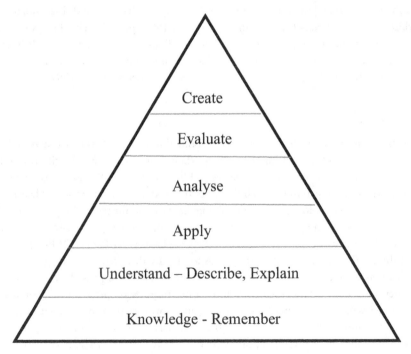

FIGURE 11.1 Bloom's revised taxonomy. Based on Anderson and Krathwohl (2001)

importantly, thinking skills, not language skills – so while deployed internally by the learner, not all stages need to be charted and checked in the target language (TL) in language teaching/learning contexts. Questions which call on the higher levels of the domain, for instance (such as asking learners' opinions or *evaluation*, the second highest level) require them to have worked through the levels cognitively, but elicit TL output fed only from this level.

Some background from the research into the link between cognition and learning is useful in order to situate Bloom's taxonomy within language learning and within the developing of materials for this. While cross-disciplinary evidence must necessarily be treated with caution in case of over-application, evidence from cognitive psychology appears to show the relationship between the depth of cognitive processing and memory/learning.

'More meaningful processing is usually associated with higher levels of recollection' (Craik, 2002, p. 316). This consolidates earlier work by the same researcher: 'It is now generally accepted that memory performance is directly and strongly linked to the nature of the processing underlying the original experience' (Lockhart & Craik, 1990, p. 109). Language practitioners were quick to spot this link to language learning: 'Meaningful material is learned faster and remembered better than information that is less meaningful' (Ghosn, 2013, p. 64).

Improved memory performance, Craik (2002) goes on to claim, with reference to other research, is associated with 'greater degrees of semantic elaboration' and 'a better fit with subjects' expertise' (2002, p. 311); in language pedagogy terms, the degree of engagement with, and relevance of, the learning material. 'To be effective for later memory, further processing must enrich the representation "meaningfully" in the broadest sense. Further processing at shallow levels of analysis does not lead to better memory' (Craik & Watkins, 1973, in Craik 2002, pp. 311–312). In pedagogical terms, involvement/interaction with the material consolidates it for learning: The rationale, not incidentally, for Task-Based learning.

Research in education and educational psychology tells a similar story; as we saw above, Bloom's taxonomy of the cognitive domain (1956) and subsequent developments from it (e.g. Anderson and Krathwohl, 2001), conceived levels of cognitive processing as a hierarchy stepped from remembering, through comprehending, applying, analysing and evaluating, up to creating (see Figure 11.1). The chief (original) aim of this taxonomy was to emphasize the importance of breadth across the categories as a 'means for determining the congruence of educational objectives, activities, and assessments in a unit, course, or curriculum' (Krathwohl, 2002, p. 212).

Krathwohl goes on to note that analyses of curricular objectives and test items have almost always shown 'a heavy emphasis on objectives requiring only recognition or recall of information, objectives that fall in the *Knowledge* category' (Krathwohl, 2002, p. 213). What he emphasizes is that 'it is objectives that involve the understanding and use of knowledge, those that would be classified in the categories from *Comprehension* to *Synthesis*, that are usually considered the most important goals of education' (Krathwohl, 2002, p. 213).

Returning to language learning materials, this raises the question as to whether this 'heavy emphasis' on recognition and recall of information is reflected in our materials as well. In an analysis of question types in ten intermediate-level course-books across four well-known global coursebook series (*Cutting Edge*, *English File*, *Inside Out* and *Headway*), Freeman (2014) detected a steady rise in what she termed 'explicit' question types (i.e. where the answer can be found stated in the same words in the text) from edition to edition (editions straddling 1986 to 2009) in all four series apart from the two books in the *English File* series. She noted, furthermore, that this rise is significant in the four books in the *Headway* series, published between 1986 and 2009 (Freeman, 2014). Alongside this, while higher-order, inferential questions were the most frequently asked question type in three of the four series, their numbers steadily fell with each revised edition of all four coursebooks, with this fall being statistically significant between some editions of *Headway* (Freeman, 2014).

The findings of other research studies are not dissimilar. Only half of the (eight) coursebooks reviewed in Tomlinson, Dat, Masuhara and Rubdy's survey review of English as a foreign language (EFL) courses for adults (2001) were considered to offer sufficient potential for cognitive challenge. This fell to three of the eight books reviewed in a subsequent survey by Masuhara, Haan, Yi and Tomlinson (2008) offering 'adult content and tasks which require intellectual and/or affective investment from the learners' (2008, p. 309). In the next survey by these research-ers (Tomlinson & Masuhara, 2013), only one coursebook (of six) scored fully in terms of potential for cognitive engagement.

What began to strike me forcefully when reviewing the research on cognitive challenge in language learning materials was the surprising failure in the materials development field to 'join the dots' and feed principles that have had a profound influence on the sphere of education – in this case, Bloom's taxonomy of the cognitive domain – into the design of language teaching materials. While the taxonomy has had some influence on the teaching of language skills, most notably reading (see, for example, Nuttall, 1982, 1996; Day & Park, 2005) where the dots have been joined (so to speak), this has been from the perspective of the *analysis* of textbook material rather than its *development*. Examples of which I am aware include Riazi and Mosalanejad's (2010) analysis of Iranian high-school English language textbooks and Freeman's (2014) mentioned above. Freeman's research drew on Bloom's taxonomy and on research on reading skills, such as Nuttall (1982, 1996) and Day and Park (2005), to trial and create her own taxonomy of question types, which she uses to do a *quantitative analysis* of the post-reading question and activity types within ten coursebooks (see above). Four of her eight question types roughly equate to levels in Bloom's taxonomy, and these will be alluded to in the course of the discussions below.

The concern of the rest of this chapter will therefore be the explication and development of a checklist for the design of language learning materials using Bloom's taxonomy (revised Anderson and Krathwohl, 2001, see Figure 11.1) as the reference point. It has long served as such in general education, as noted above, and I will exploit this, drawing on some of the matrices of verbs and activities developed to match it. The parameters of the materials design paradigm presented here are based on receptive skills, i.e. written and audio/audio-visual input, although the principles are extended/applied to other skills in the proposed tasks. Language proficiency level is, it should be noted, *not* a parameter; intellectual challenge needs to be provided at all proficiency levels: 'Despite their very limited proficiency in the language, students need the challenge and stimulation of addressing themes and topics that have adult appeal' (Lazar, 1994, p. 116). Neither is age; challenge is all the more important to children because they are still developing cognitively (see, for example, Hughes, 2013) while keeping in mind that this should, of course, be age-appropriate.

The scope of this chapter imposes two delimitations which it is important to point out: The first is omission of specific discussion of language focus/language awareness-raising activities, although these could, of course, be devised at any level of the domain. The second is coverage of the affective domain – again, a reflection of the chapter's scope and most assuredly not of its importance for language learning and materials design (see Mishan & Timmis, 2015 for a fuller treatment of this).

The necessary starting point, Bloom's revised taxonomy (Anderson and Krathwohl, 2001) was presented in Figure 11.1. To use this as a basis for the development of materials, we will look at each level in turn, and, for each, the sorts of cognitive processes will first be analysed and linguistics prompts identified. Sample language practice activities and sample questions will then be suggested (for convenience, based on a story assumed to be reasonably universally known, the fairy tale 'Little Red Riding Hood'). A summary table (Table 11.1) will, finally, be given to illustrate and collate the whole.

'Remember'

Starting from the 'base' of the triangle then, the required 'relationship' with 'knowledge' (in the case of language learning materials, the language input) at this level is simply for the learner to recognize, recall it or locate it in a text or diagram. Notably, the learner is not required to call on his/her background knowledge at this level, i.e. on anything external to the input itself (although such knowledge may be an aid to recollection). Freeman (2014) used a classification integrating this, which she termed 'textually explicit', where the answer to the question can be found stated directly ('word-matched') in the text. Recall tasks thus involve only memory checks, using such prompts as 'tell', 'list', 'draw' or memory tests: 'Recite'. Tasks might require the learner to find the information in a text, diagram or plan, etc. Other classic prompts for this level are, of course, the traditional teacher's arsenal of quantitative questions (how many . . .? how much . . .?) and wh- questions (where . . .? when . . .? what . . .? – with the possible exception of 'why . . .?' which can elicit evaluative level thinking) all of which require the learner to remember information (and/or remember where it can be found, in a written text). Learners might also be asked to make a list of this information, a timeline or fact chart.

Questions for our sample text here (assuming this information was given in the story, as it usually is) might be: *What did Little Red Riding Hood have in her basket? Where did Little Red Riding Hood's grandmother live?*

'Understand'

At the level of understanding or 'comprehending', learners are expected to be able to demonstrate an ability to interpret the input. This can be by explaining, paraphrasing or summarizing it (orally or in writing), exemplifying from it or categorizing information or facts. Freeman (2014) creates a category that is roughly equivalent, what she terms 'textually implicit', where the information required by the question can be found in the text, albeit expressed with different wording, thus requiring a minor degree of inferencing – 'an extremely important distinction in a foreign language course' (2014, p. 79). The obvious comprehension-checks, along with the classic wh- and how many/how much questions, are to ask the learner to re-tell a story or summarize the information in the input. Tasks for the sample story would be to retell the story of Little Red Riding Hood in one's own words or perhaps in a cartoon strip, or to describe or draw her grandmother, the wolf or Little Red Riding Hood herself. A more interpretive task might be to describe the clues as to who the disguised grandmother really is (big ears, big eyes, big teeth etc.). These sorts of activities illustrate that, at only the second level of the taxonomy, comprehending is not a particularly high order thinking skill, so, as argued above, the emphasis on checking it in language teaching would seem disproportionate.

'Apply'

At the third level of Bloom's six-level scale, the relationship with the input can be seen to change. 'Applying' requires learners to abstract information from the input (selecting from it, making connections between ideas) and/or draw inferences from it, often drawing on their own knowledge. This level then requires 'implementation' and change: The reapplying of extracted/interpreted information to different situations/contexts. Quite a few of what in language teaching are generally termed 'extension' tasks call on this level of cognitive processing. These often involve genreswitching: Learners might be asked to rewrite (an extract from) a story or newspaper article as a dialogue (or vice versa), or write a detailed description of a photograph. Representative tasks for our Little Red Riding Hood example would be to devise a Little Red Riding Hood board game (or digital game), or recast the story as a tabloid newspaper article under a headline such as: *Girl Hero Saves Grandma from Wolf!*

'Analyse'

At the level of 'analysis' we are well into the territory of the more complex cognitive processes, the ones which, as Krathwohl (2002, p. 217) says, are 'generally recognized as the more important and long-lasting fruits of education'. Analysis requires learners to differentiate, to break down information into simpler parts, to reorganize it and make deductions: To find evidence to support generalizations. It requires them to draw inferences and thus to detour from the text and combine their background knowledge with given information. Here, the traditional 'compare and contrast' skills so commonly called upon in academic essays appear. Thus, 'compare and contrast two alternative models of change within business organizations' is given as a typical assignment question in marketing in the coursebook *Cambridge Academic English* (Hewings & Thaine, 2012, p.48). Tasks for this level can make use of the classic repertoire of analysis instruments such as surveys and questionnaires, and then require producing information in graphic form. For our sample story, learners might devise a survey to explore their peers' knowledge of the fairy tale, or its equivalent (if one exists) in their own culture.

'Evaluate'

While considered a cognitive process in Bloom's taxonomy (e.g. 1956), evaluation can be seen to transcend cognition, crossing into the domain of 'affect', with a clear overlap between 'evaluating' and 'valuing', the third of the five levels in the taxonomy of the affective domain (Krathwohl, Bloom, & Masia, 1964). Both use as their starting points the individual's own internalized values on which they base judgements. 'Valuing', though, is more concerned with affect in that it has to do with an individual's consistency of evaluative response (to objects, phenomena etc.), to the extent of allowing him/herself to be 'perceived by others as holding the belief or value' (Krathwohl et al., 1964, p.181). Freeman in fact treats it as such, placing 'evaluation' as the higher of her two 'affect' questions (2014), which, in coursebooks, require learners to make a judgement or assessment of the input information. As a cognitive process, however, a major part of evaluating is being able to justify one's stance with reference to cultural, institutional or personal standards, so these are skills fostered at academic levels (and in examination courses): Writing a critique or review, making recommendations based on research, debating/defending a position. The following is a fairly representative assignment here: 'Write a contribution to an issue of a college magazine [. . .] devoted to the environment [. . .] You should explain why you feel climate change is a serious concern' *Cambridge English Objective Advanced* (O'Dell & Broadhead, 2012, p. 141). Little Red Riding Hood lends itself surprisingly well to evaluation activities:

- *Who do you think is really responsible for what happens to Little Red Riding Hood's grandmother? Justify your answer.*
- *Set up and conduct the trial of the huntsman for the murder of the wolf.*

'Create'

It is interesting and indeed heartening to consider that the highest-order thinking skill is one that is substantially deployed at pre- and primary school level. It is perhaps cite?

Adapt examples?

TABLE 11.1 Cognitive processes and sample activities, based on (revised) Bloom's taxonomy (Anderson & Krathwohl, 2001) and web resources

Cognitive skill level	Processes	Prompts	Sample activities	Sample questions for the story 'Little Red Riding Hood'
Creating	Based on given information; reformulating, extending, building, planning, hypothesizing, generating new patterns/structures	create, compose, predict, design, devise, formulate, imagine, hypothesize	Devise/perform role plays, advertisements, games or mazes using the input as a launching point Compose a sequel or prequel to the input (including genre/media-switch, e.g. written input transferred to aural/graphic output or newspaper article transferred to dialogue, poem, blog)	• Devise a 'maze' (using online tools if you wish) in which Little Red Riding Hood is given choices along her way. • Compose the backstory for Little Red Riding Hood, her grandmother, the wolf or the huntsman in the form of a blog, newspaper article or play
Evaluating	Making/defending judgements and arguments based on evaluation of criteria Linking to own values/ideas Critiquing/reviewing	judge, debate, justify, critique, review, argue	Write a set of rules or conventions relating to conduct in a particular situation or context, e.g. school rules, hospitality conventions in a specific culture Conduct a debate Write a critique or review	• Who do you think is really responsible for what happens to Little Red Riding Hood's grandmother? Justify your answer. • As a class or group, set up and conduct the trial of the huntsman for the murder of the wolf.

Analysing	Separating information into its component parts to identify how the parts relate to each other and the overall structure. Inferencing (and distinguishing between facts and inferences) Differentiating Organizing Deconstructing	*compare, contrast, categorize, deconstruct*	Conduct a mini-research project (design a survey, gather and analyse data)	• *Devise a survey to find out other students' knowledge of the fairy tale Little Red Riding Hood. Find out if there is an equivalent tale in their culture.*
Applying	Abstracting and reapplying to a different situation. Selecting and/or connecting information/ideas Implementing, changing	*illustrate, interpret, transfer, infer, change, complete*	Recast input as a different genre/medium, e.g. rewrite a newspaper article as a dialogue, or write a description of a photograph	• *Rewrite this story as a tabloid newspaper article under the headline:* **Girl Hero Saves Grandma from Wolf!** • *Devise a Little Red Riding Hood board/digital game*
Understanding	Determining the meaning of written/audio/graphic communication, i.e. interpreting the message	*explain, paraphrase, summarize, exemplify, categorize, predict*	Re-tell or summarize input (in written, oral or graphic form)	• *Summarize the story orally, in writing or as a comic strip.* • *Draw or describe: Little Red Riding Hood/her grandmother/ the huntsman/ the wolf* • *What are the clues that the 'grandmother' was the wolf in disguise?*
Remembering	Recalling data or information	*tell, list, draw, locate, recite*	Make a list, timeline or fact chart Answer list of factual questions	• *What did Little Red Riding Hood have in her basket?* • *Where did Little Red Riding Hood's grandmother live?*

Adapted from Mishan and Timmis (2015, p. 106)

for this reason that it is somewhat ignored or dismissed in higher-level schooling, where processes of creativity and imagination might seem too trivial to call on. Indeed, it is a truism that this capacity is nurtured at primary level, and subsequently sublimated in secondary schools with the requirements for examination cramming – which ironically works chiefly at the two base-level cognitive skills. The top level of 'creating', however, involves the input being used to launch cognitive processes such as hypothesizing, predicting, imagining, devising, formulating, combining ideas and originating new ones – in the generating of a new entity. Certain types of language learning materials/tasks work at this level, mainly 'extension' tasks which build on previous input and which often use the opportunity to extend the skills set used as well. Building on written or audio/visual input, therefore, tasks might include role plays, devising advertisements, games or mazes. For our example, this might be a maze in which Little Red Riding Hood is given choices along her way; where the path diverges in the woods; whether to enter her grandmother's cottage and so on. Prediction is also strongly creative: Composing a sequel, or alternatively, a prequel to the input, perhaps switching genre and/or medium as well (e.g. in the form of a play, a short video, a poem, a magazine or newspaper article). Little Red Riding Hood, her grandmother or the huntsman might perhaps be given a 'back-story' in the form of a short dramatic piece, or a newspaper article, or in their own blog. Roald Dahl's poem version of the story (in the collection *Revolting Rhymes*, 1982) can be seen as a classic example of a genre switch together with humorous characterizations and plot twists.

In drawing up questions for higher-level thinking skills using this table, it can be seen that the *wh-* questions and *how many/much* questions so beloved of teachers and coursebooks are mainly used at the two lower levels; suggesting a rule of thumb that the number of *wh-* questions is inversely proportional to the level of cognitive challenge. Indeed, the *wh-* question itself might be seen as one of the culprits in confining cognitive skills to lower levels – or perhaps, more fundamentally, the teacher-training conventions that train us to elicit learner participation by asking them.

Using the Checklist

While conceived with materials production in mind, the checklist is open-ended enough, it is hoped, for it to be used for all and any area of 'materials development', extending from producing original materials to evaluating, analysing or adapting existing ones. When designing materials based on this model, it is important to try to stimulate thinking skills from every level of the taxonomy, avoiding the inclination at lower proficiency levels to cluster prompts and questions on the bottom two rungs. As emphasized earlier, it is important that 'even' lower-level language learners are required to use their intellectual skills, and peak-level 'creative' tasks are routinely set for even young children. It is difficult to generalize as to the questions and tasks that might be generated for any given input, the most fruitful principle here being to use 'text-responsiveness', whereby the text itself suggests the precise tasks set. The sample questions from the fairy tale 'Little Red Riding

Hood' in the last column in Table 11.1 help to illustrate this principle with this one representative text.

Turning to its potential application for materials evaluation, the checklist can function to identify levels of cognitive challenge provided in coursebook tasks, either in materials teachers have produced for their own classroom use, or within published coursebooks (evaluation is beyond the scope of this chapter, but the reader is referred to such works as McGrath, 2002, 2013; Mishan & Timmis, 2015; Tomlinson, 2013c). Looking back at the sample text 'Japan's children play safe' from *New English File Upper Intermediate* (Oxenden & Latham-Koenig, 2008) reproduced above, the two questions on it given in the book are:

> *What are the main safety measures?*
>
> *What do you think of them?*
>
> *(Oxenden & Latham-Koenig, 2008, p. 47)*

Extrapolating from Table 11.1, the first question can be seen to default to the lower-order thinking skills of 'comprehension' and 'remembering', and in fact match Freemans's level two 'textually implicit' (2014). The second question is plainly evaluative, a higher-level skill, the two questions thus offsetting each other well in terms of a balance between comprehension check and cognitive challenge.

Since one of the chief dealings with materials that most teachers have in practice is their adaptation (see, for example, Bolster, 2014, 2015; McGrath, 2013, for evidence of the degree to which teachers adapt materials) the checklist might be most valuable as a resource for prompts for more challenging alternatives or additions to coursebook tasks. Such an addition to the questions on the *New English File* text used above, for instance, might be to ask learners to devise a news article or report for the headline 'Accident at Fantasy Kids Resort: 17 children injured'. Quite minor modifications like this can elevate conservative tasks to higher levels of cognitive challenge, achieving the more intense levels of engagement and motivation that we know to promote learning.

Finally, the delimitations noted at the beginning of this section apply. The model presented here is not, nor is it intended to be, a complete materials design 'template', but a checklist to ensure that materials provide one essential aspect of SLA, cognitive involvement.

Conclusion

An oft-repeated refrain in evaluations of coursebook materials, both empirical and anecdotal, is that they tend to underestimate learners' ability to engage intellectually in material not in their L1. In this chapter, I have explored reasons for this with reference to relevant SLA hypotheses and research, and suggested a blueprint emanating from principles of general education to address this perceived failing. As materials development as a discipline edges into the mainstream in language teacher education, with more ELT/TESOL programmes offering modules in materials design and evaluation (and see justification for this in McGrath, 2013), there is an increasing need for sets of principles, templates and taxonomies such as the one proposed here to guide practising teachers in the creation of their own materials and in the critical evaluation of those of others.

References

Anderson, L., & Krathwohl, D. R. (2001). *A taxonomy for learning, teaching and assessing: A revision of Bloom's taxonomy of educational objectives.* New York: Longman.

Bell, J., & Gower, R. (2011). Writing course materials for the world: A great compromise. In B. Tomlinson (Ed.), *Materials development in language teaching* (2nd ed., pp. 135–151). Cambridge: Cambridge University Press.

Blau, E. (1982). The effect of syntax on readability for ESL students in Puerto Rico. *TESOL Quarterly, 16*: 517–528.

Bloom, B. (1956). *Taxonomy of educational objectives: The classification of educational goals. Handbook 1: Cognitive domain.* New York: Longmans, Green.

Bolster, A. (2014). Materials adaptation of EAP materials by experienced teachers: Part I. *Folio, 16*(1), 16–22.

Bolster, A. (2015). Materials adaptation of EAP materials by experienced teachers: Part II. *Folio, 16*(2), 16–21.

Clavel-Arriotia, B., & Fuster-Márquez, M. (2014). The authenticity of real texts in advanced English language textbooks. *ELT Journal, 68*(2), 124–134.

Craik, F. (2002). Levels of processing: Past, present . . . and future. *Memory, 10*(5–6), 305–318.

Craik, F., & Watkins, M. (1973). The role of rehearsal in short-term memory. *Journal of Verbal Learning and Verbal Behavior, 12*, 599–607.

Crossley, S. A., Louwerse, M. M., McCarthy, P. M., & McNamara, D. S. (2007). A linguistic analysis of simplified and authentic texts. *The Modern Language Journal, 91*, 15–30.

Dahl, R. (1982). *Revolting rhymes.* London: Jonathan Cape.

Day, R., & Park, J.-S. (2005). Developing reading comprehension questions. *Reading in a Foreign Language, 17*, 60–73.

Dellar, H., & Walkley, A. (2008). *Innovations.* Andover, UK: Heinle Cengage Learning.

Ellis, R. (2008). *The study of second language acquisition.* Oxford: Oxford University Press.

Ellis, R. (2010). Second language research and language teaching materials. In N. Harwood (Ed.), *English language teaching materials: Theory and practice* (pp. 33–57). Cambridge: Cambridge University Press.

Freeman, D. (2014). Reading comprehension questions: The distribution of different types in global EFL textbooks. In N. Harwood (Ed.), *English language teaching textbooks: Content, consumption, production* (pp. 72–110). Basingstoke, UK: Palgrave Macmillan.

Gass, S. (1997). *Input, interaction and the second language learner.* Mahwah, NJ: Erlbaum.

Gass, S. M. (1988). Integrating research areas: A framework for second language studies 1. *Applied Linguistics, 9*(2), 198–217.

Ghosn, I.-K. (2013). Language learning for young learners. In B. Tomlinson (Ed.), *Applied linguistics and materials development* (pp. 61–74). London: Bloomsbury.

Gilmore, A. (2007). Authentic materials and authenticity in foreign language learning. *Language Teaching, 40*(2), 97–118.

Gor, K., & Long, M. (2009). Input and second language processing. In W. Ritchie & T. Bhatia (Eds.), *The new handbook of second language acquisition* (pp. 445–472). Bingley, UK: Emerald Group Publishing.

Hewings, M., & Thaine, C. (2012). *Cambridge academic English students' book: Advanced.* Cambridge: Cambridge University Press.

Hughes, A. (2013). The teaching of reading in English for young learners: Some considerations and next steps. In B. Tomlinson (Ed.), *Applied linguistics and materials development* (pp. 183–198). London: Bloomsbury.

Krashen, S. (1982). *Principles and practice in language acquisition.* New York: Pergamon.

Krashen, S. (1985). *The input hypothesis.* New York: Longman.

Krathwohl, D. R. (2002). A revision of Bloom's taxonomy: An overview. *Theory into Practice, 41*(4), 212–264.

Krathwohl, D. R., Bloom, B. S., & Masia, B. B. (1964). *Taxonomy of educational objectives: The classification of educational goals. Handbook II: Affective domain.* New York: David McKay.

Larsen-Freeman, D. (1983). The importance of input in second language acquisition. In R. Andersen (Ed.), *Pidgeonization and creolization as language acquisition.* Rowley, MA: Newbury House.

Lazar, G. (1994). Using literature at lower levels. *ELT Journal, 48*(2), 115–24.

Leow, R. (1993). To simplify or not to simplify: A look at intake. *Studies in Second Language Acquisition, 15*(3), 333–355.

Leow, R. (1997). Attention, awareness, and foreign language behavior. *Language Learning, 47*(3), 467–505.

Lockhart, R., & Craik, H. (1990). Levels of processing: A retrospective commentary on a framework for memory research. *Canadian Journal of Psychology, 44*(1), 87–112.

Long, M. (1996). The role of the linguistic environment in second language acquisition. In W. Ritchie & T. Bhatia (Eds.), *Handbook of second language acquisition.* San Diego, CA: Academic Press.

Maggi, F., Cherubin, M., & Garcia Pascual, E. (2014). Using Web 2.0 tools in CLIL. In S. Garton & K. Graves (Eds.), *International perspectives on materials in ELT* (pp. 198–215). Basingstoke, UK: Palgrave Macmillan.

Masuhara, H., Haan, N., Yi, Y., & Tomlinson, B. (2008). Adult EFL courses. *ELT Journal, 62*(3), 294–312.

McGrath, I. (2002). *Materials evaluation and design for language teaching.* Edinburgh: Edinburgh University Press.

McGrath, I. (2013). *Teaching materials and the roles of EFL/ESL teachers.* London: Bloomsbury.

Mishan, F., & Timmis, I. (2015). *Materials development for TESOL.* Edinburgh: Edinburgh University Press.

Nuttall, C. (1982). *Teaching reading skills in a foreign language.* London: Heinemann.

Nuttall, C. (1996). *Teaching reading skills in a foreign language* (2nd ed.). London: Macmillan.

O'Dell, F., & Broadhead, A. (2012). *Cambridge English objective advanced* (3rd ed.). Cambridge: Cambridge University Press.

OECD. (2011). Pisa 2009 results: Students on line: Digital technologies and performance (volume VI). http://www.oecd.org/pisa/pisaproducts/48270093.pdf/. Retrieved November 13, 2013.

Oh, S.-Y. (2001). Two types of input modification and EFL reading comprehension: Simplification versus elaboration. *Tesol Quarterly, 35,*(1), 69–96.

Oxenden, C., & Latham-Koenig, C. (2008). *New English file upper intermediate students book.* Oxford: Oxford University Press.

Prensky, M. (2009). H. sapiens digital: From digital immigrants and digital natives to digital wisdom. *Innovate, 5*(3). Also retrieved from http://www.innovateonline.info/index.php?view=article&id=705/. April 28, 2013.

Prensky, M. (2011). Digital wisdom and homo sapiens digital. In M. Thomas (Ed.), *Deconstructing digital natives* (pp. 15–29). Abingdon, UK/New York: Routledge.

Riazi, A. M., & Mosalanejad, N. (2010). Evaluation of learning objectives in Iranian high-school and pre-university English textbooks using Bloom's taxonomy. *TESL-EJ*, *13*(4), 1–16.

Sharwood-Smith, M. (1986). Comprehension vs. acquisition: Two ways of processing input. *Applied Linguistics*, (7), 159–169.

Stokes, A. (2012). ICT: The age factor. *Loud and Clear*, (*31*), 2.

Swain, M. (1985). Communicative competence: Some roles of comprensible input and comprehensible output in its development. In S. Gass, & C. Madden (Eds.), *Input in second language acquisition*. Rowley, MA: Newbury House.

Tomlinson, B. (2013a). Second language acquisition and materials development. In B. Tomlinson (Ed.), *Applied linguistics and materials development* (pp. 11–30). London: Bloomsbury.

Tomlinson, B. (2013b). *Developing materials for language teaching* (2nd ed.) London: Bloomsbury.

Tomlinson, B. (2013c). Materials evaluation. In B. Tomlinson (Ed.), *Developing materials for language teaching* (2nd ed., pp. 21–48). London: Bloomsbury.

Tomlinson, B., & Masuhara, H. (2013). Adult coursebooks. *ELT Journal*, *67*(2), 233–249.

Tomlinson, B., Dat, B., Masuhara, H., & Rubdy, R. (2001). EFL courses for adults. *ELT Journal*, *55*(1), 80–101.

Wajnryb, R. (1996). Death, taxes and jeopardy: Systematic omissions in EFL texts, or life was never meant to be an adjacency pair. Paper presented at ELICOS Association, 9th Educational Conference, Sydney.

12

WHAT ASPECTS OF CREATIVITY ENHANCEMENT DO ELT TEXTBOOKS TAKE INTO ACCOUNT?

Sasan Baleghizadeh and Zeinab Dargahi

Introduction

Writing is a difficult task both for beginning and advanced learners. Hence, it is a huge accomplishment for children when they begin writing (Puranik, Lonigan, & Kim, 2011). When we think of novice learners, particularly children, it is clear that they are still learning to control the linguistic and motor processes involved in text production. Therefore, writing for children is more difficult when compared with adults (McCutchen, 2011).

The main goal of teaching writing is to help students use this skill as a tool for communicating knowledge and expressing viewpoints and emotions. Thus, writing involves conveying meaning to other people and the act of writing itself can help refine thoughts and reshape views. As Thompson (2001) observes, "writing is a powerful means of linguistic input, output, and interaction, albeit lacking the immediacy of face-to-face communication, which enhances second language learners' acquisition" (p. 87).

In arguing for a better balance between developing knowledge about written language and language use, Grainger, Goouch, and Lambirth (2005) highlight the importance of enhancing learners' creativity and imaginative involvement in the writing task. They believe that developing creativity in writing is central to the learners' growth as writers and to their self-esteem and motivation. To develop their creativity in and through writing, learners need skills and knowledge of the form they wish to compose in, a growing assurance of themselves as writers, and the space and opportunity to develop their voices with support and encouragement. Most of the studies dealing with writing focus on a variety of elements, paying very little heed to creativity. Lack of attention to creativity for developing the writing skill will prevent learners from thinking imaginatively, generating novel ideas, and being highly motivated. Without creative thinking, learners will have very little to say, even if they do have appropriate linguistic knowledge and editorial skills.

Creativity is considered to be a psychological construct to which less attention was paid as it had often been a marginal topic in different studies until recent decades. With the emergence of the field of creativity, understanding its nature, assessing and improving it in instruction and education, and teaching learners to think creatively became important issues which drive most of the current research efforts.

Many elements are crucial in learning to write, the most important of which is creativity, which ought to be included in teaching programs (Edwards & Hiler, 1993). Beghetto and Kaufman (2011) believe that by combining the perspectives of top educators and psychologists, practical advice can be generated in order to address the challenges of supporting creativity within the classroom. Creativity is known to be one of the best predictors of children's success in learning if they are provided with a systematic training aimed at complete mastery of a particular domain, and so teachers are advised to enhance their students' writing ability through tasks and techniques which foster creative thinking.

Sternberg and Lubart (1999) have proposed a creativity model and argue that a creative work is a result of the combination and balance of three types of thinking: Synthetic, analytic, and practical. Synthetic thinking helps learners generate novel and interesting ideas to make connections between unrelated and new things in a novel way. Through synthetic thinking, learners gain the ability to successfully deal with new and unusual situations by drawing on existing knowledge and skills. Analytic thinking is typically considered to be the critical thinking ability. By fostering this way of thinking in learners, they will have the skill to analyze and evaluate ideas. Implementing analytic thinking helps learners to work out the implications of a creative idea and to test it. Besides, analytic learners also have the ability to complete academic and problem-solving tasks. Practical thinking helps learners translate theory into practice and abstract ideas into practical accomplishments. By enhancing learners' practical thinking, they will be able to convince other learners that their idea is worthy and could adapt to everyday life by drawing on existing knowledge and skills. Practical thinking enables learners to understand what needs to be done in a specific setting with perfect reasoning.

In order to develop these three capacities in learners, Sternberg and Lubart (1999) provide teachers with tasks that would help their students increase their:

- Synthetic ability through creation, imagination, discovery, invention, and prediction.
- Analytic ability through analysis, judgment, comparison, contrast, and evaluation
- Practical ability through applying, using, everyday reasoning, and practicing thoughts.

The tasks introduced by Sternberg and Lubart (1999) have a great impact on the enhancement of students' creativity and can be applied to any area of teaching, such as teaching English as a foreign language (EFL) children to write creatively.

Creativity and Second Language Teaching and Learning

Inasmuch as it is argued that creativity results in a deeper understanding among learners (Sawyer, 2004), it is widely contended that developing creativity should be an explicit part of the education process (Jackson, 2006).

Although creativity has been increasingly recognized and valued in the education literature as an effective component, there are very few studies that indicate the incorporation of creativity into the teaching and learning of a second language (L2) and research into this area has been scarce. Meera and Remya (2010), for example, examined the relationship between creativity and achievement in the English language. Their findings indicated that the role of creativity in English achievement was significant. Moreover, Otto (1998) adopted five subtasks from the Torrance test of creativity, which were consequences, unusual uses, common problems, categories, and associations. The results showed highly significant relationships between creativity and English grades. In the same vein, Sutrisno (2007) explored the relationship between creativity and achievement in learning English. The results showed a positive and significant correlation between creativity and scores on achievement tests of reading, vocabulary, and grammar.

In another study, Landry (1973) concluded that the experience of learning an L2 at the elementary school level is positively correlated with creative thinking in figural tasks, which is the subject's ability to produce a large number of different ideas by drawing figures from given stimuli. The results of his study indicated that L2 learners scored significantly higher than monolingual pupils on both variables of creativity and flexibility. Therefore, integrating creativity in L2 teaching appears not only to provide children with the ability to depart from the traditional approaches to a problem but also to supply them with possible rich resources for new, different, and creative ideas.

In his study on integrating creativity and classroom dialogues, Wegerif (2005) argued that while exploratory talk is a specific dialogical model of reason that has proved to be a useful pedagogic tool, there are educationally valuable ways of talking together that are characterized more by verbal creativity than by explicit reasoning. The results of Wegerif's study implied the need to expand the understanding of dialogical reasoning and to incorporate creativity and dialogical models in order to support the stimulation of creativity in educational contexts.

Factors Affecting L2 Writing Development

Writing is an established way of enhancing students' learning if activities are structured to elicit student reflection and creative thinking. Writing is an active learning process and is used to communicate information, to clarify thinking, and to learn and create new concepts (RCC, 2009).

According to Reilly and Reilly (2005), writing is believed to be a rational activity and the most demanding of all language skills. It is also a skill that many teachers find difficult to teach and, as a result, a skill many learners do not enjoy (Reilly & Reilly,

2005). Writing instructors have also noticed that for many learners writing is a difficult skill to acquire in their mother tongue, let alone in a foreign language. Tuan (2010) believes that normally students do not feel comfortable with a formal writing task intended for the critical eyes of someone else, who is the teacher. Thus, they find themselves in a hide-and-seek game with ideas since they have to write about what is assigned for them rather than about what bears much relevance to them.

The difficulties that students encounter are a major concern for teachers of EFL who try to provide their students with techniques for better writing. Table 12.1 highlights factors that most researchers have known to be essential for the writing development of learners.

All the mentioned factors contribute to the development of the writing process, but as Grainger et al. (2005) define writing as a creative process intertwining imagination and originality of ideas with the pursuit of purpose and judging value, it can be concluded that the important element of creativity which is central to learners' growth as writers is not considered. Grainger et al. (2005) also mention the importance of enhancing creativity and imaginative involvement in the writing task which helps learners grasp and shape the purpose of the writing activity, use their imagination, and combine new ideas in order to create a novel and creative piece of writing.

Reminder

The teaching of writing continues to occupy a major place in language pedagogy, and a large body of research has focused on factors which help learners acquire this important and complex skill effectively. Nevertheless, few studies have addressed the issue of creativity. Thus, one of the options to improve the learners' writing ability is to expose them to activities that enhance their creativity, such as tasks which increase learners' analytic, synthetic, and practical abilities (Baleghizadeh & Dargahi, 2012).

TABLE 12.1 Factors affecting L2 writing excluding creativity

Flower and Hayes, 1981	*Task environment and the three cognitive writing processes (planning, translating and reviewing)*
Zamel, 1983	Risk-taking, perceiving a sense of audience, reasoning, higher-level processing, engaging in all recursive writing processes
Borner, 1987	L2 proficiency, learners' experience, and teaching goals
Smagorinsky, 1991; Silva and Nicholls, 1993	Person knowledge, task knowledge, text knowledge, strategy knowledge
Sasaki and Hirose, 1996	L2 language proficiency
Cumming, 1998	Setting goals, organizing ideas, and expressing them
Zimmermann, 2000	Translating (formulating) factor
Franken and Haslett, 2002	Interaction with a peer
Ellis and Yuan, 2004	Pre-writing exercises, multiple drafting cycles, Interaction through instructor feedback, peer reviews
Ortega, 2004	Planning
Hyland, 2007; Kim and Kim, 2005	Genre-based pedagogies
Khoii and Tabrizi, 2011	Input enhancement

Integrating Creativity and Writing

For many writers, the compositional process needs a significant amount of time and an extensive rehearsal period. Therefore, in order to help children find their voices in their own writing, a better balance between knowledge about language and creative language use must be sought in the primary years of learning to write in another language.

Creativity is widely invoked in certain educational and other public discourses, and has been quite extensively theorized and investigated in different circles, yet it still receives little attention in discussions of young learners' writing. Craft (2005) believes that developing creativity in writing is not a fanciful extra in learning to write, but is central to learners' self-esteem and growth as writers. To develop their creativity in and through writing, learners need skills and knowledge of the form they wish to compose in, a growing assurance of themselves as writers, and the space and opportunity to develop their voices with support and encouragement. Grainger et al. (2005) also think writing involves students in communicating and conveying meaning to themselves and others, and that the act of writing itself can help in refining ways of thinking and reshaping points of view, since it allows them to hold their ideas in their hands and think of them as new and novel ones. Thus, it is essential to develop voice and verve in writing and to consider the contribution that flexible, playful, dialogic and imaginative practices can make to children's creative capacity, linguistic potential and growth as writers.

How to Foster Creativity in Children's Writing

There are many factors that enhance creativity in writing and the implementation of these elements is essential in learners' literacy programs in language classes. Some of these factors are as follows:

Using Imagination in the Creative Process of Writing

As Grainger, Goouch, and Lambirth (2003) observe, the development of imagination in handling words, ideas, and feelings helps children in the transition from improvisation to composition, as students begin to play with ideas, structures, patterns and combinations of words and sounds. This creative process including imagination involves writers in seeking solutions or a different perspective and involves them in actively fashioning, shaping, and refining the ideas generated.

Teachers' Own Creativity

The teacher's ability to interest and inspire learners deserves attention and development. Thus, teachers' playfulness, openness, and innovative ideas also need to be developed and enriched if they are to contribute imaginatively to the construction of creative learners (Grainger, 2004).

By telling tales or writing alongside the students in the classroom, teachers are freed from the traditional patterns of classroom interaction and are more personally and affectively involved, using their knowledge and skills, as well as their intuitive insights based upon experience (Grainger, 2002). Teachers can also be creative by providing plenty of playful opportunities for discussion, drama, storytelling and other explorations, in order to ensure deep learning in and through writing, and teaching about forms, functions, and features of writing can be within a motivating and empowering context which demonstrates the potential of creativity.

Affective Engagement, Participation and Motivation

Many schools have worked hard to recapture some of the elements of a more student-centered philosophy and have retained a role for creativity, participation, and motivation (OfSTED, 2002). Learners deserve to be invited into the learning experience as individuals, to become fully involved in their learning so that they can use their imagination in creative contexts. Thus, the affective dimension in writing is important, since learners' attitudes to writing influence their ability to take risks and persevere (Grainger et al., 2005).

Choice and Autonomy in Writing

To develop creativity and voice in their writing, students should not only be introduced to a rich range of existing expressive domains, but also be given time and space to explore these for themselves, making choices, taking risks, and developing their preferences and independence as writers (Grainger et al., 2005).

Creativity and Textbooks

Several aspects of learning are important to consider when thinking about education, and the most important one is creativity, which should be included in teaching programs and textbooks. Textbooks undoubtedly have a considerable influence on classroom practice, by forming the core of most teaching programs (McDonough, Shaw, & Masuhara, 2013) and 'giving guidance to teachers on both the intensity of coverage and the amount of attention demanded by particular content or pedagogical tasks' (Nunan 1991, p. 208). Textbooks may also be a means of training for teachers (Richards, 2001).

In order to provide rich and varied contexts for students to acquire, develop, and apply a broad range of knowledge, understanding and skills, the curriculum should enable students to think creatively and critically to solve problems and to make a difference for the better (Sternberg & Lubart, 1999). Thus, students need to be given the opportunity to become creative, innovative, and enterprising by their teachers and textbooks. Both have to enable students to respond creatively to opportunities, challenges, and activities. Teaching with creativity and teaching for creativity include all the characteristics of good teaching such as high motivation, high expectations,

TABLE 12.2 Writing activities to enhance creativity

Creating an imaginary character like thinking of "anger" as a person. Example: Write about his clothes, characteristics, job, food, etc. (Imagination).

Finding unusual uses for familiar items. Example: Write about the different things we can do with a book. (Discovery).

Predicting different endings for a story. Example: Write a happy and sad ending for a given story. (Prediction).

Judging the character of a story. Example: Write a judgment about the character of the story. Did he do the right thing? (Judgment).

Comparing two unrelated things. Example: Compare yourself with a robot. (Comparison).

Finding differences between two things. Example: Find the seven differences between the two pictures. (Contrast).

Everyday reasoning. Example: Write about the different ways you try to make your angry mum happy. (Reasoning).

and the ability to communicate and listen actively, as well as the ability to interest, engage, and inspire students. Creative teachers need expertise in their particular fields but they need more than this. They need techniques and textbooks that stimulate curiosity and raise self-esteem and confidence (Sternberg & Lubart, 1999).

In a recent study, Baleghizadeh and Dargahi (2012) found several examples of students' creative writing activities, as shown in Table 12.2.

The Present Study

As mentioned earlier, the writing skill is an important issue in language teaching which cannot be ignored in language classes. Among the different studies related to this issue (Galbraith, 1999), the important elements mentioned for developing the writing ability were the meaningfulness of the writing task, the relationship between the task and experience, the amount of practice done at different levels of writing, and the way the teacher sets the purpose of writing. Nevertheless, in all these studies, the element of creativity was missing. Bearing in mind the important role that creativity plays in developing writing ability, the purpose of this study is to discover whether the same lack of attention is true of textbooks. The writing activities in six general English textbooks at the elementary proficiency level are analyzed and each activity's focus on the three aspects of creativity (synthesis, analysis and practice) is observed.

Method

Textbooks

Six currently available general English textbooks, all at the elementary level, were analyzed in the study. No criteria were set for their selection, other than that they are widely used internationally. Table 12.3 lists the textbooks used.

TABLE 12.3 Textbooks used in the study

Title	Authors	Publisher	Year of Publication
English Result	M. Hancock and A. McDonald	Oxford University Press	2007
English Zone	M. Prieto and L. Robbins	McGraw-Hill	2006
Interchange (3rd ed.)	J.C.Richards, J. Hull and S. Proctor	Cambridge University Press	2005
New Headway Plus	L. and J. Soars	Oxford University Press	2006
Spectrum	D. Warshawsky and D. R. H. Byrd	Prentice Hall Regents	1993
Top-Notch	J.Saslow and A. Ascher with E. J. Kisslinger	Pearson Longman	2006

Procedure

All writing activities in each textbook were examined, including the review units. However, additional practice materials provided at the back of the textbooks and workbooks were not examined.

In this study, a creative writing activity is defined as any activity that enhances the learners' synthetic ability through imagination, invention and prediction, their analytic ability through judgment, comparison and contrast, and practical ability through everyday reasoning. For the purposes of this study, each writing activity was examined from the point of view of its creativity enhancement, namely whether it would enhance the learners' three abilities or not. Considering the three aspects of Sternberg and Lubart's (1999) creativity model, the main question that guided the authors was 'Which aspect(s) of creativity enhancement did the writer(s) of the textbooks intend the learners to gain from this writing activity?'

Results and Discussion

Table 12.4 indicates the overall results. The upper row of figures for each creativity aspect shows the raw number of activities focusing on that aspect found in each textbook. The lower row shows that aspect as a percentage of the creative activities analyzed. The total numbers of writing activities in the textbooks are also shown.

The results show that creativity enhancement is focused only in 32% of the activities in the six textbooks. The analytic aspect of creativity enhancement receives the most attention in the textbooks (19%) followed by the synthetic (10%) and the practical (4%) aspects.

Interesting differences are also revealed between the textbooks. Table 12.4 shows a comparison of the percentage of activities looking at each creativity aspect in the six textbooks. Examining the percentages of creative activities reveals that across all six textbooks, only some creativity aspects receive attention and some aspects are completely ignored. The analytic ability receives the most attention,

TABLE 12.4 Number of activities in each textbook

	Synthetic Ability			Analytic Ability			Practical Ability	Creative Activities	Total Activities
	imagination	invention	prediction	judgment	comparison	contrast	reasoning		
English Result	1 (11.11)	1 (11.11)	1 (11.11)	0 (0)	3 (33.33)	2 (22.22)	1 (11.11)	9 (56)	16
English Zone	0 (0)	0 (0)	0 (0)	1 (33.33)	1 (33.33)	1 (33.33)	0 (0)	3 (18.75)	16
Interchange	2 (50)	1 (25)	0 (0)	0 (0)	1 (25)	0 (0)	0 (0)	4 (33.33)	12
New Headway Plus	0 (0)	0 (0)	0 (0)	0 (0)	1 (100)	0 (0)	0 (0)	1 (8.5)	12
Spectrum	1 (33.33)	0 (0)	0 (0)	0 (0)	1 (33.33)	0 (0)	1 (33.33)	3 (30)	10
Top-Notch	1 (16.66)	0 (0)	0 (0)	0 (0)	3 (50)	1 (16.66)	1 (16.66)	6 (37.5)	16

while the practical ability receives the least. Furthermore, the results reveal that in textbooks such as *English Result* and *Top-Notch*, with 56% of creative activities, more attention is given to enhancing learners' creativity in writing, and that *New Headway Plus* with 8.5%, has the lowest percentage of creative activities.

In what follows, the percentages of creativity aspects in each textbook will be discussed in more detail. In *English Result*, analytic ability is focused on most (55.55%), while practical ability is focused on least (11.11%). Comparison activities as a subgroup of the analytic ability comprised 33.33% of the total creative activities, which is the highest percentage compared to other subgroups.

In *Interchange*, synthetic ability is paid attention to the most (75%), while practical ability is ignored completely. Imagination activities comprised 50% of the total creative activities in the synthetic subgroup. In *New Headway Plus*, analytic ability is the only ability which is catered for, and the other creative abilities are ignored. There is only one creative activity in the whole textbook, which features comparison, and there are no other creative writing activities found in the textbook. In *English Zone*, analytic ability is the only ability which the textbook has focused on (100%) and there are no activities related to the other two abilities. In *Spectrum*, all three abilities are focused on equally (33.33%) with the same number of activities for each. In *Top-Notch*, analytic ability is focused on the most (66.66%), while the practical and synthetic abilities receive equal attention (16.66%). Comparison activities as a subgroup of the analytic ability comprised 50% of the total creative activities, which is the highest percentage compared to other subgroups.

Conclusion and Implications

The teaching of writing continues to occupy a major role in language pedagogy and a large body of research has focused on factors which help learners acquire this complex skill effectively. However, only a few studies have addressed the creativity issue, which is known as a central factor in learners' growth as writers. Thus, one of the options to teach and develop the learners' writing ability is to boost their creativity and to expose them to creativity enhancement writing activities. The main implication of this study is that creativity has an important role in teaching learners how to write. Thus teachers, educators, teacher trainers, curriculum developers, syllabus designers and materials writers need to pay attention to this essential factor.

One of the implications of this study is for curriculum developers, who need to identify which instruments work best for developing the writing ability of learners. They could also group learners according to their level of creativity in order to inform teachers and materials writers about the beneficial methods and activities they could apply in the teaching process.

By including creativity enhancement writing activities in the curriculum, teachers and materials writers would include and use creative types of activities and methods in teaching language, especially when dealing with the writing skill. Therefore, when preparing textbooks, materials writers ought to design creative writing tasks to trigger learners' imagination, creation, analysis, evaluation, and judgment in order to place them on the right path to learning. The findings of this study suggest that a broader view of creativity enhancement needs to be adopted and that all creativity aspects should be present in teaching materials. Researchers have clearly established the fundamental importance of creativity enhancement, yet they have repeatedly found that textbooks generally provide only a limited number of writing activities that include aspects of creativity (Grainger et al., 2005). Thus, greater consideration of all aspects of creativity should result in more effective materials.

More specifically, teachers should be aware that learners' creative abilities are most likely to be developed in an atmosphere in which the teacher's creative abilities are properly engaged (NACCCE, 1999, p. 90). The teacher's playfulness, openness, and innovative ideas also need to be developed and enriched if they are to contribute imaginatively to the construction of creative learners (Grainger et al., 2005). Through training, teachers would also be aware of their own level of creativity, which would affect their teaching style. Therefore, the element of creativity should be included in teacher-training courses, to help teachers learn how to become more creative in teaching.

The present study aimed at investigating writing activities in six general English textbooks by analyzing the activities' focus on various aspects of creativity (synthesis, analysis, and practice). Nevertheless, it did not deal with the effect of creativity enhancement on other language skills, such as speaking. Besides improving their writing ability, language learners need to become more creative in the other language skills. Thus, there is room for further research to investigate whether or not ELT textbooks address the issue of creativity in other areas as well.

References

Baleghizadeh, S., & Dargahi, Z. (2012). The impact of creativity enhancement on the attitude of young Iranian EFL learners toward writing. In H. Emery & F. Gardiner-Hyland (Eds.), *Contextualizing EFL for young learners: International perspectives on policy, practice and procedure* (pp. 328–338). Dubai: TESOL Arabia Publications.

Beghetto, R. A., & Kaufman, J. C. (2011). *Nurturing creativity in the classroom.* Cambridge: Cambridge University Press.

Borner, W. (1987). Writing in the foreign language classroom: Thoughts on a model. In W. Lorscher & R. Schulze (Eds.), *Perspectives on language in performance, studies in linguistics, literacy criticism and language teaching and learning* (pp. 1336–1349). Tübingen: Narr.

Craft, A. (2005). *Creativity in schools: Tensions and dilemmas.* London: Routledge.

Cumming, A. (1998). Theoretical perspectives on writing. *Annual Review of Applied Linguistics, 18,* 61–78.

Edwards, C. P., & Hiler, C. (1993). *A teacher's guide to the exhibit: "The hundred languages of children."* Lexington, KY: College of Human Environmental Sciences, University of Kentucky.

Ellis, R., & Yuan, F. (2004). The effects of planning on fluency, complexity, and accuracy in second language narrative writing. *Studies in Second Language Acquisition, 26*(1), 59–84.

Flower, L., & Hayes, J. R. (1981). A cognitive process theory of writing. *College Composition and Communication, 32*(4), 365–387.

Franken, M., & Haslett, S. (2002). When and why talking can make writing harder. In S. Ransdell & M. Barbier (Eds.), *New directions for research in L2 writing* (pp. 209–230). Dordrecht, the Netherlands: Kluwer Academic.

Galbraith, D. (1999). Effective strategies for the teaching and learning of writing. *Learning andInstruction, 9*(2), 93–108.

Grainger, T. (2002). Storytelling: The missing link in story writing. In S. Ellis and C. Mills (Eds.), *Connecting, creating: New practices in the teaching of writing* (pp. 176–224). Leicester: United Kingdom Reading Association.

Grainger, T. (2004). Introduction: Travelling across the terrain. In T. Grainger (Ed.), *The RoutledgeFalmer reader in language and literacy* (pp.1–16). London: RoutledgeFalmer.

Grainger, T., Goouch, K., & Lambirth, A. (2003). Playing the game called writing: Children's voice and view. *English in Education, 37*(2), 4–15.

Grainger, T., Goouch, K., & Lambirth, A. (2005). *Creativity and writing: Developing voice and verve in the classroom.* London: Routledge.

Hyland, K. (2007). Genre pedagogy: Language, literacy, and L2 writing. *Journal of Second Language Writing, 16*(3), 148–164.

Jackson, N. (2006). *Creativity in higher education: Creating tipping points for cultural change* (Scholarly Paper No. 3). Guildford, UK: Centre for Excellence in Professional Training and Education, University of Surrey.

Khoii, R., & Tabrizi, A. (2011). The impact of input enhancement through multimedia on the improvement of writing ability. *ICT Language Learning, 4*(1).

Kim, Y., & Kim, J. (2005). Teaching Korean university writing class: Balancing the process and the genre approach. *Asian EFL Journal, 7*(2), 1–15.

Landry, R. G. (1973). The enhancement of figural creativity through second language learning at the elementary school level. *Foreign Language Annals, 7*(1), 111–115.

McCutchen, D. (2011). From novice to expert: Implications of language skills and writing-relevant knowledge for memory during the development of writing skill. *Journal of Writing Research, 3*(1), 51–68.

McDonough, J., Shaw, C., & Masuhara, H. (2013). *Materials and methods in ELT: A teacher's guide* (3rd ed.). Oxford: Wiley-Blackwell.

Meera, K. P., & Remya, P. (2010). Effect of extensive reading and creativity on achievement in English language. *E-journal of All India Association for Educational Research, 22*(1), 16–22.

National Advisory Committee on Creative and Cultural Education (NACCCE) (1999). *All our futures: Creativity, culture and education.* Sudbury, UK: DfEE.

Nunan, D. (1991). *Language teaching methodology.* Harlow, UK: Longman.

Office for Standards in Education (OfSTED) (2002). *The curriculum in successful primary schools* (HMI 553, October). London: OfSTED.

Ortega, L. (2004). L2 writing research in EFL contexts: Some challenges and opportunities for EFL researchers. *ALAK Newsletter.*

Otto, I. (1998). The relationship between individual differences in learner creativity and language learning success. *TESOL Quarterly, 32*(4), 763–773.

Puranik, C. S., Lonigan, C. J., & Kim, Y. (2011). Contributions of emergent literacy skills to name writing, letter writing, and spelling in preschool children. *Early Childhood Research Quarterly, 26*(4), 465–474.

Randolph Community College (RCC) (2009). *Improving student written communication skills for academic endeavors.* Asheboro, NC: Randolph Community College.

Reilly, J., & Reilly, V. (2005). *Writing with children.* Oxford: Oxford University Press.

Richards, J.C. (2001). *Curriculum development in language teaching.* Cambridge: Cambridge University Press.

Sasaki, M., & Hirose, K. (1996). Explanatory variables for EFL students' expository writing. *Language Learning, 46*(1), 137–174.

Sawyer, R. K. (2004). Creative teaching: Collaborative discussion as disciplined improvisation. *Educational Researcher, 33*(2), 12–20.

Silva, T., & Nicholls, J. C. (1993). College students as writing theorists: Goals and beliefs about the causes of success. *Contemporary Educational Psychology, 18*, 281–293.

Smagorinsky, P. (1991). The writer's knowledge and the writing process: A protocol analysis. *Research in the Teaching of English, 25*, 339–364.

Sternberg, R. J., & Lubart, T. I. (1999). The concept of creativity: Prospects and para-digms. In R. Sternberg (Ed.), *Handbook of creativity* (pp. 3–15). Cambridge: Cambridge University Press.

Sutrisno, S. (2007). *Students' creativity and its relation to English learning achievement.* Unpublished thesis. Semarang State University, Brebes.

Thompson, G. (2001). Interaction in academic writing: Learning to argue with the reader. *Applied Linguistics, 22*(1), 58–78.

Tuan, L. T. (2010). Enhancing EFL learners' writing skill via journal writing. *English Language Teaching, 3*(3), 81–88.

Wegerif, R. (2005). Reason and creativity in classroom dialogues. *Language and Education, 19*(3), 223–238.

Zamel, V. (1983). The composing processes of advanced ESL students: Six case studies. *TESOL Quarterly, 17*, 165–187.

Zimmermann, R. (2000). L2 writing: Subprocesses, a model of formulating and empirical findings. *Learning and Instruction, 10*(1), 73–99.

COMMENTS ON PART III

Brian Tomlinson

What the chapters in this section have in common is a discovery that textbook materials do not typically cater for the needs of the learners who use them. Chapters 11 and 12 are particularly concerned that EFL textbooks rarely help learners to develop and make use of such high-level skills as criticality and creativity, despite these skills featuring in most national curricula, and despite convincing evidence not only of the educational significance of these skills but also of their value in facilitating language acquisition. Chapter 10 complains about the failure of many textbooks to take into account what we know facilitates the acquisition of grammar, and Chapters 8 and 9 examine what does and does not facilitate the acquisition of vocabulary (and in particular of lexical phrases) in typical classroom materials. Nobody is accusing publishers and materials developers of wilfully ignoring research on second language acquisition, so what is it that is causing the continuing gap between what we know is likely to facilitate language acquisition and the materials that are actually developed to help learners of second and foreign languages?

In my view the main problem is that the best-selling EFL coursebooks have established a norm which is difficult and financially risky to depart from for any publisher of second language coursebooks, and which acts as an unfortunate model of good practice for ministries of education and for institutions deciding to produce their own local coursebooks. This norm features a Presentation/Practice/Production (PPP) approach, not because it has been validated by research results but because it is convenient for administrators and materials developers, and because its success in promoting short-term memory provides an illusion of learning to teachers and students, providing this learning is tested immediately and in isolation. In addition to this approach, the best-selling coursebooks feature such exercises as matching, filling-the-blank, sentence transformation, sentence completion, true/false, multiple choice and choosing correct forms. Again, they do so not because any of these exercises have ever been found to facilitate the development of communicative competence, but because they are easy for the teacher to prepare and to use both for practice and for testing, because they are easy to mark and because students are used to them and can do well on them. Such books, if published by prestigious British or American publishers, written by native speakers, packaged attractively and promoted aggressively sell in huge and profitable numbers and establish a template for future publications. We are saddled with a stereotype of the second language coursebook which is unprincipled and which is unlikely to facilitate language acquisition, because most teachers want to use it and most administrators want to buy it. And students are not going to gain from more principled and facilitative materials until SLA research findings are applied in ways which can be demonstrated not only to facilitate language acquisition but to be both teacher-friendly and administrator-friendly, to appeal to and engage students and to have the potential to make it profitable for prestigious publishers to invest in them. That is what I hope this book will inspire people to do.

PART IV
Proposals for Action

13

LANGUAGE TEACHING MATERIALS AS WORK PLANS

AN SLA PERSPECTIVE

Rod Ellis

Introduction

Language teaching materials are work plans. That is they constitute plans for activities intended to facilitate language learning. We can ask two questions about language teaching materials: (1) What kinds of work plans can be predicted to facilitate learning? and (2) Do the work plans result in activity that facilitates learning? The first question concerns the design of work plans while the second question involves evaluating their implementation. Second language acquisition (SLA) is a field of enquiry that can inform both the design and the implementation of work plans. On the whole, SLA researchers have been more interested in implementation – in particular, how the interactions that occur when a work plan is carried out foster learning. In this chapter I intend to focus on the first question by considering how SLA can inform the design or work plans. However, SLA constitutes a source of information that can only inform the design or work plans; it cannot prescribe. Nor is SLA the sole source of information. There are other relevant disciplines and, of course, teachers' own experience of what works in their own classrooms.

SLA is an academic discipline replete with controversy. There is now a plethora of theories, all of which can be argued to have some merit, but which in some respects offer fundamentally different accounts of how learners learn a second language (L2). While, in its early days, SLA was motivated by the strongly felt need to find ways of improving language pedagogy, it has increasingly become self-contained and concerned with the more abstract goal of understanding the nature of the human language faculty. Thus, increasingly, SLA and language pedagogy have grown apart, to the point where some language educators (e.g. Bolitho, 1991) dismiss SLA as having little relevance to language pedagogy. A wiser stance, however, is that of Lightbown (2000), who proposed a set of generalizations which were 'consistent with the research to date' and which could serve as a 'source of information which could help teachers set appropriate expectations for themselves and their students' (p. 431). Adopting Lightbown's perspective, I would like to propose a set of generalizations that can inform the design of work plans.

The Generalizations

The generalizations are based on a cognitive-interactionist view of L2 learning. There are other theoretical perspectives of a more social nature – in particular, sociocultural theory – which have assumed increasing importance in recent years (see Ellis, 2015) but these alternative theories are arguably of greater relevance to the implementation of work plans rather than to their design.

TEN GENERALIZATIONS ABOUT L2 ACQUISITION

1. Acquiring an L2 primarily involves the development of implicit knowledge.
2. Explicit knowledge of an L2 can play a role in both L2 use and acquisition.
3. Acquisition of implicit knowledge of an L2 takes place incidentally and involves attention to form.
4. Acquisition of explicit knowledge is mainly dependent on intentional language learning.
5. The acquisition of implicit knowledge is gradual and dynamic.
6. The acquisition of explicit knowledge takes place linearly.
7. The development of implicit knowledge takes place primarily through social interaction.
8. The development of native-speaker levels of implicit knowledge requires massive exposure to L2 input.
9. Individual learner factors play a major role in the development of both implicit and explicit knowledge. Motivation is important for both types of knowledge; language aptitude is primarily important for explicit knowledge.
10. The learner's age influences the development of implicit and explicit knowledge.

Central to cognitive-interactionist accounts is the distinction between implicit and explicit knowledge (R. Ellis, 2005). Our knowledge of how to ride a bicycle or tie a shoelace is implicit. We know how to do these but would struggle to explain how. In contrast, our knowledge of history dates or of mathematical formulae is explicit. We can tell what we know. Likewise, in the case of language, we may be able to automatically add an '-s' to third-person verbs in the present simple tense without any deliberate effort or awareness of doing so, or we may consciously draw on a rule to remind ourselves that an '-s' is needed. Thus, the fundamental difference between the two types knowledge lies in whether learners are aware of what they know. In the case of explicit knowledge, learners are aware and thus can consciously apply what they know; in the case of implicit knowledge, they are not aware and thus apply their knowledge without conscious processing. Linked to this fundamental difference is the issue of the accessibility of the two types of knowledge. Explicit knowledge consists of declarative representations that, in general, can be accessed only through controlled processing. Implicit knowledge involves procedural representations and thus can be accessed through automatic processing. Another important difference lies in the durability of the two types of knowledge. Once acquired implicit knowledge is not easily forgotten. In contrast, just as we can easily forget historical dates or mathematical formulae, so too we can easily forget explicit rules of grammar.

Generalization #1 states that 'Acquiring an L2 primarily involves the development of implicit knowledge.' This is because implicit knowledge is necessary for participating in most types of language use – in particular in conversation, but also in free writing. Learners without implicit knowledge will struggle to communicate. Generalization #2, however, acknowledges that explicit L2 knowledge also has a role to play. Learners can make use of it to consciously formulate sentences/utterances and also to monitor the correctness of their use of the L2, providing that they have sufficient time to do so. Explicit knowledge is also of value in formal language tests.

Different kinds of language learning are involved in the development of implicit and explicit knowledge as stated in Generalizations #3 and #4. Implicit knowledge is acquired incidentally. Hulstijn (2003) defines incidental acquisition as 'the "picking up" of words and structures, simply by engaging in a variety of communicative activities, in particular reading and listening activities' and intentional learning as 'the deliberate committing to memory of thousands of words . . . and dozens of grammar rules' (p. 349). Both incidental and intentional learning involve mapping linguistic forms on to their meanings – for example, mapping the s morpheme on to a noun to convey plurality. However, these two types of learning involve different kinds of awareness. Schmidt (1994) distinguished awareness in terms of 'noticing' and 'understanding'. In incidental learning, learners need to consciously attend to linguistic forms in the input they are exposed to, while focused primarily on meaning. In intentional learning, learners develop an understanding of the linguistic forms they attend to by consciously formulating rules that can account for their regularity.

The process of developing implicit knowledge is gradual and dynamic (Generalization #5). That is, learners progress slowly towards target-like use of words and structures, manifesting in the process sudden leaps and plateaus and a high level of variability where they sometimes use the target form correctly and at others resort to an earlier acquired interlanguage form. In contrast, explicit knowledge is acquired linearly (Generalization #6). That is, learners memorize words and structures in the order in which they are taught and learn them. Implicit knowledge consists of an organic, evolving system; explicit knowledge is memory of separate facts about the L2.

Generalizations #7 and #8 address how implicit knowledge is acquired. All theories of L2 acquisition emphasize the importance of social interaction. Interaction provides learners with both input that they can comprehend and opportunities to produce in the L2. In particular, when communication problems arise and learners engage in negotiation to resolve them, making input comprehensible, they are exposed to those target forms that encode just those meanings they are trying to express, and they are pushed to express themselves more clearly. Thus it is through interaction that opportunities for incidental acquisition take place. Interaction that leads to negotiation facilitates the cognitive processes involved in form–meaning mapping. However, important as interaction is, acquisition can also take place through exposure to non-interactive input, but because the acquisition of implicit knowledge is a slow, gradual process, massive amounts of input are needed. A key issue in designing work plans, therefore, is how to ensure that learners receive adequate exposure to input.

The final two generalizations (#9 and #10) address two individual learner factors that influence the acquisition of implicit and explicit knowledge. Motivation influences the acquisition of both types of knowledge. Dörnyei (2005) rightly viewed motivation as the single most important factor in language learning. One source of motivation is work plans that learners find affectively and cognitively engaging. Language aptitude (i.e. the special ability that a learner has for acquiring a language) primarily affects explicit knowledge. Thus, earners with greater aptitude – especially the ability to detect and analyse patterns in the target language – find it easier to learn and are more successful in memorizing words and learning grammatical rules. Finally, recognition needs to be given to the role that the learner's age plays in language learning. Younger learners are more adept at 'picking up' linguistic forms from the input than older learners, and hence typically acquire higher levels of proficiency in the long-term L2 (Ellis, 2015). However, they are less adept at learning explicitly and thus initially learn more slowly than older learners.

Analysing Work Plans

Tomlinson (2011) distinguishes 'analysis' and 'evaluation' in his discussion of language teaching materials. The former 'focuses on the materials and it aims to provide an objective analysis of them' whereas the latter 'focuses on the users of the materials and makes judgements about their effects' (p. 16). In this section I will focus on analysis and in the following section I will attempt a critical evaluation by drawing on the ten generalizations about L2 acquisition.

Work plans can be analysed in terms of (1) the aspect of language they target (i.e. the specific skills or linguistic features they aim to develop) and (2) the characteristics of the activities included in the work plan. I will only be concerned with (2) here and, in the main, with how work plans cater to the development of the learner's L2 knowledge system. The framework shown in Figure 13.1 is very general in nature. It is not intended to suggest that work plans can be classified neatly into the different categories. Rather the framework specifies the methodological options that can be incorporated into a work plan. In many cases a work plan

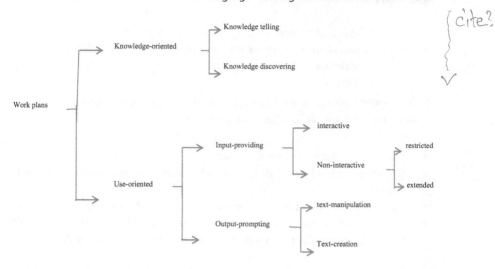

cite?

FIGURE 13.1 Framework for analysing work plans

incorporates several options, although often it is clear that a single option informs the design of the work plan. A work plan can be conceived as 'simple' (i.e. involving a single option) or 'complex' (i.e. incorporating several options).

A primary distinction is made between a work plan that incorporates a 'knowledge-oriented' option (i.e. it either provides explicit information about a target feature or guides discovery of the target feature), and one that is 'use-oriented' (i.e. specifies an activity that requires learners to make use of the L2 in some way). Use-oriented options can be distinguished in terms of whether the activity specified in the work plan is input-oriented or output-oriented. In the case of the former, a further distinction can be made between interactive and non-interactive activities. In an interactive input-based activity learners are required to process input to achieve an outcome of some kind, but can negotiate when they do not understand (for example, by requesting clarification). This kind of work plan involves what I have called input-based tasks (Ellis, 2001). In non-interactive input-based activities learners simply listen to or read texts without any need to engage in social interaction. Such activities are typically followed by comprehension questions or activities directing their attention to specific linguistic forms in the text. The texts can be 'restricted' as in a typical listening- or reading-comprehension activity or 'extended' as in a work plan that requires reading a whole book. This distinction reflects a continuum rather than binary categories. Output-prompting activities can involve 'text-manipulation' or 'text-creation'. This latter distinction is of particular significance when it comes to evaluating work plans in terms of the ten generalizations.

In a text-manipulation activity, language is treated as an <u>object</u> to be studied or practised. It has the following characteristics:

- there is a primary focus on specific linguistic forms;
- there is no communicative purpose;

- students' use of the target language is controlled;
- the outcome of the activity is a pre-determined linguistic display (i.e. the correct use of the target language).

In a text-creation activity, language is treated as a <u>tool</u> for achieving some communicative outcome. It has these characteristics:

- there is a primary focus on meaning;
- there is some kind of gap that needs to be closed (i.e. an information or opinion gap);
- students are expected to use their own linguistic and non-linguistic resources;
- the outcome of the activity is communicative (i.e. the language that results from performing the task is a means to an end, not an end in itself).

Work plans can be arranged along a continuum depending on the extent to which they allow for text-creation.

Illustrating the Framework

To illustrate use of the framework in Figure 13.1, I will analyse a number of work plans mainly chosen from selected ELT coursebooks. Often work plans occur in a sequence of work plans that incorporate a range of different options. For example, a knowledge-oriented work plan can serve as a starting point for a subsequent use-oriented work plan.

Table 13.1 illustrates two work plans that are clearly knowledge-oriented. Work plan A illustrates the *knowledge-telling option* whereas B illustrates the *knowledge-discovering option*. My impressionistic survey of popular ELT coursebooks is that there is a growing preference for the 'discovery' option although, as in work plan B, these often draw on learners' existing knowledge rather than guide them to discover something new.

Table 13.2 provides an example of a use-oriented *interactive input-based* work plan. I could not find clear examples of such work plans in the ELT coursebooks I examined, so I have included one of my own. This activity constitutes a 'task', with similar characteristics to tasks involving text-creation activities, the difference being that there is no, or minimal, requirement for production on the part of learners. By and large input-providing work plans in ELT coursebooks are of the *non-interactive input-based* kind. That is, students listen or read a text and then answer questions based on it and/ or it is mined for examples of specific linguistic forms. Texts can also serve as a basis for vocabulary and grammar out-based activities. They vary in size depending on the proficiency level of the course but at best are only of medium size. There are, of course, limits in the length of texts that can be included in a course book, but later I will suggest a way of overcoming this.

TABLE 13.1 Knowledge-oriented work plans

A	B
Grammar He may understand what is really happening. The fair could have been in any town in Europe. • Use could, may, might, must and can't to speculate about events or situations • In the present tense use modal verb + infinitive • In the past use modal verb + have + past participle *Global* (Clandfield and Benne, 2011 p. 43)	**Grammar Spot** 1. Which tense is used in these two sentences? Which verbs are regular? Which are irregular? He **laughed** a lot and **went** up to the baby. He **danced** and **sang**. Find more examples in the story and underline them. 2. What are the tenses in these sentences? What is the difference in meaning? He **laughed** when he **saw** the baby. He **was laughing** when he **saw** the baby. He **laughed** when he**'d seen** the baby. (he'd = he had) 3. Find two examples of the past Simple Passive in the story. *New Headway* (Soars and Soars, 2003, p. 23)

TABLE 13.2 An interactive input-based task

Map task

Listen to the teacher describe the locations of each of the following places on the map of the island. Write in the name of the place in the correct place on the map. If you do not understand the teacher's descriptions, you should ask for clarification.

1. Betu
2. Songa
3. Bottomless Bay
4. Mataka
5. River Ironga
6. River Ilonga
7. Iluba Mountains

TABLE 13.3 Use-oriented work plans

A	B	C
Rewrite these sentences using *so* or *such* so that the meaning stays the same.	Write five words about yourself.	Gervase Wilson-Hood lives with his large family. Here is a list of Christmas presents he bought for them. There is one present for each person.
1. This jingle is so annoying. This is _____.	**Ideas** *Your hometown; your interests; your job; your favourite place; your friends* Walk around the class. Introduce yourself to other people.	1. A diamond necklace
2. Advertising agencies come up with such weird ideas sometimes. The ideas that advertising agencies come up with are _____.	Ask questions about their words. Example *Hi, I'm Sandra. Nice to meet you. I'm Paul. What's this _____? That's my hometown.*	2. A computer game 3. A toy aeroplane 4. A designer shawl 5. A set of golf clubs 6. An Armani ladies wristwatch
Global (Clandfield and Benne, 2011, p. 81)	*First Impact* (Ellis et al., 1996)	Talk about this family. What kind of person is Gervase Wilson-Hood? Who are the people in this family? Which present did each person get?

Table 13.3 illustrates three use-oriented work plans involving output-prompting. Work plan A is entirely a *text-manipulation* activity. It manifests all four of the characteristics listed above. Work plan B, however, has elements of a text-manipulation and a text-creation activity. Arguably it does focus on meaning and perhaps too there is an information gap but the students are told what 'ideas' to focus on and an 'example' is provided so they do not have to draw much on their own linguistic resources. The outcome is a more or less pre-determined linguistic display. Work plan C (my own) more clearly involves *text-creation*; the focus is on meaning, the students have to express their own ideas about who the members of the family are and what present each person might be given, using their own linguistic resources. The outcome is a list of the family members, the present that each one received, and the students' opinions about Gervase Wilson-Hood.

Overall, then, popular coursebooks place the main focus on language as an object. Each unit is devoted to introducing and practising specific linguistic features and the meanings they convey. Typically the target features are contextualized in a reading or listening text. Knowledge-discovery is generally preferred to knowledge-telling. There is limited input. Output-prompting work plans dominate, directed at practising discrete phonological, lexical and grammatical features through text-manipulation activities. However, there are also are also some opportunities for text-creation.

To what extent, then, are these different types of work plans compatible with what is known about how languages are learned? To address this question I will now attempt an evaluation of them in terms of the ten generalizations.

Evaluating Work Plans

Knowledge-Oriented Work Plans

Knowledge-oriented work plans aim to develop explicit knowledge. Text-manipulation work plans may also contribute to explicit knowledge as they focus on the controlled use of specific linguistic features and invite learners to apply their conscious understanding of these features. Explicit knowledge plays a role in both L2 use and acquisition (Generalization #2). It is dependent on intentional learning and is acquired linearly (Generalizations 4 and 6). Thus, knowledge-oriented and text-manipulation work plans of the kinds illustrated in Tables 13.1 and 13.2 receive support from SLA theory. So too does the linear presentation of linguistic features which we find in popular ELT coursebooks – at least where explicit knowledge is concerned.

I have argued elsewhere that of the two knowledge-oriented options, discovery is to be preferred to telling. In Ellis (2010), I suggested that guiding learners to an understanding of how specific grammatical features function by means of consciousness-raising tasks is preferable to simply telling them how they work. A consciousness-raising task (such as work plan B in Table 13.1) provides learners with data and asks them to carry out some operation on the data (e.g. underlining, sorting, matching) in order to arrive at an explicit representation of a specific grammatical feature. Such tasks are likely to be more motivating than knowledge-telling, and, as Generalization #9 indicates, motivation is a key factor in successful language learning. Consciousness-raising tasks also have a learner-training function – that is, they help develop learners' language analytical ability, which learners can then deploy in self-directed intentional language learning. Research by Fotos (1994) and Mohammed (2001) has shown that consciousness-raising tasks do help learners build their explicit knowledge and that learners find them more motivating that knowledge-telling.

In Ellis (1991) I argued that if the goal is the development of explicit knowledge, consciousness-raising tasks are preferable to practice activities. Practice activities involving text-manipulation of the kind illustrated in work plan A in Table 13.3 can have a consciousness-raising function, especially if learners receive feedback on their answers, but they do not provide learners with input illustrating the use of a target feature and they do not require learners to understand how the feature works. Rather they encourage learners to make use of the explicit knowledge they have already developed. If the goal is to develop an explicit representation of how a target feature functions, production practice is unnecessary. The rationale for practice activities lies elsewhere – in helping learners to automatize their explicit knowledge so that it is available for use in communication – but, as I discuss below, it is doubtful whether they achieve this.

Generalization #2 states that explicit knowledge plays a role in both language use and acquisition. Certain types of language use – for example, careful writing – benefit from access to explicit knowledge. Cognitive models of writing propose a set of cognitive operations that operate in conjunction with working memory. Kellogg (1996), for example, distinguished 'formulation', which involves both 'planning' (i.e. conceptualizing ideas and rhetorical goals) and 'translating' (i.e. locating the language required to express the ideas), 'execution' (i.e. creating a text), and 'monitoring' (i.e. revising and editing the text). Because written production takes places off line, writers have time to draw on their explicit knowledge while 'translating' and 'monitoring'. What are needed, however, are purposeful free writing activities that provide meaningful contexts for learners to apply their explicit knowledge when 'translating' and 'monitoring'. Text-manipulation activities do not afford such a context.

Explicit knowledge can also facilitate the processes involved in the acquisition of implicit knowledge. As N. Ellis (2005) pointed out 'conscious and unconscious processes are dynamically involved together in every cognitive task and in every learning episode' (p. 340). In other words, learners make use of their explicit knowledge in the process of developing implicit knowledge. One way in which this happens is through 'noticing'. Prior explicit knowledge is not required in order to notice a specific feature in the input but it can assist it. If learners 'know' that there is an 's' on the verb in third-person present simple tense they are more likely to take note of it when they come across it in input. Similarly, prior explicit knowledge can contribute to noticing-the-gap (i.e. the difference between how learners use a linguistic feature in their own output and how the same feature is used in target-like input). Again, though, for explicit knowledge to contribute in these ways, it is necessary to create the conditions needed for the acquisition of implicit knowledge. Simply practising explicit knowledge in text-manipulation activities is unlikely to do so. Learners need to notice and notice-the-gap while they are engaged in attempts to communicate.

To sum up, work plans that are directed at developing explicit knowledge have a definite place in language teaching materials – at least for older learners. Work plans of the discovery kind are to be preferred, and it is encouraging to note that these are gaining in popularity in ELT coursebooks. Explicit knowledge plays a role in careful language use (e.g. in writing) but learners need opportunities to make use of their explicit knowledge in text-creation activities. Only in this way are conscious and unconscious processes dynamically connected. Text-manipulation activities are not likely to create such opportunities. Explicit knowledge also facilities the processes involved in the acquisition of implicit knowledge but, again, this needs to take place when learners participate in text-creation rather than in text-manipulation. Perhaps, then, work plans directed at the use of explicit knowledge should be disassociated from text-manipulation activities. By and large, however, ELT coursebooks continue to link these two types of work plans.

Input-Providing Work Plans

In a sense all the work plans in Table 13.1, Table 13.2 and Table 13.3 contain input of some kind either in the form of their rubrics or in the data comprising the different kinds of activities. If we view work plans in this way, then, there are opportunities for incidental learning that exist quite apart from their pedagogic purposes. Thus one way of evaluating work plans is in terms of the nature of the input they provide. In general, however, the input afforded by the work plans is limited in two ways. First, it is limited in quantity. Second, it is limited because the input largely consists of discrete, decontextualized sentences. In other words, the input-providing option they illustrate is of the 'restricted' kind.

An inspection of contemporary coursebooks suggests that this is a prevailing characteristic. In a typical unit of *New Headway*, for example, the only relatively extended input is to be found is in the reading passages used for practising reading comprehension and for mining linguistic features for knowledge-oriented activities of the discovery kind. Thus it is difficult to see how coursebooks of this kind can provide the massive exposure to input that the development of implicit knowledge requires (see Generalization #8). When the primary focus is on treating language as a set of objects to be studied and learned, the result is inevitably restricted input. As I noted above, this limitation is perhaps inherent in course-book materials but it is amplified by the dominance of work plans of the text-manipulation kind and also by the inclusion of substantial pictorial content that may aid motivation but often is only cosmetic in purpose. From the perspective of SLA, coursebooks can probably never provide learners with the quantity of input needed to achieve high levels of implicit knowledge. If, then, L2 acquisition primarily involves the development of implicit knowledge as claimed in Generalization #1, coursebooks replete with the types of work plans shown in Tables 13.1 and 13.3 will never be sufficient by themselves.

So the question arises as to how learners can be provided with the quantity and quality of input that is needed. The answer must lie in text-rich work plans, in particular those that require learners to read extensively and provide them with the resources to do so. Extensive reading is seen not just as a means of improving reading skills but also of developing linguistic proficiency. Krashen (2004) has consistently made the case for the 'power of reading' as a source of input for 'acquisition' (i.e. the development of implicit knowledge). He pointed out that 'language is too complex to be deliberately and consciously learned one rule or item at a time' (p. 11) and so learners need opportunities for acquiring the language incidentally through exposure. The graded reader series that many publishers offer can ensure access to both sufficient quantity of input and the kind of comprehensible input that learners need for incidental acquisition. It would be a simple matter for coursebooks such as *New Headway*, published by Oxford University Press, to include work plans that would direct students to graded readers such as those in this publisher's 'Bookworm' series, access to which could be made available online.

However, a case can be made for work plans containing restricted input – but of a different kind from those typically found in ELT coursebooks. Generalization #2 takes note of the fact that the development of implicit knowledge involves attention and that initially at least this must involve consciousness. Work plans involving what I have called 'interpretation tasks' (R. Ellis, 1995) cater to this. An interpretation task consists of structured input – that is, input that has been contrived to expose learners to specific target features and that requires learners to demonstrate they have processed it successfully by means of a non-verbal or a minimally verbal response. It serves, therefore, as a way of introducing new linguistic features and as a useful alternative to production-based activities of the text-manipulation kind. Van Patten (1996) claims that learners need to overcome the default processing strategies that prevent them from attending to specific grammatical features, and in a series of studies has shown that instruction consisting of interpretation tasks not only helps learners to process difficult features in input but also to use them in production. ELT coursebooks do contain some such work plans but they are under-used, as my own analysis of grammar practice books (Ellis, 2002) and Sommer's (2011) analysis of common EFL text books used in Germany show.

There is a lack of interactive input-based tasks of the kind illustrated in Table 13.2 in ELT coursebooks. Such tasks are ideal for younger learners and also beginner-level learners of all ages. They cater to incidental acquisition. Their interactive nature allows for the negotiation of meaning which helps learners to attend to linguistic forms while they are primarily focused on meaning (Generalization #7). In other words, such tasks create contexts that involve the real-time processing of language along with a focus on form and thus, in accordance with Generalization #3, may contribute to the development of implicit knowledge. Their interactive nature, also, is likely to enhance learners' intrinsic motivation (see Generalization #9). In short, such tasks demonstrate a high level of compatibility with several of the generalizations about L2 acquisition.

Output-Prompting Work Plans

The framework of options in Figure 13.1 distinguishes work plans involving text-manipulation and text-creation. While popular ELT coursebooks do include work plans involving text-creation these are less common than work plans that focus on text-manipulation. It would seem that the long tradition of mechanical type exercises in language teaching materials, originating in the behaviourist notion that language learning is a matter of habit-formation, is maintained in contemporary language courses. It is important to ask, therefore, what value such work plans have.

Text-manipulation materials encourage learners to treat language as a set of objects to be studied and mastered in linear fashion. In work plan A in Table 13.3 the object in focus is the use of *so* and *such*. The work plan requires students to consciously think about which word to use when rewriting the sentences. It is likely, therefore, to contribute to intentional learning and the development of explicit knowledge. Support for this type of work plan, therefore comes from those generalizations that relate to the development of explicit knowledge (i.e. Generalizations #2, #4 and #6). However, I have questioned whether text-manipulation is necessary or the most efficient way of helping learners to develop explicit knowledge. Discovery knowledge-oriented work plans can do the same job more effectively.

To justify the inclusion of text-manipulation materials it is necessary to claim that they contribute to the development of learners' implicit knowledge – namely, that by doing exercises such as that in work plan A in Table 13.3, learners will achieve control over the linguistic objects they practise to a level where they can use them in free communication. This is the assumption that underlies the popularity of text-manipulation activities in contemporary coursebooks. There is, however, little support for such an assumption in SLA. First, as stated in Generalization #3, implicit knowledge takes place incidentally, whereas text-manipulation exercises obviously encourage intentional language learning. Second, the acquisition of implicit knowledge is gradual and dynamic (Generalization #5) and therefore does not take place in a linear fashion. Third, central to the acquisition of implicit knowledge is the opportunity to engage in social interaction (Generalization #7) but text-manipulation exercises are typically completed individually and even if done collaboratively they are unlikely to generate the kinds of interaction that research shows is important for acquisition (i.e. they do not lead to negotiation). Finally, for many learners a diet of text-manipulation exercises may be demotivating and probably favours those learners with strong language analytical abilities (Generalization #9). In short, text-manipulation work plans are not the best way to ensure the development of learners' implicit knowledge.

There is an alternative position, however, that might lend support to text-manipulation materials, and it is probably this that explains their popularity in contemporary coursebooks. As Johnson (1996) noted 'there is more than one path to second language mastery' (p. 177). According to skill-learning theory, the proceduralization of declarative knowledge takes place when learners construct 'productions' consisting of condition-action pairs that can be used to initiate appropriate actions when the relevant condition applies. For example, on completing work plan A in Table 13.3, learners may succeed in forming these condition-action productions:

If you wish to intensify an adjective, use *so*; if you wish to intensify a noun use *such*.

Proceduralization, however, does not guarantee automaticity. Learners may still have to rely on controlled processing when applying the 'productions' they have internalized. To achieve automaticity learners need opportunities to practice using their 'productions' under real-operating conditions. Text-manipulation work plans may contribute to skill development by facilitating proceduralization, but text-creation activities are needed to achieve full automatization.

Thus, irrespective of whether the theoretical position informing the design of work plans is based on the implicit/explicit distinction or on skill-learning theory, text-creation activities are crucial. In the case of the former, they can be seen as sufficient in themselves to create the conditions for the development of implicit knowledge, providing that they also incorporate a focus on form. Text-manipulation activities are superfluous. Work plans such as C in Table 13.3 generate social interaction that caters to the incidental growth of implicit knowledge, when they attract learners' attention to those linguistic forms that they need to express their meanings. In task-based language teaching (TBLT), such work plans constitute the entirety of a course (see, for example, Prabhu, 1987). In the case of skill-learning theory, text-creation activities are needed to enable learners to progress from the procedural to the automatic stage so they can access their 'if-then' productions without conscious control.

Thus, a key question that must be asked of any set of language teaching materials is whether they include ample text-creation work plans. My inspection of contemporary ELT coursebooks indicates that there are relatively few self-standing text-creation work plans and that more often than not text-manipulation work plans are not followed-up with text-creation activities. In other words, on the whole it is an object-oriented rather than a tool-oriented view of language that informs these books. It is difficult to see, therefore, that they will be successful in helping learners develop the implicit knowledge (or even the automatized declarative knowledge) that they need to become confident and effective communicators in the target language. They may equip learners with explicit knowledge and perhaps also help with the construction of 'if-then' productions but without sufficient opportunities for using the language under real-operating conditions, they are unlikely to cater to the usage-based learning that leads to implicit knowledge.

Younger Learners and Work Plans

Generalization #10 points to the role of age in L2 acquisition. Thus it raises the question of what types of work plans are best suited to younger learners. Younger learners are generally credited with an enhanced ability to acquire an L2 naturally (i.e. incidentally by treating the language as a meaning-making tool). They are less adept at treating language as an object that needs to be studied, analysed, understood and memorized. In other words, it is those generalizations that relate to how implicit knowledge is acquired (i.e. #s 1, 3, 5, 6 and 7) that are more relevant to younger learners. This indicates the need for plentiful input, interactive input-based tasks and text-creation materials. These types of work plans are also of crucial importance for older learners – as I have argued above – but they should constitute the bulk (if not the entirety) of any course book for younger learners. There is less need for knowledge-oriented or text-manipulation work plans. Sadly, however, this does not appear to be the case in published materials for young learners. As in the coursebooks for older learners, we find text-manipulation work plans dominate. For example, in unit 1 of *Super Minds Students Book 1* (Puchta, Gerngross, & Lewis-Jones, 2012) the opening work plan asks learners to listen to and read some words and then say them out loud to label a picture. This is then followed by another work plan that instructs them to listen to and then chant a ready-made text.

Conclusion

The views I have expressed in this chapter may well be seen as controversial. Not all SLA researchers will agree with the ten generalizations I used as a basis for examining the design of work plans. Whether and how explicit knowledge plays a role in the development of implicit knowledge, for example, remains an area of disagreement. Whether adult learners are still capable of developing true implicit knowledge is also subject to argument. DeKeyser (2009) claims that the best adult learners can achieve is automatized production sets of the 'if-then' kind. But despite these differences, the ten generalizations do broadly reflect the cognitive-interactionist view of L2 acquisition I based them on.

I anticipate more opposition from writers of coursebooks. Perhaps I have been over hard in claiming that they over-emphasize an object-oriented view of language, and they will point to work plans in their books that do treat language as a tool. But I think it will be difficult to argue against two of my central points – namely, that their coursebooks do not provide learners with the massive amount of input needed for the gradual and dynamic acquisition of implicit knowledge, and that there is still too much reliance on text-manipulation work plans, which provide little input and meagre opportunities for the kinds of social interaction needed for implicit knowledge. In short, there is insufficient importance attached to incidental learning, even in materials for young learners. My position is that there needs to be a theoretically principled approach to balancing incidental and intentional learning for older learners and a clear emphasis on materials that cater for incidental learning by younger learners.

References

Bolitho, R. (1991). A place for second language acquisition in teacher development and in teacher education programmes. In E. Sadtono (Ed.), *Language acquisition and the second/foreign language classroom* (pp. 25–37). Singapore: Seameo Regional Language Centre.

Clandfield, L., & Benne, R. (2011). *Global*. Oxford: Macmillan Education.

DeKeyser, R. (2009). Cognitive-psychological processes in second language learning. In M. Long & C. Doughty (Eds.), *Handbook of second language teaching* (pp.119–138). Oxford: Wiley-Blackwell.

Dörnyei, Z. (2005). *The psychology of the language learner: Individual differences in second language acquisition*. Mahwah, NJ: Erlbaum.

Ellis, N. (2005). At the interface: Dynamic interactions of explicit and implicit knowledge. *Studies in Second Language Acquisition, 27*, 305–52.

Ellis, R. (1991). Grammar teaching – practice or consciousness-raising. In R. Ellis, *Second language acquisition and second language pedagogy*. Clevedon, UK: Multilingual Matters.

Ellis, R. (1995). Interpretation tasks for grammar teaching. *TESOL Quarterly, 89*, 88–105.

Ellis, R. (2001). Non-reciprocal tasks, comprehension and second language acquisition. In M. Bygate, P. Skehan, & M. Swain (Eds.), *Researching pedagogic tasks, second language learning, teaching and testing* (pp. 49–74). Harlow, UK: Longman.

Ellis, R. (2002). Methodological options in grammar teaching materials. In E. Hinkel & S. Fotos (Eds.), *New perspectives on grammar teaching in second language classrooms* (p. 155–179). Mahwah, NJ: Erlbaum.

Ellis, R. (2005). Measuring implicit and explicit knowledge of a second language: A psychometric study. *Studies in Second Language Acquisition, 27*, 141–72.

Ellis, R. (2010). Second language acquisition and language-teaching materials. In N. Harwood (Ed.), *English language teaching materials: Theory and practice* (pp. 33–57). Cambridge: Cambridge University Press.

Ellis, R. (2015). *Understanding second language acquisition* (2nd ed.). Oxford: Oxford University Press.

Ellis, R., Hegelsen, M., Browne, C., Gorsuch, G, & Schwab, J. (1996). *First impact*. Hong Kong: Longman Asia.

Fotos, S. (1994). Integrating grammar instruction and communicative language use through grammar consciousness-raising tasks. *TESOL Quarterly, 28*, 323–51.

Hulstijn, J. (2003). Incidental and intentional learning. In C. Doughty & M. Long (Eds.), *The handbook of second language acquisition* (pp. 349–381). Malden, MA: Blackwell.

Johnson, K. (1996). *Language teaching and skill learning*. Oxford: Blackwell.

Kellogg, R. (1996). A model of working memory in writing. In M. Levy & S. Ransdell. (Eds.), *The science of writing: Theories, methods, individual differences, and applications* (pp. 57–72). Mahwah, NJ: Erlbaum.

Krashen, S. (2004). *The power of reading*. Portsmouth, NH: Heinemann.

Lightbown, P. (2000). Anniversary article: Classroom SLA research and language teaching. *Applied Linguistics, 21*, 431–62.

Mohamed, N. (2001). *Teaching grammar through consciousness-raising tasks*. Unpublished MA thesis. University of Auckland, New Zealand.

Prabhu, N. S. (1987). *Second language pedagogy*. Oxford: Oxford University Press.

Puchta, H., Gerngross, G., & Lewis-Jones, P. (2012). *Super minds: Students book 1*. Cambridge: Cambridge University Press.

Schmidt, R. (1994). Deconstructing consciousness in search of useful definitions for applied linguistics. *AILA Review, 11*, 11–26.

Soars, L., & Soars, J. (2003). *New headway: Intermediate students' book*. Oxford: Oxford University Press.

Sommer, T. (2011). *An evaluation of methodological options for grammar instruction in EFL textbooks*. Heidelberg: Universitätsverlag Winter.

Tomlinson, B. (2011). Introduction: Principles and procedures of materials development. In B. Tomlinson (Ed), *Materials development in language teaching* (2nd ed., pp. 1–31). Cambridge: Cambridge University Press.

Van Patten, B. (1996). *Input processing and grammar instruction in second language acquisition*. Norwood, NJ: Ablex.

14

SUPPORTING LANGUAGE LEARNING ON THE MOVE

AN EVALUATIVE FRAMEWORK FOR MOBILE LANGUAGE LEARNING RESOURCES

Hayo Reinders and Mark Pegrum

Introduction

A number of important developments of direct relevance to mobile learning (or m-learning) took place in 2013. In that year, the number of internet-enabled mobile devices surpassed the number of desktop and laptop computers worldwide (*The Economist*, 2012); sales of smartphones surpassed sales of feature phones (Blodget & Danova, 2014); and mobile-generated traffic reached 20% of all internet traffic (Blodget & Danova, 2014), before increasing to more than 25% in the first half of 2014 (Meeker, 2014). It is timely for teachers and researchers to seek to identify and capitalize on the educational potential of these developments.

There is some disagreement over exactly what constitutes a 'mobile' as opposed to a 'portable' device, but Puentedura (2012) suggests a rule of thumb by which the latter is a device which is typically used at Point A, closed down and transported, then opened up again at Point B; while the former is a device that can be used at Point A, Point B and everywhere in between without stopping. From this perspective, today's most common mobile devices include mobile phones or cellphones (both feature phones and smartphones, with the latter running on mobile operating systems and being largely app-driven) and tablets. Older mobile devices, which are becoming less common as their functionality is subsumed into smartphones and tablets, include personal digital assistants (PDAs) and MP3 players. Newer mobile devices which are beginning to emerge include wearables such as fitness trackers (often in the form of wrist bands), smartwatches and smart glasses (or augmented-reality glasses). While laptops, especially smaller notebooks and netbooks, share some similarities with mobile devices, they in fact fall into Puentedura's portable category.

Smart mobile devices have a range of input mechanisms, thanks to the move towards natural user interfaces which can be operated by touch, gesture and voice. These devices also allow optical recognition of text, quick response (QR) codes and other augmented-reality (AR) markers; they are location-aware, thanks to inbuilt GPS receivers, compasses, gyroscopes and accelerometers; and they can pick up signals from Bluetooth, radio frequency identification (RFID) and near field communication (NFC) tags. Output modes include the visual, auditory and haptic (that is, tactile output, such as the vibration of a phone).

There are two main ways to engage in learning with a mobile device. The first involves using a general web browser to access websites, some of which may have been optimized for mobile access; the second involves downloading dedicated, single-purpose pieces of software called apps, which are normally sourced from online app stores. Apps provide a smoother, more streamlined experience, with most social media platforms and many educational services offering app versions, and increasing numbers adopting an app-first or app-only approach. At the same time, however, end users often find themselves with less control over their online experience than on the wider web 2.0, and with far less ability to move easily between apps, which effectively operate as walled gardens isolated from each other and the wider web (Pegrum, 2014). Some educators worry that the kind of active, collaborative learning facilitated by web 2.0 is being eroded by a slick, corporatized 'appification' of the web (Quitney Anderson & Rainie, 2012) which, if it progresses too far, could eventually lead to a learning landscape populated almost exclusively by individually purchased, independently used, stand-alone apps training limited sets of knowledge or skills. Fortunately, the situation is not yet so bleak.

There are two categories of *mobile resources* (whether general m-learning or specific mobile-assisted language learning [MALL] resources) available to teachers and students. First, there are *mobile materials*, in the form of websites or apps (or collections of websites or apps); and secondly, there are *mobile activities*, in the form of activities designed around websites or apps (see Table 14.1).

Mobile materials include dedicated web services and apps that are content-specific and do not require adaptation for language learning. In many cases, not only the content but the pedagogy has been designed into these sites and apps. Particularly in the case of apps, the pedagogy tends to be rather traditional, leaning towards information transmission and especially behaviourism; this is true not just of MALL apps but of educational apps in general (Murray & Olcese, 2011; Oakley et al., 2012; Searson, 2014). Some more recent apps are overlaid with social networking and sharing channels which offer more active learning options, and simple app design is now coming within the reach of teachers and students thanks to the availability of easy-to-use app-building software (Miller & Doering, 2014; Pegrum, 2014), thus increasing the collaborative, constructivist potential.

While dedicated language learning materials can be used in a stand-alone manner, they can of course also be incorporated into the design of broader *mobile activities* for language learning, which may have a more collaborative and/or constructivist orientation. Thus, a pedagogically limited information transmission app (say, an online dictionary) or a behaviourist app (say, a set of grammar drills) might form part of a larger collection or activity underpinned by a more sophisticated pedagogical design. Generic materials, like social networking services and videosharing sites, also offer many possibilities for active, collaborative learning, though they need to be adapted

TABLE 14.1 Classification of mobile learning resources

Mobile Materials	Web-based	App-based
Dedicated	Dedicated web services	Dedicated apps
Generic	Generic web services	Generic apps

Mobile Activities	
Dedicated	*May use any combination of dedicated and/or generic web services and/or apps within the design of a broader learning activity. If only generic web services and/or apps are used, they must be incorporated within the broader design of a language learning activity, which may be fully digital or blended.*

to different content areas (such as language learning) and their pedagogical use needs to be carefully considered in the overall design of a learning activity. Such learning activities may involve either a fully digital approach, or a blended approach where digital materials are combined with analogue materials in a face-to-face context.

As Burston (2014) notes, the vast majority of MALL implementations to date have been underpinned by "a behaviorist, teacher-centred, transmission model of instruction" despite the potential for "more innovative constructivist, collaborative, learner-centred instruction" (p. 344; cf. Beatty, 2013). Given the disjuncture between the promising future potential and the disappointing current reality of m-learning and MALL, it is important that educators have an evaluative framework which can guide them in assessing the benefits of the mobile resources they are considering using with their students, as well as guiding them in the design of mobile resources they may create themselves.

Evaluating MALL Resources

The evaluation of MALL resources ultimately comes down to an evaluation of the learning design of those resources. With the ongoing rollout of technology, there is a growing emphasis on the importance of learning design (Phillips, McNaught, & Kennedy, 2012; Milrad et al., 2013), with teachers increasingly being required to adopt the role of learning designers (Garcia, 2014; Hockly, 2013; Laurillard, 2012). While it is true that the nature of the available access to hardware, software and connectivity, as well as various aspects of the hardware and software itself (such as input and output mechanisms with the former, or customization options with the latter), have an impact on the learning that is possible, these elements fall outside the area of learning design and are not considered here.

The learning design can be evaluated with respect to a number of categories: The extent to which the potential educational affordances of mobile devices are exploited in the learning design (see Category 1 in our framework); the extent to which the learning design corresponds to general pedagogical approaches (Category 2); the extent to which the learning design corresponds to specific second language (L2) pedagogical approaches (Category 3); the extent to which the learning design corresponds to second language acquisition (SLA) principles (Category 4); and, finally, the extent to which the learning design takes into account affective principles (Category 5). While the measurement of learning outcomes is an important consideration in the implementation of MALL or indeed any educational resources, this is only possible post-implementation. Thus, while it may impact on subsequent reuse or redesign, it cannot influence initial use or design, and is therefore not considered here.

Category 1: Educational Affordances Exploited in Learning Design

All technologies have their own particular affordances, that is, uses to which they seem most readily to lend themselves. For Klopfer, Squire, and Jenkins (2002), the five key affordances of mobile devices are portability (which may allow distributed learning, for example), social interactivity (which may promote collaborative learning), context sensitivity (which may support situated learning), connectivity (which may foster networked learning) and individuality (which may permit differentiated learning) (cf. Klopfer & Squire, 2008). In a more recent perspective which partly echoes Klopfer et al. (2002), Dennen and Hao (2014) list four key affordances of mobile technologies: Portability, connectivity, input devices and sensors (which may promote personalized and situated learning) and recording abilities (which may support situated and immersive learning).

Pegrum (2014) has suggested that mobile devices have at least three major sets of affordances which are relevant to learning, and which subsume many of the elements described in earlier accounts. First, they allow *a linking of the local and the global*: We interact in and with our local environments while simultaneously remaining connected to global networks, from which we can learn about our local contexts and through which we can share learning generated in our local contexts (thus, for example, there is support for distributed learning, situated learning and networked learning). Second, they allow *a linking of the episodic and the extended*: We can engage in bite-sized learning whenever and wherever we find ourselves with moments of downtime, but we can connect those bite-sized chunks into extended learning by simply taking up our learning where we left it the next time a free moment arises (thus, amongst other things, there is support for autonomous learning). Third, they allow *a linking of the personal and the social*: We make individual choices about our hardware and software and can tailor our learning journeys to our own needs and preferences, but we can also hook into global networks and learning communities anytime and anywhere we please (thus, there is support for autonomous and differentiated learning but also for collaborative and networked learning, as well as for specific SLA principles such as comprehensible input and output, and negotiation of meaning).

It is also important to consider the different possible levels of mobility inherent in mobile learning. At the most basic level, only the *devices* are mobile while the *learners* and the *learning experience* are not, for example in a connected classroom where students use a class set of tablets while sitting at their desks. At a more sophisticated level, the *learners* also become mobile, for instance when they move around or between learning spaces to share their learning with peers; but while such student mobility may foster collaboration and creativity, the *learning experience* itself is not mobile in that it could take place in any space or spaces, and remains unaltered by those spaces. At a still more sophisticated level, the *learning experience* itself becomes mobile as the changing environment feeds into and alters the learning process, for example as students make annotated multimedia recordings of their surroundings which can be shared with and commented on by peers in online networks. The greater the overall level of mobility, the more fully the affordances of mobile technologies for learning are likely to be exploited, and the more closely their use is likely to align with contemporary pedagogical approaches; hence the importance of the criterion of *mobility* within Category 1 (see the framework below).

Category 2: General Pedagogical Design

As noted earlier, most MALL resources remain pedagogically very traditional, which leads Burston (2014) to comment: "MALL has yet to realize its full potential and [. . .] achieving this aim is more a matter of pedagogy than technology" (p. 344). In light of this, it is vital to consider how MALL learning design relates to established pedagogical approaches, both general and L2-specific.

Over more than a century, but particularly over the last 30–40 years, we have seen a move away from *traditional pedagogical approaches* based on information transmission and behaviourism towards *progressive approaches* such as *social constructivism* (see Burston, 2014, on constructivism in the context of MALL) and its many offshoots, like *inquiry-based learning* and *task-based learning*. These are based on the notion that individuals construct their understanding of the world by integrating new knowledge with existing knowledge as they engage in learning experiences and learning interactions with others. While this does not mean there is no place in education for information transmission or behaviourist learning – foundational content like vocabulary or grammar may be usefully consolidated in drills and simple games, for instance – there is now a widespread recognition that this cannot be the whole picture of learning. At the progressive end of the spectrum, there is much more room for the kinds of active, collaborative learning that we know to be effective. There is also room for a range of recent sociocultural approaches to learning, many of which sit comfortably with social constructivism (Pegrum, 2014). These include *situated learning*, which involves learning in real-world contexts (see, e.g., Comas-Quinn, Mardomingo, & Valentine, 2009, on situated MALL); *embodied learning*, which involves taking into account the connection between the mind, the body and the wider environment (see, e.g., Driver, 2012, on embodied MALL); *informal learning* (see, e.g., Comas-Quinn et al., 2009, on informal MALL); and of course *student-centred learning* (see, e.g., Burston, 2014, on learner-centred MALL). In addition, at this end of the spectrum there is room to incorporate a focus on the *21st-century skills* that are now regarded as increasingly essential (Gee, 2013; Mishra & Kereluik, 2011; NCTE, 2013; P21, n.d.): These are generally seen to include *creativity* and innovation, linked to entrepreneurship (Barber, Donnelly, & Rizvi, 2012; Khan, 2012; Robinson, 2011; Zhao, 2012), along with *critical thinking* and problem-solving, *collaboration* and teamwork, and *autonomy* and flexibility

(Pegrum, 2014). Naturally, there is some overlap between progressive pedagogical approaches and 21st-century skills approaches, and indeed between individual approaches and skills within these categories.

Category 3: L2 Pedagogical Design

There are a number of recent L2 pedagogical approaches which are widely regarded as particularly effective in the teaching of languages. They generally sit comfortably with social constructivism and other progressive approaches, of which they are sometimes a more specific inflection, and they generally sit comfortably with each other. The *communicative approach* represents a move towards authentic, situated interaction in line with SLA principles (see Category 4 below) (see, e.g., Pegrum, 2014, on communicative MALL). The *task-based approach* focuses on situated meaning and the achievement of real-life goals, and technology has been shown to facilitate its implementation (see, e.g., Thomas & Reinders, 2010, on task-based computer-assisted language learning [CALL]). An *intercultural (communicative) competence approach* or *intercultural literacy approach* goes beyond simply teaching and learning about other cultures and focuses on situated intercultural interactions (see, e.g., Palfreyman, 2012, on intercultural MALL).

Category 4: SLA Design

SLA research over many years has identified a number of core requirements for effective language learning. These include the need for *comprehensible input, comprehensible output, negotiation of meaning* in interaction, and *noticing* of new language, the last of which can be promoted through corrective *feedback* (e.g., Ellis, 2005). Kukulska-Hulme and Bull (2009) have linked MALL to noticing, a connection reiterated by Burston (2014), who makes a further link to constructivism. Many MALL resources capitalize on the capability of mobile devices, which at their most sophisticated can track our situated learning in real-world contexts, to provide immediate, detailed, automated feedback, which can later be complemented by human feedback (Pegrum, 2014). In fact, progressive pedagogical approaches and their specific L2 inflections can be employed in such a way as to make room for all of the above SLA principles in MALL (see, e.g., Nah, White, & Sussex, 2008, on combining progressive approaches and SLA principles in MALL).

Category 5: Affective Design

It is widely accepted that affective factors play an important role in language learning. Teachers have explored many strategies for increasing students' *engagement* and motivation through the use of interesting, relevant resources (see, e.g., Beckmann & Martin, 2013, on engagement through MALL), while simultaneously attempting to *lower students' affective filters* (see, e.g., Edge et al., 2011, on lowering affective filters through MALL).

Mobile design guidelines developed over recent years have taken many of the learning affordances and pedagogical possibilities of mobile devices into account in varying combinations (e.g., Herrington, Herrington, & Mantei, 2009; Sharples et al., 2009). Our own framework, outlined below, has a slightly different aim, as it focuses on evaluation rather than design, but it nevertheless details a set of principles which could be considered in the design phase of mobile resources.

The Framework

Based on the foregoing analysis of affordances, pedagogies and principles, we have developed a framework for evaluating the learning design of *mobile resources* for language teaching and learning, whether those resources are *mobile materials* like websites or apps, or collections of websites or apps, or *mobile activities* designed around websites or apps. It is important to evaluate a mobile resource at the macro level; that is, while a website or app used alone may be evaluated in isolation, a collection should be evaluated at the level of the whole collection, and an activity incorporating one or more websites or apps should be evaluated at the level of the whole activity.

The evaluation framework consists of five different categories, subdivided into criteria which may be rated on a continuum from 1 to 5 (with the exception of two criteria with higher possible scores, in Categories 1 and 2 respectively, as explained in the table notes). This results in a total score for each criterion, each category, and the mobile resource as a whole. Brief explanations of each category and criterion have been given in the preceding section, 'Evaluating MALL Resources'. Of course, this is necessarily an inexact science, with educators being required to estimate scores on the various continua to achieve a total. Absolute scores are not important in themselves, but where two or more resources are compared, the resource with a higher score is likely to be the one with more sophisticated pedagogical potential. Criteria or even categories considered irrelevant may be omitted, but the act of evaluating resources against multiple criteria and categories may help practitioners to improve their use – or their design – of mobile materials and activities in previously unconsidered ways.

Applying the Framework

This section presents a worked example of an evaluation conducted with the framework. In the activity being evaluated, university-level English language learners use an AR app to create a virtual campus tour for foreign visitors. Working in teams, they annotate physical objects (such as buildings and natural landscape features) with written and audio comments, which are geotagged to the relevant sites, and can be accessed in those locations by visitors taking the tour via the AR app on their mobile devices. The comments consist of historical, cultural and practical information to help visitors get to know the campus. The activity requires smartphones with wifi or 3G/4G Internet access, which can be shared among students (one per four students). The teacher and the students must know how to use an AR app, meaning that some preparation may be necessary for the teacher, followed by some pre-teaching for the students. The skills that students develop are transferable. For a description of a pilot version of this activity, see Reinders, Lakarnchua, and Pegrum (in press).

TABLE 14.2 Framework for evaluating the learning design of mobile resources for language teaching and learning

Category 1: Educational Affordances Exploited in Learning Design (__/50)

Criterion	Evaluation Continuum					Score
Local learning	1	2	3	4	5	
	little potential for local learning ⇔ much potential for local learning					
Global learning	1	2	3	4	5	
	little potential for global learning ⇔ much potential for global learning					
Episodic learning	1	2	3	4	5	
	little potential for episodic learning ⇔ much potential for episodic learning					
Extended learning	1	2	3	4	5	
	little potential for extended learning ⇔ much potential for extended learning					
Personal learning	1	2	3	4	5	
	little potential for personal learning ⇔ much potential for personal learning					
Social learning	1	2	3	4	5	
	little potential for social learning ⇔ much potential for social learning					
Mobility*	4	8	12	16	20	
	devices mobile ⇔ devices & students mobile ⇔ devices, students & learning experience mobile					

* Note: It is suggested that this criterion should be worth more than the others in this category, since it is arguably the most important, as explained under 'Evaluating MALL Resources' above.

Category 2: General Pedagogical Design (__/50)

Criterion	Evaluation Continuum					Score
Constructivist learning*	2	4	6	8	10	
	transmissive/behaviourist learning ⇔ (social) constructivist learning					
Situated learning	1	2	3	4	5	
	abstract learning ⇔ situated learning					
Embodied learning	1	2	3	4	5	
	disembodied learning ⇔ embodied learning					
Informal learning	1	2	3	4	5	
	little informal learning ⇔ much informal learning (may be alongside formal learning)					
Student-centred learning	1	2	3	4	5	
	teacher-centred learning ⇔ student-centred learning					
21st-century skills: Creative learning	1	2	3	4	5	
	uncreative learning ⇔ highly creative learning					
21st-century skills: Critical learning	1	2	3	4	5	
	uncritical learning ⇔ critical learning					

Criterion	Evaluation Continuum					Score
21st-century skills: Collaborative learning	1	2	3	4	5	
	uncollaborative learning ⇔ collaborative learning					
21st-century skills: Autonomous learning	1	2	3	4	5	
	student dependency ⇔ student autonomy					

* Note: It is suggested that this criterion should be worth more than the others in this category, since (social) constructivism is arguably today's most important pedagogical approach and in some senses sets the scene for many other progressive approaches, as explained under 'Evaluating MALL Resources' above.

Category 3: L2 Pedagogical Design (__/15)

Criterion	Evaluation Continuum					Score
Communicative learning	1	2	3	4	5	
	non-communicative learning ⇔ communicative learning					
Task-based learning	1	2	3	4	5	
	no meaning-based task focus ⇔ meaning-based task focus					
(Inter-)cultural learning	1	2	3	4	5	
	no cultural element ⇔ cultural learning ⇔ intercultural learning					

Category 4: SLA Design (__/25)

Criterion	Evaluation Continuum					Score
Comprehensible input	1	2	3	4	5	
	little comprehensible input ⇔ much comprehensible input					
Comprehensible output	1	2	3	4	5	
	little comprehensible output ⇔ much comprehensible output					
Negotiation of meaning	1	2	3	4	5	
	little negotiation of meaning ⇔ much negotiation of meaning					
Feedback (nature)	1	2	3	4	5	
	automated feedback ⇔ human feedback ⇔ automated & human feedback					
Feedback (detail)	1	2	3	4	5	
	limited feedback ⇔ detailed feedback					

Category 5: Affective Design (__/10)

Criterion	Evaluation Continuum					Score
Engagement	1	2	3	4	5	
	unengaging ⇔ highly engaging					
Affective filter	1	2	3	4	5	
	anxiety-inducing ⇔ anxiety-reducing					

Total	Overall score out of maximum 150 points

The activity was rated separately by each author and our respective scores are given. This demonstrates that small variations are likely in both the category and overall scores, reinforcing the point made earlier that this is an inexact science.

Educational Affordances Exploited in Learning Design: 41/38 Out of 50

The activity exploits both local and global learning as well as social learning, and is highly mobile. A little personal learning is possible, but the activity does not exploit either episodic or extended learning, as it is designed to be carried out only once, without follow-up.

General Pedagogical Design: 37/38 Out of 50

The activity is constructivist, situated and embodied in nature, is student-centred, requires collaboration, and leaves plenty of scope for creativity and autonomy. On the other hand, there is little scope for informal learning, and critical thinking is not foregrounded.

L2 Pedagogical Design: 12/14 Out of 15

The activity is communicative in nature, involves carrying out a task, and encourages students to consider intercultural factors in the production of their tours.

SLA Design: 15/12 Out of 25

Comprehensible output is essential in the annotations students add to the landscape, though its effectiveness will not be evident until visitors take the tour. Similarly, feedback will be delayed; it will take the form of human rather than automated feedback, but probably with little detail. Opportunities for comprehensible input and negotiation of meaning are limited to the interactions among the students, assuming they follow the instruction to interact in English.

Affective Design: 9/9 Out of 10

The activity is new for the students and involves using English for a real-life purpose, which should prove engaging. Because students are working with peers in groups away from a formal classroom environment, their affective filters should be lowered.

Total Score: 114/111 Out of 150

Although the above framework is primarily designed for evaluating resources before deciding whether to adopt them, it is of course possible to carry out evaluations before, during and after the use of resources (Breen, 1989), and our framework may contribute to all these kinds of evaluations. With MALL materials and activities, which are likely to be new to many teachers, such evaluations are extremely important in identifying potential and actual obstacles to use, and establishing professional development needs. Post-use evaluations can also include the views of the learners about their experiences with the resources, and in the case of MALL can be helpful in bringing to light technical issues (such as a lack of wireless coverage), institutional issues (such as a lack of clear policies on the use of mobile devices for learning), and personal issues (such as privacy concerns over the sharing of individuals' data). Ideally, post-use evaluations should be complemented by mechanisms for measuring improvements or changes in learning outcomes.

Conclusion

We hope to have shown that MALL carries the potential to enhance language teaching and learning in line with recent pedagogical thinking and SLA research, and that this potential can be identified and approximately quantified when deciding whether to adopt, adapt or reject MALL resources in particular teaching contexts. The framework we have introduced above foregrounds educational affordances, general pedagogical approaches, L2 pedagogical approaches, SLA principles and affective factors. While designed for evaluation of resources prior to their use, the principles in our framework could also be used to guide the development of mobile materials and mobile activities, as well as contributing to evaluating MALL resources during and after their use. Through a consistent, wide-ranging approach to evaluation, ideally in each of the pre-, during- and post-implementation phases, our understanding of the ways in which MALL resources can support language teaching and learning processes will be greatly enhanced.

References

Barber, M., Donnelly, K., & Rizvi, S. (2012). *Oceans of innovation: The Atlantic, the Pacific, global leadership and the future of education.* London: IPPR. http://www.ippr.org/images/media/files/publication/2012/09/oceans-of-innovation_Aug2012_9543.pdf

Beatty, K. (2013). Beyond the classroom: Mobile learning [in] the wider world. *The International Research Foundation for English Language Education.* http://www.tirfonline.org/english-in-the-workforce/mobile-assisted-language-learning/beyond-the-classroom-mobile-learning-the-wider-world/

Beckmann, E. A., & Martìn, M. D. (2013). How mobile learning facilitates student engagement: A case study from the teaching of Spanish. In Z. L. Berge & L. Y. Muilenburg (Eds.), *Handbook of mobile learning* (pp. 534–544). New York: Routledge.

Blodget, H., & Danova, T. (2014, March 22). The future of mobile! *Business Insider.* http://www.businessinsider.com/future-of-mobile-slides-2014-3

Breen, M. (1989). The evaluation cycle for language learning tasks. In R. K. Johnson (Ed.), *The second language curriculum* (pp. 187–206). Cambridge: Cambridge University Press.

Burston, J. (2014). MALL: The pedagogical challenges. *Computer Assisted Language Learning, 27*(4), 344–357.

Comas-Quinn, A., Mardomingo, R., & Valentine, C. (2009). Mobile blogs in language learning: Making the most of informal and situated learning opportunities. *ReCALL*, *21*(1), 96–112.

Dennen, V. P., & Hao, S. (2014). Paradigms of use, learning theory, and app design. In C. Miller & A. Doering (Eds.), *The new landscape of mobile learning: Redesigning education in an app-based world*. New York: Routledge.

Driver, P. (2012). Pervasive games and mobile technologies for embodied language learning. *International Journal of Computer-Assisted Language Learning and Teaching*, *2*(4), 50–63.

The Economist. (2012, November 21). Live and unplugged. http://www.economist.com/news/21566417-2013-internet-will-become-mostly-mobile-medium-who-will-be-winners-and-losers-live-and

Edge, D., Searle, E., Chiu, K., Zhao, J., & Landay, J. A. (2011). *MicroMandarin: Mobile language learning in context*. Presented at the Computer-Human Interaction (CHI) Conference, Vancouver, Canada, May 7–12. http://research.microsoft.com/pubs/192734/edge-chi2011-micromandarin.pdf

Ellis, R. (2005). Principles of instructed language learning. *The Asian EFL Journal Quarterly*, *7*(3), 9–24. http://www.asian-efl-journal.com/September_2005_EBook_editions.pdf

Garcia, A. (2014). Teacher agency and connected learning. In A. Garcia (Ed.), *Teaching in the connected learning classroom* (pp. 6–9). Irvine, CA: Digital Media and Learning Research Hub. http://dmlhub.net/publications/teaching-connected-learning-classroom

Gee, J. P. (2013). *The anti-education era: Creating smarter students through digital learning*. New York: Palgrave Macmillan.

Herrington, A., Herrington, J., & Mantei, J. (2009). Design principles for mobile learning. In J. Herrington, A. Herrington, J. Mantei, I. Olney, & B. Ferry (Eds.), *New technologies, new pedagogies: Mobile learning in higher education* (pp. 129–138). Wollongong, NSW: Faculty of Education, University of Wollongong. http://ro.uow.edu.au/edupapers/88

Hockly, N. (2013). Designer learning: The teacher as designer of mobile-based classroom learning experiences. *The International Research Foundation for English Language Education*. http://www.tirfonline.org/english-in-the-workforce/mobile-assisted-language-learning/designer-learning-the-teacher-as-designer-of-mobile-based-classroom-learning-experiences/

Khan, S. (2012). *The one world schoolhouse: Education reimagined*. London: Hodder & Stoughton.

Klopfer, E., Squire, K., & Jenkins, H. (2002). *Environmental detectives: PDAs as a window into a virtual simulated world*. Paper presented at the International Workshop on Wireless and Mobile Technologies in Education, Växjö, Sweden.

Klopfer, E., & Squire, K. (2008). Environmental detectives: The development of an augmented reality platform for environmental simulations. *Educational Technology Research and Development*, *56*(2), 203–228.

Kukulska-Hulme, A., & Bull, S. (2009). Theory-based support for mobile language learning: Noticing and recording. *International Journal of Interactive Mobile Technologies*, *3*(2), 12–18.

Laurillard, D. (2012). *Teaching as a design science: Building pedagogical patterns for learning and technology*. New York: Routledge.

Meeker, M. (2014). *Internet trends 2014 – Code Conference*. http://www.kpcb.com/internet-trends

Miller, C., & Doering, A. (Eds.). (2014). *The new landscape of mobile learning: Redesigning education in an app-based world*. New York: Routledge.

Milrad, M., Wong, L.-H., Sharples, M., Hwang, G.-J., Looi, C.-K., & Ogata, H. (2013). Seamless learning: An international perspective on next-generation technology-enhanced learning. In Z. L. Berge & L. Y. Muilenburg (Eds.), *Handbook of mobile learning* (pp. 95–108). New York: Routledge.

Mishra, P., & Kereluik, K. (2011). *What is 21st century learning? A review and synthesis*. Paper presented at SITE 2011, Nashville, USA, March 7–11. http://punya.educ.msu.edu/presentations/site2011/SITE_2011_21st_Century.pdf

Murray, O. T., & Olcese, N. R. (2011). Teaching and learning with iPads, ready or not? *TechTrends*, 55(6), 42–48.

Nah, K. C., White, P., & Sussex, R. (2008). The potential of using a mobile phone to access the internet for learning EFL listening skills within a Korean context. *ReCALL*, 20(3), 331–347.

NCTE (National Council of Teachers of English) [USA]. (2013). *The NCTE definition of 21st century literacies*. Position statement. [Adopted Feb. 15, 2008; updated Feb., 2013.] http://www.ncte.org/positions/statements/21stcentdefinition

Oakley, G., Pegrum, M., Faulkner, R., & Striepe, M. (2012). *Exploring the pedagogical applications of mobile technologies for teaching literacy* (Report for the Association of Independent Schools of Western Australia). http://www.education.uwa.edu.au/research/?a=2195652

P21 (Partnership for 21st Century Skills) (n.d.). *Framework for 21st century learning*. http://www.p21.org/about-us/p21-framework

Palfreyman, D. M. (2012). Bringing the world into the institution: Mobile intercultural learning for staff and students. In J. E. Díaz-Vera (Ed.), *Left to my own devices: Learner autonomy and mobile-assisted language learning* (pp.163–181). Bingley, UK: Emerald Group.

Pegrum, M. (2014). *Mobile learning: Languages, literacies and cultures*. Basingstoke, UK: Palgrave Macmillan.

Phillips, R., McNaught, C., & Kennedy, G. (2012). *Evaluating e-learning: Guiding research and practice*. New York: Routledge.

Puentedura, R. R. (2012). *Building upon SAMR*. Paper presented at Presbyterian Ladies' College, Perth, Australia, September 14.

Quitney Anderson, J., & Rainie, L. (2012). *The web is dead? . . .* Washington, DC: Pew Internet. http://pewinternet.org/~/media//Files/Reports/2012/PIP_Future_of_Apps_and_Web.pdf

Reinders, H., Lakarnchua, O., & Pegrum, M. (in press). A trade-off in learning: Mobile augmented reality for language learning. In M. Thomas & H. Reinders (Eds.), *Contemporary task-based language teaching in Asia*. London: Bloomsbury.

Robinson, K. (2011). *Out of our minds: Learning to be creative* (rev. ed.). Chichester, UK: Capstone.

Searson, M. (2014). Foreword: The failure of education's first mobile device. In C. Miller & A. Doering (Eds.), *The new landscape of mobile learning: Redesigning education in an app-based world*. New York: Routledge.

Sharples, M., Arnedillo-Sánchez, I., Milrad, M., & Vavoula, G. (2009). Mobile learning: Small devices, big issues. In N. Balacheff, S. Ludvigsen, T. de Jong, A. Lazonder, & S. Barnes (Eds.), *Technology-enhanced learning: Principles and products* (pp. 233–249). Berlin: Springer Science + Business Media.

Thomas, M., & Reinders, H. (Eds.). (2010). *Task-based language learning and teaching with technology*. London: Continuum.

Zhao, Y. (2012). *World class learners: Educating creative and entrepreneurial students*. Thousand Oaks, CA: Corwin.

15

FRAMING VOCATIONAL ENGLISH MATERIALS FROM A SOCIAL SEMIOTIC PERSPECTIVE

THE DESIGN AND USE OF ACCOUNTING ENGLISH MATERIALS

Handoyo Puji Widodo

The current study aims to document the design and use of vocational English (VE) materials situated in the Indonesian secondary vocational education sector. For this study, the design and use of language materials are referred to as language materials development. Studies in this area have long been established in the contexts of English for general purposes (EGP) and English for specific purposes (ESP) (see Tomlinson & Masuhara, 2010). In ESP programs, for instance, there has been a growing body of research investigating the design and use of ESP materials (e.g., Harwood, 2010, 2014; Tomlinson & Masuhara, 2010). A great deal of this research has been undertaken in the context of higher education, but a few studies have been carried out in the secondary vocational education sector (see Hua & Beverton, 2013; Widodo, 2015).

Moreover, there is a plethora of empirical work on how to use English language teaching (ELT) textbooks in class and studies on teacher and learner reactions to textbook materials. However, these were not specifically geared for vocational secondary school students; most of them were undertaken in the English as a second language (ESL) context where students are exposed to use of English outside the classroom, and English is officially used in educational and non–educational sites. Despite the centrality of materials in varied language teaching situations, there has been little empirical classroom-based research on the totality of ethnographic processes of language materials design that addresses needs analysis, materials creation, and materials enactment (Singapore Wala, 2013). Particularly, though some accounts of ESP materials (e.g., business English, English for medical purposes) have been discussed and reported in the literature, little is known about how VE materials (e.g., English for accounting) in the context of vocational secondary education (Harwood, 2014) are designed and enacted. To fill all these voids, this chapter reports on the design and use of VE materials, particularly accounting English materials.

Research Questions and Contributions

The impetus for the present research project has been derived from my long research interest and involvement in the area of ESP materials development since 2001. I have witnessed the fact that language materials development in both EGP and ESP programs has been a subject of interest for both language teachers and researchers since the 1980s (Dudley-Evans & John, 1998). For teachers, language materials are used as core resources, which facilitate teaching and learning, and they are also seen as the backbone of any language curriculum programs (McGrath, 2013). For researchers, language materials development is a site of research documenting such development. In book publications, language materials development has been well documented (Harwood, 2010, 2014; McGrath, 2013; Tomlinson, 2011; Widodo & Savova, 2010). For these reasons, three main questions guiding the present study include:

1. What key factors influence the design and use of VE materials?
2. What are the materials used? How are they implemented?
3. What are students' responses to the use of the materials?

These research questions aim to capture the entire design and use of VE materials. Guided by these three questions, the contributions of the current work are demonstrating how social semiotic theory is pedagogically applied to materials design and use and showing how this theory of practice contributes to language materials development in relation to sociocultural second language acquisition (SLA) theory.

VE Materials Development From a Social Semiotic Perspective

VE is one of the ESP branches. It is also called technical English. For this study, VE is used throughout the chapter. VE aims to help students in a range of specializations develop their English ability in order to function vocationally. Generally speaking, it is geared for students in vocational education (tertiary and secondary) and for company employees. In the context of the present study, VE is integral to vocational education in senior high schools in order to help students make a transition from education to employment, and in some cases to higher education. The role of VE is as an additional competence that students need to develop. Because students have diverse specializations, VE is designed based on these specializations such as accounting English, English for tourism, English for hotel hospitality, and English for computer engineering. Due to these diverse VE programs, VE materials should be specific. VE materials are defined as texts and activities, which facilitate student learning. These texts and activities are representations of the actual social practice in a particular vocational domain, such as accounting. Despite the narrow focus of VE, some studies have reported that VE contributes to language development because it is integral to EGP (Black & Yasukawa 2012; Widodo, 2015).

Informed by Hallidayan (1978) social semiotic theory (intersection between linguistics, sociology, and anthropology), views language as a tool for meaning-making confined to particular sociocultural contexts. This language-based theory of learning concurs with sociocultural SLA theory, which claims that language learning is a socialization process. In this respect, meaningful language learning means engaging students with authentic texts and activities connected to their worlds. For this study, these worlds pertain to vocational practices as social processes of understanding and creating texts mediated by language. Anchored in sociocultural SLA theory, language development and knowledge building are mediated through social mediation or interaction. Therefore, students should be engaged in dialogic interaction through small-group literature discussions (sharing and talking about texts and practices in accounting) and exploring language and genre through myriad texts. With this in mind, language learning is thought of as language socialization as a process, which results in the development of linguistic and social competences through language practice and through participatory engagement with more capable or competent agents or actors and with materials available as a semiotic resource. This argument implies that language learning involves dialogic interaction accompanied by assisted or mediated action. Thus, VE materials are defined as texts and activities, which mediate content-specific ways of meaning-making, situated in a vocational context (Moschkovich, 2002).

The Study

Research Context and Participants

A site of engagement in the current research was situated in one of the vocational secondary schools located in East Java. This school recruited 300–400 students annually and offered such vocational specializations as accounting, marketing, office management, and computer engineering, among others. English was one of the required school subjects and met twice a week. Before the current project commenced, students were taught EGP. Though the textbooks used were labeled as English for vocational purposes (EVP), the content of the textbooks focused on EGP.

Informed by a participatory action research (PAR) design (for a fuller discussion of PAR, see Hunter, Emerald, & Martin, 2013), both my research participants and I engaged in a battery of plans, continued action, critical observation, and critical reflection in relation to VE materials development. This materials development enterprise was integral to a formal educational curriculum, because the school under study shared the same vision and mission with the present research project: To equip students with VE and to help students develop their VE. The present project was intended to research and change the ways language materials were designed and was informed by a theory of practice – that is, social semiotic theory. It also involved teacher–learner reflections, reflective practice, participatory learning, and collaborative engagement.

In this PAR were involved school actors such as school administrators, teachers, and students. Both the teachers and the students were informed of the project as an investigative enterprise and as pedagogical innovation. Table 15.1 gives a short profile of participants.

TABLE 15.1 A profile of participants

Participants (Number)	Ages (Years)	Languages Spoken	Years of Teaching/ Learning	TOEFL/ TOEIC	Degrees
• English Teachers (*n* = 2)	35–50	Bahasa Indonesia and Javanese	10–20	500–570 on TOEFL	Masters in English Education
• Vocational Teachers (*n* = 2)	30–35	Bahasa Indonesia and Javanese	16	500–700 on TOEIC	Bachelor in Accounting
• Students (*n* = 57)	14–15	Bahasa Indonesia, Balinese, Javanese, and Madurese	13	350–550 on TOEIC	–

Two school administrators were also involved in the project in order to facilitate policy and remaking of curriculum materials. It is important to note that, academically, most of the accounting students could be considered high achievers. Linguistically, some of the students spoke Javanese, Madurese, and Bahasa Indonesia. The students came from families with different socioeconomic backgrounds (e.g., government employees, merchants, farmers, teachers, entrepreneurs, and casual workers).

Materials and Procedures

Situated in content-based English learning, the students were engaged in small-group literature discussions over a period of six months. This activity is also called role-based discussion, in which each of the individual students played particular roles. This task aimed to increase students' participation in sharing and talking about texts. In each of the small-group discussion sessions, the roles were rotated so that the students experienced different roles until all the topics had been discussed in scheduled class periods. The class met twice a week. Each of the class periods lasted for 120 minutes. In all the small-group discussion sessions, host groups were given the opportunity to present the chosen text to guest-group members. The students used English but also Bahasa Indonesia, due to difficulty in expressing particular ideas in English. Before engaging in this task, the students prepared their discussion and contribution within groups, but when they interacted with students from other groups they were engaged in discussions naturally and were encouraged to spontaneously use English.

Here are the roles that host- and guest-group members played during small-group literature discussions:

Host Group

- **Text Picker**: Navigate and select appropriate texts.
- **Text Master**: Understand the selected text in terms of an author's main purpose or topic, tone, mode, register, style, and main points, as well as to critique

text relevance and usefulness in relation to core vocational competencies in accounting.

- **Summarizer**: Prepare a summary of the chosen text, which wraps up key ideas in the text;
- **Language Enricher**: Provide language resources, such as links or webpages; providing grammar guides, vocabulary lists, e-dictionaries, and corpora;
- **Passage Enricher**: Recommend further readings relevant to the text discussed.

Guest Group

- **Text Assessor**: Judge if the presented text is relevant to the chosen theme;
- **Information Seeker**: Exploit information in the text by asking questions;
- **Language Observer**: Identify any unfamiliar vocabulary and grammatical patterns, which need to be learned;
- **Note-Taker and Reporter**: Jot down what has been discussed and report some main points to the whole class and to the teacher.

Small-group literature discussions were derived from what the students read. They were assigned to read one of the chosen accounting textbooks and share as well as discuss their reading. Table 15.2 gives a list of accounting textbooks.

The students were given autonomy to choose one of the textbooks based on their vocational interest. All the students engaged in sustained or extensive content-based reading spanning 6 months.

Sources of Data and Analysis

Spanning eight months, empirical data were garnered through different research instruments as shown in Table 15.3.

TABLE 15.2 A list of accounting textbooks as extensive reading (ER) materials

Author(s)	Title	Edition	Publisher
Anne Britton and Chris Waterston	*Financial accounting*	4th ed., 2006	Harlow, UK: Pearson Education
Jerry J. Weygandt, Donald E. Kieso, Paul D. Kimmel, and Agnes L. De Franco	*Hospitality financial accounting*	2nd ed., 2009	Hoboken, NJ: Wiley
Pauline Weetman	*Financial accounting: An introduction*	2011	Harlow, UK: Pearson Education
Robert Libby, Patricia A. Libby, Daniel G. Short	*Financial accounting*	7th ed., 2011	New York: McGraw-Hill/ Irwin
W. Steve Albrecht, Earl K. Stice, and James D. Stice	*Financial accounting: Concepts and applications*	7th ed., 2011	Mason, OH: South-Western Cengage Learning

TABLE 15.3 Research instruments

Instruments	Purposes	Data Providers
Documentation	Analyze all the curriculum documents	School administrators
	Examine institutional expectations	and teachers
Participant classroom observation	Record all in-class interactions	Teachers and students
	Observe how all the materials were used	
	Examine classroom discourses	
Focus groups and interviewing	Explore differing needs of schools actors such as school administrators, English teachers, vocational teachers, and students	School administrators, teachers, and students
	Explore different perceptions of materials use	
	Find out unique stories of how the participants used the materials	

All the data were qualitative and digitally recorded. Digital recording was deployed in this PAR in order to generate more contextual and rigorous data (DuFon, 2002). As a researcher, I realized that the presence of digital recorders or the act of recording itself in classroom observation, group discussion, and interview sessions might influence participants' normal behavior, the naturalness of data collection, and the natural flow of in-class interactions. I could mitigate this Observer's Paradox or Participant Reactivity (Gordon, 2013) by playing a role as an insider (co-teacher) through prolonged engagement and self-immersion and by building trust.

All the qualitative data were interpretatively analyzed, in which my beliefs, theories, values, and attitudes were involved. These data interpretations are always open, dynamic, and fluid (Wodak, 1999). Despite this, analytical tools were used to minimize the arbitrariness of interpretation. For this reason, thematic analysis and functional social semiotic analysis were used to capture meanings of data socio-historically co-constructed. All the data were analyzed through different steps of analysis: (1) data selection and coding were qualitatively analyzed using Braun and Clarke's 2006 thematic analysis and (2) all the qualitative data were interpretatively analyzed using Halliday's (1978) functional social semiotic analysis. For focused analysis, a reduction process of data analysis was required to organize and look at relevant data representing what was actually being scrutinized (Yan & He, 2012). Units of emergent data were underlined and labeled in order to omit irrelevant data. For this chapter, the data were organized and presented based on a series of action as finding themes.

Findings and Discussion

Doing Context Analysis

Both the English teachers and I conducted context analysis. Through negotiation and discussion about instruments of context analysis, we decided to use classroom observations (what both teachers and students actually did in the classroom), textbook analysis (what texts and activities both teachers and students worked on), curriculum document analysis (what institutional expectations were), and focus groups accompanied with interviews with accounting students and teachers (what accounting students' and teachers' expectations were). For this chapter, I present major data, which depicted the conditions of English teaching in the school under study. Firstly, classroom observation data shows that all the students did test-driven exercises, including listening, speaking, reading, writing, and grammar exercises. These exercises took the form of multiple choices, questions and answers, and gap fillings. All these exercises were included in the textbooks. The teachers dominated classroom interactions: The students responded to what the teachers asked them to do particular exercises. The students were rarely afforded the opportunity to share and discuss learning materials. All the listening, reading, writing, and grammar exercises were presented in a decontextualized way. For example, in writing exercises, the students were asked to write a descriptive paragraph, but no writing prompts were given. The students did not receive modeling activity, which helped them write a descriptive paragraph. In grammar exercises, the students worked on language analysis on discrete sentences, and they also identified correct English sentences. These mechanical drills focused on form only. The students did not engage in meaning making activities. All the exercises were not integral to students' vocational area; that is, accounting. Textbook analysis data demonstrated that the teachers rigidly followed the textbooks without providing the students with making adaptation or modifications of the materials. These textbook analysis data confirmed the findings gleaned from the classroom observation data that all the exercises were mechanical or drilling-based. Here is a list of exercises in students' English textbooks. The teachers and the students did these exercises in all the class periods observed.

TABLE 15.4 Exercises in students' English textbooks

Sections	Exercises
Listening	Dialog text completion, multiple-choice questions, sentence rearrangement, dictation
Speaking	Noticing and memorizing useful conversational expressions (e.g., adjacency pairs), dialog text rearrangement, memorizing and acting out the dialog texts, writing and acting out dialog texts jointly, text matching, role playing, visual text description, dialog text completion, retelling dialog texts, pronunciation drilling
Reading	Question and answer exercises, text completion
Writing	Composing short texts, sentence rearrangement, text completion, grammar error recognition and correction, text translation, sentence transformation, summary writing
Grammar	Rule presentation and memorization, rule drilling, sentence writing
Evaluation	Text completion, question and answer exercises, filling in the blanks, error recognition and correction, sentence rearrangement, description paragraph writing, narrative paragraph writing

As documented in students' interview data, most of the students reported that there was no difference between testing and learning. They identified themselves as test takers. They had no other opportunities to learn English differently. One of the student participants said that "I have studied English for grading and for passing examinations. I hoped that I would learn English, which prepared me for a better future professional or academic career because being proficient in English was an asset for me as a vocational high school leaver. In my major, we read English because most of the accounting textbooks are written in English." This evidence shows that learning English should be relevant to their vocational area. One accounting teacher reinforced that her students must be competent in English because more advanced accounting textbooks are written in English. She added that "if the students wish to learn more about their vocational subject, they need to have a good command of additional language, that is, English so that they could access more vocational knowledge. Honestly, although many textbooks are written in Bahasa Indonesia, many terminologies are adopted or borrowed from English." This empirical evidence reveals that English is a tool for vocational knowledge building. For this reason, students need to be equipped with VE.

Focus group and interview data indicate that both vocational teachers and students were concerned about English lessons, which were relevant to vocational areas. They reported that that English teachers taught students general English (GE). Vocationally speaking, students encountered accounting texts in English, but they were linguistically unprepared for learning their accounting subjects through English. The students struggled to understand vocational textbooks written in English. The vocational teachers helped the students by translating every single text. When asked why English teachers did not teach VE, they said that they needed to prepare the students for two standardized tests: A school test and a national school-leaving test.

As school administrators reported, they gave the English teachers full autonomy to develop their own English lessons and classroom materials as long as the goal was to help the students develop their English ability so that they could function in general communicative and vocationally-situated encounters. This evidence indicates that the goal of English instruction resides not only in standardized test preparation but also in development of student English ability. Therefore, the current project was timely because it could cater to multiple voices and interests of students, teachers, and school administrators. There is an urgent need for dialogic and participatory language materials development, which involved teachers and students as co-collaborators.

Collaborating With English Teachers, Students, and Vocational Teachers: The Design of Accounting English

In this project, the English teachers, accounting teachers, accounting students, and I as a consultant worked jointly on the design of materials. Before the English teachers and I designed the materials, we looked at context analysis data. Firstly, we formulated goals and purposes of VE learning. Among others, these goals were to engage students in making sense of accounting texts; to equip the students with accounting knowledge; to assist students' English ability so as to function vocationally; and to increase students' awareness of language and genre features of accounting texts. The students were asked to provide input for this goal formulation. Secondly, in every English lesson both EGP and ESP, identifying topics or themes is one of the important criteria for selecting materials because "a content topic is always the starting point for [learning]" (Huang & Morgan, 2003, p. 241). Specifying content in materials also frames topics of interest relevant to what students are currently doing in their accounting domain. Therefore, we identified topics, which were relevant to students' vocational specialization, accounting. We also involved two vocational teachers in suggesting these topics and looking at core accounting competencies. Through close analysis of accounting syllabi, we came up with a major theme, *financial accounting* because this was the focus of accounting subjects that the students learned. Based on this major theme, we decided to include such accounting topics as: *Financial statements, the income statement, the balance sheet, cash flow statements, the recording process*, and *accounting cycles*. In discussion with the accounting teachers, these topics were relevant to core competencies of students' area of specialization and related to what students were learning in accounting subjects.

The accounting teachers were also involved in selecting vocational texts because they were familiar with the content of the subject. Inviting them to select these authentic texts would meet the relevancy and usefulness of the materials. In this VE materials development, collaboration between English teachers and content teachers is common because language and content learning is mutually reinforcing. For this reason, the roles of both teachers are equally important (Lo, 2014). After we decided the topics of the materials, we discussed texts and tasks on which the students needed to work. We selected these texts and tasks, which were socially practiced in an accounting domain. In other words, both the teachers and I chose textbooks and other texts as materials based on richness of knowledge (content competence) and language (linguistic competence). We argued that language goes hand in hand with disciplinary knowledge in that it mediates the construction of disciplinary knowledge. Soon after we collected all the texts, we talked about lesson activities that engaged students in the learning of VE. In doing so, we decided to choose small group literature discussions and functional meta-language analysis among others. These in-class activities were expected to achieve our pedagogical goals as mentioned earlier. After we designed these pedagogical tasks, we consulted these with the students as co-partners of the teachers in the design of VE materials so that the students envisioned what they would learn and whether these proposed tasks met their expectations or voices articulated in a students' needs analysis session.

Making Sense and Negotiating Texts Through Small-Group Literature Discussions

In all the class periods, I co-taught with the English teachers. Before the students engaged in small-group literature discussions, we provided them with a scaffold of how to do this task. In small-group literature discussions, the students were told to form a group of 5–6 members, and discuss roles they had to play. Those who were a host group took on these roles: Text Picker, Text Master, Summarizer, Language Enricher, and Text Enricher. The students in a guest group played such roles as: Text Assessor, Information Seeker, Language Observer, Note-Taker, and Reporter. In most case, individual students played two different roles at the same time. In this section, I would like to present a subset of data demonstrating how the students participated in two small-group discussion sessions. These spontaneous discussions took place after several class periods (20 times). During the discussions, the English teachers and I walked around and recorded the discussions. We also asked them to record the activity as well. This recording was used to allow the students to reflect on their participation.

To begin with, in one small-group literature discussion session, for example, a Text Master talked about the text of the recording process for 3–5 minutes. The recording process is a generally accepted accounting practice. It is a starting point for recording all the economic events or transactions. The Text Master specifically presented economic events, which had to be recorded from an accounting perspective. When he talked about this, he attempted to invite guest group members by listing items as shown below. The Text Master said "umm . . . so that our discussion is (.) lively . . . let us discuss the following accounting case. We can discuss (.) which the items listed should be recorded or ignored . . . and we should provide (.) a justification for your response."

An information seeker of the guest group responded "Well . . . allow us to read through first." One of the guest members said "I think we should record items number 1, 2, 5, and 6 because all these items are objectively measurable resources (.) which come into or umm leave an organization or a firm." Another member of the guest group added that "making the tea and moving staff between jobs in the office do not normally . . . lead to an immediate accounting transaction." The Text Assessor provided another justification that whether particular economic transactions are recorded depends upon what can be valued reasonably in money terms. The text enricher attempted to extend the discussion by mentioning other economic transactions, which should be recorded. She listed *money received for the sales, production materials bought*, and *borrowing money from the bank*. The text master concluded that "to identify (.) whether certain transactions are recorded or ignored . . . think of three major business activities

TABLE 15.5 The recording of economic events or transactions

Event / transaction	Recorded	Ignored
1. Selling one of the organization's cars		
2. Paying the wages		
3. Making the tea		
4. Moving staff between jobs in the office		
5. Incurring a fine for polluting a local river		
6. Paying the fine		

TABLE 15.6 Student list of business transactions

Economic events/transactions	Operating	Investing	Financing
Borrowing money from the bank			
Buying production materials			
Incurring a fine for polluting a local river			
Paying the fine			
Paying the wages			
Receiving money for the sale			
Selling one of the organization's cars			

like operating, investing, and financing . . . So, making the tea and moving staff do not fall into any of these activities." Then, a Summarizer drew a conclusion that "we can create another table to classify (.) whether the items we discussed belong to the three major business activities." Here is another text that the Summarizer created.

Generally speaking, the students of two groups played the assigned roles very well. They participated in small-group discussions by contributing ideas to the discussions. For example, based on the classroom observation data above, the students focused on content instead of form. The students could extend the presented text by creating multiple texts, such as drawing a table to discuss whether particular economic events should be recorded or ignored in an accounting system and a table classifying economic events based on three major business activities. To work on this issue, the students need to have sufficient accounting literacy. As observed, the students were literate in generally accepted accounting practice. They were familiar with economic transactions, which were subject to the recording process in an accounting term. The recording of economic transaction is a process of transforming transaction data into useful accounting information. All the students reported that sharing and discussing a variety of accounting texts led to knowledge building. In addition, they admitted that they experienced the actual use of English in accounting texts. They realized that understanding texts also led to understanding of generally accepted accounting practice. One of the accounting students (Ria) recounted that "being exposed to a variety of accounting texts helped me develop my vocational knowledge. At the same time, I also developed my English ability. Now, learning vocational English looks like 'killing two birds with one stone.' I feel that the purpose of learning English becomes clear." Another student, Yul, argued that sharing and discussing accounting texts in English challenged her to contribute ideas to the discussion because she played roles agreed before the small-group literature discussion began.

In another small-group discussion, the students talked about *control of cash*. They discussed how to create a journal entry text based on this text. The following dialog snapshot demonstrates how three accounting students made sense of and negotiated the text. One of the students initiated this discussion. She noticed this accounting text, *control of cash*.

As shown in the classroom observation data (verbatim transcription), the students engaged in making sense of the *control of cash* text. Their discussion came from

TABLE 15.7 Student engagement in meaning-making

Participants	Turns	
Student A (Yul)	1	I got this portion of text, err, from the textbook entitled *Financial Accounting: Concepts and Applications* on page 225 ((*looking at the textbook*)) . . . I find this text interesting . . . In this text (.) we have to provide all the journal entries and compute net sales.
Student B (Ran)	2	But let us list key concepts\
Student C (Ria)	3	Can I list *cash accounts receivable* and *sales*?
Student A (Yul)	4	Ria, that's good . . . These entities correspond to $100,000 for credit or accounts receivable and $40,000 for cash
Student B (Ran)	5	How about paying attention to this sentence "Customers who purchased on credit received sales discounts totaling $2,700 when paying for $90,000 of the goods purchased" ((*This student was reading the text, Control of Cash*))
Student C (Ria)	6	We need to reduce (.) $90,000 of the goods purchased by (.) $2,700 . . . So, the total cash is $87–300.
Student B (Ran)	7	So, the accounts receivable remains $90–000.
Student A (Yul)	8	We still got another number [umm] $4,500 (.) which means sales returns . . . What do you think?
Student C (Ria)	9	Yes I do agree . . . but the cash is (.) $4,500.
Student B (Ran)	10	So gross sales come from $100–000 and $40–000. The total gross sales are $140–000 (.) These sales are reduced by sales discounts ($2–900) and sales returns ($4–500) respectively.
Student C (Ria)	11	We can conclude that (.) the net sales are $132,800.

their reading of the chosen textbook. They focused on meaning instead of on form. In Turn 1, one of the students invited her peers to find out net sales and create a journal entry. First, they started by talking about key business entities, which represent control of cash. They attempted to find a solution by identifying numbers in order to find the total net sales. This turn-by-turn interaction showed how the students negotiated what counted as accounting computation and tried to meet generally accepted accounting practice. From this discussion, the students seem to be literate in accounting computation. One of the participants (Ria) admitted that before she discussed the text, she read it carefully. She also identified key terms such as *credit and cash sales, sales discounts, credit received,* and *sales returns.* She was aware that understanding key accounting terms allowed her to make sense of the text. She viewed her peers as collaborators in meaning-making of the text. All the students felt that engaging in small-group literature discussions led to knowledge construction and allowed them to connect one text to another. This evidence can be seen in the text (Figure 15.1) created by the student who played the role of Summarizer. This student created a journal entry as stated in the previous text.

As shown in Figure 15.1, the students collaboratively created another text, which came out of sharing and discussion of the previous text. This evidence shows that the students engaged in transforming a verbal text into a visually presented vocational text. It also confirms that vocational terms or vocabulary conveys key

Cash	40,000	
Accounts Receivable	100,000	
Sales		140,000
Cash	87,300	
Sales Discounts	2,700	
Accounts Receivable		90,000
Sales Returns	4,500	
Cash		4,500
Gross Sales ($100,000 + $40,000)		$140,000
Sales Discounts		−2,700
Sales Returns		−4,500
Net Sales		$132,800

FIGURE 15.1 Accounting text 2, a journal entry

accounting concepts. The students could communicate knowledge and ideas using the language of accounting. They were literate in accounting as social practice. This suggests that learning an additional language such as English has a lot to do with attention to content or knowledge particularly in the ESP context. In this respect, the students engaged in the construction or production of vocational content. Language is viewed as a tool for communicating this vocational knowledge. In other words, understanding vocational knowledge is a semiotic process, connecting what the students knew (accounting knowledge) to what the students experienced (students' accounting literacy practice).

Exploring the Language and Genre of Accounting Through Functional Analysis of Text

In addition to engaging in vocational knowledge building or construction, the students worked on textual analysis. This textual analysis aimed to assist the students to develop their language ability. It has been reported that this contributes positively to the understanding and construction of disciplinary texts (see Fang & Schleppegrell, 2008). Through a functional meta-language analysis of accounting texts, the students needed to become familiar with specialist vocabulary associated with accounting so that they could read and understand accounting terms and texts. Through this analysis, the students were fully aware of how to communicate vocational knowledge and concepts using the language of accounting. For this study, I report how the students explored the language and genre of accounting texts (Class Period #21).

At the beginning, I guided the students on how to analyze a text. For instance, I asked the students to identity themes in the sample text shown in Figure 15.1. In this text, there are three different themes: *The income statement, accountants,* and *Maxidrive's net income*. These themes convey different meanings. The first theme describes the purpose of *the income statement*. The use of brackets indicates other terms associated with *the income statement*. The second theme shows the preferred terms used by accountants. The construct of *net incomes* or *net earnings* is still related to the income statement. The third theme tells the reader about the purpose of net

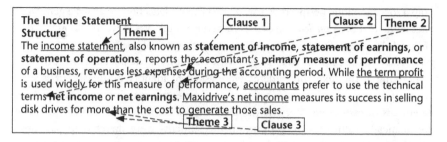

FIGURE 15.2   Accounting text 3, *The Income Statement.* Adapted from Libby, Libby and Short (2011, p. 10)

income. Though this thematic progression is divergent, the main construct of the text is the income statement, which involves the human actor and a sub-concept of the income statement. Then, I asked the students to identify types of clauses in the text, such as a simple clause (1), a complex clause (2), and a subordinate clause (3).

The central language feature of the text is verb processes. I showed the students that the text contains four types of *present* verb processes, such as a verbal process (*report*), relational processes (*is*), a mental process (*prefer*), and doing processes (*use* and *measure*). I moved on to explain why particular verb processes were used. For example, the word, *prefer*, indicates preference. The actor, *accountants*, has a logical semantic relation, because only humans can have a preference. Afterwards, I guided the students on how to identify the tone of the text. I asked the students to look back to major verb processes, though some evaluative words or language appraisal (e.g., attitudes, judgments, appreciation) such as *primary*, *widely*, and *success* were used. Drawing on such major verb processes as *report*, *is*, *prefer*, *use*, and *measure*, the tone of the text is descriptive or informative. These are the examples of how I guided language features of the text. To help the students notice or pay close attention to target language features, I provided a guide sheet as shown in Table 15.8.

The students were afforded autonomy in deciding the language features on which they focused. They could make a decision on areas of language they discussed with their peers. In addition to showing the students how to analyze language properties

TABLE 15.8 Guide sheet of functional meta-language analysis

Types of Meaning	Functional Meta-Language Analysis
Experiential meaning	Analyze participants, processes, and circumstances
Textual meaning	• Analyze clause themes
	• Analyze nominalization
	• Analyze cohesive devices
Interpersonal meaning	• Analyze mood
	• Analyze modality
	• Analyze language appraisal

Adapted from Fang and Schleppegrell (2008)

from a social semiotic perspective, I scaffolded the students how to analyze genre features in the text of *a cash flow statement* extracted from Libby, Libby, and Short's (2011) *Financial Accounting*. *Statement of cash flows* is a sub-genre of *financial statements*. In this genre analysis, the students were taught what constitutes a statement of cash flows.

Looking at the text, the students were asked to identify business entities such as operating activities, investing activities, and financing activities, which represent statements of cash flows. Because the purpose of cash flow statements is to know the financial health of an organization, the students were directed to pay close attention to the standing of cash at both beginning of year and end of year. In short, genre analysis helped the students become fully aware of representation of cash flow statements in an accounting term.

Now, I would like to present how three students talked about the language and genres of an accounting text, *Control of Cash* as presented earlier. These students analyzed language and genre features in order to create a journal entry and find a solution of *net sales* (refer to Figure 15.1 above).

Table 15.9 shows that the students analyzed both language and genre features purposively. They learned a variety of technical vocabulary, which makes up a journal entry. They jointly constructed a text of a journal entry and found a solution of net sales. They noticed functional properties of the text (e.g., circumstances and content vocabulary) in order to complete two tasks, to create a journal entry, and to find net sales. It is evident that understanding language and genre of accounting texts could help the students complete accounting tasks. The functional meta-language analysis guided the students on how to use language in accounting practices.

Drawing on student engagement in joint construction of accounting texts and in the functional meta-language analysis task, all the students found these activities useful. They perceived both vocabulary and grammar as tools for meaning-making and for doing accounting tasks. Yul admitted that "before I learned a functional meta-language analysis, I viewed vocabulary and grammar as separable from texts. Now, I understand that vocabulary and grammar are the skeleton of texts. They are crucial components of text construction." This evidence demonstrates change in student beliefs of vocabulary and grammar. Another student (Ria) admitted that "I have learned grammar in action. I used grammar for reading and understanding accounting texts. I see vocabulary as integral to grammar. Grammar is a vehicle for putting vocabulary together to communicate ideas or knowledge." All the students recognized the social roles of vocabulary and grammar because they are always in the text. They found learning language through texts engaging and enjoyable. They were also familiar with the concept of genres as a rhetorical tool for constructing accounting knowledge or information. Most of the students perceived genres as functional moves, which serve to organize texts. They also argued that genres determine what is conventionally acceptable in accounting or what counts as the balance sheet, the income statement, or a statement of cash flows, for example. Thus, all the student participants were positive about the learning of language and genre through the exploration of myriad accounting texts. This learning is a continuation of small-group literature discussions derived from extensive reading.

TABLE 15.9 Student–student interaction in functional meta-language analysis

Participants	Turns	
Student A (Yul)	1	Let us explore language and genre features of the text we discussed.
Student B (Ran)	2	This text consists of five main sentences (.) I can read two. Yul and Ria, you can read one or two . . . What do you think?
Student C (Ria)	3	That's a good idea! I can read the third and fourth sentences\
Student A (Yul)	4	I will read the last sentence.
Student B (Ran)	5	Let us move on.
Student C (Ria)	6	Can I start sharing–what I noticed?
Yul and Ran	7	Please go on.
Student C (Ria)	8	In the first sentence (.) I noticed **respectively**. This circumstance of manner refers to ((*looking at the text*)) credit and cash sales ($100,000 and $40,000).
Student A (Yul)	9	Yes . . . the dictionary ((*looking up the word in a digital dictionary*)) tells that the word **respectively** is used to mention (.) two entities or items listed in the order\
Student B (Ran)	10	So . . . we can add (.) both credit and cash err both are considered as (.) **revenues**.
Student C (Ria)	11	Let me continue sentence no. 2 . . . The second sentence tells us the event of **purchase** . . . The customers received sales discounts of $2,700 ((*reading her note*)) because they made payment by credit. The word **discount** indicates (.) reduction of the goods purchased.
Student A (Yul)	12	We can subtract . . . $90–000 by $2,700. **The actual sales** received are $87–300 ((*reading her note*))
Student C (Ria)	13	I got it (.) Let me share my analysis for the third and fourth sentences. Sentence no. 3 tells us about a future event of **balance payment** ((*reading her note*)). Sentence no. 4 shows **sales returns** of $4,500 ((*reading her note*)). This also is another **reduction of sales** because of **cash payment**.
Student A (Yul)	14	Perfect, Ria (.) Now, it is my turn. The last sentence tells us umm about two tasks we have to do . . . The first task is **to provide** all the journal entries and the second task is **to compute** net sales ((*reading the text, Control of Cash*))
Student C (Ria)	15	The last sentence tells us (.) we create a genre of a journal entry . . . based on all the transactions done like **credit and cash sales** (paid by credit and cash), **sales discounts**, and **sales returns** ((*reading her note*)).
Student B (Ran)	16	Yes . . . this journal entry should show **net sales**.

This is a good example of how the learning of VE implicates different language skills that the students learned.

To conclude, all the students view language as a tool for understanding and constructing knowledge. They also contend that learning English becomes more meaningful because they talk about knowledge through language, not about the language in a discrete way. The students perceive the language not as a stand-alone skill, but as integral to content/vocational knowledge or information. In other words, English is seen as a tool for understanding and building knowledge as well as communicating this knowledge.

Conclusion

This chapter has shown how VE materials were jointly designed and how accounting students engaged with VE materials, texts, and tasks. The implications of these findings suggest that VE not only aims to provide students with technical vocabulary, but it is also geared to use this language for vocational knowledge building. In addition, the learning of ESP also prepares students for understanding how technical or vocational vocabulary or terms construct key vocational concepts. The second implication of the study is that ESP teachers need to familiarize students with functional meta-language analysis in order to increase their awareness of language and genre features, which construct vocational texts. In addition, this language and genre awareness helps students use appropriate language in vocational discourses (see Widodo, 2015). Taken together, texts (sources of language), social practices (media for the actual use of language), contexts (genres: Social and cultural conventions of how texts, language, and social practices are embodied), and language (a tool for meaning-making and participating in social practices) are essential components of ESP materials development. To extend this scholarship, more studies on VE materials development are needed in the future.

Acknowledgements

The current research project received financial support from the University of Adelaide, Australia. I am thankful to the school and the participants who volunteered to take part in the project. My sincere gratitude is due to my PhD supervisors, Dr. Peter Mickan and Dr. John Walsh, for encouraging me to investigate materials development from a social semiotic perspective.

Transcription Symbols

(.) short pause; . . . normal pause; \ falling accent; (( )) non-linguistic events; ? question remarks; – truncated talks; ( ) particular word/phrase; and **bold** particular expressions

References

Black, S., & Yasukawa, K. (2012). Shared delivery: Integrating ELT in Australian vocational education. *ELT Journal, 66*, 347–355.

Braun, V., & Clarke, V. (2006). Using thematic analysis in psychology. *Qualitative Research in Psychology, 3*, 77–101.

Dudley-Evans, T., & St. John, M. (1998). *Developments in English for specific purposes: A multidisciplinary approach*. Cambridge: Cambridge University Press.

DuFon, M. A. (2002). Video recording in ethnographic SLA research: Some issues of validity in data collection. *Language Learning & Technology, 6*(1), 40–59.

Fang, Z., & Schleppegrell, M. J. (2008). *Reading in secondary content areas: A language-based pedagogy.* Ann Arbor, MI: University of Michigan Press.

Gordon, C. (2013). Beyond the observer's paradox: The audio-recorder as a resource for the display of identity. *Qualitative Research, 13,* 299–317.

Halliday, M. A. K. (1978). *Language as social semiotic.* London: Edward Arnold.

Harwood, N. (Ed.) (2010). *English language teaching materials: Theory and practice.* Cambridge: Cambridge University Press.

Harwood, N. (Ed.). (2014). *English language teaching textbooks: Content, consumption, production.* Basingstoke, U.K: Palgrave Macmillan.

Hua, T.-L., & Beverton, S. (2013). General or vocational English courses for Taiwanese students in vocational high schools? Students' perceptions of their English courses and their relevance to their future career. *Educational Research for Policy and Practice, 12,* 101–120.

Huang, J., & Morgan, G. (2003). A functional approach to evaluating content knowledge and language development in ESL students' science classification texts. *International Journal of Applied Linguistics, 13,* 234–262.

Hunter, L., Emerald, E., & Martin, G. (2013). *Participatory activist research in the globalised world: Social change through the cultural professions.* New York: Springer.

Libby, R., Libby, P. A., & Short, D. G. (2011). *Financial accounting* (7th ed.). New York: McGraw-Hill/Irwin.

Lo, Y. Y. (2014). Collaboration between L2 and content subject teachers in CBI: Contrasting beliefs and attitudes. *RELC Journal, 45,* 181–196.

McGrath, I. (2013). *Teaching materials and the roles of EFL/ESL teachers: Practice and theory.* London: Bloomsbury.

Moschkovich, J. N. (2002). A situated and sociocultural perspective on bilingual mathematics learners. *Mathematical Thinking and Learning, 4,* 189–212.

Singapore Wala, D. A. (2013). Publishing a coursebook: Completing the materials development circle. In B. Tomlinson (Ed.), *Developing materials for language teaching* (pp. 141–161). London: Bloomsbury.

Tomlinson, B. (2011). *Materials development in language teaching* (2nd ed.). Cambridge: Cambridge University Press.

Tomlinson, B., & Masuhara, H. (Eds.) (2010). *Research for materials development in language learning: Evidence for best practice.* London: Bloomsbury.

Widodo, H. P. (2015). Designing and implementing task-based vocational English (VE) materials: Text, language, task, and context. In H. Reinders and M. Thomas (Eds.), *Contemporary task-based language learning and teaching (TBLT) in Asia: Challenges, opportunities and future directions* (pp. 291–312). London: Bloomsbury.

Widodo, H. P., & Savova, L. (2010). *The Lincom guide to materials design in ELT.* Munich: Lincom Europa.

Wodak, R. (1999). Critical discourse analysis at the end of the 20th century. *Research on Language and Social Interaction, 32,* 185–193.

Yan, C., & He, C. (2012). Bridging the implementation gap: An ethnographic study of English teachers' implementation of the curriculum reform in China. *Ethnography and Education, 7*(1), 1–19.

16

CORPUS-BASED MATERIALS DEVELOPMENT FOR TEACHING AND LEARNING PRAGMATIC ROUTINES

Kathleen Bardovi-Harlig and Sabrina Mossman

Introduction

In this chapter we discuss the use of spoken corpora for the development of materials for the teaching of pragmatic routines. Pragmatic routines are linguistic realizations of social conventions that form part of a speaker's pragmalinguistic competence. They often indicate what speech act is being performed. Pragmatic routines such as *That's right, You're right, That's true,* and *I agree* signal agreements and *Yeah, but* and *I agree, but* signal disagreements. Kasper and Blum-Kulka (1993) have observed that pragmatic routines may be a source of difficulty for second language (L2) learners. Kecskes (2003) and Bardovi-Harlig (2009) have empirically tested Kasper and Blum-Kulka's observation. Success with pragmatic routines depends in part on the expressions themselves (some expressions like *Nice to meet you,* and *You too!* seem to be learned before others, e.g., *Nice to see you* and *Thanks for having me*) and on the tasks used to evaluate knowledge (multiple-choice tasks, Rover, 2012, score higher than production tasks, Kecskes, 2003; Bardovi-Harlig, 2009). Higher proficiency learners and learners with greater interaction with conversation in the target language with both native speakers and other learners are also more successful than learners with lower proficiency and less interaction (Bardovi-Harlig & Bastos, 2011).

In spite of the predicted difficulties, it has also been shown that the acquisition of pragmatic routines can be facilitated through instruction that includes the presentation of routines in context. English as a second language (ESL) students (classroom learners in a mixed host and classroom environment) who were presented with expressions in context with focused noticing exercises, both with production activities (Bardovi-Harlig, Mossman, & Vellenga, 2015a) and without (Bardovi-Harlig & Vellenga, 2012) demonstrated improved production of pragmatic routines by their performance in timed oral conversation simulations. Advanced EFL students who received contextualized input, explicit metapragmatic instruction, production activities, and feedback showed improvement from instruction by their performance on role plays (House, 1996).

One of the challenges in the instruction of pragmatics has been the well-known lack of pragmatic authenticity in commercially available materials. Developing reasonably authentic materials for the teaching of pragmatics has been an abiding goal of pragmatics research (see, for example, Bardovi-Harlig, 2001; Bardovi-Harlig & Mahan-Taylor, 2003; Cohen & Ishihara, 2013; Houck & Tatsuki, 2011; Ishihara & Cohen, 2010; Ishihara, this volume; Tatsuki & Houck, 2010, and numerous reviews of pragmatics in commercial materials.) The outlook for learning or teaching L2 pragmatic routines from commercial materials is no better. Pragmatic routines often appear in decontextualized boxes headed by a banner similar to "useful expressions" (Bardovi-Harlig, Mossman, & Vellenga, 2015b). Although providing alternative expressions may be desirable, context is crucial in pragmatics for both acquisition and use. For instance, the phrase *I was wondering if* presented as part of an authentic academic service encounter at the computer center rather than in isolation in a box demonstrates the appropriateness of the phrase in that context. Moreover, the lists also include pragmatic routines which may be infrequent and/ or pragmatically risky (that is, negative and direct; for example, disagreement routines such as *That's completely wrong* and *That's crazy* were modeled by the major textbook series *Quest Intro* and *Pathways 4,* respectively). Thus, the lack of materials and the demonstrated success of instruction make the effort of developing materials to teach pragmatic routines worthwhile.

Drawing on general principles of SLA and L2 pedagogy, this chapter focuses on developing materials that provide (1) input (as a necessity, as a model, and as meaningful and motivating exposure to language); (2) fidelity of input to the target language; and (3) input and activities consistent with L2 acquisition processes.

Input Necessity

Exposure to input is necessary for SLA (VanPatten & Williams, 2007) and more valuable when it includes rich and meaningful exposure to language in use (Tomlinson, 2013).

We argue that input necessity can only be met if input fidelity is also met. That is, the input should reflect the language that is used by the speech community.

Input Fidelity

What is selected for instruction should "reflect the actual behavior of TL [target language] speakers in communicative contexts" (Valdman, 1989; VanPatten 2002).

Input and Activities Consistent With L2 Acquisition Processes

Give learners the opportunity to notice how the L2 is used (Schmidt, 1993; Tomlinson, 2013). Learners' output (speech) often follows predictable paths with predictable stages in the acquisition of a given structure (VanPatten & Williams, 2007).

We demonstrate how various corpora can be used in the development of pragmatically appropriate teaching materials and illustrate the principles of working with pragmatic routines. These steps include (1) selecting the corpus, (2) identifying expressions, (3) extracting examples, (4) preparing corpus excerpts for teaching, (5) developing noticing activities and (6) developing production activities.

Why Use Corpora in the Teaching of Pragmatic Routines?

The use of corpora in language teaching has been advocated by other materials developers and corpus experts (e.g., Reppen, 2010). Many corpora are tagged for grammatical features, which is not the case for pragmatic features such as speech acts, back channels, or repair. Nevertheless, the lexical nature of routines makes corpora good resources for materials development. Pragmatic routines can be searched for, and this is something at which corpora excel.

Using corpora to develop materials for the teaching of pragmatic routines addresses two of the central goals of developing pragmatically authentic materials: Input necessity and input fidelity. The use of corpora can help materials developers ascertain the frequency of use of certain pragmatic routines and can also provide the contexts for the expressions. That is not to claim, however, that all natural context is immediately clear or suitable for instructional purposes, and we discuss how to work with corpora in the following sections. In addition, the existence of a variety of free online corpora which are readily available offers an accessible resource for teachers and program-level materials developers who very likely do not have the time to conduct data collection of their own.

Developing Materials for Pragmatic Routines

Selecting the Corpus

In this section we consider working with three types of spoken corpora: An academic corpus, a conversation corpus, and a television corpus. An academic corpus is ideal for academic purposes programs (such as the English for academic purposes [EAP] context in which we teach). Both the conversational corpus and the TV corpus offer examples of social talk. We will discuss each type of corpus, and their advantages, in turn. All of the corpora are free and easily accessible, and can be used by teachers with ease after a brief online introduction.

An Academic Corpus

The Michigan Corpus of Academic Spoken English (MICASE; Simpson, Briggs, Ovens, & Swales 2002; http://quod.lib.umich.edu/m/micase) contains 1.8 million words of transcribed speech from almost 200 hours of recordings from the University of Michigan. The transcribed speech events include lectures, classroom discussions, lab sections, seminars, advising sessions, and service encounters.

Considering mode, context, speakers, and region is crucial in corpus selection. We used MICASE in order to develop materials focused on agreeing, disagreeing, and clarification in academic group work for an EAP program (Bardovi-Harlig, Mossman, & Vellenga, 2015b). For that project, we needed a corpus of spoken English, in an academic setting, whose speakers were the age of our students, and which was geographically appropriate.

One of the primary advantages of MICASE is that it is very easy to use with no training. MICASE has both browse and search functions that allow users to browse through transcripts that meet certain criteria, or to search for specific words or expressions in the corpus. MICASE provides attributes for both speakers and transcripts, and the user can select specific attributes as search criteria. Speaker attributes include academic role, native-speaker status and first language (L1), and transcript attributes include speech event type and interactivity rating. To search, the user types a word or expression into the search box. A list of sentences containing the expression will appear on the screen, with the expression highlighted in the center. MICASE provides the total number of occurrences and the total number of transcripts along with the frequency and other statistical information about the word or expression. The larger context and the entire transcript is available for each use.

Conversational Corpora

The second corpus we consider here is the 249,000-word Santa Barbara Corpus of Spoken American English (Du Bois, Chafe, Meyer, Thompson, Englebretson, & Martey, 2000–2005; http://www.linguistics.ucsb.edu/research/santa-barbara-corpus). This corpus is based on a large body of recordings of naturally occurring spoken interaction from all over the United States. It contains recordings from people of different regional origins, ages, occupations, genders, and ethnic and social backgrounds. The predominant form of language use is face-to-face conversation, but the corpus also includes other speech events including telephone conversations, card games, food preparation, on-the-job talk, classroom lectures, sermons, story telling, and town hall meetings. The Santa Barbara Corpus provides the main source of data for the spontaneous spoken portions of the American component of the International Corpus of English.

This corpus allows learners to peek behind closed doors, giving them access to authentic language that is used in private interactions among people who are very close to each other. This provides a useful contrast to the language of an academic corpus where the situations and relationships dictate different sociopragmatic rules. The corpus includes detailed demographic information including age, gender, hometown and state, state of residence at the time of data collection, level of education, years of education, occupation, and ethnicity. Each conversation is accompanied by a summary that usually includes information about the relationship between the speakers. This is very useful in determining the register of the conversation and the use of pragmatic routines. The transcripts are annotated in great detail providing non-verbal and prosodic information, and for many of the conversations audio recordings are also available.

The 61 transcripts are available for free download. These files can be consolidated into a single, searchable document using common word processing or portable document-editing software programs. The user can also keep multiple copies of the transcripts, with and without the annotations, to be used for different purposes. When searching for pragmatic formulas, it is more useful to remove the annotations.

As with MICASE, to search the Santa Barbara Corpus once the document has been created, the user can search for the entire expression or an element of the expression if there are variations. For example, a search for *you mind* returns all instances of *would you mind, do you mind,* and just *you mind*. With 249,000 words, the Santa Barbara Corpus is large enough to provide usable examples, but small enough to be manually searchable once the results have been returned. Thus, in looking for requests, a search for *would you* yields 45 instances, but it is easy to read through these instances and eliminate all the uses of the phrase that are not requests. The format in which the results are displayed will depend on the software. Some programs allow the user to specify how closely matched the results need to be to the original word or phrase.

TV Corpora

The third type of corpus that we consider here consists of fan-based transcriptions of television shows. These vary from the spontaneous data found in the academic and conversational corpora in that they are scripted, but importantly, these too are authentic cultural texts and exist for entertainment, quite independently of language learning and teaching (Bardovi-Harlig, 2015). They are authentic scripted sources meant to represent conversation. Quaglio (2009) demonstrated that one sitcom, *Friends*, had characteristics that made it quite similar to spontaneous conversation in the American conversation portion of the Longman Grammar Corpus, a finding replicated by Al-Surmi (2012).

An advantage of these corpora is the online availability of the shows that correspond to the transcripts, so students can watch as well as read or listen. Transcripts and TV shows can be used together. A number of studies on the effect of instruction on pragmatics have used TV shows and their transcripts as input (e.g., Silva, 2003, *Friends*; Alcón Soler, 2005, *Stargate*).

For the television corpus, we use a 500,000-word US corpus available on the Lexical Tutor website (http://www.lextutor.ca/conc/eng/; in the concordance select "TV-Marlise"). The television corpus was compiled by applied linguistics graduate students at Concordia University, Montreal. The corpus contains ten TV shows – five comedies (*How I Met Your Mother, The Office, Seinfeld, Two and a Half Men,* and *Frasier*) and five dramas (*Alias, Desperate Housewives, Grey's*

Anatomy, Lost, and *Prison Break*). The sub-corpora from the ten shows were compiled by downloading transcripts freely available on the Internet. Stage prompts and other non-spoken material in the transcripts were deleted manually by the compilers; this step leads to more accurate word counts. (A quick Internet search yields the transcript with speakers identified.) About 50,000 words are included for each show; the number of episodes represented in each ranged from 11 to 18 (due to differences in show length and amounts of talk that occurred in them). The comedy and drama sub-corpora amounted to about 250,000 words each. News broadcasts, commentaries or talk shows were not included in the corpus.

The Lexical Tutor has a concordance program which permits the user to search for a key word, such as "sorry" and a second word such as "late" to the right or the left of the key word (for a pragmatic routine such as "sorry I'm late"). The program returns a numbered concordance list with the pragmatic routine in the center and text on either side. Each line can be read in context and the fuller context can be found by clicking on the key word.

Partial Concordance List for *Do You Mind* (Lexical Tutor)

```
005. confidential. Do you MIND if I ask why? To be perfectly honest,
006. Hey, listen. Do you MIND if we stop at the next motel? It's only like,
007. behind you. Do you MIND if I check my email? No, not at all.
008. get through. Do you MIND if I take it? No, no. Go right ahead.
```

Identifying Pragmatic Routines

Candidate pragmatic routines can be identified in at least three ways: L2 textbooks, research, and local data collection or observation. Many teachers (and students) may like the convenience of starting with the textbook. In one materials development project, we compiled lists of pragmatic routines for agreements, disagreements, and clarifications from EAP textbooks that had been selected for special prominence in textboxes (Bardovi-Harlig, Mossman, & Vellenga, 2014). In another, we observed community use of conventional expressions (pragmatic routines that are highly favored for specific contexts, Bardovi-Harlig, 2009) and used these as target expressions in the TV-based instructional materials we developed (Bardovi-Harlig & Vellenga, 2012).

After generating an initial list of pragmatic routines, the next step is to compare the list to the routines found in the corpus. We read the examples to include only the relevant uses of the routine, we note the number of occurrences of each expression (raw #) and the number of texts in which it occurs (to make sure an expression is both frequent and used by multiple speakers), and then calculate a frequency rate by dividing the raw score by the size of the corpus (1.8 million words, MICASE; 249,000 for the Santa Barbara corpus, and 500,000 for the TV corpus). Biber and colleagues have defined the lower limit for "frequent" for multiword units as occurring between 10 occurrences/million words (Biber, Johansson, Leech, Conrad, & Finegan 1999) and 40 occurrences/million words (Biber, Conrad, & Cortes 2004).

To illustrate these steps, we consider request routines presented by ESL textbooks which include *Can you do me a favor, Could you give me a hand . . . , Could you possibly . . . , Do you mind (if), Would it be OK if, Would you mind (if), Would you mind (v-ing), I wonder if, I was wondering if you'd mind* (Interchange 3, Ventures 4, True Colors 2, All Star 3), in addition to *Can I* and *Could you* also given in *Interchange 3*.

In is important to note that textbooks may present longer expressions than speakers use. For example, the EAP textbooks that we worked with presented *I think that's right, I think you're right, You're right about that* and *That sounds good to me* as common expressions. When searched in MICASE, *You're right about* only occurred twice and *I think you're right* did not occur at all. However, *You're right* occurred 139 times in 50 different transcripts. In the Santa Barbara Corpus none of the longer expressions were produced except for two instances of *I think you're right*, but there were fourteen instances of *you're right*. In this set of request routines, *I was wondering if you would mind* is highly mitigated and was not found in any corpus that we searched.

The textbook recommendations for pragmatic routines for requests are given in the left-hand column of Table 16.1 with the attested shortened form underlined and the three corpora are listed in the top row. The greatest use of the pragmatic routines suggested by the commercial textbooks comes from the TV corpus, but even so, only four of the seven request routines were used, and three of those were used in shortened form.

TABLE 16.1 Frequency of pragmatic routines for requests

Textbook (shortened corpus form underlined)	TV Corpus	MICASE	Santa Barbara
Can you <u>do me a favor</u>	8 (16/million); 3 requests (would/could you do me a favor; 1 do me a favor, 5 directives (do me a favor)	0	0
Would <u>you mind</u> (if) . . .	17 (34/million)	7	1 (friends)
Could you <u>give me a hand</u>	6 uses with requests (12/million)	1 could you give me a hand	0
Could you possibly	0	1 directive (not a request, writing conference)	0
Do you mind	13 requests (26/million) (plus 6 directives)	2 requests	0
Would it be OK/okay	0	0 hits for requests	0
I wonder if	0	0 w/ requests	1 (restaurant)
I was wondering if	0 hits	5 requests	0

In the Santa Barbara Corpus where the majority of the interactions are conversations between friends and family, the requests are even shorter and more direct. Thus, there are almost no instances of the full expressions presented in the textbooks, with the exception of *I wonder if* which occurred once in an interaction with a server at a restaurant, and *would you mind* which occurred once between friends. Even the shortened versions, that yielded numerous results in the MICASE corpus, did not appear in the Santa Barbara corpus, where most of the speakers are familiar and close to each other. Instead, requests and directives are much less mitigated and include direct questions using *can I* (49; 196/million), *can we* (3), *could you* (23; 92/million), *can you* (7; 28/million), *will you* (7; 28/million), and *would you* (5; 20/million). Interactions from the conversational corpus show the simplicity of social interactions in contrast to those of an academic setting.

From Santa Barbara

JUNE: Hi.
REBECCA: Hi.
JUNE: Can I sit with you?
REBECCA: Sure.

From MICASE (SVC999MX148):

SU-f: Hi Becky.
SU-f: Hi (Peter Sarah) what's up. hanging in there? <*LAUGH*>
SU-m: Hi this book's on reserve for, Bio three-oh-eight <u>I was wondering if</u> I could get this.
S9:   Yes

Extracting Examples

Both MICASE and Lexical Tutor create a list (or concordance) with the expressions or key words that can be clicked on to see the full context. The contexts can then be extracted to be used as input for noticing activities and production. The goal is to select relatively clear examples that can be followed without reading the entire transcript, that have relatively comprehensible topics, and that include an unambiguous use of the expression and a clear referent. The following example provides a sample of the input for an agreement (the transcript ID refers to the MICASE identifier). In this example, only the speaker identification format has been modified.

Agreement (That's True)

A: I remember it had to be really really big because we had to add all the solids.
B: I don't know.

A: Yeah, it wasn't too much bigger, maybe fifteen hundred gallons or something.
B: Oh, yeah that's true.

Transcript ID: SGR195SU127

This example is straightforward, but others require slight modification to increase their utility as conversation models.

Whereas vocabulary and density of the discussion may present occasional challenges for identifying excerpts to serve as input (see the next section for ways to deal with these), the conversational nature of the Santa Barbara Corpus presents different issues. Because of the authentic, personal nature of the conversations, some of the topics and language used may not be considered appropriate for the classroom. Another consideration is that in some cases the target speech acts may be inserted into a conversation; in effect, there can be two conversational streams at one time. In this excerpt, Frank's turns (in italics) constitute a request sequence, while Melissa's turns discuss political views.

MELISSA: The political views, and all this other stuff, and they just talked about it, on and on and on and on and on. And so Mom told me never ever to ask,
FRANK: *Maybe I'll have tea.*
MELISSA: anything about that again.
FRANK: *Could you grab me a box of tea?*
MELISSA: That was Grandpa Flynn. I asked him something about the Democratic Platform.

Preparing Excerpts for Teaching

The next step is to ensure the clarity of the excerpts once they have been extracted from the longer conversations. The challenges of vocabulary, simultaneous turns, non-sequential or off-topic contributions, repetition, and repair can be addressed by simplifying a transcript to highlight the pragmatic routine (cf. Ishihara & Cohen, 2010). Turns that contain the target expression should *not* be modified, but rather should appear in the teaching materials exactly as they do in the corpus.

Especially in an academic corpus it may be necessary to substitute common words for technical words to increase comprehensibility (e.g. *sunfish* for *centrarchid* in a biology transcript). In both the conversation and the academic spoken corpus many people may talk at the same time, and they may be talking about different things (as Frank and Melissa do in the example above); TV shows also contain examples of multiple strands in one conversation. To enhance the salience of the corpus examples, delete non-sequential turns from multi-party conversations, and reduce repetition, repair, overlap, false starts, and unfinished sentences. This is particularly true for requests, which can be integrated into an ongoing conversation as we saw above. Another example of this can be seen below where there appear to be three conversations occurring simultaneously. The part of the conversation dealing with requests is in italics. This example shows the original conversation, the deleted portions, and the transcript presented to the students.

MAUREEN: *Gail, would you go downstairs,*
STEPHANIE: everything.
MAUREEN: there are two bottles of,
ERIKA: Wasn't   Fast   Times   at   Ridgemont
              High . . . filmed there too?
MAUREEN: burgundy in the refrigerator, *and bring up*
              a roll of paper towels,
STEPHANIE: Fast Times at Ridgemont High,
MAUREEN: since we're X>,
STEPHANIE: um,
GAIL: *Okay.*
MAUREEN: *Gail, would you go downstairs,*
~~STEPHANIE: everything.~~
~~MAUREEN: there are two bottles of,~~
~~ERIKA: Wasn't   Fast   Times   at   Ridgemont~~
              ~~High . . . filmed there too?~~
~~MAUREEN: burgundy in the refrigerator,~~ *and bring up*
              a roll of paper towels,
~~STEPHANIE: Fast Times at Ridgemont High,~~
MAUREEN: since we're X>,
~~STEPHANIE: um,~~
GAIL: *Okay.*
MAUREEN: *Gail, would you go downstairs, and bring up*
              a roll of paper towels, since we're X>
GAIL: *Okay.*

The final step in preparing the excerpts is to prepare the audio or video presentation. One way is to rerecord modified excerpts or excerpts for which the audio was not available. Riddiford and Newton (2010) provided high-quality audio of selected recorded conversations from their workplace corpus and Bardovi-Harlig, Mossman, and Vellenga (2015b) followed suit with rerecordings of simplified academic group work. Using TV excerpts, the original video from which the modified input was created can be presented once the students are familiar with the targeted sequences; they may be more able to follow the non-linear development of conversations and seeing the speakers on video will help. Although compiling examples takes time, this step results in a collection of authentic conversations that are representative of the instructional target and can be used (and reused) in many ways.

Developing Noticing Activities

The four previous steps yield authentic, contextualized, and pragmatically valuable excerpts that can be used to help learners notice the use, form, and contrast between expressions. It is at this point that good materials engage acquisition.

It is not sufficient for learners to have a list of expressions; they must be contextualized. In this section we offer three examples of noticing activities for a
variety of types of classroom instruction on pragmatics. (For the development of
a unit with a single focus, academic group work, using MICASE see Bardovi-
Harlig, Mossman, & Vellenga, 2015b.) Most noticing opportunities include both
use (the sociopragmatics of the routines) and form (the pragmalinguistics of the
pragmatic routines).

Noticing Use

This first example illustrates one principle we use with noticing exercises, which is
to have the student write down some aspect of the directed noticing so that we are
confident that the noticing occurred. This excerpt from the Santa Barbara corpus
shows an interaction at a restaurant that can be used in noticing exercises for both
use and form.

ROSEMARY:	Which one are you having.
SHERRY:	I'm having this.
ROSEMARY:	Oh.
BETH:	But I want a salad with it.
SERVER:	What type of dressing?
BETH:	I'll have a Caesar salad.
SERVER:	Caesar's
SERVER:	And what did you want ma'am?
ROSEMARY:	A BLT croissant. And ice tea with no lemon.
SERVER:	Kay. What type of salad soup or fries?
ROSEMARY:	Can I have clam chowder for my soup?
SERVER:	Mhm.
ROSEMARY:	Okay. Soup.
SERVER:	And you wanted the ke- –the kebab here, steak and pasta kebab?
BETH:	That's what I wanted, yeah.
ROSEMARY:	. . . And what are you having Sherry?
SHERRY:	I wonder if I can get salad and half a sandwich, instead of soup and half a sandwich.
SERVER:	Sure.
SHERRY:	Can I just get salad . . . like . . . green salad or whatever?
SERVER:	White whole-wheat sourdough or rye?
SHERRY:	Um whole-wheat.
SERVER:	And did you want um, what type of dressing on your salad?
SHERRY:	Um, do you have ranch?
SERVER:	Mhm.
SHERRY:	Okay.
ROSEMARY:	What kind of sandwich are you getting?
SHERRY:	I'll take that.

Noticing Activity Instructions:

1. Rosemary, Beth, and Sherry are at a restaurant. Read their conversation and underline all the expressions they use to order their food. How many different kinds of ordering expressions do they use? Write the number here: _____.

2. Sometimes people say *I'll have* or *I'll take* when they order something. In this conversation, Sherry uses more words to order her food. What long expression does she use? _____

    Why do you think she uses a long expression instead of a short one? Discuss this with your classmate. (Instructor can then call on students to give their explanations.)

Noticing the Form

Instruction can also provide explicit metapragmatic information focusing on the form of the expressions. For example, when teaching agreements for academic discussion (Bardovi-Harlig, Mossman, & Vellenga, 2015b), we pointed out that some agreement expressions are personal, such as *You're right* and *You make a good point*, and some are impersonal, such as *That's right* and *That's a good point*. Some expressions do not have a corresponding personal expression: *That's true,* but not *#You're true*. To increase the salience of this distinction, students read several excerpts and then indicate whether an expression is impersonal or personal. Students can also complete a table that leads them to notice that *#You're true,* does not occur in the examples.

Noticing Contrasting Expressions

Two expressions that contrast in American English, but are often equated by learners, are *Nice to meet you* which is part of an introduction, and *Nice to see you* which is part of greetings and closings. *Nice to meet you* tends to be over-generalized by learners into *Nice-to-see-you* contexts (Bardovi-Harlig, 2014). The essential difference between them is that *meet* is used with new acquaintances, and *see* is used with continuing relationships. We can use the corpora to provide input and focused noticing activities to heighten the differences in use between the two. *Nice to meet you* is frequent in the TV corpus, occurring 41 times (82/million); an alternative, *Good to meet you*, occurs five times (10/million). All of the *Nice to meet you* tokens are used in cases of introductions. *Nice to see you* occurs 7 times (14/million), and *Good to see* you occurs 23 times (46/million).

Because learners are very good at using *Nice to meet you* for introductions, the focus of instruction is on helping students recognize that the routine is limited to introductions, and to give them an alternative expression for greetings and closings. The goal in presenting these excerpts is to answer two questions:

> When do the speakers say "Nice/Good to <u>meet</u> you?"
> When do they say "Nice/Good to <u>see</u> you"? How do you know?

The following excerpts from the TV corpus illustrate the difference in use. In the first, Laura and her friend know each other, but Laura and George do not.[1] Compare what Jerry says to Laura, and what Laura says to George.

[suddenly a woman approaches Jerry from behind and puts her hands over Jerry's eyes]

LAURA:	Guess who?
JERRY:	Hey, hey.
LAURA and JERRY:	Heeeey! [they take each other's hands]
JERRY:	It's good to see you.
LAURA:	Hi.
JERRY:	This is my friend George.
LAURA:	[Shakes George's hand] Hi, how nice to meet you.
GEORGE:	Hi, how are you?

http://www.seinfeldscripts.com/TheSeinfeldChronicles.htm

In this excerpt from *Frasier* Niles uses *Nice to see you* once it has been established that he has already met Roz (Season 1, Episode 4).[2]

NILES:	Hello, I don't believe we've met.
ROZ:	Yes we have, Niles, three or four times. Roz Doyle.
NILES:	Oh, of course. It was at the . . . it was during the . . . well, I'm far too successful to feel awkward. Where did we meet?
ROZ:	The radio station.
NILES:	Ah, I'll take your word for it. Nice to see you again.

The excerpts provide evidence that the expressions are used in different social contexts, and they also provide explicit metapragmatic commentary from the characters themselves about appropriate usage which paves the way to class discussions.

Developing Production Activities

Giving students an opportunity to produce is important (Swain & Lapkin, 1995; Cohen & Ishihara, 2013) for pragmatics because these pragmatic routines are part of conversation. Among other benefits, production allows learners to notice the gap between what they want to say and what they can say. Production activities can be ordered from more to less supported; we will consider three, a board game, a TV turn completion, and a role play. For the first two, the students can check their own or each other's production with the corpus.

One activity that is both dynamic and entertaining is a board game that can easily be created by using an online template or a basic word-processing program. A more controlled version of the board game would be to have scenes from the TV shows in the corpus to which learners respond to as characters; these can either be variable assignments through drawing a card or predetermined by the token the student chooses which represents a character. In a less controlled version, the squares on the board can contain relationships such as family members, teacher, friend, co-worker; and different request scenarios can be printed on cards. After rolling the dice, landing on a square, and drawing a card, learners perform the request described on the card by selecting one of the expressions they have learned from the corpus.

There are various ways to modify and implement a game such as this, depending on the desired focus. If, for example, the teacher wishes to focus on register, points can be assigned when the selected expression is considered appropriate for the relationship. A different strategy may involve assigning points for using an appropriate request form that has not already been produced. Games such as these give all learners an opportunity to take a turn rather than just the more talkative ones, who often do most of the talking during classroom group activities. Students can compare responses to cross-indexed scenes or transcripts provided by the teachers.

In another lesson, students get to play "TV star" and act out the scenes from the television shows used in the corpus. The instructor plays the scene from the show where the target language appears. Students are told whose role they will play and that they should respond as that character, using an expression they have learned when the video stops and it is their character's turn. For example, in the excerpt we saw earlier from *Seinfeld*, students are told they will play the role of Laura when the video stops.

JERRY AND LAURA: Heeeey!
JERRY: It's good to see you.
LAURA: Hi.
JERRY: This is my friend George.
[Video pauses, students respond with Laura's turn]
GEORGE: Hi, how are you?

A greater challenge would be to have learners play Jerry's role when he greets Laura and to contrast the two expressions, *Nice to* {*meet*/*see*} *you*, following the noticing exercise. The request excerpts from the previous section could also be used for production. Learners could be given the opportunity to produce request strategies across contexts. This is a good opportunity to learn that requests to friends, service encounters (at the library), and restaurants are distinct request contexts.

Whatever the target expression, a series of clips can be played with short scene-setting statements for each one. After the activity is completed, students can watch all the clips in their original format to compare their answers. This activity can be implemented in multiple ways depending on the available technology. If students are in a computer lab, they can respond individually and record their responses. Otherwise, the video can be played for the class as a whole and they can play the roles in unison or take turns. If the instructor does not have video-editing software that would allow for the removal of the section of the video with the target language, the instructor can stop the video immediately before the phrase is uttered, the students can respond, and then the instructor can play the video and they can immediately hear if they said the same thing. Students can also record themselves on their smart phones.

A variation of "TV star" can be used as a warm-up production activity before the expressions are presented in noticing activities. Students can be told they are TV stars acting out a scene for a popular TV show. The instructor then provides just the context from the video clip and the students act out the scene. The video with the original scene is then introduced as part of a noticing activity. This is followed by a second opportunity for students to act out the scene on their own. There are many ways to implement "TV star."

Role-play activities can give students an opportunity to use different types of pragmatic routines in different contexts. Students can take the role of characters from the TV corpus, conversation corpus, or the academic corpus in the first round of role plays. In the second round, they can play themselves in a variety of situations. Role plays also give students watching them a more challenging speech event to judge and discuss.

What to Expect From Learner Production of Pragmatic Routines

Implementation of instruction using these types of materials engages the L2 acquisition process. We have found that after instruction students use the pragmatic routines more appropriately and that their speech acts are clearer and more readily recognized, even when the target expression is not used. Although the pragmatic routines that we work with are frequent and typical, not every student is developmentally ready to produce the grammar of the expressions. However, they can easily produce the key words and should be encouraged when they use them in the appropriate contexts. Agreement expressions *That's true* and *I agree* are sometimes realized as *That true* and *I'm agree* and the clarification expression *What do you mean* may be produced as *What you mean* (Bardovi-Harlig, Mossman, & Vellenga, 2015a). Instruction that helps students match pragmatic routines with contexts helps build their sociopragmatics in the L2.

Learners who are already experimenting with expressions may also work on the form during instruction, which helps develop their pragmalinguistics. For example we found that students who produced identifiable but non-target-like forms such as *I'm sorry for being lating* and *Thank you very much for inviting Ø* before instruction produced *I'm sorry I was late* and *Thanks for inviting me* after instruction (Bardovi-Harlig & Vellenga, 2012). Like everything in language acquisition, pragmatic routines and expressions are subject to acquisitional stages. Even though pragmatic routines can be valuable pragmatic resources for knowing what to say, they may very well not be learned "whole," but rather they often reflect the grammar of the learner. As our examples show, these stages also give way to target-like production. When the learners use them in expected contexts, they still convey the pragmatic intent of their contributions, even with interlanguage forms.

Meaningful communicative lessons allow learners to make use of instruction at their own level and rate. Some learners may be faster at making sociopragmatic connections and others at pragmalinguistic development. With authentic input and noticing opportunities, learners are free to notice form, meaning, and context for their current needs.

Conclusion

Corpora provide two important resources for materials developers, namely frequency information and authentic language use that serves as input. The availability of transcripts eliminates the need for teachers to transcribe spoken language for materials development. Authentic audio is often provided, and TV shows can be easily located online to supplement written and audio materials to provide crucial visual clues to context of use. Hopefully developing materials for teaching pragmatic routines using corpus resources will bring us one step closer to developing better materials to teach pragmatics more generally.

Acknowledgments

We thank Marlise Horst for bringing the TV corpus to our attention, and Tom Cobb for sending us the corpus file. Thanks to Yunwen Su and Kyle Swanson for comments on an earlier version of this chapter.

Notes

1 Recall that the TV-Marlise corpus does not indicate the turn breaks or the speakers. We consulted http://www.seinfeldscripts.com/TheSeinfeldChronicles.htm to verify the turns and speakers.
2 In order to establish the turns, teachers can use a search engine to locate the TV episode by entering a unique expression or phrase from the conversation and the name of the TV show (e.g., "nice to see you" Frasier). The search will return fan-based transcription websites and videos for episodes that contain the desired expression.

References

Alcón-Soler, E. (2005). Does instruction work for learning pragmatics in the EFL context? *System, 33*, 417–435.

Al-Surmi, M. (2012). Authenticity and TV shows: A multidimensional analysis perspective. *TESOL Quarterly, 46*, 671–694.

Bardovi-Harlig, K. (2001). Pragmatics and second language acquisition. In R. Kaplan (Ed.), *The Handbook of Applied Linguistics* (pp.182–192). Oxford: Oxford University Press.

Bardovi-Harlig, K. (2009). Conventional expressions as a pragmalinguistic resource: Recognition and production of conventional expressions in L2 pragmatics. *Language Learning, 59*, 755–795.

Bardovi-Harlig, K. (2014). Awareness of meaning of conventional expressions in second language pragmatics. *Language Awareness, 23*, 41–56.

Bardovi-Harlig, K. (2015). Operationalizing conversation in studies of instructional effects in L2 pragmatics. *System, 48*, 21–34.

Bardovi-Harlig, K., & Bastos, M.-T. (2011). Proficiency, length of stay, and intensity of interaction and the acquisition of conventional expressions in L2 pragmatics. *Intercultural Pragmatics*, *8*, 347–384.

Bardovi-Harlig, K., & Mahan-Taylor, R. (2003). *Teaching pragmatics*. Washington, DC: United States Department of State. http://draft.eca.state.gov/education/engteaching/pragmatics.htm

Bardovi-Harlig, K., & Vellenga, H. E. (2012). The effect of instruction on conventional expressions in L2 pragmatics. *System*, *40*, 77–89.

Bardovi-Harlig, K., Mossman, S., & Vellenga, H. E. (2015a). The effect of instruction on pragmatic routines in academic discussion. *Language Teaching Research*, *19*, 324–350.

Bardovi-Harlig, K., Mossman, S., & Vellenga, H. E. (2015b). Developing corpus-based materials to teach pragmatic routines. *TESOL Journal*, *6*, 499–526.

Biber, D., Conrad, S., & Cortes, V. (2004). If you look at . . . : Lexical bundles in university teaching and textbooks. *Applied Linguistics*, *25*, 371–405.

Biber, D., Johansson, S., Leech, G., Conrad, S., & Finegan, E. (1999). *Longman grammar of spoken and written English*. London: Longman.

Cobb. T. (n.d.) Corpus concordance English [Computer software] at: http://www.lextutor.ca/conc/eng/. Accessed November 16, 2014.

Cohen, A. D., & Ishihara, N. (2013). Pragmatics. In B. Tomlinson (Ed.), *Applied linguistics and materials development* (pp. 113–126). London: Bloomsbury Academic.

Du Bois, J. W., Chafe, W. L., Meyer, C., Thompson, S. A., Englebretson, R., & Martey, N. (2000–2005). *Santa Barbara corpus of spoken American English. Parts 1–4*. Philadelphia, PA: Linguistic Data Consortium.

Houck, N. R., & Tatsuki, D. H. (Eds.) (2011). *Pragmatics: Teaching natural conversation*. New York: TESOL.

House, J. (1996). Developing pragmatic fluency in English as a foreign language: Routines and metapragmatic awareness. *Studies in Second Language Acquisition*, *18*, 225–252.

Ishihara, N., & Cohen, A. D. (2010). *Teaching and learning pragmatics: Where language and culture meet*. London: Longman.

Kasper, G., & Blum-Kulka, S. (1993). Interlanguage pragmatics: An introduction. In G. Kasper & S. Blum-Kulka (Eds.), *Interlanguage pragmatics* (pp. 1–17). Oxford: Oxford University Press.

Kecskes, I. (2003). *Situation-bound utterances in L1 and L2*. Berlin: Mouton.

Quaglio, P. (2009). Television dialogue: The sitcom *Friends* vs. natural conversation. Philadelphia, PA: John Benjamins.

Reppen, R. (2010). *Using corpora in the language classroom*. Cambridge: Cambridge University Press.

Riddiford, N., & Newton, J. (2010). *Workplace talk in action – An ESOL resource*. Wellington: School of Linguistics and Applied Language Studies, Victoria University of Wellington.

Rover, C. (2012). What learners get for free: Learning of routine formulae in ESL and EFL environments. *ELT Journal*, *66*, 10–21.

Schmidt, R. (1993). Consciousness, learning and interlanguage pragmatics. In G. Kasper & S. Blum-Kulka (Eds.), *Interlanguage pragmatics* (pp. 21–42). Oxford: Oxford University Press.

Silva, A. (2003). The effects of instruction on pragmatic development: Teaching polite refusals in English. *Second Language Studies*, *22*, 55–106.

Simpson, R. C., Briggs, S. L., Ovens, J., & Swales, J. M. (2002). *The Michigan corpus of academic spoken English*. Ann Arbor, MI: The Regents of the University of Michigan.

Swain, M., & Lapkin, S. (1995). Problems in output and cognitive processes they generate: A step towards second language learning. *Applied Linguistics*, *16*, 371–391.

Tatsuki, D. H., & N. R. Houck (Eds.). (2010). *Pragmatics: Teaching speech acts*. New York: TESOL.

Tomlinson, B. (2013). Second language acquisition and materials development. In B. Tomlinson (Ed.), *Applied linguistics and materials development* (pp. 11–29). London: Bloomsbury Academic.

Valdman, A. (1989). The elaboration of pedagogical norms for second language learners in a conflictual diglossia situation. In S. Gass, C. Madden, D. Preston, & L. Selinker (Eds.), *Variation in second language acquisition* (pp. 15–34). Clevedon, UK: Multilingual Matters.

Van Patten, B. (2002). Communicative classrooms, processing instruction, and pedagogical norms. In S. M. Gass, K. Bardovi-Harlig, S. Magnan, & J. Walz (Eds.), *Pedagogical norms for second and foreign language teaching* (pp. 105–118). Amsterdam: John Benjamins.

Van Patten, B., & Williams, J. (2007). Introduction: The nature of theories. In B. Van Patten & J. Williams (Eds.), *Theories in second language acquisition* (pp. 57–75). Mahwah, NJ: Erlbaum.

17

WHY ONE-SIZE-FITS-ALL IS NOT FIT FOR PURPOSE

THE PROBLEM WITH MASS-PRODUCED TEACHING MATERIALS, AND HOW ONE MIGHT CREATIVELY AND SENSITIVELY CONFRONT THIS PROBLEM

Kevin Ottley

Introduction

Having spent almost twenty years in English language teaching (ten of which have been in English for academic purposes (EAP)) I have long had doubts about the suitability of mass-produced teaching materials – a feeling which has become more pronounced as, for the last two years, I have been teaching mono-national groups of students in Iraqi Kurdistan. English language teaching (ELT) materials are produced for an international market, for international students, and, this being the case, they too frequently rely upon a one-size-fits-all philosophy: They assume that all learners are "aspirational, urban, middle-class, well-educated, westernized computer users" (Tomlinson & Masuhara, 2013, p. 248). But at the margins this all-too-simplistic philosophy becomes stretched, even threadbare, with the danger that learners come to feel disenfranchized, bored and demotivated by content which assumes all international students are the same – same interests, same aspirations, same fashions, same desires.

The current study offers, I hope, a solution to the problem outlined above. First, I will give a sketch of the region I have been employed in for the last two years, highlighting the reasons why I have needed to create my own teaching materials. Second, I will discuss the theoretical background behind the selection of teaching materials, exploring here the arguments which have encouraged me in my pursuit of relevance. Following this, I will provide a summary of an interview that was conducted in order for me to gain an insight into the *local* point of view, namely, with a focus group of foundation students drawn from a university in the region where I was employed. Finally, I will offer a preview of some of the materials I have produced.

Kurdistan, and the Need for Relevant Teaching Materials

August, 2012: Sadly for its people, Kurdistan is in the news again.

I'm not, I must confess, a great follower of current affairs. In fact, I only ever see or hear the news accidentally – while flicking through the TV channels for example or, more usually, when my teenage daughter bangs on Radio 1 in the house and half-hourly news bulletins punctuate the music and inane DJ chatter.

When I'm on holiday I'm a zero follower of current affairs. In the summer of 2014, therefore, I was completely unaware of the rapid advances that the armies of the Islamic State of Iraq and Syria (ISIS) had been making; until, that is, while driving back from a holiday in France I finally gave in to my daughter's request that we tune into Radio 1, and I was brought up to date with the alarming news coming out of a region I had worked in for two years and was planning to return to in two weeks – ISIS armies had routed Kurdish fighters and had taken the Mosul dam, advanced columns of ISIS were only thirty kilometres from the capital of the Iraqi Kurdistan region, Erbil, and within Erbil itself the population were preparing to do what they had done as recently as 1991 (but which had seemed unthinkable during the two years I had lived in the country) – arm and fight, while at the same time being ready to flee to the mountains in the north of the country.

In early October I was back in Kurdistan, helping to set up an English foundation programme for a university in the region. But although the military situation had stabilized (at least with regard to the southern and western frontiers of Iraqi Kurdistan), the detritus of the summer campaigns was everywhere. On the road from Kirkuk to Sulaymaniyah (Slemani) I got chatting with a young Iraqi Arab serving me a sandwich; he had been in his final year of a business degree at a university south of Baghdad but, fearing for his personal safety, had fled with his family: They had been allowed into Erbil but he hadn't, and he was now earning less than $10 a day working at a roadside food stall. In Soran city centre, I talked with a couple in their twenties: He had been employed by the judiciary in Mosul, but when ISIS took the city he crossed into Kurdistan with his pregnant wife, and was now living off his savings. I visited Diana (Diyana) in the north of the region, where the community's small church is now home to dozens of Christian families, survivors of an exodus from the Nineveh plains around Mosul, where, prior to the incursions of ISIS, members of Christian, Arab and Yazidi religions had lived peacefully side-by-side for centuries.

But what, you might well be asking, has this preamble to do with ELT or materials development?

When I first started teaching academic English on a foundation course in Kurdistan, I quickly became aware that the students were not really motivated by the materials I was expected to teach from. Even, much of it was alien. According to Ka-Ming Yuen (2011), learning a second language (L2) means learning about different strands of the culture in which it is used, adding that in language textbooks a "tourist's perspective" of the culture, usually simple and superficial, is put forward, with the focus being on topics such as food and transport. But while this might work with some success with a general English syllabus, by its very nature an English for academic purposes (EAP) course requires texts more demanding and more intellectually sophisticated. And here is the challenge. The further one goes along the spectrum from simple and superficial themes (such as food and transport) and towards more sophisticated topics, the more likely one is to lose universality and accessibility and, thus, the engagement and motivation of the students.

This was very true of the resources I was expected to use on my foundation course in Kurdistan. To take one example: The learning aim of a lesson was cohesion in writing by using 'it' and 'this' – a noble attempt by the authors, it has to be said, to coax teachers and learners away from the dull and often painful (and unnatural and clunky) repetition of discourse markers such as 'therefore', 'thus', 'with reference to' and so on. Unfortunately, the context of the lesson was Romanesque architecture, which my students, none of whom had ever travelled beyond Turkey, knew nothing about: Great for German or French learners of English, or, possibly, for international students studying in a European country, but a completely irrelevant subject for Iraqi Kurds. And another example – a lesson about noticing signposting language in public speaking, again a very useful content given that the students I was teaching would need to be able to take effective notes from lectures in English in their undergraduate years, was introduced in a context about the moral issues regarding research into genetics, a subject which might well lead to cultural/ethical complications for students from particular religious backgrounds. In short, although the content of the lesson material was good and useful for my students, its subject matter was not. I knew immediately that the creative element of my teaching skills, in the widest sense, was going to be tested.

To be fair, other material in the textbooks I was given was good – topics such as video games, emotional intelligence and TV all promised potential. Bell and Gower (1998) rightly argue that no coursebooks can cater fully for the needs of the learners, and that with global markets the needs of individual students and teachers can never be satisfied. To this we might drop in a quote from Thornbury (2013), namely that materials "need to be mediated by the teachers . . . so they can be made to accommodate the lives and needs of the students". To mediate means, of course, to negotiate in order to agree on a solution or compromise: At which juncture one needs to ask with whom are we negotiating: Who are the stakeholders in the teaching/learning experience? Ka-Ming Yuen (2011) is right when she argues that authors and publishers need to take on board the opinions of teachers and schools when developing teaching material, but this is hardly the quick fix which might be needed when one arrives in a new region and is presented with teaching material not wholly fit for purpose.

Perhaps, then, we teachers need to invite another stakeholder into the discussion, one who, I'm afraid, usually isn't at the table when it comes to planning a syllabus. According to Widdows and Voller (1991), curriculum reform generally should be modified to take into account learner opinions; more pointedly still, Nuttall (1996) recommends students themselves be canvassed in order to find out what their interests are. I'm not suggesting that students' personal interests should help form a syllabus (that would prove exhausting and confusing), but topics relating to their cultural and national background, their history and identity, could and should be employed.

And this is what I set out to do. Although a new nation politically, the Kurdish people have a rich and diverse history. Also, the region of Iraqi Kurdistan, although geographically no larger than the Republic of Ireland, contains a powerful assortment of peoples. Furthermore, Iraqi Kurdistan is a country which borders three powerful entities, each, it might be argued, possessing their own distinctive and often competing ideologies – Turkey, Iran and the Arab world. Also, Iraqi Kurdistan is undergoing rapid economic development, with the result that old and new, traditional and modern, exist side by side. Finally, and critically, because of its new-nation status, Kurds in Iraq are very aware of themselves, their identity and their future. And as my introductory preamble should make clear, the culture of the Kurds, their society and its customs, their history, is alive and vital in the present, not merely for Kurdistan but for the entire region. To paraphrase T. S. Eliot, "History is now and Kurdistan."

Plenty of potential, then, for teaching material.

The Selection of Materials: Relevance and Appropriateness

In his work *Materials evaluation and design for language teaching* (2002), Ian McGrath includes a list of criteria for the selection of authentic texts, these being: Relevance; intrinsic interest of topic/theme; cultural appropriateness; linguistic demands; cognitive demands; logistical considerations; quality and exploitability. It is no accident that relevance heads the list, for as McGrath goes on to note, "if [a text's] use cannot be justified on the grounds of relevance . . . it should not be used at all" (2002, p. 106). It is worth remembering that the main focus of any language class is not content but language (or, within EAP, an academic skill, maybe); this being the case, why labour the point with a text which the students are just not interested in? Better, surely, to select material which is exciting and engaging? Hence the second item in McGrath's list: Intrinsic interest of topic/theme, one which can never be separated from relevance. Many years ago, in Germany, I was expected to teach an English for specific purposes (ESP) class to a group of lively secretaries and administration staff in a petrochemical plant. The material I was provided with was relevant to their work, but was dull and heavy, for both the students and their teacher. Also, the specific content of it, i.e. technical vocabulary, was already well known to them – this was their job after all – and they weren't that interested in spending their weekly English class talking about work. Having consulted with the students (see below), it was decided to keep the framework provided by the teaching material but to ditch its specific content, instead delivering the syllabus in a context with which they were familiar and happy. Thus, a lesson about telephone etiquette, the original version of which necessitated the students improvising a role-play in which xxx tonnes of chemicals may or may not have been supplied by such and such a date, became instead a role-play in which exactly the same telephoning vocabulary and expressions were introduced, but for which a different and more engaging context was used – following up an online order for clothes for a wedding, if I remember correctly. As McGrath notes, "if a text is patently not going to interest learners, however relevant it is, it should be replaced by one that will" (2002, p. 106).

The next item on McGrath's list is cultural appropriateness. I am glad that McGrath uses the positive form of the word, and not its negative relation. If my own experience is anything to go by, far too often instructors on teaching of ELT courses make a song and dance about which subjects to avoid in class – the usual suspects being sex and gender issues, religion, politics, history, and nationalism, and related 'controversial' themes. While I agree that it might be a good idea to avoid the subject of religion when teaching a class which includes, for example, both Sunni and Shi'ite Muslims, as well as steering clear of nationalistic and historical texts if the class includes students from both sides of the national divide in Cyprus (and these are just two personal examples from many), I would argue that common sense should be one's guide in this area, and not proscription. As we shall see, I personally have got a lot of mileage out of these supposed 'subjects-to-avoid' when teaching in Kurdistan – and it is worth noting here that a typical university EAP class in Kurdistan will include Muslims and Christians, Sunnis and Shi'ites, Kurds from Iraq, Iran and Syria, and Arabs – as I have enjoyed similar success in England with mixed-national groups: For example, although Saudi women are barred from driving in their own country, Saudi female students in the UK will nevertheless espouse strong views on this and other gender-related topics. Rather than just ban certain subjects from the classroom, my advice would be to dip one's toes into the waters of controversy and gauge the mood of the river. Often, it is the more controversial subjects which guarantee a response from students; and is this not what a teacher of English is seeking?

Before going on to address the critical question of what subjects we might include in our teaching, it is worth first looking at the extent to which research into second language acquisition (SLA), especially with reference to affective and cognitive engagement, supports the principles under discussion. First, in support of his Input Hypothesis, Krashen (1989) argues that the best method of maximizing vocabulary growth is through reading for pleasure, and it is to be hoped that learners get more pleasure from reading about subjects they are familiar with than from prescribed texts. And this needn't be limited to vocabulary acquisition only: According to Saville-Troike (2012, p. 205), a prior knowledge of content and context "allow[s] learners to guess the meanings of words they have not encountered before, and to make sense out of larger chunks of written and oral text". This is known as top-down processing. Furthermore, Lightbown and Spada (2013) correctly point out that a key difference between first language (L1) acquisition and L2 acquisition is time – i.e., learners have limited exposure to a second language. We need, thus, to encourage more second language use, receptive and productive, outside of traditional learning zones such as the classroom. I would argue that my principles achieve this, in the following ways. First, a learner is more likely to follow up and find more examples of English if the subject is recognizable and stimulating. Second, they will also learn to compare the qualities of a variety of Englishes they will encounter (e.g. if a text is written by a non-native speaker or not). Third, they will learn to contextualize register – for example, they will recognize that a song lyric when translated is colloquial because that was its original context.

This brings us to the question of what subjects we might include in our teaching. If we are working as a teacher in a new country we will find ourselves at a loss, initially, about where to drink and eat, shop, and what places of interest to visit. A solution might be to get hold of a map and a guide book – assuming these exist and are legible (in Kurdistan they don't). A better idea however might be to simply ask the students for advice. You might even want to incorporate this into a lesson. Tomlinson (n.d.) observes correctly that "Most of the events and places described in [a] textbook are inevitably located at a huge distance from the students." We know this is true: A general English (GE) textbook I have just grabbed from the shelf has a nice exercise on basic directions and prepositions of place and movement, but is located in and around Trafalgar Square in London. Tomlinson argues that where possible we should localize teaching content, a principle which is surely not difficult to apply to a lesson about directions – simply use Google Maps. And if we introduce this under the theme of 'Directions to local places of interest' or 'How to find a good restaurant' we will achieve the double purpose of teaching the target language and guaranteeing ourselves a busy weekend that concludes with a good meal!

We might want to extend this basic tactic of knowledge-gathering into a strategy for lesson planning – i.e. we can canvass learner opinions as to what 'local' content we could introduce into the classroom. This is not radical or novel: Widdows and Voller (1991) have argued that L2 curriculum reform should be modified to take into account the opinions of learners, an observation which can be placed in the wider context of learner beliefs and opinions having a part to play in course design (Nunan, 1988; Nuttall, 1996). Accomplishing this need not be difficult. We often undertake needs analyses at the commencement of a course in order to investigate the students' language ability and educational requirements; why not, then, introduce a *subject* analysis? Such a task needn't be over-formal or even extra to teaching; with a little imagination it might even form the basis of the first few hours of class time. The results will surely be worthwhile: Not only does the teacher gain a valuable insight into the culture of the country s/he will be working in, but s/he will also learn about student interests. And the outcome is precious, at least from a teaching point of view: You have gathered a wealth of subject ideas which, when fed into your syllabus, should prove relevant and stimulating for the students.

The Student Point of View: A Focus Group

A further means of knowledge gathering is to speak to the learners in a formal environment. When I realized that a lot of the teaching material I was given in Kurdistan was not going to work, I set about organizing a focus group in order to ascertain what the student interests and opinions might be. A focus group was chosen mainly for the reason put forward by Laws (2003, p. 299): I desired to know "how people *think* about an issue". The qualitative approach ensured that insights into the students' views could be sought, and any ambiguities arising during the interview could be immediately clarified. Hayes's (2000) advice that focus groups need to be balanced according to gender and ethnic status was noted: A group should be as representative as possible. Accordingly, I invited to the group seven students, these comprising: Two Christians, four Muslims (three Sunnis and one Shi'ite), and one student who professed no religious affiliation; six of the students were Kurds, one of whom was originally from Iran, and one was an Arab from Mosul; four were female and three were male. The interview lasted for 50 minutes and was conducted in a classroom normally used for the students' EAP classes. It was recorded.

I opened the discussion with a very general question: I asked if it were possible to use local interest subjects in either an EAP or GE class. The response was positive. One student noted that Kurdish culture was "very diverse," adding, "we have also many other components of this culture . . . we have a big history and many things happen in this history," the implication being that this could provide a rich storehouse of potential teaching material. This was followed by another student making the common-sense assertion that, "if I am talking about something I'm interested in and engaged with I know something about it [and] I'll be more confident." The talk then became focused on presentations. One student immediately hit the nail on the head with the remark that "[if] know what we want to talk about . . . we will have more information about it and more knowledge about it," the point being that what is assessed on their EAP module is language skills and not content, so why demotivate the students with a potentially random and irrelevant subject? At least give the students a list of topics, argued another student, and they choose one which is relevant and appropriate to their lives. I then learned that in a previous semester the students had needed to give an assessed presentation on the subject of gender bias in higher education, but the papers they had to work from were case studies from California and Alaska. What compounded their frustration meanwhile was the fact that for the mock presentations they had been able to pick their own subject.

I asked the students: If they were free to choose their own local subject themes, which might they prefer? Gender issues – from female and male participants – was popular, as were public transportation, film, society generally, and music. Both gender issues and public transportation are in Kurdistan what we might call cutting-edge, and I will cover these themes when I preview some of my materials.

Given that the students were young (aged 19–23) one would expect them to be interested in film and music, and they made clear that they believed the subjects could be exploited for teaching material. Of the latter, one participant argued that because many Kurdish-made films have been translated into English, students could benefit from watching them while simultaneously reading the English text; and because these subtitles are not perfect, the students could practise their English by improving on the originals. Added to this, it was observed that English reviews of well-known (to the students) Kurdish films might become an exercise whereby the original text is changed into academic English. Regarding music, it was again noted that original Kurdish lyrics could be translated into English. Further to this, the point was made that because many Kurdish songs have a strong narrative element "we can discuss it, we have knowledge about it, we can share our ideas." Also, the idea was put forward that Kurdish song lyrics, because they deal with many different subjects, could be used as a launchpad in order to explore other themes, in particular the subject of gender roles.

Most generally, the students noted that there is a lot of discussion in the Kurdish media about their society, how it is developing, and especially regarding the theme of tradition versus modernization, and that this might be exploited for English learning activities and tasks. An example which was offered was the subject of the singer, Dashne Morad. Although born in Iraqi Kurdistan, Dashne (as she is universally known in Kurdistan) moved to the Netherlands when she was nine, later working for Kurdistan TV (a Kurdish satellite station based in Iraqi Kurdistan which is popular with expatriate communities in Holland and Germany), and fronting a series of shows where taboo subjects such as non-marital romantic relationships were debated. Dashne followed this with a career in pop music, releasing an album and producing a stage show which included the kinds of sexually suggestive dance moves more usually associated with home-grown US and European singers. Needless to say, Dashne polarizes opinion in Iraqi Kurdistan (opinions which do not necessarily split conveniently along a young/old divide). And where there is controversy, there is debate. As one participant noted, "with Dashne . . . it is tradition versus progression."

Lesson Previews

I started my EAP course in Kurdistan with a sequence of lessons designed to explore how the main body of a discursive essay is constructed. To this end, I needed first to select a context. Essentially, what underlines this approach is the notion of critical thinking. Here the deficit view that many international students are unable to think critically – because they are from a culture which lacks an evident democratic tradition, because they do not wish to challenge group harmony, or on account of their youth simply – needs to be challenged. As Alexander notes, "The task for the teacher is to discover a context in which students are familiar or comfortable with analysing and thinking critically and to devise ways to bring this thinking, along with the appropriate language, into the academic context." (Alexander et al., 2008, p. 17) Looked at this way, critical thinking should not be difficult to achieve.

For my class, I have the students sit in small groups and ask them to brainstorm vocabulary based on two words, *traditional* and *modern*. After a few minutes the students are requested to transfer the vocabulary into recognizable contexts (for example, transport and fashion) and to come up with lists of contrasting subthemes. Music is volunteered as a context (if not, it is volunteered by the teacher!). Some general feedback is encouraged, a few example ideas are noted on the whiteboard, and the subject of music is selected to carry the lesson forward. I ask the students to supply me with some names of traditional Kurdish singers and we take a vote on which one to look for on YouTube; we then do the same for modern Kurdish singers. It is guaranteed that Dashne will be mentioned. Once we have watched a sample of a Dashne music video, I take a show of hands to find out who likes her or not (I keep the question general, i.e., I do not ask who likes her *music* or not) and form the students into groups, each containing pro- and anti-Dashne factions. Having allowed them to argue this out for a little while, I encourage the students to try to order their ideas into sensible themes. Finally, I hand out a list of quotes about Dashne that I have collected from the Internet and get the students to add these to the themes they already have. We can now begin to mould this material into paragraphs (with supporting ideas and quotations) and to structure the whole.

Another lesson I have devised is based around the subject of public transport; it introduces the connected skills of summarizing and editing. Public transport is to urban Kurds what the weather is to the British – a source of both amusement and grief; the difference, however, is that while the British have too much weather (which is why, possibly, it is such a popular topic for conversation) the Kurds have very little public transport. There are taxis, cheap and generally efficient, which will scuttle you around and between the cities and major towns, and within the main population centres there does exist a bus service of sorts, but this is unreliable: There are no timetables, the buses leaving when they are full, and they disappear altogether once dusk falls. Add to this the traffic jams, huge, dirty, loud and unyielding. That is the public transport issue in Iraqi Kurdistan.

On a Kurdish-interest website I found an article, *Transportation system needs modernization*. There are plans, it appears, to develop a tram network for Kurdistan's three largest cities, Erbil, Sulaymaniyah and Duhok. At the time of writing an Italian company was conducting a feasibility study into building a tram system for Erbil: A route network was being debated. The article was full of ideas and was a great discussion piece; unfortunately, it was cobbled together from a plethora of formal and anecdotal sources and was as poorly organized as, well, the Erbil bus system.

I begin the lesson with a warmer, asking the class to debate the advantages and disadvantages of introducing different public transport systems into a busy city – an underground rail network, a tram system, a local train network and a monorail system. Having set the scene, the students are requested to read the entire article, at the same time summarizing each paragraph in no more than five words. Because a lot of duplication will be encountered (such is the nature of the original), they are also asked to order the whole text around four main points or sub-subjects, this task being consolidated with the whole group debating what the four points should be. The students are next required to eliminate all superfluous detail and, by using the four sub-subjects as a guide, edit the entire article (the original is one thousand words) down to about 300–350 words, before ordering the text which remains into the four main points. At this stage the class have: Read the article and summarized each paragraph; identified the four main points of the text; edited the text from a thousand to about 350 words in length; and organized the remaining text into what will become four paragraphs. Finally, a previous lesson about paragraph structuring is recalled, and, working in pairs or small groups, the students need to write a topic sentence for one of the paragraphs, as well as debating amongst themselves the ideas which are needed for supporting sentences. Eventually, the paragraph can be written. I finish the lesson with a relaxing change of pace, asking each small group to devise their own route map for an Erbil tram network.

As noted previously, gender is a popular issue in Iraqi Kurdistan, especially amongst its younger population. Women have played a prominent role in the history of Kurdistan, politically, culturally, and militarily, and this continues to this day; the first female judge in the Middle East was a Kurd, Zakiyya Hakki, women *peshmerga* fight alongside men in armed campaigns, and the parliament in Erbil includes a minimum number of female MPs – at least 30% according to the region's constitution. But visit Erbil's main bazaar, drink a sweet tea or order a kebab, take a bus or taxi, journey outside of Erbil (or Sulaymaniyah) to the plains or into the mountains, and you might be left wondering not where the women are – they are present in droves, easily recognizable in their black burqas and tight-fitting headscarves (the styles are more relaxed amongst younger women) – but what they do, beyond, that is, traditional domestic-related duties: One sees very few women in 'visible' jobs such as shopkeeping and driving. A number of Iraqi Kurds, having grown up (like Dashne) in Western countries, have experienced first-hand the different conditions which Western females enjoy when compared with Middle Eastern women, and like many of their home-grown compatriots, male and female, they often give voice to the feeling that their lives are constrained by tradition. A good launchpad, then, for a lesson.

The aim of a lesson I have developed on this subject is based around the teaching of cohesion in texts, but attempts to draw students away from the trap of overusing relevant discourse markers such as 'and' and 'but'; another aim is to avoid repetition. It is worth bearing in mind that the English word *text* is derived from the Latin *texere*, meaning 'to weave', and while a study of texts involves an unpicking, as it were, of a variety of interwoven threads, successful writing means knowing about how to stitch the threads together correctly, and, importantly, understanding that patterning is not about effect, but strength. The lesson introduces students to the noticing, recognition and practice of a variety of pronouns and determiners which, in writing, enforce cohesion in a text, usually by referring anaphorically to a previous word or concept.

For the 'warmer' stage of the lesson I show the class two photographs taken in Erbil, one inside the bazaar, the other of one of the many modern shopping malls which have sprung up in the last years, and ask them to reflect on the differences between the two. I give some guide questions, encouraging the students to think about what is sold, about the shopping experience generally, who is seen in these places, and who works in them. I next hand out the first paragraph of an article I discovered in an English-language Kurdish newspaper, *The Kurdish Globe*: This introduces a discussion about how and why the Kurdish regional government is attempting to encourage more women into traditionally male-reserve occupations. The short text includes two cohesive devices, 'it' and 'this', the former referring to a previously mentioned basic concept, the latter indicating a more extensive and general idea: The students are encouraged to identify both. In order to reinforce the task, more paragraphs with more cohesive devices (including 'these', 'those', 'their' and 'they') are handed out, the students being encouraged to attack the original text with a bright red pen and to draw arrows indicating which parts of the article are being referred. After some whole-class feedback, a list of connected sentences is presented – "The text is taken from a newspaper" / "The subject of the text is women in Kurdistan" / The text argues that women in Kurdistan are a valuable economic resource," etc. – and the students need to produce a paragraph which replaces the underlined phrases with one of the cohesive devices already introduced.

Conclusion

The aim of this article has been not to criticize the publishers of English language teaching materials (I, for one, would struggle without them), but rather, first, to point out the flaws inherent in the production of mass-market teaching materials, and, second, how one might creatively and sensitively deal with their limitations – creatively, that is, for the teacher (who is, we hope, excited about engaging with the students' culture), and sensitively for the students. I need to add that I am not arguing for a complete overhaul of teaching materials, but presenting instead a means of embellishing them. One hopes this might be done institutionally, but, failing that, a teacher would need to achieve this for her/himself (time constraints notwithstanding).

The arguments I offer for a justification to the approach I have written about here are, I believe, sound and even commonsensical – my means of production while in Kurdistan have enabled me not only to investigate and explore the culture of this country, but have given me an insight into the character and mindset of my students, which for any teacher must be considered priceless. And when I teach one of the lessons I have previewed above, my students are usually engaged and motivated; at least more so than when I am teaching from materials they cannot relate to culturally.

We are told, repeatedly, that the contemporary world is a global village. This is nonsense. The world is as it has always been – a collection of societies, regions, and countries which, while possessing points of uniformity and similarity, are at the same time unique and special. A career in ELT can provide a passport to these places, at least for the individual who is hardworking, creative, imaginative, and willing to learn. I recommend that these qualities – all of them – be invested in the production of teaching materials.

Finally, it is a fact that as English becomes more popular in 'developing' countries, a larger number of local teachers are required to supply demand: This is already the case in Kurdistan. To what extent this will shape the future of coursebooks remains to be seen. But to what extent local teachers of English are already adapting materials for their classes, and how, offers itself as a subject for further research.

References

Alexander, O., Argent, S., & Spencer, J. (2008). *EAP essentials: A teacher's guide to principles and practice*. London: Garnet Publishing.

Bell, J., & Gower, R. (1998). Writing course materials for the world: A great compromise. In B. Tomlinson (Ed.), *Materials development in English language teaching* (pp. 116–129). Cambridge: Cambridge University Press.

Hayes, N. (2000). *Doing psychological research: Gathering and analysing data*. Buckingham: Open University Press.

Krashen, S. (1989). We acquire vocabulary and spelling by reading: Additional evidence for the input hypothesis. *Modern Language Journal, 73*(4), 440–464.

The Kurdish Globe (2011). Kurdistan: Kurdish women will transform the economy. http://www.peacewomen.org/news_article.php?id=3540&type=news/. Accessed May 30, 2013.

Kurdistan Adventures (2013). Transportation system needs modernization. http://blog.kurdistan-adventures.com/2012/05/22/transportation-system-needs-modernization/. Accessed May 25, 2013.

Laws, S., Harper, C., & Marcus, R. (2003). *Research for development*. London: Sage Publications.

Lightbown, P. M., & Spada, N. (2013) *How languages are learned*. Oxford: Oxford University Press.

McGrath, I, (2002). *Materials evaluation and design for language teaching*. Edinburgh: Edinburgh University Press.

Nunan, D. (1988). *The learner-centred curriculum*. Cambridge: Cambridge University Press.

Nuttall, C. (1996). *Teaching reading skills in a foreign language*. Oxford: Macmillan Heinemann.

Saville-Troike, M. (2012). *Introducing second language acquisition*. Cambridge: Cambridge University Press.

Thornbury, S. (2013). *ELT journal signature event: Published course materials don't reflect the lives of learners*. http://iatefl.britishcouncil.org/2013/sessions/. Accessed April 13, 2013.

Tomlinson, B., & Masuhara, H. (2013). Survey review: Adult coursebooks. *ELT Journal*, *67*(2), 233–248.

Widdows, S., and Voller, P. (1991). PANSI: A survey of the ELT needs of Japanese university students. *Cross Currents*, *18*, 127–141.

Yuen, Ka-Ming (2011). The representation of foreign cultures in English textbooks. *ELT Journal*, *65*(4), 458–466.

18

WHEN IT'S NOT WHAT YOU DO, BUT THE WAY THAT YOU DO IT

HOW RESEARCH INTO SECOND LANGUAGE ACQUISITION CAN HELP TEACHERS TO MAKE THE MOST OF THEIR CLASSROOM MATERIALS

Pauline Foster and Ann-Marie Hunter

Introduction

The links between what research may reveal about second language acquisition (SLA) and the uses a language teacher or classroom materials writer may make of it all are, alas, neither neat nor straightforward. This state of affairs is probably inevitable for a variety of reasons: The researcher is constrained by limited resources of time and money, as well the need to control variables (age, proficiency, language background) which might influence results or render them suspect; the teacher meanwhile is constrained by the curriculum, and by management or student preferences; and lastly the materials writer is constrained by what the marketplace and publishers will tolerate. It's also probably true to say that a certain amount of suspicion of research outcomes exists in the pedagogic world, partly because these may arise from an environment very unlike a classroom and from materials whose design may suit a volunteer group of language 'guinea pigs' but not an authentic group of students. Certainly, it was not uncommon in the earlier days of language classroom research for the leap from lab findings to classroom applications to be promoted without sufficient regard to their generalizability or practical implications. A nice example of this is the work on comprehensible input and the negotiation of meaning in the 1970s, 80s and 90s as Krashen's (1985) Input Hypothesis was reshaped into Long's Interaction Hypothesis (1996), and the pedagogical implications had to be reshaped as well. From the opposite camp, the situation is not helped by expecting research to be the handmaiden of pedagogy (Sheen, 2006) for whom the *raison d'être* of an SLA study is that of provider of classroom improvements. This is a limitation that few SLA researchers would agree to.

Focusing more narrowly on the design of language teaching materials, it is not hard to see why the impact of research findings might be slow to take hold here. While research studies can have a rather restricted currency (a couple of publications or conference presentations and then perhaps oblivion), teaching materials hang on for years. They are expensive to produce and expensive to buy. A school which has invested in the latest set of books is not going to throw these out and replace them, even if research has shown that their assumptions about SLA are not really justified. Every language school surely has shelves of dog-eared materials still doing the rounds. This is not necessarily a bad thing because teachers are not necessarily slavish followers of the material writer's designs. Classroom experience makes them able to judge what goes down well and what does not, what is feasible and what is not, what is too long or too short, too difficult or too easy for particular groups of learners. Materials are chopped, tweaked, reworded and rearranged to fit them better to particular pedagogic circumstances. It should be noted however that inexperienced teachers, or those set in their ways, or those compelled by massive workloads to follow a prescribed book, are likely to lack the ability, energy or opportunity to put their own stamp on materials.

This chapter will argue that evolving SLA theory or recent empirical observations do not necessarily require different classroom materials, but can instead suggest different implementations of existing materials. We will look specifically at three lines of research that are promising in this regard – pre-task planning time, post-task transcriptions and task repetition – and their impact on learners' spoken fluency, complexity and accuracy. To do this, we start with a consideration of how a model of speaking in a second language (L2) is helpful in conceptualizing speaking and laying the foundations for research into it.

Speaking in a Second Language

For many years now, Levelt's (1989) model of speech production has been the most important reference point for SLA researchers interested in L2 oral performance. In brief, the model posits three main stages in speech production. Speakers *conceptualize* the pre-verbal message that they would like to communicate, they draw on their linguistic knowledge to *formulate* this message, and they *articulate* it in spoken language. This model is supported by a self-monitoring mechanism which allows the speaker to make online adjustments at any of these stages. In a first language (L1) this three-part model works speedily and efficiently, due in large part to the speaker's automatic processing at the formulation and articulation stages, and parallel processing at all stages. That is to say, while a speaker is articulating a message, she is at the same time formulating the next one and conceptualizing the one after that.

L2 speakers, on the other hand, do not have similar linguistic knowledge, or indeed automatic processing in formulation and articulation, and they require more time to deliver messages. Real-time communication however affords no extra time for processing, and as a result the slower L2 production appears laboured. According to Wang, (2014), L2 instruction should therefore seek:

> To provide learners with opportunities to overcome time pressure, access their linguistic knowledge as effectively as possible, practice these forms and

functions, proceduralise them in long term memory, and ultimately improve L2 speaking proficiency.

(p. 32)

In order to attempt to address how this might be done, researchers have needed to find a way of measuring speaking ability which links to Levelt's model (1989). The result has been a three-dimensional profile that describes high-proficiency speech as being relatively free from error, lexically and structurally rich and delivered in a smooth and effortless manner (Skehan, 1998), in other words, the three dimensions of complexity, accuracy and fluency (henceforth, CAF). According to Housen and Kuiken (2009), CAF measures are now common performance descriptors for L2 proficiency tests, as well as general measures to track progress in L2 learning.

In an L1, the three dimensions of performance and the three parts of Levelt's model do not compete for attentional resources, but this is not true in low to intermediate L2 proficiency. At these levels, the normal human characteristic of limited attention and limited working memory means that focusing on one area of CAF may mean that another suffers. This notion has been described by Skehan's 'trade-off hypothesis' (1998) which suggests that in L2 accuracy may be at odds with fluency, and both of these with complexity. However, Skehan further suggests that certain task types and task conditions might relieve the pressure on a learner's attention and even influence where it is directed.

Research into what task types and implementation conditions can predictably affect CAF has been an active SLA field for some time. Our space to explore the details of this research is rather too short to go into detail but we can report some generalized observations: Tasks based on concrete or familiar information advantage accuracy and fluency; tasks with a clear structure advantage accuracy and fluency; interactive tasks advantage accuracy and complexity; tasks requiring information manipulation lead to higher complexity; narrative tasks elicit higher complexity but lower accuracy and fluency; personal information tasks encourage higher accuracy and fluency. Research has also pointed to the CAF benefits of certain teacher interventions: Task repetition increases fluency; pre-task planning is associated with greater fluency and complexity; post-task activities (or even the anticipation of a post-task activity) is related to greater accuracy, as is giving learners time to plan whilst carrying out the task. Housen et al. (2012) have a good overview of this rich literature.

Findings like these have two practical implications for pedagogy: (1) materials could be created which include the specific types of tasks identified as beneficial to CAF development; and (2) teachers could be aware of how to implement tasks to get the most from them. In other words, it is not always *what* materials teachers use that can manipulate CAF, but rather *how* they are organized. The rest of this chapter will be devoted to the three specific procedures found to influence CAF and which could be exploited in a wide range of contexts with learners of any level of proficiency. This chapter will, we hope, suggest to teachers some powerful, multi-purpose, empirically supported strings to their bows.

Pre-Task Planning

Starting with exploratory studies by Rod Ellis (1987) and Graham Crookes (1989), there is now a considerable body of research into the impact of planning time on a learner's spoken language (e.g. Foster & Skehan, 1996, 1999; Mehnert, 1998; Ortega,1999; Skehan & Foster, 1997; Wigglesworth 1997; Yuan & Ellis 2003). These studies compared the spoken language of learners who had been given time to plan a task (varying from 1 minute to 10 minutes) to the spoken language of learners who had had to extemporize. The results across these studies are broadly similar; pre-task planning is consistently associated with greater syntactic complexity, greater fluency, and sometimes with greater accuracy. These effects are relatively short-lived, being greatest during the first five minutes and weakening thereafter.

To fill in with a bit more detail, we can take the 1996 study by Foster and Skehan on the impact of planning time on the spoken performance of low- to intermediate-level L2 English learners doing three kinds of task: Personal information exchange, narrative and decision making. These represented rising degrees of cognitive complexity, with the progressively less familiar and less predictable content of the narrative and decision-making tasks requiring more of the learners' attention than the highly predictable and familiar content of the personal information exchange task. Learners were recorded doing these three tasks in pairs, in their usual classes, either with or without time to plan. The results showed that pre-task planning time impacted most dramatically on their pausing. The mean number of pauses greater than 0.5 seconds (which are very noticeable in speech) was significantly higher for the non-planners compared to the planners across all three tasks. The mean total silence during a 5-minute performance – arrived at by adding all the pauses together – was even more significantly higher for the non-planners. The figures show that students without time to plan had to resort to pausing for (astonishingly) up to 30 seconds while they mustered their linguistic resources to complete, or even initiate, an utterance. Those with planning time were able to get through these tasks without such yawning gaps.

The impact of planning time on syntactic complexity was similar (time to plan results in more complex language) but it was more layered because the interplay with cognitive demands of the task was more evident, so we will deal with this outcome in more detail. Syntactic complexity was measured by an index of subordination, i.e. the ratio of the number of independent grammatical propositions to the number of clauses. Thus the simplest language has a subordination ratio of one clause to one proposition: *I like coffee. He makes it. It is bad.* Subordinated language has a ratio of more than one clause to one proposition: *Because I am a coffee snob, I don't like the way he makes it.* As noted, Foster and Skehan's study revealed that the time to plan beforehand significantly increased syntactic complexity across all three tasks used, with this difference increasing in line with the increasing cognitive demands of the tasks. The least demanding task (the personal information exchange) resulted in the lowest level of syntactic subordination in the unplanned condition (a ratio of 1:1.1), and the smallest increase in the planned condition (1:1.22).

The most cognitively demanding task (the narrative) resulted in the highest level of syntactic subordination in the unplanned condition (1:1.22), and the greatest increase in the planned condition (1:1.55). In other words, the least taxing task done without time to plan resulted in language that was almost as simple as language can be, while the most taxing task done with time to plan resulted in language in which over half the propositions involved a subordinate clause.

This cross-sectional snapshot of language performance does not, of course, prove anything in terms of language development. It does demonstrate, though, that learners are capable of putting together more fluent and more complex language when they are not thrown straight into a task. With pre-task planning time they are able to absorb the details of the task, reflect upon what is required of them to transact it, and allow themselves attentional space to retrieve grammatical and lexical items from memory. Without pre-task planning time, the demands of understanding the task instructions *and* the task content compete for limited attentional resources, resulting in the speaker's need to resort to simple propositions, and/or lapse into silence. All this fits well with the research finding of Van Patten (1990), who showed that listeners cannot easily or naturally attend to both language form and meaning at the same time. Given a choice, learners opt for meaning over form, an instinct which plays into pidginization and eventual fossilization (Schumann, 1978; Selinker, 1972).

From a teaching perspective, it's important that learners engaged in an interactive classroom task do not follow an instinct to prioritize meaning over form and thereby risk lapsing into pidginized or formulaic language. The point is more to get them to speak at the 'top of their game', as it were, so that the 'top of their game' becomes easier to achieve. Pre-task planning time, even as short as one minute, has been shown to support this, by reducing the need to pause and enabling learners to engage their cutting-edge interlanguage through more complex propositions. Task type also plays a role here. Setting learners cognitively undemanding tasks gives little scope for complex propositions, and little scope for a planning time effect. This may be fine for lower-level learners with limited L2 resources, but for those with greater resources, the challenge of a more demanding task coupled with the time to access and display newer lexical and syntactic knowledge can be argued as more supportive of L2 development.

The pedagogic message from SLA research into planning time is therefore twofold. First, rather than requiring learners to get going on a task as soon as you blow the whistle, allow them some minutes to think about it. Secondly, be aware of the cognitive demands of the task – whether it requires only well-known and oftrehearsed subject matter, or the transfer of new information which neither speaker not listener has encountered before, or the need to weigh up alternatives and justify a choice against opposing views. This combination of implementation conditions is predicted to support learners in producing a more fluent, more ambitious and more developed spoken performance.

All this can be incorporated into any classroom plan that involves interactive task materials. If the task is a balloon debate, for example, where learners are assigned a character to defend against being thrown out of the balloon, the planning time can be a solitary pondering of what to say and how to say it, or done in a group where all learners with the same assigned character pool their ideas, using the L2. At the end of the planning time, let's say ten minutes, all notes are taken away, balloon groups are formed with one learner for each character, and they commence their debate. This is a cognitively and linguistically demanding task for which complex propositions are useful in persuading the others in the group not to throw you out. The planning time, together with the cognitive demands of the debate, can supply an environment with the greatest chance of learners being able to speak to the best of their current ability, and this in turn provides necessary practice at complex argument through complex and fluent language.

There is one caveat: The Foster and Skehan results detected a trade-off between accuracy and complexity. The most ambitious scores in terms of propositional complexity were related to a decline in accuracy. This inverse relationship did not show up in other planning studies, where accuracy and complexity increased in parallel. So while the overall message is that pre-task planning time changes learner language in ways that are supportive of both these aspects of SLA, there is possibly a limit beyond which across-the-board benefits give way to competition between them.

Post-Task Activities

The idea behind the effectiveness of a post-task activity is that learners will perform with greater attention to their language, and therefore greater accuracy, if they know that it leads into a following task, such as public performance or a transcription activity. This idea is much less researched than pre-task planning, but one recent study has thrown up some intriguing results.

Foster and Skehan (2013) conceptualized a post-task condition as a transcription activity. Twenty-three pairs of low to intermediate students of English were recorded doing a narrative and decision-making task, one week apart, during their normal class times. Half of these students were given an audio file of their task performance to take home to transcribe, the other half were not. The students were therefore in one of two implementation conditions: The experimental group did task one, then transcribed their performance, then one week later did task two, and then again transcribed that performance. The control group also did tasks one and two a week apart, but were not given any recordings and did not do any transcriptions. The order of the two tasks was counterbalanced across the weeks to avoid a task effect, and for simplicity's sake we report here on the outcomes of the first week only. The analysis is therefore of the first task performance, *before* any transcription is done. The students in the post-task condition differ from those in the non-post-task condition only in that they knew they would be taking a recording home and transcribing it.

A reliable accuracy quotient is a tricky thing to capture in research of this nature; there are many ways to do it, all with their own weak spots. Accordingly,

Foster and Skehan chose to use two. The first was a straightforward measure which expresses error-free clauses (EFC) as a percentage of overall clauses. The second was more nuanced; short clauses are disproportionately likely to be error-free compared to longer ones, so all clauses were categorized according to their number of words and then the longest clause length at which a learner was at least 70% accurate could be calculated. Results showed that for both these measures the post-task condition was associated with higher accuracy. For the narrative task, the mean EFC score for the non–post-task group was 47%, compared to 56% for the post-task group; for the decision-making task, the mean EFC score for the non–post-task group was 59%, compared to 70% for the post-task group. The other measure showed heightened accuracy in the post-task condition. In the narrative, the longest clause which the non–post-task group could manage with 70% accuracy was only 1.73 words, rising to 3.50 words for the post-task group. For the decision-making task, the longest clause which the non–post-task group could manage with 70% accuracy was 2.64 words, rising to 5.10 words for the post-task group.

In sum, the addition of a post–task requirement was associated with significantly higher accuracy on both tasks, on both measures. This suggests that a learner's attention to language form can be influenced by the anticipation of an additional activity that will follow the task itself. Fundamentally, the post-task condition reminds participants that a task is not an end in itself, but is an integral part of something connecting to wider pedagogic concerns. The post-taskers' heightened attention to form, revealed by their more accurate language, was achieved without the guidance of a teacher but simply by the foreknowledge that the task extended into another activity in which their previous performance would be under their own scrutiny. They appear to have been induced by the task implementation condition to process language in a way that encourages interlanguage development. And interestingly, this heightened focus-on-form was achieved without any loss of fluency or complexity; in other words, there was no trade-off.

With the advent of cheap and ubiquitous recording devices (in the developed world at least) it has become possible for students to make, store and retrieve audio files of their real-time L2 performance. In contrast to even the very recent past, when recording equipment was bulky, expensive and intrusive, classroom interactions can be captured discreetly and securely downloaded to a laptop by technophiles and technophobes alike. Free software, such as Soundscriber, has made transcription a very much faster job. It would therefore be a relatively simple matter for teachers to encourage students to record themselves, and then produce a transcript. While collecting the data for their study, Foster and Skehan found that students were enthusiastic about listening to themselves speaking English, enjoyed the transcription exercise, and were fascinated by locating their mistakes. So, given that this kind of post-task activity has been demonstrated to raise levels of accuracy through a heightened attention to form, and is likely to be enjoyable, it seems like an excellent idea to exploit pedagogically. It can attach itself to any materials where students are interacting with the teacher or fellow students.

Task Repetition

Task repetition requires learners to repeat the same, or a slightly modified, task (Bygate & Samuda, 2005). Although, the word 'repetition' may conjure up images of behaviourist drills, it is important to note that what we refer to as 'task repetition' or 'task rehearsal' does not mean verbatim repetition. Instead, it means the repetition of a communicative task, in the full knowledge that the exact language used in each iteration of the task will vary (Pinter, 2007). We illustrate with an example from everyday life. A student is having problems running particular software on her new laptop, which was paid for by the department. It's a complex problem and she is not an expert in computers, so she approaches the head of the department for advice. The head asks her a number of questions but is too busy to take the issue further, and so gives the student the number of the IT department. The student calls the IT department and explains the whole thing again. The IT technician asks a few different questions and comes to the conclusion that she should contact the service centre for the laptop manufacturer. She does this and explains the problem once again. The service centre employee transfers her to another colleague . . . and so on. Clearly, the student does not repeat exactly the same speech with each of her three interlocutors, nor have the words written down, but responds to the particular questions. We might imagine that the quality of the student's third explanation is different from the first; this is a complicated problem, she isn't confident with computer lingo, so the first time she may struggle a little, hesitate and search for particular words. However, by the time she is talking to the laptop service centre, she has overcome some of these difficulties, and is using quicker, more efficient and detailed speech.

What this example describes is real-life L1 task repetition. Classroom-based (L2) task repetition works in much the same way. When learners are asked to perform a task, they typically first focus on the message content, scanning their memory for appropriate language to cope with it. This takes time, and the resulting utterance may be slow and hesitant. This initial performance, however, establishes familiarity with the semantic content of the message and the linguistic demands of the task. If learners are then given the chance to repeat the task, this familiarity allows them to move their attention away from message content to the selection and monitoring of suitable language. Therefore, through task repetition, learners may be helped to integrate the competing demands of being fluent, accurate and suitably complex (Ellis, 2009).

Research into task repetition has reported an impact on oral complexity (Ahmadian & Tavakoli, 2011; Ahangari & Birjandi, 2010), on accuracy (Bygate, 1996; Lynch & Maclean, 2000, 2001; Wang, 2014), and on fluency (Ahangari & Birjandi, 2010; Wang, 2014). A number of studies have found that all three areas were affected by task repetition simultaneously (see Wang, 2014 for a recent example). In addition, task repetition may also facilitate improvements in discursive complexity (Bygate & Samuda, 2005), morphosyntax (Gass et al., 1999) and pronunciation (Lynch & Maclean, 2000, 2001). More recently, it has been suggested that task repetition, as it provides students with the opportunity to perform at higher-than-usual levels of fluency, may result in the proceduralization of language and *long-term* fluency development (de Jong & Perfetti, 2011).

The fluency-enhancing potential of task repetition is particularly intriguing because, while many language learners aspire to become fluent in an L2, it is a source of frustration that while their knowledge of the target language increases, they are not able to access it quickly and efficiently in real-time communication. Research has thrown up a number of possibilities for this. It has been argued that massive amounts of interactive experience – such as is gained in immersion or study-abroad settings – may be necessary to proceduralize L2 linguistic knowledge and therefore to increase fluency (DeKeyser, 2007). However, DeKeyser also notes that even in study-abroad contexts, fluency often fails to develop, as students may not interact sufficiently with native speakers round them. Furthermore, as not all students around the world are able or willing to travel to the target-language country, an alternative needs to be offered by more formal, classroom-based instruction. Rossiter et al. (2010) discovered, however, that many of the existing materials currently available to teachers are insufficient for promoting oral fluency; task repetition might, therefore, fill the gap.

While task repetition may be seen as a good all-rounder in terms of CAF and, with growing empirical support, may even be the key to unlocking long-term fluency development, when Hunter (in preparation) surveyed 54 language teachers, she found that, although they conceded that repetition could be beneficial to SLA, they feared that it would appear contrived and be boring to boot. But, as we showed in the illustration of the student asking about her laptop problems, rehearsal is an entirely natural (though not always entirely welcome) part of our lives (Bygate & Samuda, 2005). We rehearse before formal interviews and presentations, and informal explanations and apologies; we tell the same anecdote many times; we go through our symptoms over and over again with different members of the medical profession. There is nothing contrived about this. As for boring the students (suggested by Plough & Gass, 1993, and also by Gass et al., 1999), Lynch and Maclean (2000, 2001) found that students actually valued the opportunity to repeat the task, and Pinter (2007) reported that her two young subjects mentioned feeling more relaxed and confident in their third performance. She also noted that the children 'clearly enjoyed the task and seeing the improvements between the performances gave them a real sense of satisfaction' (Pinter, 2007, p. 200). In the same vein, a recent study (Hunter, in preparation), which used a poster-carousel task (see below), found the response from follow-up focus groups to be generally positive, with many students expressing gratitude for having the opportunity to repeat the task, and some even seeming to be aware of the potential CAF benefits: "The more we repeat the same subject, the more we use phrase (*sic*) that we would like to use . . . [the second and third times] we add different phrases . . . we add our comments . . . we get used to the story so we become more confident about it."

If it is going to work in the classroom, there is obviously a need for task repetition to be embraced as beneficial by teachers and learners alike. Recording, transcription and reflection on the differences between first and subsequent performances may be one way to win support for this task repetition. Feedback from the teacher may also maintain students' interest and increase their confidence in the procedure. Sheppard (2006) reports that if feedback is given to support task repetition, gains in CAF (notably accuracy) are magnified and may transfer to other tasks. Feedback was identified by a number of students in Hunter (in preparation) as something which would make the procedure more worthwhile for them. Feedback could come from the teacher, or from other students, or (as noted above) the students could record their first performance and listen to it before subsequent performances. Along similar lines, Hawkes (2012) reports that task repetition can be used to highlight problematic areas for students and a focus-on-form stage. A further way to maintain students' involvement would be to consider adding time pressure, having students perform their repetitions in decreasing amounts of time (also known as the 4/3/2 technique, see Nation, 1989). Using non-identical tasks of the same type is another suggestion; Takimoto (2012) showed that while bigger CAF gains are seen in exact task repetition, improvements are also observed when the *type* of task is repeated. This would mean that teachers could have students present, for example, three *different* narratives or have interviews for three different jobs. Finally, there is the *carousel* presentation, which maintains the ecological validity or authenticity of repetition in the classroom by allowing students to repeat a task with a different interlocutor each time. Genuine communication is preserved, as the performance is novel for each listener, and the speaker has a new audience with each repetition. Below are three practical examples of tasks typical of many current text books which could be rejigged as carousel repetitions.

Interview Carousel

Many language textbooks include job interview tasks. This will typically involve listening to an extract from a successful interview, discussing appropriate behaviour and language for an interview and then taking part in an interview role play. In order to include an element of task repetition, the teacher could tweak the role-play stage to enable each student to take part in four or five interviews instead of one. This could be seen as interview stages for the same job or it could be for a number of different jobs. To set this up the teacher would give out the job descriptions as normal and split the class into As and Bs. The As prepare the questions they would like to ask their candidates and the Bs prepare to fit their real-life experience to the job description (or invent a profile for themselves). When they are ready, the interviewees are assigned an interviewer and the interview begins. After five minutes the interviewees thank the interviewers and move in a clockwise direction to the next available interviewer. The process repeats itself until the interviewers have seen each of the candidates. At this point the candidates can leave the room while the interviewers get their heads together and choose the best candidate.

Poster/Powerpoint Carousel

This is adapted from Lynch and Maclean (2000, 2001). Presentations and presentation skills are another popular classroom task type, usually involving the learners listening to a presentation, identifying useful language and then making a presentation to the whole class (presenting a new product, marketing strategy, etc). This could easily be manipulated to include task repetition. The teacher asks pairs of students to prepare presentations, in the form of Powerpoint slides (if a language lab is available) or using posters (if not). Then, rather than have the students present to the whole class, the teacher divides the pairs into As and Bs. The As stay with their poster/Powerpoint while the Bs move in a clockwise direction to the next poster/Powerpoint. The As make their presentation using the poster/Powerpoint as a guide, and answer the Bs' questions. When they have finished, the Bs move in a clockwise direction to the next poster/Powerpoint. The As now have to present for a second time to a new interlocutor. The process repeats until the Bs have returned to their original partner. At this point, the As and Bs swap over and the Bs make the presentation while the As go visiting the other presentations.

Comic-strip Carousel

Another familiar task type in language textbooks is narration. The formats are various, but involve some example of storytelling in the form of a listening text followed by language work, which might, in turn, be followed by a speaking activity in which students tell a partner another narrative. In this example, pairs of students are presented with an authentic written narrative. (A good source for these is www.theguardian.co.uk/experience). Each pair in the class works with a different text. The students are given time to sort out the key moments in the narrative, and are able to look up vocabulary they are unsure of. They reduce the story to six key moments. Students are then asked to create a six-frame comic strip with each of these six moments taking up one frame. The process then follows that of the poster carousel above, with pairs being split into As and Bs and each presenting the story to multiple visitors who could, for example, be playing the role of a journalist.

Conclusion

As noted in the introduction, materials developers cannot be expected to keep up with changing tides in SLA research, and language schools cannot be expected to throw out materials every year or so. This chapter has argued that for developments in SLA to make an impact on teaching, new material is not necessarily required. We have given examples of how current understandings of CAF can be applied to existing materials without too much effort. We have also argued that experienced teachers are accustomed to adapting materials that might have become old-fashioned or are unpopular for whatever reason. Therefore, advising teachers to adapt their materials in ways which research has shown to promote students' language development would seem entirely feasible, affordable and beneficial. What is not to like about that?

References

Ahangari, S., & Birjandi, P. (2010). Effects of task repetition on the fluency, complexity and accuracy of Iranian EFL learners' oral discourse. *The Asian EFL Journal, 10*, 28– 52.

Ahmadian, M. J., & Tavakoli, M. (2011). The effects of simultaneous use of careful online planning and task repetition on accuracy, fluency, and complexity of EFL learners' oral production. *Language Teaching Research, 15*, 35–59.

Bygate, M. (1996). Effects of task repetition: Appraising the development of second language learners. In J. Willis & D. Willis (Eds.), *Challenge and change in language teaching* (pp. 136–146). London: Macmillan.

Bygate, M. & Samuda, V. (2005). Integrative planning through the use of task repetition. In R. Ellis (Ed.), *Planning and task performance in a second language* (pp.37–74). Amsterdam: John Benjamins.

Crookes, G. (1989). Planning and interlanguage variation. *Studies in Second Language Acquisition, 11*(4), 367–383.

de Jong, N., & Perfetti, C. A. (2011). Fluency training in the ESL classroom: An experimental study of fluency development and proceduralization. *Language Learning, 61*, 533–568.

DeKeyser, R. M. (2007). *Practice in a second language: Perspectives from applied linguistics and cognitive psychology*. Cambridge: Cambridge University Press.

Ellis, R. (1987). Interlanguage variability in narrative discourse: Style shifting in the use of the past tense. *Studies in Second Language Acquisition, 9*, 12–20.

Ellis, R. (2009). The differential effects of three types of task planning on the fluency, complexity and accuracy in L2 oral production. *Applied Linguistics, 30*, 474–509.

Foster, P., & Skehan, P. (1996). The influence of planning and task type on second language performance. *Studies in Second Language Acquisition, 18*, 229–323.

Foster, P., & Skehan, P. (1999). The influence of planning and focus of planning on task-based performance. *Language Teaching Research, 3*, 215–247.

Foster, P., & Skehan, P. (2013) The effects of post-task activities on the accuracy of language during task performance. *Canadian Modern Language Review, 69*, 249–273.

Gass, S., Mackey, A., Alvarez-Torres, M., & Fernandez, M. (1999). The effects of task repetition on linguistic output. *Language Learning, 49*, 549–581.

Hawkes, M. L. (2012). Using task repetition to direct learner attention and focus on form. *ELT Journal, 66*, 327–336.

Housen, A., & Kuiken, F. (2009). Complexity, accuracy, and fluency in second language acquisition. *Applied Linguistics, 30*, 461–473.

Housen, A., Folkert, K., & Vedder, I. (Eds.) (2012). *Dimensions of L2 performance and proficiency: Complexity, accuracy and fluency in SLA*. Amsterdam/Philadelphia: John Benjamins.

Hunter, A. (in preparation). Exploring teachers' and students' opinions of task repetition in the language classroom.

Kormos, J. (2006). *Speech production and second language acquisition*. Mahwah, NJ: Erlbaum.

Krashen, S. D. (1985). *The input hypothesis*. London/New York: Longman.

Levelt, W. (1989). *Speaking: From intention to articulation*. Cambridge, MA: MIT Press.

Long, M. H. (1996). The role of linguistic environment in second language acquisition. In W. Ritchie and T. K. Bhatia (Eds.), *Handbook of second language acquisition* (pp. 413–468). San Diego: Academic Press.

Lynch, T., & Maclean, J. (2000). Exploring the benefits of task repetition and recycling for classroom language learning. *Language Teaching Research, 4*, 221–250.

Lynch, T., & Maclean, J. (2001). A case of exercising: Effects of immediate task repetition on learners' performance. In M. Bygate, P. Skehan, & M. Swain (Eds.), *Researching pedagogic tasks: Second language learning, teaching and testing* (pp. 141–162). Harlow, UK: Pearson Longman.

Mehnert, U. (1998). The effects of different lengths of planning time on second language performance. *Studies in Second Language Acquisition, 20,* 83–108

Nation, P. (1989). Improving speaking fluency. *System, 17,* 377–384.

Ortega, L. (1999). Planning and focus on form in L2 oral performance. *Studies in Second Language Acquisition, 21,* 109–148.

Pinter, A. (2007). Some benefits of peer–peer interaction: 10-year-old children practising with a communication task. *Language Teaching Research, 11,* 189–207.

Plough, I., & Gass, S. (1993). Interlocutor familiarity: Effects on interactional structure. In G. Crookes & S. Gass (Eds.), *Tasks and language learning: Integrated theory and practice* (pp. 35–56). Philadelphia, PA: Multilingual Matters.

Rossiter, M. J., Derwing, T. M., Manimtim, L. G., & Thomson, R. I. (2010). Oral fluency: The neglected component in the communicative language classroom. *Canadian Modern Language Review, 66,* 583–606.

Schumann, J. (1978). The pidginisation process: A model for second language acquisition. Rowley, MA: Newbury House

Selinker, L. (1972). Interlanguage. *International Review of Applied Linguistics, 10,* 209–30.

Sheen, R. (2006). Review of VanPatten, B., Williams, J., Rott S., & Overstreet, M. Form-meaning connections in SLA. *Applied Linguistics, 27,* 538–542.

Sheppard, C. (2006). The effects of instruction directed at the gaps second language learners noticed in their oral production. Unpublished PhD dissertation. University of Auckland, New Zealand.

Skehan, P. (1998). *A cognitive approach to language learning.* Oxford: Oxford University Press.

Skehan, P. & Foster, P. (1997). Task type and task processing conditions as influences on foreign language performance. *Language Teaching Research, 1,* 185–211.

Takimoto, M. (2012). Assessing the effects of identical task repetition and task-type repetition on learners' recognition and production of second language request downgraders. *Intercultural Pragmatics, 9,* 71–96.

Van Patten, B. (1990). Attending to form and content in the input. *Applied Linguistics, 12,* 287–301.

Wang, Z. (2014). On-line time pressure manipulations. *Processing Perspectives on Task Performance, 5,* 27.

Wigglesworth, G. (1997). An investigation of planning time and proficiency level on oral test discourse. *Language Testing, 14,* 85–106.

Yuan, F., & Ellis, R. (2003). The effect of pre-task planning and online planning on fluency, complexity, and accuracy in L2 oral production. *Applied Linguistics, 24,* 1–27.

COMMENTS ON PART IV

Brian Tomlinson

The proposals for action in Part IV are all principled and practical suggestions for what could be done to bring materials and their classroom use closer to what we know facilitates language acquisition and the development of communicative competence. They all involve, though, materials developers and/or teachers taking actions which they are unfamiliar with and insufficiently informed about. The proposals in Chapters 13, 14 and 15 would involve both materials developers and teachers increasing their knowledge of SLA research and theory and developing skills in the application of principled criteria to the evaluation and adaptation/revision of materials. The actions suggested in Chapters 16, 17 and 18 would require materials developers to seek, to gain and to apply new knowledge to their development of classroom materials, and teachers to do the same in relation to the classroom use of the materials they have at their disposal and the materials which they create themselves for their learners. None of the capabilities outlined above are beyond the ability of materials developers and teachers; they are just not in their current repertoires. I hope that reading this book will help materials developers and teachers to become aware of and to develop some of the capabilities outlined. But reading about a capability does not automatically lead to proficient performance of the capability.

What is needed are courses and workshops in which materials developers and teachers are informed about relevant SLA theories, are given opportunities to evaluate them against their experience and beliefs, are given opportunities to apply those theories they value, and then return to their jobs to apply theories for real within the constraining contexts in which they work.

What is also needed are courses and workshops (and ideally observations) in which applied linguists learn more about the constraining realities of teaching second or foreign languages in real classrooms, and in which they are given opportunities to reappraise their research in the light of what they have discovered and to develop research projects in partnership with materials developers and teachers.

Ideally each of the courses and workshops hoped for would aim to achieve all the objectives described for materials developers, teachers and applied linguists outlined above and would also achieve the vital objective of bringing the three groups closer together in their knowledge, their capabilities, their aspirations and their endeavours.

Certainly some action is necessary for, as chapter after chapter in this book reveals, there is too great a discrepancy between what typically happens in second and foreign language classrooms and what we know could happen to increase the chances of language learners acquiring their target language and being able to use it effectively for the purposes they need and/or want it for.

CONCLUSION

Brian Tomlinson

This is a book which describes a situation which is far from ideal, a situation in which we know that materials for the learning of second and foreign languages could easily be made more effective, and in which we actually do know how to make them more effective, too. This is not quite as bad as knowing how to develop a treatment which could cure a damaging disease and not developing it. But it does mean that we are continuing to help many learners all over the world to gain very little from their investment of time (and often money) in attempting to acquire another language.

The situation is not quite as desperate, though, as my opening paragraph suggests. There are indications that teachers and materials developers are becoming more aware of findings in SLA research, and that applied linguists are becoming more aware of the realities of classroom teaching of languages, as well as of the need to make their findings and theories more easily accessible for teachers and materials developers. Organizations like MATSDA, IATEFL, TESOL, RELC and JALT arrange conferences which attract teachers, materials developers and applied linguists and whose programmes are containing more and more presentations on research on the principled evaluation, adaptation, development and use of language learning materials. In addition, new classroom materials are beginning to show some indications of the application of relevant SLA findings and theories with, for example, activities offering more opportunities for personalization, for interaction and for choice becoming more prevalent (see, for example, Tomlinson & Masuhara, 2013). This is especially true on materials development projects in countries and institutions which have decided to stop depending on what they consider to be unsuitable global coursebooks and to develop locally relevant materials themselves. I know of national projects in Bulgaria, Ethiopia, Morocco, Namibia, Russia and Romania, of locally published coursebooks in China, Norway and Singapore and of institutional projects in Turkey and in Vietnam which have achieved a closer match with SLA findings than most global coursebooks have done. Of course, in many of these cases they have the advantage that they do not have to make commercial profits. However they do have to face the problem of teachers teaching new books in old ways (see, for example, Daoyi & Zhaoyi, 2015; Thomas & Reinders, 2015). This danger highlights the need for teacher training, both initial and in-service, to introduce teachers to approaches which do match what we know facilitates language acquisition, rather than only to the approaches typically featured in global coursebooks and/or traditionally used in the area.

In my Preface to this book I mentioned that there had been 'no book which focuses specifically on the interaction between SLA theory and materials development for language learning', and I commented that this was 'a serious gap in the literature and has contributed, in my view, to an impoverishment of both SLA research and materials development practice'. I hope you feel that this book has gone some way to closing this gap, and that you will work with us to improve the interaction between the field of second language acquisition and the field of materials development for language learning. One way of doing this is to contribute to a MATSDA Conference (www.matsda.org), as our conferences are dedicated to a bringing together of researchers, teachers, materials writers and publishers. Another way is to present and to publish papers reporting on or proposing specific actions to foster such interaction. If you have any such projects in action or in mind I would be very happy to hear about them at <brianjohntomlinson@gmail.com>.

References

Daoyi, L., & Zhaoyi, W. (Eds.) (2015). *English language education in China: Past and present.* Beijing: People's Education Press.

Thomas, M., & Reinders, H. (Eds.) (2015). *Contemporary task-based language teaching in Asia.* London: Bloomsbury.

Tomlinson, B., & Masuhara, H. (2013). Review of adult ELT textbooks. *ELT Journal,* 67(2), 233–249.

INDEX